to: Dear
my friend Cynthia L.
from: Tina T.
God bless you!'.
11/2/16

C. G. Finney.

C H A R L E S   G .   F I N N E Y

AN AUTOBIOGRAPHY

---

*The action-packed life story
of the New York lawyer
who became one of America's most effective
and controversial evangelists.*

Previously published in English with the title "Charles G. Finney – An Autobiography" 1908. Fleming H. Revell Company. New Jersey, USA.

© Copyright 2016 by Pavel Gurzhiy. All rights reserved.
Edited by Pavel Gurzhiy
Word of Revival
www.wordofrevival.com
Design by Brothers Printing, Inc.

ISBN - 978-1-5323-0740-9 (hard cover)
Printed in China

CONTENTS

FOREWORD

"I bought this book at the public library, it's over a hundred years old", – with these words, my friend handed me a thick book with pages that had turned yellow from age. It was Charles Finney's autobiography. The book was published in 1908.

When I started reading this book, I knew I was holding a masterpiece of Christian history of the nineteenth century. Charles Finney's life was – a vivid example, of how God is as strong and mighty today as He was in the apostolic age. It is impossible to remain indifferent, seeing how, throughout the span of this man's ministry, the Holy Spirit led him, and how the hand of God saved hundreds of thousands of sinners through him. While reading this book, I was compelled many times to stop, amazed and greatly inspired by what I just read, I would turn to God in prayer, pleading with Him to pour out the Spirit of revival on our generation as He did on theirs.

A great desire was born within me to publish this masterwork in a modern format. I believe that this book will bring a blessing to all who read it. Let the example of this man's life, who dedicated himself entirely to serving God, ignite many souls.

I believe God wants to do infinitely more in our days than He did for the generations before us. Christ is calling us to leave behind our church programs, carnal methods and to get on our knees. The Holy Spirit alone is able to wake-up the church from its slumber, save sinners and transform society.

I am praying that the Lord will find sincere intercessors whom He would use as vessels to act and contribute to the emergence of a great revival in our generation!

Pavel Gurzhiy

CHAPTER 1

BIRTH AND
EARLY EDUCATION

*You have prayed enough since
I have attended these meetings
to have prayed the devil out of Adams.*

IT has pleased God in some measure to connect my name and labors with an extensive movement of the church of Christ, regarded by some as a new era in its progress, especially in relation to revivals of religion. As this movement involved, to a considerable extent, the development of views of Christian doctrine which had not been common, and was brought about by changes in the means of carrying forward the work of evangelization, it was very natural that some misapprehension should prevail in regard to these modified statements of doctrine, and the use of these measures; and consequently that, to some extent, even good men should call in question the wisdom of these measures and the soundness of these theological statements; and that ungodly men should be irritated, and for a time should strenuously oppose these great movements.

I have spoken of myself as connected with these movements; but only as one of the many ministers and other servants of Christ, who have shared prominently in promoting them. I am aware that by a certain portion of the church I have been considered an innovator, both in regard to doctrine and measures; and that many have looked upon me as rather prominent, especially in assailing some of the old forms of theological thought and expression, and in stating the doctrines of the Gospel in many respects in new language.

I have been particularly importuned, for a number of years, by the friends of those revivals with which my name and labors have been connected, to write a history of them. As so much misapprehension has prevailed respecting them, it is thought that the truth of history demands a statement from myself of the doctrines that were preached, so far as I was concerned; of the measures used, and of the results of preaching those doctrines and the use of those measures.

My mind seems instinctively to recoil from saying so much of myself as I shall be obliged to do, if I speak honestly of those revivals and of my relation to them. For this reason, I have declined, up to this time, to undertake such a work. Of late the trustees of Oberlin College have laid the matter before me, and urged me to undertake it. They, together with numerous other friends in this country and in England, have urged that it was due to the cause of Christ, that a better understanding should exist in the church than has hitherto existed, in regard especially to the revivals that occurred in central New York and elsewhere, from 1821 and onward for several years, because those revivals have been most misrepresented and opposed.

I approach the subject, I must say, with reluctance, for many reasons. I have kept no diary, and consequently must depend on my memory. It is true, that my memory is naturally very tenacious, and the events that I have witnessed in revivals of religion have made a very deep impression on my mind; and I remember, with great distinctness, many more than I shall have time to communicate. Everyone who has witnessed powerful revivals of religion is aware that many cases of conviction and conversion are daily occurring, of the greatest interest to the people in the midst of whom they occur. Where all the facts and circumstances are known, a thrilling effect is often produced; and such cases are frequently so numerous that if all the highly interesting facts of even one extended revival, in a single locality, should be narrated, it would fill a large volume.

I do not propose to pursue this course in what I am about to write. I shall only sketch such an outline as will, upon the whole, give a tolerably clear idea of the type which these revivals took on; and shall only relate a few of the particular instances of conversion which occurred in different places. I shall also endeavor to give such an account of the doctrines which were preached, and of the measures which were used, and shall mention such facts, in general, as will enable the church hereafter, partially at least, to estimate the power and purity of those great works of God.

But I hesitate to write a narrative of those revivals, because I have often been surprised to find how much my own remembrance of facts differs from the recollection of other persons who were in the midst of those scenes. Of course I must state the facts as I remember them. A great many of those events have been often referred to by myself in preaching, as illustrative of the truths that I was presenting to the people. I have been so often reminded of them, and have so often referred to them in all the years of my ministry, that I cannot but have strong confidence that I remember them substantially as they occurred. If I shall in any case misstate the facts, or if in any case my recollections shall differ widely from those of others, I trust that the church will believe that my statements are in entire accordance with my present remembrance of those facts. I am now (1867-1868) seventy-five years old. Of course, I remember things that transpired many years ago more definitely than those of recent occurrence. In regard to the doctrines preached, so far as I was concerned, and the means used to promote the revivals, I think I cannot be mistaken.

To give any intelligible account of the part which I was called to act in those scenes, it is necessary that I should give a little history of the manner in which I came to adopt the doctrinal views which I have long held and preached, and which have been regarded by many persons as objectionable.

I must commence by giving a very brief account of my birth, and early circumstances and education, my conversion to Christ, my study of theology, and my entering upon the work of the ministry. I am not about to write an autobiography, let it be remembered; and shall enter no farther into a relation of the events of my own private life than shall seem necessary to give an intelligible account of the manner in which I was led, in relation to these great movements of the church.

I was born in Warren, Litchfield county, Connecticut, August 29, 1792. When I was about two years old, my father removed to Oneida county, New York, which was, at that time, to a great extent, a wilderness. No religious privileges were enjoyed by the people. Very few religious books were to be had. The new settlers, being mostly from New England, almost immediately established common schools; but they had among them very little intelligent preaching of the Gospel. I enjoyed the privileges of a common school, summer and winter, until I was fifteen or sixteen years old I believe; and advanced so far as to be supposed capable of teaching a common school myself, as common schools were then conducted.

My parents were neither of them professors of religion, and, I believe, among our neighbors there were very few religious people. I seldom heard a sermon, unless it was an occasional one from some traveling minister, or some miserable holding forth of an ignorant preacher who would sometimes be found in that country. I recollect very well that the ignorance of the preachers that I heard was such, that the people would return from meeting and spend a considerable time in irrepressible laughter at the strange mistakes which had been made and the absurdities which had been advanced.

In the neighborhood of my father's residence we had just erected a meeting house and settled a ministry when my father was induced to remove again into the wilderness skirting the southern shore of Lake Ontario, a little south of Sackett's Harbor. Here again I lived for several years, enjoying no better religious privileges then I had in Oneida county.

When about twenty years old I returned to Connecticut, and from thence went to New Jersey, near New York city, and engaged in teaching. I taught and studied as best I could; and twice returned to New England and attended a high school for a season. While attending the high school I meditated going to Yale College. My preceptor was a graduate of Yale, but he advised me not to go. He said it would be a loss of time, as I could easily accomplish the whole curriculum of study pursued at that institution, in two years; whereas it would cost me four years to graduate. He presented such considerations as prevailed with me, and as it resulted, I failed to pursue my school education any farther at that time. However, afterward I acquired some knowledge of Latin, Greek, and Hebrew. But I was never a classical scholar, and never possessed so much knowledge of the ancient languages as to think myself capable of independently criticizing our English translation of the Bible.

The teacher to whom I have referred, wished me to join him in conducting an academy in one of the Southern States. I was inclined to accept his proposal, with the design of pursuing and completing my studies under his instruction. But when I informed my parents, whom I had not seen for four years, of my contemplated movement south, they both came immediately after me, and prevailed on me to go home with them to Jefferson county, New York. After making them a visit, I concluded to enter, as a student, the law office of Squire W., at Adams, in that county. This was in 1818.

Up to this time I had never enjoyed what might be called religious privileges. I had never lived in a praying community, except during the periods when I was attending the high school in New England; and the religion in that place was of a type not at all calculated to arrest my attention. The preaching was by an aged clergyman, an excellent man, and greatly beloved and venerated by his people; but he read his sermons in a manner that left no impression whatever on my mind. He had a monotonous, humdrum way of reading what he had probably written many years before.

To give some idea of his preaching, let me say that his manuscript sermons were just large enough to put into a small Bible. I sat in the gallery, and observed that he placed his manuscript in the middle of his Bible, and inserted his fingers at the places where were to be found the passages of Scripture to be quoted in the reading of his sermon. This made it necessary to hold his Bible in both hands, and rendered all gesticulation with his hands impossible. As he proceeded he would read the passages of Scripture where his fingers were inserted, and thus liberate one finger after another until the fingers of both hands were read out of their places. When his fingers were all read out, he was near the close of the sermon. His reading was altogether unimpassioned and monotonous; and although the people attended very closely and reverentially to his reading, yet, I must confess, it was to me not much like preaching.

When we retired from meeting, I often heard the people speak well of his sermons; and sometimes they would wonder whether he had intended any allusion, in what he said, to what was occurring among them. It seemed to be always a matter of curiosity to know what he was aiming at, especially if there was anything more in his sermon than a dry discussion of doctrine. And this was really quite as good preaching as I had ever listened to in any place. But anyone can judge whether such preaching was calculated to instruct or interest a young man who neither knew nor cared anything about religion.

When I was teaching school in New Jersey, the preaching in the neighborhood was chiefly in German. I do not think I heard half a dozen sermons in English during my whole stay in New Jersey, which was about three years. Thus when I went to Adams to study law, I was almost as ignorant of religion as a heathen. I had been brought up mostly in the woods. I had very little regard to the Sunday, and had no definite knowledge of religious truth.

I received my education at Adams under the ministry of Rev. George W. Gale, from Princeton, New Jersey. Soon after I went there, he became pastor of the Presbyterian Church in that place. His preaching was of the old school type; that is, it was thoroughly Calvinistic; and whenever he came out with the doctrines, which he seldom did, he would preach what has been called hyper-Calvinism. He was, of course, regarded as highly orthodox; but I was not able to gain very much instruction from his preaching. As I sometimes told him, he seemed to me to begin in the middle of his discourse, and to assume many things which to my mind needed to be proved. He seemed to take it for granted that his hearers were theologians, and therefore that he might assume all the great and fundamental doctrines of the Gospel. But I must say that I was rather perplexed than edified by his preaching. I had never, until this time, lived where I could attend a stated prayer meeting. As one was held by the church near our office every week, I used to attend and listen to the prayers, as often as I could be excused from business at that hour.

In studying elementary law, I found the old authors frequently quoting the Scriptures, and referring especially to the Mosaic Institutes, as authority for many of the great principles of common law. This excited my curiosity so much that I went and purchased a Bible, the first I had ever owned; and whenever I found a reference by the law authors to the Bible, I turned to the passage and consulted it in its connection. This soon led to my taking a new interest in the Bible, and I read and meditated on it much more than I had ever done before in my life. However, much of it I did not understand.

Mr. Gale was in the habit of dropping in at our office frequently, and seemed anxious to know what impression his sermons had made on my mind. I used to converse with him freely; and I now think that I sometimes criticized his sermons unmercifully. I raised such objections against his positions as forced themselves upon my attention. In conversing with him and asking him questions, I perceived that his own mind was, as I thought, mystified; and that he did not accurately define to himself what he meant by many of the important terms that he used. Indeed, I found it impossible to attach any meaning to many of the terms which he used with great formality and frequency. What did he mean by repentance? Was it a mere feeling of sorrow for sin? Was it altogether a passive state of mind, or did it involve a voluntary element? If it was a change of mind, in what respect was it a change of mind? What did he mean by the term regeneration? What did such language mean when applied to a spiritual change? What did he mean by faith? Was it merely an intellectual state? Was it merely a conviction, or persuasion, that the things stated in the Gospel were true? What did he mean by sanctification? Did it involve any physical change in the subject, or any physical influence on the part of God? I could not tell, nor did he seem to me to know himself, in what sense he used these and similar terms. We had a great many interesting conversations; but they seemed rather to stimulate my own mind to inquiry, than to satisfy me in respect to the truth.

But as I read my Bible and attended the prayer meetings, heard Mr. Gale preach, and conversed with him, with the elders of the church, and with others from time to time, I became very restless. A little consideration convinced me that I was by no means in a state of mind to go to heaven if I should die. It seemed to me that there must be something in religion that was of infinite importance; and it was soon settled with me, that if the soul was immortal I needed a great change in my inward state to be prepared for happiness in heaven. But still my mind was not made up as to the truth or falsehood of the Gospel and of the Christian religion. The question, however, was of too much importance to allow me to rest in any uncertainty on the subject.

I was particularly struck with the fact that the prayers that I had listened to, from week to week, were not, that I could see, answered. Indeed, I understood from their utterances in prayer, and from other remarks in their meetings, that those who offered them did not regard them as answered. When I read my Bible I learned what Christ had said in regard to prayer, and answers to prayer. He had said, "Ask, and you shall receive, seek and you shall find, knock and it shall he opened unto you. For everyone that asks receives, and he that seeks finds, and to him that knocks it shall be opened." I read also what Christ affirms, that God is more willing to give his Holy Spirit to them that ask him, than earthly parents are to give good gifts to their children. I heard them pray continually for the outpouring of the Holy Spirit, and not often confess that they did not receive what they asked for.

They exhorted each other to wake up and be engaged, and to pray earnestly for a revival of religion, asserting that if they did their duty, prayed for the outpouring of the spirit, and were in earnest, that the spirit of God would be poured out, that they would have a revival of religion, and that the impenitent would be converted. But in their prayer and conference meetings they would continually confess, substantially, that they were making no progress in securing a revival of religion. This inconsistency, the fact that they prayed so much and were not answered, was a sad stumbling block to me. I knew not what to make of it. It was a question in my mind whether I was to understand that these persons were not truly Christians, and therefore did not prevail with God; or did I misunderstand the promises and teachings of the Bible on this subject, or was I to conclude that the Bible was not true? There was something inexplicable to me; and it seemed, at one time, that it would almost drive me into skepticism. It seemed to me that the teachings of the Bible did not at all accord with the facts which were before my eyes.

On one occasion, when I was in one of the prayer meetings, I was asked if I did not desire that they should pray for me! I told them, no; because I did not see that God answered their prayers. I said, "I suppose I need to be prayed for, for I am conscious that I am a sinner; but I do not see that it will do any good for you to pray for me; for you are continually asking, but you do not receive. You have been praying for a revival of religion ever since I have been in Adams, and yet you have it not. You have been praying for the Holy Spirit to descend upon yourselves, and yet complaining of your leanness." I recollect having used this expression at that time: "You have prayed enough since I have attended these meetings to have prayed the devil out of Adams, if there is any virtue in your prayers. But here you are praying on, and complaining still." I was quite in earnest in what I said, and not a little irritable, I think, in consequence of my being brought so continually face to face with religious truth; which was a new state of things to me.

But on farther reading of my Bible, it struck me that *the reason why their prayers were not answered, was because they did not comply with the revealed conditions upon which God had promised to answer prayer; that they did not pray in faith,* in the sense of expecting God to give them the things that they asked for.

This thought, for some time, lay in my mind as a confused questioning, rather than in any definite form that could be stated in words. However, this relieved me, so far as queries about the truth of the Gospel were concerned; and after struggling in that way for some two or three years, my mind became quite settled that whatever mystification there might be either in my own or in my pastor's mind, or in the mind of the church, the Bible was, nevertheless, the true word of God. This being settled, I was brought face to face with the question whether I would accept Christ as presented in the Gospel, or pursue a worldly course of life. At this period, my mind, as I have since known, was so much impressed by the Holy Spirit, that I could not long leave this question unsettled; nor could I long hesitate between the two courses of life presented to me.

CHAPTER 2

CONVERSION TO CHRIST

I had intellectually believed the Bible before;
but never had the truth been in my mind
that faith was a voluntary trust
instead of an intellectual state.

On a Sunday evening in the autumn of 1821, I made up my mind that I would settle the question of my soul's salvation at once, that if it were possible I would make my peace with God. But as I was very busy in the affairs of the office, I knew that without great firmness of purpose, I should never effectually attend to the subject. I therefore, then and there resolved, as far as possible, to avoid all business, and everything that would divert my attention, and to give myself wholly to the work of securing the salvation of my soul. I carried this resolution into execution as sternly and thoroughly as I could. I was, however, obliged to be a good deal in the office. But as the providence of God would have it, I was not much occupied either on Monday or Tuesday; and had opportunity to read my Bible and engage in prayer most of the time.

But I was very proud without knowing it. I had supposed that I had not much regard for the opinions of others, whether they thought this or that in regard to myself; and I had in fact been quite singular in attending prayer meetings, and in the degree of attention that I had paid to religion, while in Adams. In this respect I had not been so singular as to lead the church at times to think that I must be an anxious inquirer. But I found, when I came to face the question, that I was very unwilling to have anyone know that I was seeking the salvation of my soul. When I prayed I would only whisper my prayer, after having stopped the keyhole to the door, lest someone should discover that I was engaged in prayer. Before that time, I had my Bible lying on the table with the law books; and it never had occurred to me to be ashamed of being found reading it, any more than I should be ashamed of being found reading any of my other books.

But after I had addressed myself in earnest to the subject of my own salvation, I kept my Bible, as much as I could, out of sight. If I was reading it when anybody came in, I would throw my law books upon it, to create the impression that I had not had it in my hand. Instead of being outspoken and willing to talk with anybody and everybody on the subject as before, I found myself unwilling to converse with anybody. I did not want to see my minister, because I did not want to let him know how I felt, and I had no confidence that he would understand my case, and give me the direction that I needed. For the same reasons I avoided conversation with the elders of the church, or with any of the Christian people. I was ashamed to let them know how I felt, on the one hand; and on the other, I was afraid they would misdirect me. I felt myself shut up to the Bible.

During Monday and Tuesday my convictions increased; but still it seemed as if my heart grew harder. I could not shed a tear; I could not pray. I had no opportunity to pray above my breath; and frequently I felt, that if I could be alone where I could use my voice and let myself out, I should find relief in prayer. I was shy, and avoided, as much as I could, speaking to anybody on any subject. I endeavored, however, to do this in a way that would excite no suspicion, in any mind, that I was seeking the salvation of my soul. Tuesday night I had become very nervous; and in the night a strange feeling came over me as if I was about to die. I knew that if I did I should sink down to hell; but I quieted myself as best I could until morning.

At an early hour I started for the office. But just before I arrived at the office, something seemed to confront me with questions like these: indeed, it seemed as if the inquiry was within myself, as if an inward voice said to me, "What are you waiting for? Did you not promise to give your heart to God? And what are you trying to do?

Are you endeavoring to work out a righteousness of your own?" Just at this point the whole question of Gospel salvation opened to my mind in a manner most marvelous to me at the time. I think I then saw, as clearly as I ever have in my life, the reality and fullness of the atonement of Christ. I saw that his work was a finished work; and that instead of having, or needing, any righteousness of my own to recommend me to God, I had to submit myself to the righteousness of God through Christ. Gospel salvation seemed to me to be an offer of something to be accepted; and that it was full and complete; and that all that was necessary on my part, was to get my own consent to give up my sins, and accept Christ. Salvation, it seemed to me, instead of being a thing to be wrought out, by my own works, was a thing to be found entirely in the Lord Jesus Christ, who presented himself before me as my God and my Savior.

Without being distinctly aware of it, I had stopped in the street right where the inward voice seemed to arrest me. How long I remained in that position I cannot say. But after this distinct revelation had stood for some little time before my mind, the question seemed to be put, "Will you accept it now, today?" I replied, "Yes; I will accept it today, or I will die in the attempt."

North of the village, and over a hill, lay a piece of woods, in which I was in the almost daily habit of walking, more or less, when it was pleasant weather. It was now October, and the time was past for my frequent walks there. Nevertheless, instead of going to the office, I turned and bent my course toward the woods, feeling that I must be alone, and away from all human eyes and ears, so that I could pour out my prayer to God.

But still my pride must show itself. As I went over the hill, it occurred to me that someone might see me and suppose that I was going away to pray. Yet probably there was not a person on earth that would have suspected such a thing, had he seen me going. But so great was my pride, and so much was I possessed with the fear of man, that I recollect that I skulked along under the fence, till I got so far out of sight that no one from the village could see me. I then penetrated into the woods, I should think, a quarter of a mile, went over on the other side of the hill, and found a place where some large trees had fallen across each other, leaving an open place between. There I saw I could make a kind of closet. I crept into this place and knelt down for prayer. As I turned to go up into the woods, I recollect to have said, "I will give my heart to God, or I never will come down from there." I recollect repeating this as I went up — "I will give my heart to God before I ever come down again."

But when I attempted to pray I found that my heart would not pray. I had supposed that if I could only be where I could speak aloud, without being overheard, I could pray freely. But lo! when I came to try, I was dumb; that is, I had nothing to say to God; or at least I could say but a few words, and those without heart. In attempting to pray I would hear a rustling in the leaves, as I thought, and would stop and look up to see if somebody were not coming. This I did several times.

Finally, I found myself verging fast to despair. I said to myself, "I cannot pray. My heart is dead to God, and will not pray." I then reproached myself for having promised to give my heart to God before I left the woods. When I came to try, I found I could not give my heart to God. My inward soul hung back, and there was no going out of my heart to God. I began to feel deeply that it was too late; that it must be that I was given up of God and was past hope. The thought was pressing me of the rashness of my promise, that I would give my heart to God that day or die in the attempt. It seemed to me as if that was binding upon my soul; and yet I was going to break my vow. A great sinking and discouragement came over me, and I felt almost too weak to stand upon my knees.

Just at this moment I again thought I heard someone approach me, and I opened my eyes to see whether it was so. But right there the revelation of my pride of heart, as the great difficulty that stood in the way, was distinctly shown to me. An overwhelming sense of my wickedness in being ashamed to have a human being see me on my knees before God, took such powerful possession of me, that I cried at the top of my voice, and exclaimed that I would not leave that place if all the men on earth and all the devils in hell surrounded me. "What!" I said, "such a degraded sinner I am, on my knees confessing my sins to the great and holy God; and ashamed to have any human being, and a sinner like myself, find me on my knees endeavoring to make my peace with my offended God!" The sin appeared awful, infinite. It broke me down before the Lord.

Just at that point this passage of Scripture seemed to drop into my mind with a flood of light: "Then shall ye go and pray unto me, and

I will hearken unto you. Then shall ye seek me and find me, when ye shall search for me with all your heart." I instantly seized hold of this with my heart. I had intellectually believed the Bible before; but never had the truth been in my mind that faith was a voluntary trust instead of an intellectual state. I was as conscious as I was of my existence, of trusting at that moment in God's veracity. Somehow I knew that that was a passage of Scripture, though I do not think I had ever read it. I knew that it was God's word, and God's voice, as it were, that spoke to me. I cried to Him, "Lord, I take thee at thy word. Now thou knows that I do search for thee with all my heart, and that I have come here to pray to thee; and thou hast promised to hear me."

That seemed to settle the question that I could then, that day, perform my vow. The Spirit seemed to lay stress upon that idea in the text, "When you search for me with all your heart." The question of when, that is of the present time, seemed to fall heavily into my heart. I told the Lord that I should take him at his word; that he could not lie; and that therefore I was sure that he heard my prayer, and that he would be found of me. He then gave my many other promises, both from the Old and the New Testament, especially some most precious promises respecting our Lord Jesus Christ. I never can, in words, make any human being understand how precious and true those promises appeared to me. I took them one after the other as infallible truth, the assertions of God who could not lie. They did not seem so much to fall into my intellect as into my heart, to be put within the grasp of the voluntary powers of my mind; and I seized hold of them, appropriated them, and fastened upon them with the grasp of a drowning man.

I continued thus to pray, and to receive and appropriate promises for a long time, I know not how long. I prayed till my mind became so full that, before I was aware of it, I was on my feet and tripping up the ascent toward the road. The question of my being converted, had not so much as arisen to my thought; but as I went up, brushing through the leaves and bushes, I recollect saying with emphasis, *"If I am ever converted, I will preach the Gospel."*

I soon reached the road that led to the village, and began to reflect upon what had passed; and I found that my mind had become most wonderfully quiet and peaceful. I said to myself. "What is this? I must have grieved the Holy Ghost entirely away. I have lost all my conviction. I have not a particle of concern about my soul; and it must be that the Spirit has left me." "Why!" thought I, "I never was so far from being concerned about my own salvation in my life." Then I remembered what I had said to God while I was on my knees — that I had said I would take him at his word; and indeed I recollected a good many things that I had said, and concluded that it was no wonder that the Spirit had left me; that for such a sinner as I was to take hold of God's word in that way, was presumption if not blasphemy. I concluded that in my excitement I had grieved the Holy Spirit, and perhaps committed the unpardonable sin.

I walked quietly toward the village; and so perfectly quiet was my mind that it seemed as if all nature listened. It was on the 10th of October, and a very pleasant day. I had gone into the woods immediately after an early breakfast; and when I returned to the village I found it was dinner time. Yet I had been wholly unconscious of the time that had passed; it appeared to me that I had been gone from the village but a short time.

But how was I to account for the quiet of my mind? I tried to recall my convictions, to get back again the load of sin under which I had been laboring. But all sense of sin, all consciousness of present sin or guilt, had departed from me. I said to myself, "What is this, that I cannot arouse any sense of guilt in my soul, as great a sinner as I am?" I tried in vain to make myself anxious about my present state. I was so quiet and peaceful that I tried to feel concerned about that, lest it should be a result of my having grieved the Spirit away. But take any view of it I would, I could not be anxious at all about my soul, and about my spiritual state. The repose of my mind was unspeakably great. I never can describe it in words. The thought of God was sweet to my mind, and the most profound spiritual tranquility had taken full possession of me. This was a great mystery; but it did not distress or perplex me.

I went to my dinner, and found I had no appetite to eat. I then went to the office, and found that Squire W. had gone to dinner. I took down my bass-viol, and, as I was accustomed to do, began to play and sing some pieces of sacred music. But as soon as I began to sing those sacred words, I began to weep. It seemed as if my heart was all liquid; and my feelings were in such a state that I could not hear my own voice in singing without causing my sensibility to overflow. I wondered at this, and tried to suppress my tears, but could not. After trying in vain to suppress my tears, I put up my instrument and stopped singing.

After dinner we were engaged in removing our books and furniture to another office. We were very busy in this, and had but little conversation all the afternoon. My mind, however, remained in that profoundly tranquil state. There was a great sweetness and tenderness in my thoughts and feelings. Everything appeared to be going right, and nothing seemed to ruffle or disturb me in the least. Just before evening the thought took possession of my mind, that as soon as I was left alone in the new office, I would try to pray again — that I was not going to abandon the subject of religion and give it up, at any rate; and therefore, although I no longer had any concern about my soul, still I would continue to pray.

By evening we got the books and furniture adjusted; and I made up, in an open fireplace, a good fire, hoping to spend the evening alone. Just at dark Squire W., seeing that everything was adjusted, bade me goodnight and went to his home. I had accompanied him to the door; and as I closed the door and turned around, my heart seemed to be liquid within me. All my feelings seemed to rise and flow out; and the utterance of my heart was, "I want to pour my whole soul out to God." The rising of my soul was so great that I rushed into the room back of the front office, to pray.

There was no fire, and no light, in the room; nevertheless, it appeared to me as if it were perfectly light. As I went in and shut the door after me, it seemed as if I met the Lord Jesus Christ face to face. It did not occur to me then, nor did it for some time afterward, that it was wholly a mental state. On the contrary it seemed to me that I saw him as I would see any other man. He said nothing, but looked at me in such a manner as to break me right down at his feet. I have always since regarded this as a most remarkable state of mind; for it seemed to me a reality, that he stood before me, and I fell down at his feet and poured out my soul to him. I wept aloud like a child, and made such confessions as I could with my choked utterance. It seemed to me that I bathed his feet with my tears; and yet I had no distinct impression that I touched him, that I recollect.

I must have continued in this state for a good while; but my mind was too much absorbed with the interview to recollect anything that I said. But I know, as soon as my mind became calm enough to break off from the interview, I returned to the front office, and found that the fire that I had made of large wood was nearly burned out. But as I turned and was about to take a seat by the fire, I received a mighty baptism of the Holy Ghost. Without any expectation of it, without ever having the thought in my mind that there was any such thing for me, without any recollection that I had ever heard the thing mentioned by any person in the world, the Holy Spirit descended upon me in a manner that seemed to go through me, body and soul. I could feel the impression, like a wave of electricity, going through and through me. Indeed, it seemed to come in waves and waves of liquid love for I could not express it in any other way. It seemed like the very breath of God. I can recollect distinctly that it seemed to fan me, like immense wings.

No words can express the wonderful love that was shed abroad in my heart. I wept aloud with joy and love; and I do not know but I should say, I literally bellowed out the unutterable gushing of my heart. These waves came over me, and over me, and over me, one after the other, until I recollect I cried out, "I shall die if these waves continue to pass over me." I said, "Lord, I cannot bear any more;" yet I had no fear of death.

How long I continued in this state, with this baptism continuing to roll over me and go through me, I do not know. But I know it was late in the evening when a member of my choir — for I was the leader of the choir — came into the office to see me. He was a member of the church. He found me in this state of loud weeping, and said to me, "Mr. Finney, what ails you?" I could make him no answer for some time. He then said, "Are you in pain?" I gathered myself up as best I could, and replied, "No, but so happy that I cannot live."

He turned and left the office, and in a few minutes returned with one of the elders of the church, whose shop was nearly across the way from our office. This elder was a very serious man; and in my presence had been very watchful, and I had scarcely ever seen him laugh. When he came in, I was very much in the state in which I was when the young man went out to call him. He asked me how I felt, and I began to tell him. Instead of saying anything, he fell into a most spasmodic laughter. It seemed as if it was impossible for him to keep from laughing from the very bottom of his heart.

There was a young man in the neighborhood who was preparing for college, with whom I had been very intimate. Our minister, as I afterward learned, had repeatedly talked with him on the subject of religion, and warned him against being misled by me. He informed him that I was a very careless young man about religion; and he thought that if he associated much with me his mind would be diverted, and he would not be converted. After I was converted, and this young man was converted, he told me that he had said to Mr. Gale several times, when he had admonished him about associating so much with me, that my conversations had often affected him more, religiously, than his preaching. I had, indeed, let out my feelings a good deal to this young man.

But just at the time when I was giving an account of my feelings to this elder of the church, and to the other member who was with him, this young man came into the office. I was sitting with my back toward the door, and barely observed that he came in. He listened with astonishment to what I was saying, and the first I knew he partly fell upon the floor, and cried out in the greatest agony of mind, "Do pray for me!" The elder of the church and the other member knelt down and began to pray for him; and when they had prayed, I prayed for him myself. Soon after this they all retired and left me alone.

The question then arose in my mind, "Why did Elder B. laugh so? Did he not think that I was under a delusion, or crazy?" This suggestion brought a kind of darkness over my mind; and I began to query with myself whether it was proper for me — such a sinner as I had been — to pray for that young man. A cloud seemed to shut in over me; I had no hold upon anything in which I could rest; and after a little while I retired to bed, not distressed in mind, but still at a loss to know what to make of my present state. Notwithstanding the baptism I had received, this temptation so obscured my view that I went to bed without feeling sure that my peace was made with God.

I soon fell asleep, but almost as soon awoke again on account of the great flow of the love of God that was in my heart. I was so filled with love that I could not sleep. Soon I fell asleep again, and awoke in the same manner. When I awoke, this temptation would return upon me, and the love that seemed to be in my heart would abate; but as soon as I was asleep, it was so warm within me that I would immediately awake. Thus I continued till, late at night. When I awoke in the morning the sun had risen, and was pouring a clear light into my room. Words cannot express the impression that this sunlight made upon me. Instantly the baptism that I had received the night before, returned upon me in the same manner. I arose upon my knees in the bed and wept aloud with joy, and remained for some time too much overwhelmed with the baptism of the Spirit to do anything but pour out my soul to God. It seemed as if this morning's baptism was accompanied with a gentle reproof, and the Spirit seemed to say to me, "Will you doubt?" "Will you doubt?" I cried, "No! I will not doubt; I cannot doubt." He then cleared the subject up so much to my mind that it was in fact impossible for me to doubt that the Spirit of God had taken possession of my soul.

In this state I was taught the doctrine of justification by faith, as a present experience. That doctrine had never taken any such possession of my mind, that I had ever viewed it distinctly as a fundamental doctrine of the Gospel. Indeed, I did not know at all what it meant in the proper sense. But I could now see and understand what was meant by the passage, "Being justified by faith, we have peace with God through our Lord Jesus Christ." I could see that the moment I believed, while up in the woods all sense of condemnation had entirely dropped out of my mind; and that from that moment I could not feel a sense of guilt or condemnation by any effort that I could make. My sense of guilt was gone; my sins were gone; and I do not think I felt any more sense of guilt than if I never had sinned.

This was just the revelation that I needed. I felt myself justified by faith; and, so far as I could see, I was in a state in which I did not sin. Instead of feeling that I was sinning all the time, my heart was so full of love that it overflowed. My cup ran over with blessing and with love; and I could not feel that I was sinning against God. Nor could I recover the least sense of guilt for my past sins. Of this experience I said nothing that I recollect, at the time, to anybody; that is, of this experience of justification.

CHAPTER 3

BEGINNING OF HIS WORK

Nothing could compare with the worth of souls,
and no labor could be so sweet,
and no employment so exalted,
as that of holding up Christ to a dying world.

THIS morning, of which I have just spoken, I went down into the office, and there I was having the renewal of these mighty waves of love and salvation flowing over me, when Squire W. came into the office. I said a few words to him on the subject of his salvation. He looked at me with astonishment, but made no reply whatever, that I recollect. He dropped his head, and after standing a few minutes left the office. I thought no more of it then, but afterward found that the remark I made pierced him like a sword; and he did not recover from it till he was converted.

Soon after Mr. W. had left the office, Deacon B. came into the office and said to me, "Mr. Finney, do you recollect that my cause is to be tried at ten o'clock this morning? I suppose you are ready?" I had been retained to attend this suit as his attorney. I replied to him, "Deacon B. I have a retainer from the Lord Jesus Christ to plead his case, and I cannot plead yours." He looked at me with astonishment, and said, "What do you mean?" I told him, in a few words, that I had enlisted in the cause of Christ; and then repeated that I had a retainer from the Lord Jesus Christ to plead his case, and that he must go and get somebody else to attend his lawsuit; I could not do it. He dropped his head, and without making any reply, went out. A few moments later, in passing the window, I observed that Deacon B. was standing in the road, seemingly lost in deep meditation. He went away, as I afterward learned, and immediately settled his suit. He then betook himself to prayer, and soon got into a much higher religious state than he had ever been in before.

I soon walked out of the office to converse with those whom I should meet about their souls. I had the impression, which has never left my mind, that God wanted me to preach the Gospel, and that I must begin immediately. I somehow seemed to know it. If you ask me how I knew it, I cannot tell how I knew it, any more that I can tell how I knew that was the love of God and the baptism of the Holy Ghost which I had received. I did somehow know it with a certainty that was past all possibility of doubt. And so I seemed to know that the Lord commissioned me to preach the gospel.

When I was first convicted, the thought had occurred to my mind that if I was ever converted I should be obliged to leave my profession, of which I was very fond, and go to preaching the Gospel. This at first stumbled me. I thought I had taken too much pains, and spent too much time and study in my profession to think now of becoming a Christian, if by doing so I should be obliged to preach the Gospel. However, I at last came to the conclusion that I must submit that question to God; that I had never commenced the study of law from any regard to God, and that I had no right to make any conditions with him; and I therefore had laid aside the thought of becoming a minister, until it was sprung in my mind, as I have related, on my way from my place of prayer in the woods.

But now after receiving these baptisms of the Spirit I was quite willing to preach the Gospel. More than that, I found that I was unwilling to do anything else. I had no longer any desire to practice law. Everything in that direction was shut up, and had no longer any attractions for me at all. I had no disposition to make money. I had no hungering and thirsting after worldly pleasures and amusements in any direction. My whole mind was taken up with Jesus and his salvation; and the world seemed to me of very little consequence. Nothing, it seemed to me, could be put in competition with the worth of souls; and no labor, I thought, could be so sweet, and no employment so exalted, as that of holding up Christ to a dying world.

With this impression, as I said, I sallied forth to converse with any with whom I might meet. I first dropped in at the soul of a shoemaker, who was a pious man, and one of the most praying Christians, as I thought, in the church. I found him in conversation with a son of one of the elders of the church; and this young man was defending Universalism[1]. Mr. W., the shoemaker, turned to me and said, "Mr. Finney, what do you think of the argument of this young man; "and he then stated what he had been saying in defense of Universalism[1]. The answer appeared to me so ready that in a moment I was enabled to blow his argument to the wind. The young man saw at once that his argument was gone; and he rose up without making any reply, and went suddenly out. But soon I observed, as I stood in the middle of the room, that the young man, instead of going along the street, had passed around the shop, had climbed over the fence, and was steering straight across the fields toward the woods. I thought no more of it until evening, when the young man came out, and appeared to be a bright convert, giving a relation of his experience. He went into the woods, and there, as he said, gave his heart to God.

I spoke with many persons that day, and I believe the Spirit of God made lasting impressions upon every one of them. I cannot remember one whom I spoke with, who was not soon after converted. Just at evening I called at the house of a friend, where a young man lived who was employed in distilling whiskey. The family had heard that I had become a Christian; and as they were about to sit down to tea, they urged me to sit down and take tea with them. The man of the house and his wife were both professors of religion. But a sister of the lady, who was present, was an unconverted girl; and this young man of whom I have spoken, a distant relative of the family, was a professed Universalist. He was rather an outspoken and talkative Universalist, and a young man of a good deal of energy of character.

I sat down with them to tea, and they requested me to ask a blessing. It was what I had never done; but I did not hesitate a moment, but commenced to ask the blessing of God as we sat around the table. I had scarcely more than begun before the state of these young people rose before my mind, and excited so much compassion that I burst into weeping, and was unable to proceed. Everyone around the table sat speechless for a short time, while I continued to weep. Directly, the young man moved back from the table and rushed out of the room.

---

1 Universalism – a doctrine that all human beings will eventually be saved. Universalists generally deny existence of literal hell and eternal punishment.

He fled to his room and locked himself in, and was not seen again till the next morning, when he came out expressing a blessed hope in Christ. He has been for many years an able minister of the Gospel.

In the course of the day, a good deal of excitement was created in the village by its being reported what the Lord had done for my soul. Some thought one thing, and some another. At evening, without any appointment having been made that I could learn, I observed that the people were going to the place where they usually held their conference and prayer meetings. My conversion had created a good deal of astonishment in the village. I afterward learned that some time before this some members of the church had proposed, in a church meeting, to make me a particular subject of prayer, and that Mr. Gale had discouraged them, saying that he did not believe I would ever be converted; that from conversing with me he had found that I was very much enlightened upon the subject of religion, and very much hardened. And furthermore, he said he was almost discouraged; that I led the choir, and taught the young people sacred music; and that they were so much under my influence that he did not believe that, while I remained in Adams, they would ever be converted.

I found after I was converted, that some of the wicked men in the place had hid behind me. One man in particular, a Mr. C., who had a pious wife, had repeatedly said to her, "If religion is true, why don't you convert Finney? If you Christians can convert Finney, I will believe in religion."

An old lawyer by the name of M., living in Adams, when he heard it rumored that day that I was converted, said that it was all a hoax; that I was simply trying to see what I could make Christian people believe.

However, with one consent the people seemed to rush to the place of worship. I went there myself. The minister was there, and nearly all the principal people in the village. No one seemed ready to open the meeting; but the house was packed to its utmost capacity. I did not wait for anybody, but arose and began by saying that I then knew that religion was from God. I went on and told such parts of my experience as it seemed important for me to tell. This Mr. C., who had promised his wife that if I was converted he would believe in religion, was present. Mr. M., the old lawyer, was also present. What the Lord enabled me to say seemed to take a wonderful hold upon the people.

Mr. C. got up, pressed through the crowd, and went home, leaving his hat. Mr. M. also left and went home, saying I was crazy. "He is in earnest," said he, "there is no mistake; but he is deranged, that is clear."

As soon as I had done speaking, Mr. Gale, the minister, arose and made a confession. He said he believed he had been in the way of the church; and then confessed that he had discouraged the church when they had proposed to pray for me. He said also that when he had heard that day that I was converted, he had promptly said that he did not believe it. He said he had no faith. He spoke in a very humble manner.

I had never made a prayer in public. But soon after Mr. Gale was through speaking, he called on me to pray. I did so, and think I had a good deal of enlargement and liberty in prayer. We had a wonderful meeting that evening; and, from that day, we had a meeting every evening for a long time. The work spread on every side.

As I had been a leader among the young people, I immediately appointed a meeting for them, which they all attended — that is, all of the class with which I was acquainted. I gave up my time to labor for their conversion; and the Lord blessed every effort that was made, in a very wonderful manner. They were converted one after another, with great rapidity; and the work continued among them until but one of their number was left unconverted.

The work spread among all classes; and extended itself, not only through the village, but out of the village in every direction. My heart was so full that, for more than a week, I did not feel at all inclined to sleep or eat. I seemed literally to have meat to eat that the world knew nothing of. I did not feel the need of food, or of sleep. My mind was full of the love of God to overflowing. I went on in this way for a good many days, until I found that I must rest and sleep, or I should become insane. From that point I was more cautious in my labors; and ate regularly, and slept as much as I could.

The word of God had wonderful power; and I was every day surprised to find that the few words, spoken to an individual, would stick in his heart like an arrow.

After a short time, I went down to Henderson, where my father lived, and visited him. He was an unconverted man; and only one of the family, my youngest brother, had ever made a profession of religion. My father met me at the gate and said, "How do you do, Charles?" I replied, "I am well, father, body and soul. But, father, you are an old man; all your children are grown up and have left your house; and I never heard a prayer in my father's house." Father dropped his head, and burst into tears, and replied, "I know it, Charles; come in and pray yourself."

We went in and engaged in prayer. My father and mother were greatly moved; and in a very short time thereafter they were both hopefully converted. I do not know but my mother had had a secret hope before; but if so, none of the family, I believe, ever knew it.

I remained in that neighborhood, I think, for two or three days, and conversed more or less with such people as I could meet with. I believe it was the next Monday night, they had a monthly concert of prayer in that town. There were there a Baptist church that had a minister, and a small Congregational church without a minister. The town was very much of a moral waste, however; and at this time religion was at a very low level.

My youngest brother attended this monthly concert of which I have spoken, and afterward gave me an account of it. The Baptists and Congregationalists were in the habit of holding a union monthly concert. But few attended, and therefore it was held at a private house. On this occasion they met, as usual, in the parlor of a private house. A few of the members of the Baptist church, and a few Congregationalists, were present.

The deacon of the Congregational church was a spare, feeble old man, by the name of M. He was quiet in his ways, and had a good reputation for piety; but seldom said much upon the subject. He was a good specimen of a New England deacon. He was present, and they called upon him to lead the meeting. He read a passage of Scripture according to their custom. They then sung a hymn, and Deacon M. stood up behind his chair, and led in prayer. The other persons present, all of them professors of religion, and younger people, knelt down around the room. My brother said that Deacon M. began as usual in his prayer, in a low, feeble voice; but soon began to wax warm and to raise his voice, which became tremulous with emotion. He proceeded to pray with more and more earnestness, till soon he began to rise upon his toes and come down upon his heels; and then to rise upon his toes and drop upon his heels again, so that they could feel the jar in the room. He continued to raise his voice, and to rise upon his toes, and come down upon his heels more emphatically. And as the spirit of prayer led him onward he began to raise his chair together with his heels, and bring that down upon the floor; and soon he raised it a little higher, and brought it down with still more emphasis. He continued to do this, and grew more and more engaged, till he would bring the chair down as if he would break it to pieces.

In the meantime, the brethren and sisters that were on their knees, began to groan, and sigh, and weep, and agonize in prayer. The deacon continued to struggle until he was about exhausted; and when he ceased, my brother said that no one in the room could get off from his knees. They could only weep and confess, and all melt down before the Lord. From this meeting the work of the Lord spread forth in every direction all over the town. And thus it spread at that time from Adams as a center, throughout nearly all the towns in the county.

I have spoken of the conviction of Squire W. in whose office I studied law. I have also said that when I was converted, it was in a grove where I went to pray. Very soon after my conversion, several other cases of conversion occurred that were reported to have taken place under similar circumstances; that is, persons went up into the grove to pray, and there made their peace with God. When Squire W. heard them tell their experience, one after the other, in our meetings, he thought that he had a parlor to pray in; and that he was not going up into the woods, to have the same story to tell that had been so often told. To this, it appeared, he strongly committed himself. Although this was a thing entirely immaterial in itself; yet it was a point on which his pride had become committed, and therefore he could not get into the kingdom of God.

I have found in my ministerial experience a great many cases of this kind; where upon some question, perhaps immaterial in itself, a sinner's pride of heart would commit him. In all such cases the dispute must be yielded, or the sinner never will get into the kingdom of God. I have known persons to remain for weeks in great tribulation of mind, pressed by the Spirit; but they could make no progress till the point upon which they were committed was yielded. Mr. W. was the first case of the kind that had ever come to my notice.

After he was converted, he said the question had frequently come up when he was in prayer; and that he had been made to see that it was pride that made him take that stand, and that kept him out of the kingdom of God. But still he was not willing to admit this, even to himself. He tried in every way to make himself believe, and to make God believe, that he was not proud. One night, he said, he prayed all night in his parlor that God would have mercy on him; but in the morning he felt more distressed than ever. He finally became enraged that God did not hear his prayer, and was tempted to kill himself. He was so tempted to use his pen-knife for that purpose, that he actually threw it as far as he could, that it might be lost, so that this temptation should not prevail. He said that, one night, on returning from meeting, he was so pressed with a sense of his pride, and with the fact that it prevented his going up into the woods to pray, that he was determined to make himself believe, and make God believe, that he was not proud; and he sought around for a mud puddle in which to kneel down, that he might demonstrate that it was not pride which kept him from going into the woods. Thus he continued to struggle for several weeks.

But one afternoon I was sitting in our office, and two of the elders of the church with me; when the young man that I had met at the shoemaker's shop, came hastily into the office, and exclaimed as he came, "Squire W. is converted!" and proceeded to say: "I went up into the woods to pray, and heard someone over in the valley shouting very loud. I went up to the brow of the hill, where I could look down, and I saw Squire W. pacing to and fro, and singing as loud as he could sing; and every few moments he would stop and clap his hands with his full strength, and shout, 'I will rejoice in the God of my salvation!' Then he would march and sing again; and then stop, and shout, and clap his hands." While the young man was telling us this, behold, Squire W. appeared in sight, coming over the hill. As he came down to the foot of the hill we observed that he met Father T., as we all called him, an aged Methodist brother. He rushed up to him, and took him right up in his arms. After setting him down, and conversing a moment, he came rapidly toward the office. When he came in, he was in a profuse perspiration — he was a heavy man, and he cried out, "I've got it! I've got it!" clapped his hands with all his might, and fell upon his knees and began to give thanks to God. He then gave us an account of what had been passing in his mind, and why he had not obtained a hope before. He said as soon as he gave up that point and went into the woods, his mind was relieved; and when he knelt down to pray, the

Spirit of God came upon him and filled him with such unspeakable joy that it resulted in the scene which the young man witnessed. Of course from that time Squire W. took a decided stand for God.

Toward spring the older members of the church began to abate in their zeal. I had been in the habit of rising early in the morning, and spending a season of prayer alone in the meeting house; and I finally succeeded in interesting a considerable number of brethren to meet me there in the morning for a prayer meeting. This was at a very early hour; and we were generally together long before it was light enough to see to read. I persuaded my minister to attend these morning meetings. But soon they began to be remiss; whereupon I would get up in time to go around to their houses and wake them up. Many times I went round and round, and called the brethren that I thought would be most likely to attend, and we would have a precious season of prayer. But still the brethren, I found, attended with more and more reluctance; which fact greatly tried me.

One morning I had been around and called the brethren up, and when I returned to the meeting house but few of them had got there. Mr. Gale, my minister, was standing at the door of the church, and as I came up, all at once the glory of God shone upon and round about me, in a manner most marvelous. The day was just beginning to dawn. But all at once a light perfectly ineffable shone in my soul, that almost prostrated me to the ground. In this light it seemed as if I could see that all nature praised and worshipped God except man. This light seemed to be like the brightness of the sun in every direction. It was too intense for the eyes. I recollect casting my eyes down and breaking into a flood of tears, in view of the fact that mankind did not praise God. I think I knew something then, by actual experience, of that light that prostrated Paul on his way to Damascus. It was surely a light such as I could not have endured long.

When I burst out into such loud weeping, Mr. Gale said, "What is the matter, brother Finney?" I could not tell him. I found that he had seen no light; and that he saw no reason why I should be in such a state of mind. I therefore said but little. I believe I merely replied, that I saw the glory of God; and that I could not endure to think of the manner in which he was treated by men. Indeed, it did not seem to me at the time that the vision of his glory which I had, was to be described in words. I wept it out; and the vision, if it may be so called, passed away and left my mind calm.

I used to have, when I was a young Christian, many seasons of communing with God which cannot be described in words. And not unfrequently those reasons would end in an impression by my mind like this: "Go, see that thou tell no man." I did not understand this at the time, and several times I paid no attention to this injunction; but tried to tell my Christian brethren what communications the Lord had made to me, or rather what seasons of communion I had with him. But I soon found that it would not do to tell my brethren what was passing between the Lord and my soul. They could not understand it. They would look surprised, and sometimes, I thought, incredulous; and I soon learned to keep quiet in regard to those divine manifestations, and say but little about them.

I used to spend a great deal of time in prayer; sometimes, I thought, literally praying "without ceasing." I also found it very profitable, and felt very much inclined to hold frequent days of private fasting. On those days I would seek to be entirely alone with God, and would generally wander off into the woods, or get into the meeting house, or somewhere away entirely by myself.

Sometimes I would pursue a wrong course in fasting, and attempt to examine myself according to the ideas of self-examination then entertained by my minister and the church. I would try to look into my own heart, in the sense of examining my feelings; and would turn my attention particularly to my motives, and the state of my mind. When I pursued this course, I found invariably that the day would close without any perceptible advance being made. Afterwards I saw clearly why this was so. Turning my attention, as I did, from the Lord Jesus Christ, and looking into myself, examining my motives and feelings, my feelings all subsided of course. But whenever I fasted, and let the Spirit take his own course with me, and gave myself up to let him lead and instruct me, I universally found it in the highest degree useful. I found I could not live without enjoying the presence of God; and if at any time a cloud came over me, I could not rest, I could not study, I could not attend to anything with the least satisfaction or benefit, until the medium was again cleared between my soul and God.

I liked my profession a lot. But as I have said, when I was converted all was dark in that direction, and I had, no more, any pleasure in attending to law business. I had many very pressing invitations to conduct lawsuits, but I uniformly refused. I did not dare to trust myself in the excitement of a contested lawsuit; and furthermore, the business itself of conducting other people's controversies, appeared odious and offensive to me.

The Lord taught me, in those early days of my Christian experience, many very important truths in regard to the spirit of prayer. Not long after I was converted, a woman with whom I had boarded — though I did not board with her at this time, was taken very sick. She was not a Christian, but her husband was a professor of religion. He came into our office one evening, being a brother of Squire W., and said to me, "My wife cannot live through the night." This seemed to plant an arrow, as it were, in my heart. It came upon me in the sense of a burden that crushed me, the nature of which I could not at all understand; but with it came an intense desire to pray for that woman. The burden was so great that I left the office almost immediately, and went up to the meeting house, to pray for her. There I struggled, but could not say much. I could only groan loud and deep.

I stayed a considerable time in the church, in this state of mind, but got no relief. I returned to the office; but could not sit still. I could only walk the room and agonize. I returned to the meeting house again, and went through the same process of struggling. For a long time, I tried to get my prayer before the Lord; but somehow words could not express it. I could only groan and weep, without being able to express what I wanted in words. I returned to the office again, and still found I was unable to rest; and I returned a third time to the meeting house. At this time the Lord gave me power to prevail. I was enabled to roll the burden upon him; and I obtained the assurance in my own mind that the woman would not die, and indeed that she would never die in her sins.

I returned to the office. My mind was perfectly quiet; and I soon left and retired to rest. Early the next morning the husband of this woman came into the office. I inquired how his wife was. He, smiling said, "She's alive, and to all appearance better this morning." I replied, "Brother W., she will not die with this sickness; you may rely upon it. And she will never die in her sins." I do not know how I was made sure of this; but it was in some way made plain to me, so that I had no doubt that she would recover. She did recover, and soon after obtained a hope in Christ.

At first I did not understand what this exercise of mind that I had passed through, was. But shortly after in relating it to a Christian brother he said to me, "Why, that was the travail of your soul." A few minutes' conversation, and pointing me to certain scriptures, gave me to understand what it was.

Another experience which I had soon after this, illustrates the same truth. I have spoken of one young woman as belonging to the class of young people of my acquaintance, who remained unconverted. This attracted a good deal of attention; and there was considerable conversation among Christians about her case. She was naturally a charming girl, and very much enlightened on the subject of religion, but she remained in her sins.

One of the elders of the church and myself agreed to make her a daily subject of prayer, to continue to present her case at the throne of grace, morning, noon, and evening, until she was either converted, or should die, or we should be unable to keep our covenant. I found my mind greatly exercised about her; and more and more, as I continued to pray for her. I soon found, however, that the elder who had entered into this arrangement with me, was losing his spirit of prayer for her. But this did not discourage me. I continued to hold on with increasing importunity. I also availed myself of every opportunity to converse plainly and searchingly with her on the subject of her salvation.

After I had continued in this way for some time, one evening I called to see her just as the sun was setting. As I came up to the door I heard a shriek from a female voice, and a scuffling and confusion inside the door; and stood and waited for the confusion to be over. The lady of the house soon came and opened the door, and held in her hand a portion of a book, which had evidently been torn in two. She was pale and very much agitated. She held out that portion of the book which she had in her hand, and said, "Mr. Finney, don't you think my sister has become a Universalist?" The book was a defense of Universalism. Her sister had detected her reading it in a private way, and tried to get it away from her; and it was the struggle to obtain that book which I had heard. I received this information at the door; whereupon I declined to go in. It struck me very much in the same way as had the announcement that the sick woman, already mentioned, was about to die. It loaded me down with great agony. As I returned to my room, at some distance from that house, I felt almost as if I should stagger under the burden that was on my mind; and I struggled, and groaned, and agonized, but could not frame to present the case before God in words, but only in groans and tears.

It seemed to me that the discovery that young woman, instead of being converted, was becoming a Universalist, so astounded me that I could not break through with my faith, and get hold of God in reference to her case. There seemed to be a darkness banging over the question, as if a cloud had risen up between me and God, in regard to prevailing for her salvation. But still the Spirit struggled within me with groanings that could not be uttered. However, I was obliged to retire that night without having prevailed. But as soon as it was light I awoke; and the first thought that I had was to beseech the God of grace again for that young woman. I immediately arose and fell upon my knees. No sooner was I upon my knees than the darkness gave way, and the whole subject opened to my mind; and as soon as I plead for her God said to me, "Yes! yes!" If he had spoken with an audible voice, it would not have been more distinctly understood than was this word spoken within my soul. It instantly relieved all my solicitude. My mind became filled with the greatest peace and joy; and I felt a complete certainty that her salvation was secure.

I drew a false inference, however, in regard to the time; which indeed was not a thing particularly impressed upon my mind at the time of my prayer. Still I expected her to be converted immediately; but she was not. She remained in her sins for several months. In its proper place I shall have occasion to speak of her conversion. I felt disappointed, at the time, that she was not converted at once; and was somewhat staggered upon the question whether I had really prevailed with God in her behalf.

Soon after I was converted, the man with whom I had been boarding for some time, who was a magistrate, and one of the principal men in the place, was deeply convicted of sin. He had been elected a member of the legislature of the state. I was praying daily for him, and urging him to give his heart to God. His conviction became very deep; but still, from day to day, he deferred submission, and did not obtain a hope. My solicitude for him increased.

One afternoon several of his political friends had a protracted interview with him. On the evening of the same day I attempted again to carry his case to God; as the urgency in my mind for his conversion had become very great. In my prayer I had drawn very near to God. I do not remember ever to have been in more intimate communion with the Lord Jesus Christ than I was at that time. Indeed, his presence was so real that I was bathed in tears of joy, and gratitude, and love; and in this state of mind I attempted to pray for this friend. But the moment I did so, my mouth was shut. I found it impossible to pray a word for him. The Lord seemed to say to me, "No; I will not hear." An anguish seized upon me; I thought at first it was a temptation. But the door was shut in my face. It seemed as if the Lord said to me, "Speak no more to me of that matter." It pained me beyond expression. I did not know what to make of it.

The next morning, I saw him; and as soon as I brought up the question of submission to God, he said to me, "Mr. Finney, I shall have nothing more to do with it until I return from the legislature. I stand committed to my political friends to carry out certain measures in the legislature, that are incompatible with my first becoming a Christian; and I have promised that I will not attend to the subject until after I have returned from Albany."

From the moment of that exercise the evening before, I had no spirit of prayer for him at all. As soon as he told me what he had done, I understood it. I could see that his convictions were all gone, and that the Spirit of God had left him. From that time, he grew more careless and hardened than ever. When the time arrived he went to the legislature; and in the Spring he returned an almost insane Universalist. I say almost insane, because, instead of having formed his opinions from any evidence or course of argument, he told me this: he said, "I have come to that conclusion, not because I have found it taught in the Bible, but because such a doctrine is so opposed to the carnal mind. It is a doctrine so generally rejected and spoken against, as to prove that it is distasteful to the carnal, or unconverted mind." This was astonishing to me. But everything else that I could get out of him was as wild and absurd as this. He remained in his sins, finally fell into decay, and died at last, as I have been told, a dilapidated man, and in the full faith of his Universalism.

CHAPTER 4

HIS DOCTRINAL EDUCATION AND OTHER EXPERIENCES AT ADAMS

*I proposed that we should pray in private
for the revival of God's work;
that we should pray at sunrise, at noon,
and at sunset, in our closets…
No other means were used
for the revival of God's work.*

Soon after I was converted I called on my pastor, and had a long conversation with him on the atonement. He was a Princeton student, and of course held the limited view of the atonement — that it was made for the elect and available to none else. Our conversation lasted nearly half a day. He held that Jesus suffered for the elect the literal penalty of the Divine law; that he suffered just what was due to each of the elect on the score of retributive justice. I objected that this was absurd; as in that case he suffered the equivalent of endless misery multiplied by the whole number of the elect. He insisted that this was true. He affirmed that Jesus literally paid the debt of the elect, and fully satisfied retributive justice. On the contrary it seemed to me that Jesus only satisfied public justice, and that that was all that the government of God could require.

I was however but a child in theology. I was but a novice in religion and in Biblical learning; but I thought he did not sustain his views from the Bible, and told him so. I had read nothing on the subject except my Bible; and what I had there found upon the subject, I had interpreted as I would have understood the same or like passage in a law book. I thought he had evidently interpreted those texts in conformity with an established theory of the atonement. I had never heard him preach the views he maintained in that discussion. I was surprised in view of his positions, and withstood them as best I could.

He was alarmed, I dare say, at what appeared to him to be my obstinacy. I thought that my Bible clearly taught that the atonement was made for all men. He limited it to a part. I could not accept this view, for I could not see that he fairly proved it from the bible. His rules of interpretation did not meet my views. They were much less definite and intelligible than those to which I had been accustomed in my law studies. To the objections which I urged, he could make no satisfactory reply. I asked him if the Bible did not require all who hear the gospel to repent, believe the Gospel, and be saved. He admitted that it did require all to believe, and be saved. But how could they believe and accept a salvation which was not provided for them?

We went over the whole field of debate between the old and new school divines, upon the subject of atonement, as my subsequent theological studies taught me. I do not recollect to have ever read a page upon the subject except what I had found in the Bible. I had never, to my recollection, heard a sermon or any discussion whatever upon the question. This discussion was often renewed, and continued through my whole course of theological studies under him. He expressed concern lest I should not accept the orthodox faith. I believe he had the strongest conviction that I was truly converted; but he felt the greatest desire to keep me within the strict lines of Princeton theology. He had it fixed in his mind that I should be a minister; and he took pains to inform me that if I did become a minister, the Lord would not bless my labors, and his Spirit would not bear witness to my preaching, unless I preached the truth. I believed this myself. But this was not to me a very strong argument in favor of his views; for he informed me — but not in connection with this conversation, that he did not know that he had ever been instrumental in converting a sinner. I had never heard him preach particularly on the subject of the atonement; I think he feared to present his particular views to the people. His church, I am sure, did not embrace his view of a limited atonement.

After this we had frequent conversations, not only on the question of the atonement, but on various theological questions, of which I shall have occasion to speak more fully hereafter.

I have said that in the spring of the year the older members of the church began manifestly to decline in their eagerness and zeal for God. This greatly oppressed me, as it did also the young converts generally. About this time, I read in a newspaper an article under the head of, "A revival revived." The substance of it was, that in a certain place there had been a revival during the winter; that in the spring it declined; and that upon earnest prayer being offered for the continued out-pouring of the Spirit, the revival was powerfully revived. This article set me into a flood of weeping. I was at that time boarding with Mr. Gale, and I took the article to him. I was so overcome with a sense of the divine goodness in hearing and answering prayer, and with a felt assurance that he would hear and answer prayer for the revival of his work in Adams, that I went through the house weeping aloud like a child. Mr. Gale seemed surprised at my feelings, and my expressed confidence that God would revive his work. The article made no such impression on him as it did on me.

At the next meeting of the young people, I proposed that we should pray in private for the revival of God's work; that we should pray at sunrise, at noon, and at sunset, in our closets, and continue this for one week; when we should come together again and see what farther was to be done. No other means were used for the revival of God's work. But the spirit of prayer was immediately poured out wonderfully upon the young converts. Before the week was out I learned that some of them, when they would attempt to observe this season of prayer, would lose all their strength and be unable to rise to their feet, or even stand upon their knees in their closets; and that some would lie prostrate on the floor, and pray with unutterable groanings for the out-pouring of the Spirit of God.

The Spirit was poured out, and before the week ended all the meetings were thronged; and there was as much interest in religion, I think, as there had been at any time during the revival.

And here, I am sorry to say, a mistake was made, or, perhaps I should say, a sin committed, by some of the older members of the church, which resulted in great evil. As I afterward learned, a considerable number of the older people resisted this new movement among the young converts. They were jealous of it. They did not know what to make of it, and felt that the young converts were getting out of their place, in being so forward and so urgent upon the older members of the church. This state of mind finally grieved the Spirit of God. It was not long before alienations began to arise among these older members of the church, which finally resulted in great evil to those who had allowed themselves to resist this latter revival. The young people held out well. The converts, so far as I know, were almost universally sound, and have been thoroughly efficient Christians.

In the Spring of this year, 1822, I put myself under the care of the Presbytery as a candidate for the Gospel ministry. Some of the ministers urged me to go to Princeton to study theology, but I declined. When they asked me why I would not go to Princeton, I told them that my pecuniary circumstances forbade it. This was true; but they said they would see that my expenses were paid. Still I refused to go; and when urged to give them my reasons, I plainly told them that I would not put myself under such an influence as they had been under; that I was confident they had been wrongly educated, and they were not ministers that met my ideal of what a minister of Christ should be. I told them this reluctantly, but I could not honestly withhold it. They appointed my pastor to superintend my studies. He offered me the use of his library, and said he would give what attention I needed to my theological studies.

But my studies, so far as he was concerned as my teacher, were little else than controversy. He held to the old school doctrine of original sin, or that the human constitution was morally depraved. He held also, that men were utterly unable to comply with the terms of the Gospel, to repent, to believe, or to do anything that God required them to do; that while they were free to all evil, in the sense of being able to commit any amount of sin, yet they were not free to perform any good; that God had condemned men for their sinful nature; and for this, as well as for their transgressions, they deserved eternal death.

He held also that the influences of the Spirit of God on the minds of men were physical, acting directly upon the substance of the soul; that men were passive in regeneration; and in short he held all those doctrines that logically flow from the fact of a nature sinful in itself. These doctrines I could not receive. I could not receive his views on the subject of atonement, regeneration, faith, repentance, the slavery of the will, or any of the kindred doctrines. But of these views he was quite tenacious; and he seemed sometimes not a little impatient because I did not receive them without question. He used to insist that if I would reason on the subject, I should probably land in infidelity. And then he would remind me that some of the students who had been at Princeton had gone away infidels, because they would reason on the subject, and would not accept the confession of faith, and the teaching of the doctors at that school. He furthermore warned me repeatedly, and very feelingly, that as a minister I should never be useful unless I embraced the truth, meaning the truth as he believed and taught it.

I am sure I was quite willing to believe what I found taught in the Bible, and told him so. We used to have many protracted discussions; and I would often come from his study greatly depressed and discouraged, saying to myself, "I cannot embrace these views come what will. I cannot believe they are taught in the Bible." And several times I was on the point of giving up the study for the ministry altogether.

There was but one member of the church to whom I opened my mind freely on this subject; and that was Elder H., a very godly, praying man. He had been educated in Princeton views, and held pretty strongly the higher doctrines of Calvinism. Nevertheless, as we had frequent and protracted conversations, he became satisfied that I was right; and he would call on me frequently to have seasons of prayer with me, to strengthen me in my studies, and in my discussions with Mr. G., and to decide me more and more firmly that, come what would, I would preach the gospel.

Several times he fell in with me when I was in a state of great depression, after coming from Mr. Gale's study. At such times he would go with me to my room; and sometimes we would continue till a late hour at night crying to God for light and strength, and for faith to accept and do his perfect will. He lived more than three miles from the village; and frequently he has stayed with me till ten or eleven o'clock at night, and then walked home. The dear old man! I have reason to believe that he prayed for me daily as long as he lived.

After I got into the ministry and great opposition was raised to my preaching, I met Elder H. at one time, and he alluded to the opposition, and said, "Oh! my soul is so burdened that I pray for you day and night. But I am sure that God will help. Go on," he said, "go on, brother Finney; the Lord will give you deliverance."

One afternoon Mr. Gale and I had been conversing for a long time on the subject of the atonement, and the hour arrived for us to attend the conference meeting. We continued our conversation on that subject until we got into the house. As we were early, and very few persons had arrived, we continued our conversation. The people kept coming in; and they would sit down and listen with the greatest attention to what we were saying. Our discussion was very earnest, though I trust conducted in a Christian spirit. The people became more and more interested in hearing our discussion, and when we proposed to stop and commence our meeting, they earnestly begged us to proceed with our discussion and let that be our meeting. We did so; and spent the whole evening, I think very much to the satisfaction of those present, and I trust to their permanent edification.

After I had been studying theology for a few months, and Mr. Gale's health was such that he was unable to preach; a Universalist minister came in and began to promote his objectionable doctrines. The impenitent part of the community seemed very much disposed to hear him, and finally people became so interested that there was a large number that seemed to be shaken in their minds, in regard to the commonly received views of the Bible. In this state of things, Mr. Gale, together with some of the elders of his church, desired me to address the people on the subject, and see if I could not reply to the arguments of the Universalist. The great effort of the Universalist was of course to show that sin did not deserve endless punishment. He inveighed against the doctrine of endless punishment as unjust, infinitely cruel and absurd. God was love; and how could a God of love punish men endlessly?

I arose in one of our evening meetings and said, "This Universalist preacher holds forth doctrines that are new to me, and I do not believe they are taught in the Bible. But I am going to examine the subject, and if I cannot show that his views are false, I will become a Universalist myself." I then appointed a meeting the next week, at which time I proposed to deliver a lecture in opposition to his views. The Christian people were rather startled at my boldness in saying that I would be a Universalist, if I could not prove that his doctrines were false. However, I felt sure that I could.

When the evening came for my lecture, the house was crowded. I took up the question of the justice of endless punishment, and discussed it through that and the next evening. There was general satisfaction with the presentation. The Universalist himself found that the people were convinced that he was wrong, and then he took another tack. Mr. Gale, together with his school of theology, maintained that the atonement of Christ was the literal payment of the debt of the elect, a suffering of just what they deserved to suffer; so that the elect were saved upon principles of exact justice; Christ, so far as they were concerned, having fully answered the demands of the law. The Universalist seized upon this view, assuming that this was the real nature of the atonement. He had only to prove that the atonement was made for all men, and then he could show that all men would be saved; because the debt of all mankind had been literally paid by the Lord Jesus Christ, and Universalism would follow on the very ground of justice; for God could not justly punish those whose debt was paid.

I saw, and the people saw — those of them who understood Mr. Gale's position, that the Universalist had got him into a tight place. For it was easy to prove that the atonement was made for all mankind; and if the nature and value of the atonement were as Mr. Gale held, universal salvation was an inevitable result.

This again carried the people away; and Mr. Gale sent for me and requested that I should go on and reply to him further. He said he understood that the question on the ground of law was settled; but now I must answer his argument upon the ground of the Gospel. I said to him, "Mr. Gale, I cannot do it without contradicting your views on that subject, and setting them all aside. With your views of the atonement he cannot be answered. For if you have the right view of the atonement, the people can easily see that the Bible proves that Christ died for all men, for the whole world of sinners; and therefore unless you will allow me to sweep your views of the atonement all away, I can say nothing to any purpose." "Well," said Mr. Gale, "it will never do to let the thing remain as it is. You may say what you please; only go on and answer him in your own way. If I find it necessary to preach on the subject of the atonement, I shall be obliged to contradict you." "Very well," said I, "let me but show my views, and I can answer the Universalist; and you may say to the people afterward what you please."

I then appointed to lecture on the Universalists argument founded on the Gospel. I delivered two lectures upon the atonement.

In these I think I fully succeeded in showing that the atonement did not consist in the literal payment of the debt of sinners, in the sense which the Universalist maintained; that it simply rendered the salvation of all men possible, and did not of itself lay God under obligation to save anybody; that it was not true that Christ suffered just what those for whom he died deserved to suffer; that no such thing as that was taught in the Bible, and no such thing was true; that, on the contrary, Christ died simply to remove an insurmountable obstacle out of the way of God's forgiving sinners, so as to render it possible for him to proclaim a universal amnesty, inviting all men to repent, to believe in Christ, and to accept salvation; that instead of having satisfied retributive justice, and borne just what sinners deserve, Christ had only satisfied public justice, by honoring the law, both in his obedience and death, thus rendering it safe for God to pardon sin, to pardon the sins of any man and of all men who would repent and believe in him. I maintained that Christ, in his atonement, merely did that which was necessary as a condition of the forgiveness of sin; and not that which canceled sin, in the sense of literally paying the indebtedness of sinners.

This answered the Universalist, and put a stop to any further proceedings or excitement on that subject. But what was very striking, these lectures secured the conversion of the young woman for whom, as I have said, such earnest and agonizing prayer had been offered. This was very astonishing to Mr. Gale; for the evidence was that the Spirit of God had blessed my views of the atonement. This, I think, staggered him considerably in regard to the correctness of his view. I could see, in conversing with him, that he felt very much surprised that this view of the atonement should be instrumental in converting that young woman.

After many such discussions with Mr. Gale in pursuing my theological studies, the presbytery was finally called together at Adams to examine me; and, if they could agree to do so, to license me to preach the Gospel. This was in March 1824. I expected a severe struggle with them in my examination; but I found them a good deal softened. The manifest blessing that had attended my conversations, and my teaching in prayer and conference meetings, and in these lectures of which I have spoken, rendered them, I think, more cautious than they would otherwise have been in getting into any controversy with me. In the course of my examination they avoided asking any such questions as would naturally bring my views into collision with theirs. When they had examined me, they voted unanimously to license me to preach. Unexpectedly to myself they asked me if I received the confession of faith of the Presbyterian church. I had not examined it — that is, the large work containing the catechism and confession. This had made no part of my study. I replied that I received it for substance of doctrine, so far as I understood it. But I spoke in a way that plainly implied, I think, that I did not pretend to know much about it. However, I answered honestly, as I understood it at the time. They heard the trial sermons which I had written, on texts which had been given me by the presbytery; and went through with all the ordinary details of such an examination.

At this meeting of presbytery I first saw Rev. Daniel Nash, who is generally known as "Father Nash." He was a member of the presbytery. A large congregation was assembled to hear my examination. I got in a little late, and saw a man standing in the pulpit speaking to the people, as I supposed. He looked at me, I observed, as I came in; and was looking at others as they passed up the aisles. As soon as I reached my seat and listened, I observed that he was praying. I was surprised to see him looking all over the house, as if he were talking to the people; while in fact he was praying to God. Of course it did not sound to me much like prayer; and he was at that time indeed in a very cold and back-slidden state. I shall have occasion frequently to mention him hereafter.

The next Sunday after I was licensed, I preached for Mr. Gale. When I came out of the pulpit he said to me. "Mr. Finney, I shall be very much ashamed to have it known, wherever you go, that you studied theology with me." This was so much like him, and like what he had repeatedly said to me, that I made little or no reply to it. I held down my head, and felt discouraged, and went my way. He afterwards viewed this subject very differently; and told me that he blessed the Lord that in all our discussion, and in all he had said to me, he had not had the least influence to change my views. He very frankly confessed his error in the manner in which he had dealt with me; and said that if I had listened to him I should have been ruined as a minister. The fact is that Mr. Gale's education for the ministry had been entirely defective. He had imbibed a set of opinions, both theological and practical, that were a strait jacket to him. He could accomplish very little or nothing if he carried out his own principles. I had the use of his library, and searched it thoroughly on all the questions of theology, which came up for examination; and the more I examined the books, the more was I dissatisfied.

I had been used to the close and logical reasonings of the judges, as I found them reported in our law works; but when I went to Mr. Gale's old school library, I found almost nothing proved to my satisfaction. I am sure it was not because I was opposed to the truth, but I was dissatisfied because the positions of these theological authors were unsound and not satisfactorily sustained. They often seemed to me to state one thing and prove another, and frequently fell short of logically proving anything. I finally said to Mr. Gale, "If there is nothing better than I find in your library to sustain the great doctrines taught by our church, I must be an infidel." And I have always believed that had not the Lord led me to see the fallacy of those arguments, and to see the real truth as presented in the Scriptures; especially had he not so revealed himself to me personally that I could not doubt the truth of the Christian religion, I should have been forced to be an infidel.

At first, being no theologian, my attitude in respect to his peculiar views was rather that of negation or denial, than that of opposing any positive view to his. I said, "Your positions are not proved." I often said, "They are unsusceptible of proof." So I thought then, and so I think now. But after all, he would insist upon it that I ought to defer to the opinions of the great and good men who, after much consultation and deliberation, had come to those conclusions; that it was unbecoming in me, a young man, bred to the profession of law, and having no theological education, to oppose my views to those of the great men and profound theologians, whose opinions I found in his library. He urged that if I persisted in having my intelligence satisfied, on those points, with argument, I should become an infidel. He believed that the decisions of the church ought to be respected by a young man like myself, and that I should surrender my own judgment to that of others of superior wisdom. Now I could not deny that there was a good deal of force in this; but still I found myself utterly unable to accept doctrine on the ground of authority. If I tried to accept those doctrines as mere dogmas, I could not do it. I could not be honest in doing it; I could not respect myself in doing it. Often when I left Mr. Gale, I would go to my room and spend a long time on my knees over my Bible. Indeed, I read my Bible on my knees a great deal during those days of conflict, beseeching the Lord to teach me his own mind on those points. I had nowhere to go but directly to the Bible, and to the philosophy or workings of my own mind, as revealed in consciousness. My views took on a positive type but slowly. At first I found myself unable to receive his peculiar views; and then gradually formed views of my own in opposition to them, which appeared to me to be unequivocally taught in the Bible.

But not only were Mr. Gale's theological views such as to cripple his usefulness; his practical views were equally erroneous. Hence he prophesied, with respect to my views, every kind of evil. He assured me, that the Spirit of God would not approve and cooperate with my labors; that if I addressed men as I told him I intended to, they would not hear me; that if they came for a short time, they would soon become offended, and my congregation would all fall off; that unless I wrote my sermons I should immediately become stale and uninteresting, and could not satisfy the people; and that I should divide and scatter instead of building up the congregation, wherever I preached. Indeed, I found his views to be almost the reverse of those which I entertained, on all such practical questions relating to my duty as a minister.

I do not wonder, and did not at the time, that he was shocked at my views and purposes in relation to preaching the gospel. With his education it could not be otherwise. He followed out his views with very little practical result. I pursued mine, and by the blessing of God the results were the opposite of those which he predicted. When this fact came out clearly, it completely upset his theological and practical ideas as a minister. This result, as I shall mention in its place, at first annihilated his hope as a Christian, and finally made him quite another man as a minister.

But there was another defect in brother Gale's education, which I regarded as fundamental. If he had ever been converted to Christ, he had failed to receive that divine anointing of the Holy Ghost that would make him a power in the pulpit and in society, for the conversion of souls. He had fallen short of receiving the baptism of the Holy Ghost, which is indispensable to ministerial success.

When Christ commissioned his apostles to go and preach, he told them to abide at Jerusalem till they were endued with power from on high. This power, as everyone knows, was the baptism of the Holy Ghost poured out upon them on the day of Pentecost. This was an indispensable qualification for success in their ministry. I did not suppose then, nor do I now, that this Baptism was simply the power to work miracles. The power to work miracles and the gift of tongues were given as signs to attest the reality of their divine commission. But the baptism itself was a divine purifying, an anointing bestowing on them a divine illumination, filling them with faith, and love, with peace and power; so that their words were made sharp in the hearts of god's enemies, quick and powerful, like a two-edged sword. This is an indispensable qualification of a successful ministry; and I have often been surprised and pained that to this day so little stress is laid upon this qualification for preaching Christ to a sinful world. Without the direct teaching of the Holy Spirit, a man will never make much progress in preaching the Gospel. The fact is, unless he can preach the Gospel as an experience, present religion to mankind as a matter of consciousness, his speculations and theories will come far short of preaching the Gospel.

I have said that Mr. Gale afterward concluded that he had not been converted. That he was a sincere, good man, in the sense of honestly holding his opinions, I do not doubt. But he was sadly defective in his education, theologically, philosophically and practically; and so far as I could learn, his spiritual state, he had not the peace of the Gospel, when I sat under his ministry.

Let not the reader, from anything that I have said, suppose that I did not love Mr. Gale, and highly respect him. I did both. He and I remained the firmest friends, so far as I know, to the day of his death. I have said what I have in relation to his views, because I think it applicable, I am afraid I must say, to many of the ministers even of the present day. I think that their practical views of preaching the Gospel, whatever their theological views may be, are very defective indeed; and that their want of unction, and of the power of the Holy Ghost, is a radical defect in their preparation for the ministry. I say not this censoriously; but still I would record it as a fact which has long been settled in my mind, and over which I have long had occasion to mourn. And as I have become more and more acquainted with the ministry in this and other countries, I am persuaded that, with all their training, and discipline, and education, there is a lack in practical views of the best way of presenting the Gospel to men, and in adapting means to secure the end; and especially in their want of the power of the Holy Ghost.

I have spoken at considerable length of my protracted controversy with my theological teacher, Mr. Gale. Upon reflection I think that I should state a little more definitely some of the points upon which we had so much discussion. I could not receive that theological fiction of imputation. I will state, as nearly as I can, the exact ground that he maintained and insisted upon. First, he maintained that the guilt of Adam's first transgression is literally imputed to all his posterity; so that they are justly sentenced and exposed to eternal damnation for Adam's sin. Secondly, he maintained that we received from Adam, by natural generation, a nature wholly sinful, and morally corrupt in every faculty of soul and body; so that we are totally unable to perform any act acceptable to God, and are necessitated by our sinful nature to transgress his law, in every action of our lives. And this, he insisted, is the estate into which all men fell by the first sin of Adam. For this sinful nature, thus received from Adam by natural generation, all mankind is also sentenced to, and are deserving of eternal damnation. Then, thirdly, in addition to this, he maintained that we are all justly condemned and sentenced to eternal damnation for our own unavoidable transgression of the law. Thus we find ourselves justly subject to a triple eternal damnation.

Then the second branch of this wonderful imputation is as follows: The sin of all the elect, both original and actual — that is, the guilt of Adam's sin, together with the guilt of their sinful nature, and also guilt of their personal transgressions, are all literally imputed to Christ; and therefore the divine government regarded him as an embodiment of all the sins and guilt of the elect, and treated him accordingly; that is, the Father punished the Son precisely as much as all the elect deserved. Hence their debt being thus fully discharged by the punishment of Christ, they are saved upon principles of "exact justice."

The third branch of this wonderful theological fiction is as follows: First — The obedience of Christ to the divine law is literally imputed to the elect; so that in him they are regarded as having always perfectly obeyed the law. Secondly — His death for them is also imputed to the elect; so that in him they are regarded as having fully suffered all that they deserve on account of the guilt of Adam's sin imputed to them, and on account of their sinful nature, and also on account of all their personal transgressions. Thirdly — Thus by their surety the elect have first perfectly obeyed the law; and then they have by and in their surety suffered the full penalty to which they were subject in consequence of the guilt of Adam's sin imputed to them, and also the guilt of their sinful nature, with all their blame worthiness for their personal transgressions. Thus they have suffered in Christ, just as if they had not obeyed in him. He, first, perfectly obeys for them, which obedience is strictly imputed to them, so that they are regarded by the government of God as having fully obeyed in their surety; secondly, he has suffered for them the penalty of the law, just as if no obedience had been rendered; thirdly, after the law has been doubly satisfied, the elect are required to repent as if no satisfaction had been rendered; fourthly, payment in full having been rendered twice over, the discharge of the elect is claimed to be an act of infinite grace. Thus the elect are saved by grace on principles of justice, so that there is strictly no grace or mercy in our forgiveness, but the whole grace of our salvation is found in the obedience and sufferings of Christ. It follows that the elect may demand their discharge on the score of strict justice. They need not pray for pardon or forgiveness; it is all a mistake to do so. This inference is my own; but it follows, as everyone can see, irresistibly, from what the confession of faith itself asserts, that the elect are saved on principles of exact and perfect justice.

I found it impossible to agree with Mr. Gale on these points. I could not but regard and treat this whole question of imputation as a theological fiction. Upon these points we had constant discussion, in some shape, during the whole course of my study.

I do not recollect that Mr. Gale ever insisted that the confession of faith taught these principles, as I learned that it did when I came to study it. I was not aware that the rules of the presbytery required them to ask a candidate if he accepted the Presbyterian confession of faith. As soon as I learned what were the unambiguous teachings of the confession of faith upon these points, I did not hesitate on all suitable occasions to declare my dissent from them. I repudiated and exposed them. Wherever I found that any class of persons were hidden behind these dogmas, I did not hesitate to demolish them, to the best of my ability.

I have not caricatured these positions of Mr. Gale, but have stated them, as nearly as I can, in the very language in which he would defend them, when I presented them to him in controversy. He did not pretend that they were rational, or that they would bear reasoning upon. Hence he infested that my reasoning would lead me into infidelity. But I insisted that our reason was given us for the very purpose of enabling us to justify the ways of God; and that no such fiction of imputation could by any possibility be true.

Of course there were many other points that were so related to these as necessarily to come under discussion, upon which we had a good deal of controversy, but our controversy always turned upon this as the foundation. If man had a sinful nature, then regeneration must consist in a change of nature. If man's nature was sinful, the influence of the Holy Spirit that must regenerate him, must be physical and not moral. If man had a sinful nature, there was no adaptation in the gospel to change his nature, and consequently no connection, in religion, between means and end.

This brother Gale sternly held; and consequently in his preaching he never seemed to expect, nor even to aim at converting anybody, by any sermon that I ever heard him preach. And yet he was an able preacher as preaching was then estimated. The fact is, these dogmas were a perfect strait-jacket to him. If he preached repentance, he must be sure before he sat down, to leave the impression on his people that they could not repent. If he called them to believe he must be sure to inform them that, until their nature was changed by the Holy Spirit, faith was impossible to them. And so his orthodoxy was a perfect snare to himself and to his hearers. I could not receive it. I did not so understand my Bible; nor could he make me see that it was taught in the Bible.

When I came to read the confession of faith, and saw the passages that were quoted to sustain these peculiar positions, I was absolutely ashamed of it. I could not feel any respect for a document that would undertake to impose on mankind such dogmas as those, sustained, for the most part, by passages of Scripture that were totally irrelevant; and not in a single instance sustained by passages which, in a court of law, would have been considered at all conclusive. But the presbytery, so far as I know, were all of one way of thinking at that time. They subsequently, however, I believe, all gave in; and when Mr. Gale changed his views. I heard no more from any of the members of the presbytery in defense of those views.

CHAPTER 5

PREACHING AS A MISSIONARY

At evening her husband returned,
and learned from herself what had taken place.
He was greatly enraged,
and swore he would "kill Finney."

Having had no regular training for the ministry I did not expect
or desire to labor in large towns or cities, or minister to cultivated
congregations. I intended to go into the new settlements and preach
in schoolhouses, and barns, and groves, as best I could. Accordingly,
soon after being licensed to preach, for the sake of being introduced
to the region where I proposed to labor, I took a commission, for six
months, from a female missionary society located in Oneida county. I
went into the northern part of Jefferson county, and began my labors
at Evans' Mills, in the town of Le Ray.

At this place I found two churches, a small Congregational
church without a minister, and a Baptist church with a minister. I
presented my credentials to the deacons of the church. They were very
glad to see me, and I soon began my labors. They had no meeting
house; but the two churches worshipped alternately in a large stone
schoolhouse, large enough, I believe, to accommodate all the children
in the village. The Baptists occupied the house one Sunday, and
the Congregationalists the next; so that I could have the house but
every other Sunday, but could use it evenings as often as I pleased. I

therefore divided my Sundays between Evans' Mills and Antwerp, a village some sixteen or eighteen miles still farther north.

I will relate first some facts that occurred at Evans' Mills, during that season; and then give a brief narrative of the occurrences at Antwerp. But as I preached alternately in these two places, these facts were occurring from week to week in one or the other of these localities. I began, as I said, to preach in the stone schoolhouse at Evans' Mills. The people were very much interested, and thronged the place to hear me preach. They extolled my preaching; and the little Congregational church became very much interested, and hopeful that they should be built up, and that there would be a revival. More or less convictions occurred under every sermon that I preached; but still no general conviction appeared upon the public mind.

I was very much dissatisfied with this state of things; and at one of my evening services, after having preached there two or three Sundays, and several evenings in the week, I told the people at the close of my sermon, that I had come there to secure the salvation of their souls; that my preaching, I knew, was highly complimented by them; but that, after all, I did not come there to please them but to bring them to repentance; that it mattered not to me how well they were pleased with my preaching, if after all they rejected my Master; that something was wrong, either in me or in them; that the kind of interest they manifested in my preaching was doing them no good; and that I could not spend my time with them unless they were going to receive the Gospel. I then, quoting the words of Abraham's servant, said to them, "Now will you deal kindly and truly with my master? If you will, tell me; and if not, tell me, that I may turn to the right hand or to the left." I turned this question over, and pressed it upon them, and insisted upon it that I must know what course they proposed to pursue. If they did not purpose to become Christians, and enlist in the service of the Savior, I wanted to know it that I might not labor with them in vain. I said to them, "You admit that what I preach is the Gospel. You profess to believe it. Now will you receive it? Do you mean to receive it, or do you intend to reject it? You must have some mind about it. And now I have a right to take it for granted, in as much as you admit that I have preached the truth, that you acknowledge your obligation at once to become Christians. This obligation you do not deny; but will you meet the obligation? Will you discharge it? Will you do what you admit you ought to do? If you will not, tell me; and if you will, tell me, that I may turn to the right hand or to the left."

After turning this over till I saw they understood it well, and looked greatly surprised at my manner of putting it, I then said to them, "Now I must know your minds, and I want that you who have made up your minds to become Christians, and will give your pledge to make your peace with God immediately, should rise up; but that, on the contrary, those of you who are resolved that you will not become Christians, and wish me so to understand, and wish Christ so to understand, should sit still." After making this plain, so that I knew that they understood it, I then said: "You who are now willing to pledge to me and to Christ, that you will immediately make your peace with God, please rise up. On the contrary, you that mean that I should understand that you are committed to remain in your present attitude, not to accept Christ — those of you that are of this mind, may sit still." They looked at one another and at me, and all sat still just as I expected.

After looking around upon them for a few moments, I said, "Then you are committed. You have taken your stand. You have rejected Christ and his Gospel; and ye are witnesses one against the other, and God is witness against you all. This is explicit and you may remember as long as you live, that you have thus publicly committed yourselves against the Savior, and said, 'We will not have this man, Christ Jesus, to reign over us.'" This is the purport of what I urged upon them, and as nearly in these words as I can recollect. When I thus pressed them they began to look angry, arose, and started for the door. When they began to move, I paused. As soon as I stopped speaking they turned to see why I did not go on. I said, "I am sorry for you; and will preach to you once more, the Lord willing, tomorrow night."

They all left the house except Deacon McC. who was a deacon of the Baptist church in that place. I saw that the Congregationalists were confounded. They were few in number and very weak in faith. I presume that every member of both churches who was present, except Deacon McC., was taken aback, and concluded that the matter was all over — that by my imprudence I had dashed and ruined all hopeful appearances. Deacon McC. came up and took me by the hand and smiling said, "Brother Finney, you have got them. They cannot rest under this, rely upon it. The brethren are all discouraged," said he; "but I am not. I believe you have done the very thing that needed to be done, and that we shall see the results." I thought so myself, of course. I intended to place them in a position which, upon reflection, would make them tremble in view of what they had done. But for that evening and the next day they were full of wrath. Deacon McC. and myself agreed upon the spot, to spend the next day in fasting and prayer — separately in the morning, and together in the afternoon. I learned in the course of the day that the people were threatening me — to ride me on a rail, to tar and feather me, and to give me a walking paper, as they said. Some of them cursed me; and said that I had put them under oath, and made them swear that they would not serve God; that I had drawn them into a solemn and public pledge to reject Christ and his Gospel. This was no more than I expected. In the afternoon Deacon McC. and I went into a grove together, and spent the whole afternoon in prayer. Just at evening the Lord gave us great enlargement, and promise of victory. Both of us felt assured that we had prevailed with God; and that, that night, the power of God would be revealed among the people.

As the time came for meeting, we left the woods and went to the village. The people were already thronging to the place of worship; and those that had not already gone, seeing us go through the villages turned out of their stores and places of business, or threw down their ball clubs where they were playing upon the green, and packed the house to its utmost capacity.

I had not taken a thought with regard to what I should preach; indeed, this was common with me at that time. The Holy Spirit was upon me, and I felt confident that when the time came for action I should know what to preach. As soon as I found the house packed, so that no more could get in, I arose, and I think, without any formal introduction of singing, opened upon them with these words: "Say to the righteous that it shall be well with him; for they shall eat the fruit of their doings. Wo to the wicked! it shall be ill with him; for the reward of his hands shall be given him." The Spirit of God came upon me with such power, that it was like opening an artillery battery upon them. For more than an hour, and perhaps for an hour and a half, the word of God came through me to them in a manner that I could see was carrying all before it. It was a fire and a hammer breaking the rock; and as the sword that was piercing to the dividing asunder of soul and spirit. I saw that a general conviction was spreading over the whole congregation. Many of them could not hold up their heads. I did not call that night for any reversal of the action they had taken the night before, nor for any committal of themselves in any way; but took it for granted, during the whole of the sermon, that they were committed against the Lord. Then I appointed another meeting, and dismissed the congregation.

As the people withdrew, I observed a woman in the arms of some of her friends, who were supporting her, in one part of the house; and I went to see what was the matter, supposing that she was in a fainting fit. But I soon found that she was not fainting, but that she could not speak. There was a look of the greatest anguish in her face, and she made me understand that she could not speak. I advised the women to take her home, and pray with her, and see what the Lord would do. They informed me that she was Miss G., sister of the well-known missionary, and that she was a member of the church in good standing, and had been for several years.

That evening, instead of going to my usual lodgings, I accepted an invitation, and went home with a family where I had not before stopped overnight. Early in the morning I found that I had been sent for to the place where I was supposed to be, several times during the night, to visit families where there were persons under awful distress of mind. This led me to sally forth among the people, and everywhere I found a state of wonderful conviction of sin and alarm for their souls.

After lying in a speechless state about sixteen hours, Miss G.'s mouth was opened, and a new song was given her. She was taken from the horrible pit of miry clay, and her feet were set upon a rock; and it was true that many saw it and feared. It occasioned a great searching among the members of the church. She declared that she had been entirely deceived; that for eight years she had been a member of the church, and thought she was a Christian, but, during the sermon the night before, she saw that she had never known the true God; and when his character arose before her mind as it was then presented, her hope "perished," as she expressed it, "like a moth." She said, such a view of the holiness of God was presented, that like a great wave it swept her away from her standing, and annihilated her hope in a moment.

I found at this place a number of deists[1]; some of them men of high standing in the community. One of them was a keeper of a hotel

---

1 - *Deism – the belief that God created the universe but remains apart from it and permits his creation to administer itself through natural laws. Deism rejects supernatural aspects of religion.*

in the village; and others were respectable men, and of more than average intelligence. But they seemed banded together to resist the revival. When I ascertained exactly the ground they took, I preached a sermon to meet their wants; for on the Sunday they would attend my preaching. I took this for my text: "Suffer me a little, and I will show you that I have yet to speak on God's behalf. I will bring my knowledge from afar, and I will ascribe righteousness to my Maker." I went over the whole ground, so far as I understood their position; and God enabled me to sweep it clean. As soon as I had finished and dismissed the meeting, the hotel keeper, who was the leader among them, came frankly up to me, and taking me by the hand, said, "Mr. Finney, I am convinced. You have met and answered all my difficulties. Now I want you to go home with me, for I want to converse with you." I heard no more of their infidelity; and if I remember right, that class of men were nearly, or quite, all converted.

There was one old man in this place, who was not only an infidel, but a great railer at religion. He was very angry at the revival movement. I heard every day of his railing and blaspheming, but took no public notice of it. He refused altogether to attend meeting. But in the midst of his opposition, and when his excitement was great, while sitting one morning at the table, he suddenly fell out of his chair in a fit of apoplexy. A physician was immediately called, who, after a brief examination, told him that he could live but a very short time; and that if he had anything to say, he must say it at once. He had just strength and time, as I was informed, to stammer out, "Don't let Finney pray over my corpse." This was the last of his opposition in that place.

During that revival my attention was called to a sick woman in the community, who had been a member of a Baptist church, and was well-known in the place; but people had no confidence in her piety. She was fast failing with the consumption; and they begged me to call and see her. I went, and had a long conversation with her. She told me a dream which she had when she was a girl, which made her think that her sins were forgiven. Upon that she had settled down, and no argument could move her. I tried to persuade her, that there was no evidence of her conversion, in that dream. I told her plainly that her acquaintances affirmed that she had never lived a Christian life, and had never evinced a Christian temper; and I had come to try to persuade her to give up her false hope, and see if she would not now accept Jesus Christ that she might be saved. I dealt with her as kindly as I could, but did not fail to make her understand what I meant. But she took great offense; and after I went away complained that I tried to get away her hope and distress her mind; that I was cruel to try to distress a woman as sick as she was, in that way — to try to disturb the repose of her mind. She died not long afterward. But her death has often reminded me of Dr. Nelson's book called, "The Cause and Cure of Infidelity." When this woman came to be actually dying, her eyes were opened; and before she left the world she seemed to have such a glimpse of the character of God, and of what heaven was, and of the holiness required to dwell there, that she shrieked with agony, and exclaimed that she was going to hell. In this state, as I was informed, she died.

While at this place, one afternoon, a Christian brother called on me and wished me to visit his sister, who, as he informed me, was fast failing with consumption, and was a Universalist. Her husband, he said, was a Universalist, and had led her into Universalism. He said he had not asked me to go and see her when her husband was at home, because he feared that he would abuse me; as he was determined that his wife's mind should not be disturbed on the question of universal salvation. I went, and found her not at all at rest in her views of Universalism; and during my conversation with her, she gave up these views entirely, and appeared to embrace the Gospel of Christ. I believe she held fast to this hope in Christ till she died.

At evening her husband returned, and learned from herself what had taken place. He was greatly enraged, and swore he would "kill Finney." As I learned afterward, he armed himself with a loaded pistol, and that night went to meeting where I was to preach. Of this, however, I knew nothing at the time. The meeting that evening was in a schoolhouse out of the village. The house was very much packed, almost to suffocation. I went on to preach with all my might; and almost in the midst of my discourse I saw a powerful looking man, about in the middle of the house, fall from his seat. As he sunk down he groaned, and then cried or shrieked out, that he was sinking to hell. He repeated that several times. The people knew who he was, but he was a stranger to me. I think I had never seen him before.

Of course this created a great excitement. It broke up my preaching; and so great was his anguish that we spent the rest of our time in praying for him. When the meeting was dismissed his friends helped him home. The next morning, I inquired for him; and found that he had spent a sleepless night, in great anguish of mind, and that at the early dawn he had gone forth, they knew not whither. He was not heard from till about ten o'clock in the morning. I was passing up the street, and saw him coming, apparently from a grove at some distance from the village. He was on the opposite side of the street when I first saw him, and coming toward me. When he recognized me, he came across the street to meet me. When he came near enough, I saw that his countenance was all in a glow. I said to him, "Good morning Mr. C.." "Good morning," he replied. "And," said I, "how do you feel in your mind this morning?" "Oh, I do not know," he replied; "I have had an awfully distressed night. But I could not pray there in the house; and I thought if I could get alone, where I could pour out my voice with my heart, I could pray. In the morning I went into the woods; but when I got there," said he, "I found I could not pray. I thought I could give myself to God; but I could not. I tried, and tried, till I was discouraged," he continued. "Finally I saw that it was of no use; and I told the Lord that I found myself condemned and lost; that I had no heart to pray to him, and no heart to repent; that I found I had hardened myself so much that I could not give my heart to him, and therefore I must leave the whole question to him. I was at his disposal, and could not object to his doing with me just as it seemed good in his eyes, for I had no claim to his favor at all. I left the question of my salvation or damnation wholly with the Lord." "Well, what followed?" I inquired. "Why," said he, "I found I had lost all my conviction. I got up and came away, and my mind was so still and quiet that I found the Spirit of God was grieved away, and I had lost my conviction. "But," said he, "when I saw you my heart began to burn and grow hot within me; and instead of feeling as if I wanted to avoid you, I felt so drawn that I came across the street to see you." But I should have said that when he came near me, he leaped, and took me right up in his arms, and turned around once or twice, and then set me down. This preceded the conversation that I have just related. After a little further conversation, I left him. He soon came into a state of mind that led him to indulge a hope. We heard no more of his opposition.

At this place I again saw Father Nash, the man who prayed with his eyes open, at the meeting of presbytery, when I was licensed. After he was at presbytery he was taken with inflamed eyes; and for several weeks was shut up in a dark room. He could neither read nor write, and, as I learned, gave himself up almost entirely to prayer. He had a terrible overhauling in his whole Christian experience; and as soon as he was able to see, with a double black veil before his face, he sallied forth to labor for souls. When he came to Evans' Mills he was full of the power of prayer. He was another man altogether from what he had been at any former period of his Christian life. I found that he had "a praying list," as he called it, of the names of persons whom he made subjects of prayer every day, and sometimes many times a day. And praying with him, and hearing him pray in meeting, I found that his gift of prayer was wonderful, and his faith almost miraculous.

There was a man by the name of D., who kept a low tavern in a corner of the village, whose house was the resort of all the opposers of the revival. The bar-room was a place of blasphemy; and he was himself a most profane, ungodly; abusive man. He went railing about the streets respecting the revival; and would take particular pains to swear and blaspheme whenever he saw a Christian. One of the young converts lived almost across the way from him; and he told me that he meant to sell and move out of that neighborhood, because every time he was out of doors and D. saw him, he would come out and swear, and curse, and say everything he could to wound his feelings. He had not, I think, been at any of our meetings. Of course he was ignorant of the great truths of religion, and despised the whole Christian enterprise.

Father Nash heard us speak of this Mr. D. as "a hard case;" and immediately put his name upon his praying list. He remained in town a day or two, and went on his way, having in view another field of labor. Not many days afterward, as we were holding an evening meeting with a very crowded house, who should come in but this notorious D.? His entrance created a considerable movement in the congregation. People feared that he had come in to make a disturbance. The fear and abhorrence of him had become very general among Christians, I believe; so that when he came in, some of the people got up and retired. I knew his countenance, and kept my eye upon him; I very soon became satisfied that he had not come in to oppose, and that he was in great anguish of mind. He sat and writhed upon his seat, and was very uneasy. He soon arose, and tremblingly asked me if he might say a few words. I told him that he might. He then proceeded to make one of the most heart-broken confessions that I almost ever heard. His confession seemed to cover the whole ground of his treatment of God, and of his treatment of Christians, and of the revival, and of everything good.

This thoroughly broke up the fallow ground in many hearts. It was the most powerful means that could have been used, just then, to give an impetus to the work. D. soon came out and professed a hope, abolished all the revelry and profanity of his bar-room; and from that time, as long as I stayed there, and I know not how much longer, a prayer meeting was held in his bar-room nearly every night.

CHAPTER 6

REVIVAL AT EVANS' MILLS
AND ITS RESULTS

I thought that Jesus could teach me to read;
and I asked him if he would not
please to teach me to read his Word.

A little way from the village of Evans' Mills, was a settlement of Germans, where there was a German church with several elders, and a considerable membership, but no minister, and no regular religious meetings. Once each year they were in the habit of having a minister come up from the Mohawk Valley, to administer the ordinances of baptism and the Lord's supper. He would catechize their children, and receive such of them as had made the required attainments in knowledge. This was the way in which they were made Christians. They were required to commit to memory the catechism, and to be able to answer certain doctrinal questions; whereupon they were admitted to full communion in the church. After receiving the communion, they took it for granted that they were Christians, and that all was safe. This is the way in which that church had been organized and continued.

They requested me to go out there and preach. I consented; and the first time I preached I took this text: "Without holiness no man shall see the Lord." The whole settlement gathered together; and the schoolhouse where they worshipped was filled to its utmost capacity. They could understand English well. I began by showing, what holiness is not. Under this head I took everything that they considered to be religion, and showed that it was not holiness at all. In the second place I showed what holiness is. I then showed, thirdly, what is intended by seeing the Lord; and then, why those that had no holiness could never see the Lord — why they could never be admitted to his presence, and be accepted of him. I then concluded with such pointed remarks as were intended to make the subject go home. And it did go home by the power of the Holy Ghost. The sword of the Lord slew them on the right hand and on the left.

In a very few days it was found that the whole settlement was under conviction; elders of the church and all were in the greatest consternation, feeling that they had no holiness. At their request I appointed a meeting for inquiry, to give instruction to inquirers. This was in their harvest time. I held the meeting at one o'clock in the afternoon, and found the house literally packed. People had thrown down the implements with which they were gathering their harvest, and had come into the meeting. As many were assembled as could be packed in the house. I took a position in the center of the house, as I could not move around among them; and asked them questions, and encouraged them to ask questions. They became very much interested, and were very free in asking questions, and in answering the questions which I asked them. I seldom ever attended a more interesting or profitable meeting than that.

I recollect that one woman came in late, and sat near the door. When I came to speak to her, I said, "You look unwell." "Yes," she replied, "I am very sick, I have been in bed until I came to meeting. But I cannot read; and I wanted to hear God's word so much that I got up and came to meeting." "How did you come?" I inquired. She replied, "I came on foot." "How far is it?" was the next inquiry. "We call it three miles," she said. On inquiry I found that she was under conviction of sin, and had a most remarkably clear apprehension of her character and position before God. She was soon after converted, and a remarkable convert she was. My wife said that she was one of the most remarkable women in prayer that she ever heard pray; and that she repeated more Scripture in her prayers than any person she ever heard.

I addressed another, a tall dignified looking woman, and asked her what was the state of her mind. She replied immediately that she had given her heart to God; and went on to say that the Lord had taught her to read, since she had learned how to pray. I asked her what she meant. She said she never could read, and never had known her letters. But when she gave her heart to God, she was greatly distressed that she could not read God's word. "But I thought," she said, "that Jesus could teach me to read; and I asked him if he would not please to teach me to read his Word." Said she, "I thought when I had prayed that I could read. The children have a Testament, and I went and got it; and I thought I could read what I had heard them read." "But," said she, "I went over to the school ma'am, and asked her if I read right; and she said I did; and since then," said she, "I can read the Word of God for myself."

I said no more; but thought there must be some mistake about this, as the woman appeared to be quite in earnest, and quite intelligent in what she said. I took pains, afterwards to inquire of her neighbors about her. They gave her an excellent character; and they all affirmed that it had been notorious that she could not read a syllable until after she was converted. I leave this to spoke for itself; there is no use in theorizing about it. Such, I think, were the undoubted facts.

But the revival among the Germans resulted in the conversion of the whole church, I believe, and of nearly the whole community of Germans. It was one of the most interesting revivals that I ever witnessed.

While I was laboring at this place, the presbytery was called together to ordain me, which they did. Both churches were so strengthened, and their numbers so greatly increased, that they soon went forward and built each of them a commodious stone meeting house, and I believe have had a healthy state of religion there since that time. I have not been there for many years.

I have only narrated some of the principal facts that I remember as connected with this revival. But I would farther say respecting it, that a wonderful spirit of prayer prevailed among Christians, and great unity of feeling. The little Congregational church, as soon as they saw the results of the next evening's preaching, recovered themselves; for they had been scattered, discouraged, and confounded the night before. They rallied and took hold of the work as best they could; and though a feeble and inefficient band, with one or two exceptions, still they grew in grace, and in the knowledge of the Lord Jesus Christ, during that revival.

The German woman of whom I have spoken as being sick when she came to the meeting of inquiry, united with the Congregational church. I was present and received her to the church. A very affecting incident, I recollect, occurred at the time she gave a relation of her Christian experience. There was a Jewish woman belonging to that church, by the name of S., a very godly woman, of ripe age, and piety. We had been sitting for a long time, and, hearing the narration of the experience of one after another who came forward as candidates for admission to the church. At length this German woman arose and related her experience. It was one of the most touching, childlike, interesting Christian experiences that I ever listened to. As she was going on with her narrative, I observed that old Mrs. S. rose up from her place, and as the house was filled, crowded her way around as best she could. At first I supposed she was going out of doors. I was so occupied myself with the woman's narrative, that I was barely conscious of Mrs. S.'s moving in that direction. As soon as she came near to where the woman stood relating her experience, she stepped forward, and threw her arms around her neck and burst into tears, and said, "God bless you, my dear sister! God bless you!" The woman responded with all her heart; and such a scene as followed, so unpremeditated, so natural, so childlike, so overflowing with love — it melted the congregation on every side to tears. They wept on each other's necks. It was too moving a scene to be described in words.

The doctrines preached were those which I have always preached as the Gospel of Christ. I insisted upon the voluntary total moral depravity of the unregenerate; and the unalterable necessity of a radical change of heart by the Holy Ghost, and by means of the truth. *I laid great stress upon prayer as an indispensable condition of promoting the revival.* The atonement of Jesus Christ, his divinity, his divine mission, his perfect life, his vicarious death, his resurrection, repentance, faith, justification by faith, and all the kindred doctrines, were discussed as thoroughly as I was able, and pressed home, and were manifestly made efficacious by the power of the Holy Ghost.

The means used were simply preaching, prayer and conference meetings, much private prayer, much personal conversation, and meetings for the instruction of earnest inquirers. These, and no other means, were used for the promotion of that work. There was no appearance of fanaticism, no bad spirit, no divisions, no heresies, no schisms. Neither at that time, nor certainly so long as I was acquainted at that place, was there any result of that revival to be lamented, nor any feature of it that was of questionable effect.

I have spoken of cases of intensified opposition to this revival. One circumstance, I found, had prepared the people for this opposition, and had greatly embittered it. I found that region of country what, in the western phrase, would be called, "a burnt district." There had been, a few years previously, a wild excitement passing through that region, which they called a revival of religion, but which turned out to be spurious. I can give no account of it except what I heard from Christian people and others. It was reported as having been a very extravagant excitement; and resulted in a reaction so extensive and profound, as to leave the impression on many minds that religion was a mere delusion. A great many men seemed to be settled in that conviction. Taking what they had seen as a specimen of a revival of religion, they felt justified in opposing any thing looking toward the promoting of a revival.

I found that it had left among Christian people some practices that were offensive, and calculated rather to excite ridicule than any serious conviction of the truth of religion. For example, in all their prayer meetings I found a custom prevailing like this: every professor of religion felt it a duty to testify for Christ. They must "take up the cross," and say something in meeting. One would rise and say in substance: "I have a duty to perform which no one can perform for me. I arise to testify that religion is good; though I must confess that I do not enjoy it at present. I have nothing in particular to say, only to bear my testimony; and I hope you will all pray for me." This concluded, that person would sit down and another would rise and say, about to the same effect: "Religion is good; I do not enjoy it; I have nothing else to say, but I must do my duty. I hope you will all pray for me." Thus the time would be occupied, and the meeting would pass off with very little that was more interesting than such remarks as these. Of course the ungodly would make sport of this.

It was in fact ridiculous and repulsive. But the impression was so rooted in the public mind that this was the way to hold a prayer and conference meeting, and that it was the duty of every professor of religion, whenever an opportunity was afforded, to give such testimony for God, that I was obliged, for the purpose of getting rid of it, to hold no such meetings. I appointed every meeting, consequently, for preaching. When we were assembled, I would begin by singing, and then would pray myself. I would then call on one or two others to pray, naming them. Then I would name a text, and talk for a while. Then, when I saw that an impression was made, I would stop and ask one or two to pray that the Lord might fasten that on their minds. I would then proceed with my talk, and after a little, stop again and ask some one or two to pray. Thus I would proceed, not throwing the meeting open at all for remarks on the part of the brethren and sisters. Then they would go away without being in bondage, feeling that they had neglected their duty in not bearing testimony for God. Thus most of our prayer meetings were not so in name. As they were appointed for preaching, it was not expected that they would be thrown open for everyone to speak; and in this way I was enabled to overcome that silly method of holding meetings, that created so much mirth and ridicule on the part of the ungodly.

After the revival took thorough hold in this place, and those things occurred that I have named, opposition entirely ceased so far as I could learn. I spent more than six months at this place and at Antwerp, laboring between the two plates; and for the latter part of the time I heard nothing of open opposition.

I have spoken of the doctrines preached. I should add, that I was obliged to take much pains in giving instruction to inquirers. The practice had been, I believe, universal, to set anxious sinners to praying for a new heart, and to using means for their own conversion. The directions they received either assumed or implied that they were very willing to be Christians, and were taking much pains to persuade God to convert them. I tried to make them understand that God was using the means with them, and not they with Him; that God was willing, and they were unwilling; that God was ready, and they were not ready. In short, I tried to shut them up to present faith and repentance, as the thing which God required of them, present and instant submission to his will, present and instant acceptance of Christ. I tried to show them that all delay was only an evasion of present duty; that all praying for a new heart, was only trying to throw the responsibility of their conversion upon God; and that all efforts to do duty, while they did not give their hearts to God, were hypocritical and delusive.

During the whole six months that I labored in that region, I rode on horseback from town to town, and from settlement to settlement, in various directions, and preached the Gospel as I had opportunity. When I left Adams my health had run down a good deal. I had coughed blood; and at the time I was licensed, my friends thought that I could live but a short time. Mr. Gale charged me, when I left Adams, not to attempt to preach more than once a week, and then to be sure not to speak more than half an hour at a time. But instead of this, I visited from house to house, attended prayer meetings, and preached and labored every day, and almost every night, through the whole season. Before the six months were completed my health was entirely restored, my lungs were sound, and I could preach two hours, and two hours and a half, and longer, without feeling the least fatigue. I think my sermons generally averaged nearly or quite two hours. I preached out of doors; I preached in barns; I preached in schoolhouses; and a glorious revival spread all over that new region of country.

All through the earlier part of my ministry especially, I used to meet from ministers a great many rebuffs and reproofs, particularly in respect to my manner of preaching. I have said that Mr. Gale, when I preached for him immediately after I was licensed, told me that, he should be ashamed to have anyone know that I was a pupil of his. The fact is, their education had been so entirely different from mine, that they disapproved of my manner of preaching, very much. They would reprove me for illustrating my ideas by reference to the common affairs of men of different pursuits around me, as I was in the habit of doing. Among farmers and mechanics, and other classes of men, I borrowed my illustrations from their various occupations. I tried also to use such language as they would understand. I addressed them in the language of the common people. I sought to express all my ideas in few words, and in words that were in common use.

Before I was converted I had a different tendency. In writing and speaking, I had sometimes allowed myself to use ornate language. But when I came to preach the Gospel, my mind was so anxious to be thoroughly understood, that I studied in the most earnest manner, on the one hand to avoid what was vulgar, and on the other to express my thoughts with the greatest simplicity of language.

This was extremely contrary to the notions which at that time prevailed among ministers, and even yet prevail to a very great extent. In reference to my illustrations they would say, "Why don't you illustrate from events of ancient history, and take a more dignified way of illustrating your ideas?" To this, of course, I replied, that if my illustrations brought forward anything that was new and striking, the illustration itself would rather occupy the minds of the people, than the truth which I wished to illustrate. And in respect to the simplicity of my language, I defended myself by saying, that my object was not to cultivate a style of oratory that should soar above the heads of the people, but to make myself understood; and that therefore I would use any language adapted to this end, and that did not involve coarseness or vulgarity.

About the time that I left Evans' Mills our presbytery met, and I attended the meeting. I left the revival work at the particular request of some brethren, and went over to the presbytery. The brethren had heard of my manner of preaching — those of them who had not heard me preach. The presbytery met in the morning, and went on with the transaction of business; and after our recess for dinner, as we assembled in the afternoon, the mass of the people came together and filled the house. I had not the remotest thought of what was in the minds of the brethren of the presbytery. I therefore took my seat in the crowd, and waited for the meeting of the presbytery to be opened.

As soon as the congregation was fairly assembled, one of the brethren arose and said: "The people have come together manifestly to hear preaching; and I move that Mr. Finney preach a sermon." This was seconded, and unanimously carried. I saw in a moment that it was the design of the brethren of the presbytery to put me on trial, that they might see if I could do as they had heard that I did — get up and preach on the spur of the moment, without any previous preparation. I made no apology or objection to preaching; for I must say that my heart was full of it, and that I wanted to preach. I arose and stepped into the aisle; and looking up to the pulpit, I saw that it was a high, small pulpit, up against the wall. I therefore stood in the aisle and named my text: "Without holiness no man shall see the Lord." The Lord helped me to preach. I walked up and down the broad aisle; and the people were evidently interested and much moved.

But after the meeting one of the brethren stepped up to me and said: "Brother Finney, if you come up our way, I should like to have you preach in some of our school districts. I should not like to have you preach in our church. But we have got schoolhouses in some of the districts, away from the village — I should like to have you preach in some of those." I mention this to show what their ideas were of my method of preaching. But how completely they were in the dark in regard to the results of that method of addressing people! They used to complain that I let down the dignity of the pulpit: that I was a disgrace to the ministerial profession; that I talked like a lawyer at the bar; that I talked to the people in a colloquial manner; that I said "you," instead of preaching about sin and sinners, and saying "they;" that I said "hell," and with such an emphasis as often to shock the people; furthermore, that I urged the people with such vehemence, as if they might not have a moment to live; and sometimes they complained that I blamed the people too much. One doctor of divinity told me that he felt a great deal more like weeping over sinners, than blaming them. I replied to him that I did not wonder, if he believed that they had a sinful nature, and that sin was entailed upon them, and they could not help it.

After I had preached some time, and the Lord had everywhere added his blessing, I used to say to ministers, whenever they contended with me about my manner of preaching, and desired me to adopt their ideas and preach as they did, that I dared not make the change they desired. I said, "Show me a more excellent way. Show me the fruits of your ministry; and if they so far exceed mine as to give me evidence that you have found a more excellent way, I will adopt your views. But do you expect me to abandon my own views and practices, and adopt yours, when you yourselves cannot deny that, whatever errors I may have fallen into, or whatever imperfections there may be in my preaching, in style, and in everything else, yet the results justify my methods?" I would say to them: "I intend to improve all I can; but I never can adopt your manner of preaching the Gospel, until I have higher evidence that you are right and I am wrong."

They used to complain, oftentimes, that I was guilty of repetition in my preaching. I would take the same thought and turn it over and over, and illustrate it in various ways. I assured them that I thought it was necessary to do so, to make myself understood; and that I could not be persuaded to relinquish this practice by any of their arguments. Then they would say, "you will not interest the educated part of your congregation." But facts soon silenced them on this point. They found that, under my preaching, judges, and lawyers, and educated men were converted by scores; whereas, under their methods, such a thing seldom occurred.

CHAPTER 7

REMARKS UPON MINISTERIAL EDUCATION

All ministers may be, and ought to be,
so filled with the Holy Spirit that all who hear them
shall be impressed with the conviction that
"God is in them of a truth."

In what I say upon this subject I hope my brethren will not impute to me any other motive than a kind and benevolent regard for their highest usefulness. I have always taken their criticisms kindly, and given them credit for benevolent intentions. Now I am an old man, and many of the results of my views and methods are known to the public. Is it out of place in me to speak freely to the ministry, upon this subject? In reply to their objections, I have sometimes told them what a judge of the supreme court remarked to me, upon this subject. "Ministers," said he, "do not exercise good sense in addressing the people. They are afraid of repetition. They use language not well understood by the common people. Their illustrations are not taken from the common pursuits of life. They write in too elaborated a style, and read without repetition, and are not understood by the people." "Now," said he, "if lawyers should take such a course, they would ruin themselves and their cause." "When I was at the bar," he added, "I used to take it for granted, when I had before me a jury of respectable men, that I should have to repeat over my main positions about as many times as there were persons in the jury-box. I learned that unless I did so, illustrated, and repeated, and turned the main points over — the main points of law and of evidence, I should lose my cause." "Our object," he said, "in addressing a jury, is to get their minds settled before they leave the jury-box; not to make a speech in language but partially understood by them; not to let ourselves out in illustrations entirely above their apprehension; not to display our oratory, and then let them go. We are set on getting a verdict. Hence we are set upon being understood. We mean to convince them; and if they have doubts as to the law, we make them understand it, and rivet it in their minds. In short, we expect to get a verdict, and to get it upon the spot; so that when they go to their room, it will be found that they have understood us, and that they have been convinced by the facts and arguments. If we do not thus take pains to urge home every thought and every word, and every point, so as to lodge it in their convictions, we are sure to lose our cause. We must overcome their prejudices; we must overcome their ignorance; we must try to overcome even their interest, if they have any, against our client." "Now," said he, "if ministers would do this, the effects of their preaching would be unspeakably different from what they are. They go into their study and write a sermon; they go into their pulpit and read it, and those that listen to it but poorly understand it. Many words used they will not understand, until they go home and consult their dictionaries. They do not address the people, expecting to convince them, and to get their verdict in favor of Christ, upon the spot. They seek no such object. They rather seem to aim at making fine literary productions, and displaying great eloquence and an ornate use of language." Of course I do not profess, at this distance of time, to give the exact language used by the judge; but I have given his remarks in substance, as made to me at the time.

I never entertained the least hard feeling toward my brethren for the roughness with which they often treated me. I knew that they were very anxious to have me do good; and really supposed that I should do much more good, and much less evil, if I should adopt their views. But I was of a different opinion.

I could mention many facts illustrative of the views of ministers, and of the manner in which they sometimes treated me. When I was preaching in Philadelphia, for example, Dr., the celebrated temperance lecturer from Connecticut, came there and heard me preach. He was indignant at the manner in which I let down the dignity of the pulpit.

His principal conversation, however, was with Mr. Patterson, with whom, at the time, I labored. He insisted upon it that I should not be allowed to preach till I had a ministerial education; that I should stop preaching and go to Princeton and learn theology, and get better views of the way in which the Gospel should be preached.

Let not anything I say on this subject leave the impression on any mind, that I thought either my views or my methods perfect, for I had no such thought. I was aware that I was but a child. I had not enjoyed the advantages of the higher schools of learning; and so conscious had I been all along that I lacked those qualifications that would make me acceptable, especially to ministers, and I feared to the people in large places, that I had never had any higher ambition or purpose than to go into the new settlements and places where they did not enjoy the Gospel. Indeed, I was often surprised myself, in the first year of my preaching, to find it so edifying and acceptable to the most educated classes. This was more than I had expected, greatly more than my brethren had expected, and more than I had dared to hope myself. I always endeavored to improve in everything in which I discovered myself to be in error. But the longer I preached, the less reason had I to think that my error lay in the direction in which it was supposed to lie, by my brother ministers.

The more experience I had, the more I saw the results of my method of preaching, the more I conversed with all classes, high and low, educated and uneducated, the more was I confirmed in the fact that God had led me, had taught me, had given me right conceptions in regard to the best manner of winning souls. I say that God taught me; and I know it must have been so; for surely I never had obtained these notions from man. And I have often thought that I could say with perfect truth, as Paul said, that I was not taught the Gospel by man, but by the Spirit of Christ himself. And I was taught it by the Spirit of the Lord in a manner so clear and forcible, that no argument of my ministerial brethren, with which I was plied so often and so long, had the least weight with me.

I mention this as a matter of duty. For I am still solemnly impressed with the conviction, that the schools are to a great extent spoiling the ministers. Ministers in these days have great facilities for obtaining information on all theological questions; and are vastly more learned, so far as theological, historical, and Biblical learning is concerned, than they perhaps ever have been in any age of the world. Yet with all their learning, they do not know how to use it. They are, after all, to a great extent, like David in Saul's armor. A man can never learn to preach except by preaching.

But one great thing above all others ministers need, and that is sincereness. If they have a reputation to secure and to nurse, they will do but little good. Many years ago a beloved pastor of my acquaintance, left home for his health, and employed a young man, just from the seminary, to fill his pulpit while he was absent. This young man wrote and preached as splendid sermons as he could. The pastor's wife finally ventured to say to him, "You are preaching over the heads of our people. They do not understand your language or your illustrations. You bring too much of your learning into the pulpit." He replied, "I am a young man. I am cultivating a style. I am aiming to prepare myself for occupying a pulpit and surrounding myself with a cultivated congregation. I cannot descend to your people. I must cultivate an elevated style." I have had my thought and my eye upon this man ever since. I am not aware that he is yet dead; but I have never seen his name connected with any revival, amidst all the great revivals that we have had, from year to year, since that time; and I never expect to, unless his views are radically changed, and unless he addresses the people from an entirely different stand-point, and from entirely different motives.

I could name ministers who are yet alive, old men like myself, who were greatly ashamed of me when I first began to preach because I was so undignified in the pulpit, used such common language, addressed the people with such directness, and because I aimed not at all at ornament, or at supporting the dignity of the pulpit.

Dear brethren they were; and I always felt in the kindest manner toward them, and do not know that in a single instance I was ruffled or angry at what they said. I was from the very first aware that I should meet with this opposition; and that there was this wide gulf in our views, and would be in practice, between myself and other ministers. I seldom felt that I was one of them, or that they regarded me as really belonging to their fraternity. I was bred a lawyer. I came right forth from a law office to the pulpit, and talked to the people as I would have talked to a jury.

It was very common, as I learned, among ministers in my earlier years of preaching, to agree among themselves that if I were to succeed in the ministry, it would bring the schools into disrepute; and men would come to think it hardly worthwhile to support them with their funds, if a man could be accepted as a successful preacher without them. Now I never had a thought of undervaluing the education furnished by colleges or theological seminaries; though I did think, and think now, that in certain respects they are greatly mistaken in their modes of training their students. They do not encourage them to talk to the people, and accustom themselves to extemporaneous addresses to the people in the surrounding country, while pursuing their studies. Men cannot learn to preach by study without practice. The students should be encouraged to exercise, and prove, and improve, their gifts and calling of God, by going out into any places open to them, and holding Christ up to the people in earnest talks. They must thus learn to preach. Instead of this, the students are required to write what they call sermons, and present them or criticism; to preach, that is, read them to the class and the professor. Thus they play preaching. No man can preach in this manner. These so-called sermons will of course, under the criticism they receive, degenerate into literary essays. The people have no respect for such sermons, as sermons. This reading of elegant literary essays, is not to them preaching. It is gratifying to literary taste, but not spiritually edifying. It does not meet the wants of the soul. It is not calculated to win souls to Christ. The students are taught to cultivate a fine, elevated style of writing. As for real eloquence, that gushing, impressive, and persuasive oratory, that naturally flows from an educated man whose soul is on fire with his subject, and who is free to pour out his heart to a waiting and earnest people, they have none of it.

A reflecting mind will feel as if it were infinitely out of place to present in the pulpit to immortal souls, hanging upon the verge of everlasting death, such specimens of learning and rhetoric. They know that men do not do so on any subject where they are really in earnest. The captain of a fire company, when a city is on fire, does not read to his company an essay or exhibit a fine specimen of rhetoric, when he shouts to them and directs their movements. It is a question of urgency, and he intends that every word shall be understood. He is entirely in earnest with them; and they feel that criticism would be out of place in regard to the language he uses.

So it always is when men are entirely in earnest. Their language is in point, direct and simple. Their sentences are short, cogent, powerful. The appeal is made directly for action; and hence all such discourses take effect. This is the reason why, formerly, the ignorant Methodist preachers, and the earnest Baptist preachers produced so much more effect than our most learned theologians and divines. They do so now. The impassioned utterance of a common exhorter will often move a congregation far beyond anything that those splendid exhibitions of rhetoric can effect. Great sermons lead the people to praise the preacher. Good preaching leads the people to praise the Savior.

Our theological schools would be of much greater value than they are, if they were much more practical. I heard a theological teacher read a sermon on the importance of extemporaneous preaching. His views on that subject were correct; but his practice entirely contradicted them. He seemed to have studied the subject, and to have attained to practical views of the highest importance. But yet I have never known one of his students, in practice, to adopt those views. I have understood that he says that if he were to begin his life anew as a preacher, he would practice according to his present views; and that he laments that his education was wrong in this respect, and consequently his practice has been wrong.

In our school at Oberlin our students have been led — not by myself, I am bound to say — to think that they must write their sermons; and very few of them, notwithstanding all I could say to them, have the courage to launch out, and commit themselves to extemporaneous preaching. They have been told again and again: "You must not think to imitate Mr. Finney. You cannot be Finneys."

Ministers do not like to get up and talk to the people as best they can, and break themselves at once into the habit of talking to the people. They must preach; and if they must preach in the common acceptation of the term, they must write. Hence, according to that view, I have never preached. Indeed, people have often said to me: "Why, you do not preach. You talk to the people." A man in London went home from one of our meetings greatly convicted. He had been a skeptic; and his wife seeing him greatly excited, said to him, "Husband, have you been to hear Mr. Finney preach?" He replied: "I have been to Mr. Finney's meeting. He doesn't preach; he only explains what other people preach." This, in substance, I have heard over and over again.

"Why!" they say, "anybody could preach as you do. You just talk to the people. You talk as if you were as much at home as if you sat in the parlor." Others have said: "Why it doesn't seem like preaching; but it seems as if Mr. Finney had taken me alone, and was conversing with me face to face."

Ministers generally avoid preaching what the people before them will understand as addressed particularly to them. They will preach to them about other people, and the sins of other people, instead of addressing them and saying, "You are guilty of these sins;" and, "The Lord requires this of you." They often preach about the Gospel instead of preaching the Gospel. They often preach about sinners instead of preaching to them. They studiously avoid being personal, in the sense of making the impression on anyone present that he is the man. Now I have thought it my duty to pursue a different course; and I always have pursued a different course. I have often said, "Do not think I am talking about anybody else; but I mean you, and you, and you."

Ministers told me at first that people would never endure this; but would get up and go out, and never come to hear me again. But this is all a mistake. Very much, in this as in everything else, depends on the spirit in which it is said. If the people see that it is said in the spirit of love, with a yearning desire to do them good; if they cannot call it an ebullition of personal animosity, but if they see, and cannot deny that it is telling the truth in love; that it is coming right home to them to save them individually, there are very few that will continue to resent it. If at the time they feel pointed at and rebuked, nevertheless the conviction is upon them that they needed it, and it will surely ultimately do them great good.

I have often said to people, when I saw that they looked offended, "Now you resent this and you will go away and say that you will not come again; but you will. Your own convictions are on my side. You know that what I tell you is true; and that I tell it for your own good; and that you cannot continue to resent it." And I have always found this to be true.

My experience has been, that even in respect to personal popularity, "honesty is the best policy" in a minister; that if he means to maintain his hold upon the confidence, and respect, and affection of any people, he must be faithful to their souls. He must let them see that he is not courting them for any purpose of popularity, but that he is trying to save their souls. Men are not fools. they have no solid respect for a man that will go into the pulpit and preach smooth things. They cordially despise it in their inmost souls. And let no man think that he will gain permanent respect, that he will be permanently honored by his people, unless as an ambassador of Christ he deals faithfully with their souls.

The great argument in opposition to my views of preaching the Gospel was, that I should not give nearly so much instruction to the people, as I should if I wrote my sermons. They said I would not study; and consequently, although I might succeed as an evangelist, when I labored but a few weeks or months in a place, still it would never do for a pastor to preach extemporaneously.

Now I have the best of reasons for believing that preachers of written sermons do not give their people so much instruction as they think they do. The people do not remember their sermons. I have in multitudes of instances heard people complain — "I cannot carry home anything that I hear from the pulpit." They have said to me in hundreds of instances: "We always remember what we have heard you preach. We remember your text, and the manner in which you handled it; but written sermons we cannot remember."

I have been a pastor now for many years — indeed, ever since 1832; and I have never heard any complaint that I did not instruct the people. I do not believe it is true that my people are not as well instructed, so far as pulpit instruction is concerned, as those people are who sit under the preaching of written sermons. It is true that a man may write his sermons without studying much; as it is true that he may preach extemporaneously without much study or thought. Many written sermons, that I have heard, manifested anything but profound, accurate thought.

My habit has always been to study the Gospel, and the best application of it, all the time. I do not confine myself to hours and days of writing my sermons; but my mind is always pondering the truths of the Gospel, and the best ways of using them. I go among the people and learn their wants. Then, in the light of the Holy Spirit, I take a subject that I think will meet their present necessities. I think intensely on it, and pray much over the subject on Sunday morning, for example, and get my mind full of it, and then go and pour it out to the people. Whereas one great difficulty with a written sermon is, that a man after he has written it, needs to think but little of the subject. He needs to pray but little. He perhaps reads over his manuscript Saturday evening, or Sunday morning; but he does not feel the necessity of being powerfully anointed, that his mouth may be opened and filled with arguments, and that he may be enabled to preach out of a full heart. He is quite at ease. He has only to use his eyes and his voice, and he can preach, in his way. It may be a sermon that has been written for years; it may be a sermon that he has written, every word of it, within the week. But on Sunday-day there is no freshness in it. It does not come necessarily new and fresh, and as an anointed message from God to his heart, and through his heart to the people.

I am prepared to say, most solemnly, that I think I have studied all the more for not having written my sermons. I have been obliged to make the subjects upon which I preached familiar to my thoughts, to fill my mind with them, and then go and talk them off to the people. I simply note the heads upon which I wish to dwell in the briefest possible manner and in language not a word of which I use, perhaps, in preaching. I simply jot down the order of my propositions, and the petitions which I propose to take; and in a word, sketch an outline of the remarks and inferences with which I conclude.

But unless men will try it, unless they will begin and talk to the people, as best they can, keeping their hearts full of truth and full of the Holy Ghost, they will never make extemporaneous preachers. I believe that half an hour's earnest talk to the people from week to week, if the talk be pointed, direct, earnest, logical, will really instruct them more than the two labored sermons that those who write, get off to their people on the Sunday. I believe the people would remember more of what is said, be more interested in it, and would carry it away with them to be pondered, vastly more than they do what they get from the labored written sermons.

I have spoken of my method of preparing for the pulpit in more recent years. When I first began to preach, and for some twelve years of my earliest ministry, I wrote not a word; and was most commonly obliged to preach without any preparation whatever, except what I got in prayer. Oftentimes I went into the pulpit without knowing upon what text I should speak, or a word that I should say. I depended on the occasion and the Holy Spirit to suggest the text, and to open up the whole subject to my mind; and certainly in no part of my ministry have I preached with greater success and power. If I did not preach from inspiration, I don't know how I did preach. It was a common experience with me, and has been during all my ministerial life, that the subject would open up to my mind in a manner that was surprising to myself. It seemed that I could see with intuitive clearness just what I ought to say; and whole platoons of thoughts, words, and illustrations, came to me as fast as I could deliver them. When I first began to make "skeletons," I made them after, and not before I preached. It was to preserve the outline of the thought which had been given me, on occasions such as I have just mentioned. I found when the Spirit of God had given me a very clear view of a subject, I could not retain it, to be used on any other occasion, unless I jotted down an outline of the thoughts. But after all, I have never found myself able to use old skeletons in preaching, to any considerable extent, without remodeling them, and having a fresh and new view of the subject given me by the Holy Spirit. I almost always get my subjects on my knees in prayer; and it has been a common experience with me, upon receiving a subject from the Holy Spirit, to have it make so strong an impression on my mind as to make me tremble, so that I could with difficulty write. When subjects are thus given me that seem to go through me, body and soul, I can in a few moments make out a skeleton that shall enable me to retain the view presented by the Spirit; and I find that such sermons always tell with great power upon the people.

Some of the most telling sermons that I have ever preached in Oberlin, I have thus received after the bell had rung for church; and I was obliged to go and pour them off from my full heart, without jotting down more than the briefest possible skeleton, and that sometimes not covering half the ground that I covered in my sermon.

I tell this, not boastfully, but because it is a fact, and to give the praise to God, and not to any talents of my own. Let no man think that those sermons which have been called so powerful, were productions of my own brain, or of my own heart, unassisted by the Holy Ghost. They were not mine, but from the Holy Spirit in me.

And let no man say that this is claiming a higher inspiration than is promised to ministers, or than ministers have a right to expect. For I believe that all ministers, called by Christ to preach the Gospel, ought to be, and may be, in such a sense inspired, as to "preach the

Gospel with the Holy Ghost sent down from heaven." What else did Christ mean when he said, "Go and disciple all nations; and lo! I am with you always, even unto the end of the world?" What did he mean when he said, speaking of the Holy Spirit, "He shall take of mine and show it unto you?" "He shall bring all things to your remembrance, whatsoever I have said unto you?" What did he mean when he said, "If any man believes in me, out of his belly shall flow rivers of living water?" "This spoke he of the Spirit, that they which believe on him should receive." All ministers may be, and ought to be, so filled with the Holy Spirit that all who hear them shall be impressed with the conviction that "God is in them of a truth."

CHAPTER 8

REVIVAL AT ANTWERP

If I had had a sword in each hand,
I could not have cut them off
their seats as fast as they fell.

I must now give some account of my labors, and their result, at Antwerp, a village north of Evans' mills. I arrived there in April, and found that no religious services, of any kind, were held in the town. The land in the township belonged to a Mr. P., a rich landholder residing in Ogdensburg. To encourage the settlement of the township, he had built a brick meeting house. But the people had no mind to keep up public worship and therefore the meeting house was locked up, and the key was in the possession of a Mr. C., who kept the village hotel.

I very soon learned that there was a Presbyterian church in that place, consisting of but few members. They had, some years before, tried to keep up a meeting at the village, on Sunday. But one of the elders who conducted their Sunday meetings, lived about five miles out of the village, and was obliged, in approaching the village, to pass through a Universalist settlement. The Universalists had broken up the village meeting, by rendering it impossible for Deacon R., as they called him, to get through their settlement to meeting. They would even take off the wheels of his carriage; and finally they carried their opposition so far that he gave up attending meetings at the village; and all religious services at the village, and in the township, so far as I could learn, were relinquished.

I found Mrs. C., the landlady, a pious woman. There were two other pious women in the village, a Mrs. H., the wife of a merchant, and a Mrs. R., the wife of a physician. It was on Friday, if I remember right, that I arrived there. I called on those pious women and asked them if they would like to have a meeting. They said that they would, but they did not know that it would be possible. Mrs. H. agreed to open her parlor that evening, for a meeting, if I could get anybody to attend. I went about and invited the people, and secured the attendance, I think, of some thirteen in her parlor. I preached to them; and then said, that, if I could get the use of the village school house, I would preach on Sunday. I got the consent of the trustees; and the next day an appointment was circulated around among the people, for a meeting at the school house Sunday morning.

In passing around the village I heard a vast amount of profanity. I thought I had never heard so much in any place that I had ever visited. It seemed as if the men, in playing ball upon the green, and in every business place that I stepped into, were all cursing and swearing and damning each other. I felt as if I had arrived upon the borders of hell. I had a kind of awful feeling, I recollect, as I passed around the village on Saturday. The very atmosphere seemed to me to be poison; and a kind of terror took possession of me.

I gave myself to prayer on Saturday, and finally urged my petition till this answer came: "Be not afraid, but speak, and hold not thy peace; for I am with thee, and no man shall set on thee to hurt thee. For I have much people in this city." This completely relieved me of all fear. I found, however, that the Christian people there were really afraid that something serious might happen, if religious meetings were again established in that place. I spent Saturday very much in prayer; but passed around the village enough to see that the appointment that had been given out for preaching at the schoolhouse, was making quite an excitement.

Sunday morning, I arose and left my lodgings in the hotel; and in order to get alone, where I could let out my voice as well as my heart, I went up into the woods at some distance from the village, and continued for a considerable time in prayer. However, I did not get relief, and went up a second time; but the load upon my mind increased, and I did not find relief. I went up a third time; and then the answer came. I found that it was time for meeting, and went immediately to the schoolhouse. I found it packed to its utmost capacity. I had my pocket Bible in my hand, and read to them this text: "God so loved the world that he gave his only begotten son, that whosoever believeth in him might not perish but have everlasting life." I cannot remember much that I said; but I know that the point on which my mind principally labored, was the treatment which God received in return for his love. The subject affected my own mind very much; and I preached and poured out my soul and my tears together.

I saw several of the men there from whom I had, the day before, heard the most awful profanity. I pointed them out in the meeting, and told what they said — how they called on God to damn each other. Indeed, I let lose my whole heart upon them. I told them they seemed "to howl blasphemy about the streets like hell-hounds;" and it seemed to me that I had arrived "on the very verge of hell." Everybody knew that what I said was true, and they quailed under it. They did not appear offended; but the people wept about as much as I did myself. I think there were scarcely any dry eyes in the house.

Mr. C., the landlord, had refused to open the meeting house in the morning. But as soon as these first services closed, he arose and said to the people that he would open the meeting house in the afternoon.

The people scattered, and carried the information in every direction; and in the afternoon the meeting house was nearly as much crowded as the schoolhouse had been in the morning. Everybody was at meeting; and the Lord let me loose upon them in a wonderful manner. My preaching seemed to them to be something new. Indeed, it seemed to myself as if I could rain hail and love upon them at the same time; or in other words, that I could rain upon them hail, in love. It seemed as if my love to God, in view of the abuse which they heaped upon him, sharpened up my mind to the most intense agony. I felt like rebuking them with all my heart, and yet with a compassion which they could not mistake. I never knew that they accused me of severity; although I think I never spoke with more severity, perhaps, in my life.

But the labors of this day were effectual to the conviction of the great mass of the population. From that day, appoint a meeting when and where I would, anywhere round about, and the people would throng to hear. The work immediately commenced and went forward with great power. I preached twice in the village church on Sunday, attended a prayer meeting at intermission, and generally preached somewhere, in a schoolhouse in the neighborhood, at five o'clock in the afternoon.

On the third Sunday that I preached there, an aged man came to me as I was entering the pulpit, and asked me if I would not go and preach in a schoolhouse in his neighborhood, about three miles distant; saying that they had never had any services there. He wished me to come as soon as I could. I appointed the next day, Monday, at five o'clock in the afternoon. It was a warm day. I left my horse at the village, and thought I would walk down, so that I should have no trouble in calling along on the people, in the neighborhood of the schoolhouse. However, before I reached the place, having labored so hard on the Sunday, I found myself very much exhausted, and sat down by the way and felt as if I could scarcely proceed. I blamed myself for not having taken my horse.

But at the appointed hour I found the schoolhouse full, and I could only get a standing-place near the open door. I read a hymn; and I cannot call it singing, for they seemed never to have had any church music in that place. However, the people pretended to sing. But it amounted to about this: each one bawled in his own way. My ears had been cultivated by teaching church music; and their horrible discord distressed me so much that, at first, I thought I must go out. I finally put both hands over my ears, and held them with my full strength. But this did not shut out the discords. I stood it, however, until they were through; and then I cast myself down on my knees, almost in a state of desperation, and began to pray. The Lord opened the windows of heaven, and the spirit of prayer was poured out, and I let my whole heart out in prayer. I had taken no thought with regard to a text upon which to preach; but waited to see the congregation. As soon as I had done praying, I arose from my knees and said: "Up, get you out of this place; for the Lord will destroy this city." I told them I did not recollect where that text was; but I told them very nearly where they would find it, and then went on to explain it. I told them that there was such a man as Abraham, and who he was; and that there was such a man as Lot, and who he was; their relations to each other; their separating from each other on account of differences between their herdsmen; and that Abraham took the hill country, and Lot settled in the valley of Sodom. I then told them how exceedingly wicked Sodom became, and what abominable practices they fell into. I told them that the Lord decided to destroy Sodom, and visited Abraham, and informed him what he was about to do; that Abraham prayed to the Lord to spare Sodom, if he found so many righteous there; and the Lord promised to do so for their sakes; that then Abraham besought him to save it for a certain less number, and the Lord said he would spare it for their sakes; that he kept on reducing the number, until he reduced the number of righteous persons to ten; and God promised him that, if he found ten righteous persons in the city, he would spare it. Abraham made no farther request, and Jehovah left him. But it was found that there was but one righteous person there, and that was Lot, Abraham's nephew. "And the men said to Lot, hast thou here any besides? Son-in-law, and thy sons, and thy daughters, and whatsoever thou hast in the city, bring them out of this place; for we will destroy this place, because the cry of them is great before the face of the Lord; and the Lord has sent us to destroy it."

While I was relating these facts I observed the people looking as if they were angry. Many of the men were in their shirt sleeves; and they looked at each other and at me, as if they were ready to fall upon me and chastise me on the spot. I saw their strange and unaccountable looks, and could not understand what I was saying, that had offended them. However, it seemed to me that their anger rose higher and higher, as I continued the narrative. As soon as I had finished the narrative, I turned upon them and said, that I understood that they had never had a religious meeting in that place; and that therefore I had a right to take it for granted, and was compelled to take it for granted, that they were an ungodly people. I pressed that home upon them with more and more energy, with my heart full almost to bursting.

I had not spoken to them in this strain of direct application, I should think, more than a quarter of an hour, when all at once an awful solemnity seemed to settle down upon them; the congregation began to fall from their seats in every direction, and cried for mercy. If I had had a sword in each hand, I could not have cut them off their seats as fast as they fell. Indeed, nearly the whole congregation were either on their knees or prostrate, I should think, in less than two minutes from this first shock that fell upon them. Every one prayed for himself, who was able to speak at all.

Of course I was obliged to stop preaching; for they no longer paid any attention. I saw the old man who had invited me there to preach, sitting about in the middle of the house, and looking around with utter amazement. I raised my voice almost to a scream, to make him hear, and pointing to him said, "Can't you pray?" He instantly fell upon his knees, and with a stentorian voice poured himself out to God; but he did not at all get the attention of the people. I then spoke as loud as I could, and tried to make them attend to me. I said to them, "You are not in hell yet; and now let me direct you to Christ." For a few moments I tried to hold forth the Gospel to them; but scarcely any of them paid any attention. My heart was so overflowing with joy at such a scene that I could hardly contain myself. It was with much difficulty that I refrained from shouting, and giving glory to God.

As soon as I could sufficiently control my feelings I turned to a young man who was close to me, and was engaged in praying for himself, laid my hand on his shoulder, thus getting his attention, and preached in his ear Jesus. As soon as I got his attention to the cross of Christ, he believed, was calm and quiet for a minute or two, and then broke out in praying for the others. I then turned to another, and took the same course with him, with the same result; and then another, and another. In this way I kept on, until I found the time had arrived when I must leave them, and go and fulfill an appointment in the village. I told them this, and asked the old man who had invited me there, to remain and take charge of the meeting, while I went to my appointment. He did so. But there was too much interest, and there were too many wounded souls, to dismiss the meeting; and so it was held all night. In the morning there were still those there that could not get away; and they were carried to a private house in the neighborhood, to make room for the school. In the afternoon they sent for me to come down there, as they could not yet break up the meeting.

When I went down the second time, I got an explanation of the anger manifested by the congregation during the introduction of my sermon the day before. I learned that the place was called Sodom, but I knew it not; and that there was but one pious man in the place, and him they called Lot. This was the old man that invited me there. The people supposed that I had chosen my subject, and preached to them in that manner, because they were so wicked as to be called Sodom. This was a striking coincidence; but so far as I was concerned, it was altogether accidental.

I have not been in that place for many years. A few years since, I was laboring in Syracuse, in the state of New York. Two gentlemen called upon me one day; one an elderly man; the other not quite fifty years of age. The younger man introduced the older one to me as Deacon W., elder in his church; saying that he had called on me to give a hundred dollars to Oberlin College. The older man in his turn introduced the younger, saying, "This is my minister, the Rev. Mr. Cross. He was converted under your ministry." Whereupon Mr. Cross said to me: "Do you remember preaching at such a time in Antwerp, and in such a part of the town, in the schoolhouse, in the afternoon, and that such a scene, describing it, occurred there?" I said, "I remember it very well, and can never forget it while I remember anything." "Well," said he, "I was then but a young man, and was converted in that meeting." He has been many years a successful minister. Several of his children have obtained their education in our college in Oberlin.

As nearly as I can learn, although that revival came upon them so suddenly, and was of such a powerful type, the converts were sound, and the work permanent and genuine. I never heard of any disastrous reaction as having taken place.

I have spoken of the Universalists having prevented Deacon R. from attending religious meetings on Sunday, in the village of Antwerp, by taking off the wheels of his carriage. When the revival got its full strength, Deacon R. wanted me to go and preach in that neighborhood. Accordingly, I made an appointment to preach on a certain afternoon, in their schoolhouse. When I arrived I found the schoolhouse filled, and Deacon R. sitting near a window, by a stand with a Bible and hymn book on it. I sat down beside him, then arose and read a hymn, and they sung after a fashion. I then engaged in prayer, and had great access to the throne of grace. I then arose and took this text: "You serpents, generation of vipers, how can you escape the damnation of hell?"

I saw that Deacon R. was very uneasy; and he soon got up and went and stood in the open door. As there were some boys near the door, I supposed, at the time, that he had gone to keep the boys still. But I afterward learned that it was through fear. He thought that if they set upon me, he would be where he could escape. From my text he concluded that I was going to deal very plainly with them; and he had been made quite nervous with the opposition which he had met with from them, and wanted to keep out of their reach. I proceeded to pour myself out upon them with all my might; and before I was through, there was a complete upturning of the very foundations of Universalism, I think, in that place. It was a scene that almost equaled that of which I have spoken, in Sodom. Thus the revival penetrated to every part of the town, and some of the neighboring towns shared in the blessing. The work was very precious in this place.

When we came to receive the converts, after a great number had been examined, and the day approached for their admission, I found that several of them had been brought up in Baptist families, and asked them if they would not prefer to be immersed. They said they had no choice; but their parents would prefer to have them immersed. I told them I had no objection to immersing them, if they thought it would please their friends better, and themselves as well. Accordingly, when Sunday came, I arranged to baptize by immersion, during the intermission. We went down to a stream that runs through the place; and there I baptized, I should think, a dozen or more.

Among the converts was also a considerable number whose friends were Methodists. On Saturday I learned that some Methodist people were saying to the converts, "Mr. Finney is a Presbyterian. He believes in the doctrine of election and predestination; but he has not preached it here. He dares not preach it, because if he should, the converts would not join his church." This determined me to preach on the doctrine of election, the Sunday morning previous to their joining the church. I took my text, and went on to show, first, what the doctrine of election is not; secondly, what it is; thirdly, that it is a doctrine of the Bible; fourthly, that it is the doctrine of reason; fifthly, that to deny it, is to deny the very attributes of God; sixthly, that it opposes no obstacle in the way of the salvation of the non-elect; seventhly, that all men may be saved if they will; and lastly, that it is the only hope that anybody will be saved; and concluded with remarks.

The Lord made it exceedingly clear to my own mind, and so clear to the people, that, I believe, it convinced the Methodists themselves. I never heard a word said against it, or a word of dissatisfaction with the argument. While I was preaching, I observed a Methodist sister with whom I had become acquainted, and whom I regarded as an excellent Christian woman, weeping, as she sat near the pulpit stairs.

I feared that I was hurting her feelings. After the close of the meetings she remained sitting and weeping; and I went to her and said to her, "Sister, I hope I have not injured your feelings." "No," said she, "you have not injured my feelings, Mr. Finney; but I have committed a sin. No longer ago than last night, my husband, who is an impenitent man, was arguing this very question with me; and maintaining, as best he could, the doctrine of election." Said she, "I resisted it, and told him that it was not true. And now, today, you have convinced me that it is true; and instead of forming any excuse for my husband, or anybody else, it is the only hope I can have that he will be saved, or anybody else." I heard no farther objection to the converts joining a church that believed in the doctrine of election.

There were a great many interesting cases of conversion in this place; and there were two very striking cases of instantaneous recovery from insanity during this revival. As I went into meeting in the afternoon of one Sunday, I saw several ladies sitting in a pew, with a woman dressed in black who seemed to be in great distress of mind; and they were partly holding her, and preventing her from going out. As I came in, one of the ladies came to me and told me that she was an insane woman; that she had been a Methodist, but had, as she supposed, fallen from grace; which had led to despair, and finally to insanity. Her husband was an intemperate man, and lived several miles from the village; and he had brought her down and left her at meeting, and had himself gone to the tavern. I said a few words to her; but she replied that she must go; that she could not hear any praying, or preaching, or singing; that hell was her portion, and she could not endure anything that made her think of heaven.

I cautioned the ladies, privately, to keep her in her seat, if they could, without her disturbing the meeting. I then went into the pulpit and read a hymn. As soon as the singing began, she struggled hard to get out. But the ladies obstructed her passage; and kindly but persistently prevented her escape. After a few moments she became quiet; but seemed to avoid hearing or attending at all to the singing. I then prayed. For some little time, I heard her struggling to get out; but before I had done she became quiet, and the congregation was still. The Lord gave me a great spirit of prayer, and a text; for I had no text settled upon before. I took my text from Hebrews: "Let us come boldly unto the throne of grace, that we may obtain mercy and find grace to help in time of need."

My object was to encourage faith, in ourselves, and in her; and in ourselves for her. When I began to pray, she at first made quite an effort to get out. But the ladies kindly resisted, and she finally sat still, but held her head very low, and seemed determined not to attend to what I said. But as I proceeded she began gradually to raise her head, and to look at me from within her long black bonnet. She looked up more and more until she sat upright, and looked me in the face with intense earnestness. As I proceeded to urge the people to be bold in their faith, to launch out, and commit themselves with the utmost confidence to God, through the atoning sacrifice of our great High Priest, all at once she startled the congregation by uttering a loud shriek. She then cast herself almost from her seat, held her head very low, and I could see that she "trembled very exceedingly." The ladies in the pew with her, partly supported her, and watched her with manifest prayerful interest and sympathy. As I proceeded she began to look up again, and soon sat upright, with face wonderfully changed, indicating triumphant joy and peace. There was such a glow upon her countenance as I have seldom seen in any human face. Her joy was so great that she could scarcely contain herself till meeting was over; and then she soon made everybody understand around her, that she was set at liberty. She glorified God, and rejoiced with amazing triumph. About two years after, I met with her, and found her still full of joy and peace.

The other case of recovery was that of a woman who had also fallen into despair and insanity. I was not present when she was restored; but was told that it was almost or quite instantaneous, by means of a baptism of the Holy Spirit. Revivals of religion are sometimes accused of making people mad. The fact is, men are naturally mad on the subject of religion; and revivals rather restore them, than make them mad.

During this revival, we heard much of opposition to it from Gouverneur, a town about twelve miles, I believe, farther north. We heard that the wicked threatened to come down and mob us, and break up our meetings. However, of course, we paid no attention to that; and I mention it here only because I shall have occasion soon to notice a revival there. Having received the converts, and having labored in Antwerp together with Evans' Mills, until the fall of the year, I sent and procured for them, a young man by the name of Denning, whom they settled as pastor. I then suspended my labors at Antwerp.

CHAPTER 9

RETURN TO EVANS' MILLS

*I went on preaching, from day to day,
and from night to night;
and there was a powerful revival.*

At this time, I was earnestly pressed to remain at Evans' Mills, and finally gave them encouragement that I would abide with them, at least one year. Being engaged to marry, I went from there to Whitestown, Oneida county, and was married in October, 1824. My wife had made preparations for housekeeping; and a day or two after our marriage I left her, and returned to Evans' Mills, to obtain conveyance to transport our goods to that place. I told her that she might expect me back in about a week.

The fall previous to this, I had preached a few times, in the evening, at a place called Perch River, still farther northwest from Evans' Mills about a dozen miles. I spent one Sunday at Evans' Mills, and intended to return for my wife, about the middle of that week. But a messenger from Perch River came up that Sunday, and said there had been a revival working its way slowly among the people ever since I preached there; and he begged me to go down and preach there, at least once more. I finally sent an appointment to be there Tuesday night. But I found the interest so deep that I stayed and preached Wednesday night, and Thursday night; and I finally gave up returning that week, for my wife, and continued to preach in that neighborhood.

The revival soon spread in the direction of Brownville, a considerable village several miles, I think, in a southwestern direction from that place. Finally, under the pressing invitation of the minister and church at Brownville, I went there and spent the winter, having written to my wife, that such were the circumstances that I must defer coming for her, until God seemed to open the way.

At Brownville there was a very interesting work. But still the church was in such a state that it was very difficult to get them into the work. I could not find much that seemed to me to be sound-hearted piety; and the policy of the minister was really such as to forbid anything like a general sweep of a revival. I labored there that winter with great pain, and had many serious obstacles to overcome. Sometimes I would find that the minister and his wife were away from our meetings, and would learn afterwards that they had stayed away to attend a party.

I was the guest at that place of a Mr. B., one of the elders of the church, and the most intimate and influential friend of the minister. One day as I came down from my room, and was going out to call on some inquirers, I met Mr. B. in the hall; and he said to me, "Mr. Finney, what should you think of a man that was praying week after week for the Holy Spirit, and could get no answer?" I replied that I should think he was praying from false motives. "But from what motives," said he, "should a man pray? If he wants to be happy, is that a false motive?" I replied, "Satan might pray with as good a motive as that;" and then quoted the words of the Psalmist: "Uphold me with thy free spirit. Then will I teach transgressors thy ways, and sinners shall be converted unto thee." "See!" said I, "the Psalmist did not pray for the Holy Spirit that he might be happy, but that he might be useful, and that sinners might be converted to Christ." I said this and turned and went immediately out; and he turned very short and went back to his room.

I remained out till dinner time; and when I returned, he met me, and immediately began to confess. "Mr. Finney," said he, "I owe you a confession. I was angry when you said that to me; and I must confess that I hoped I should never see you again. What you said," he continued, "forced the conviction upon me, that I never had been converted, that I never had had any higher motive than a mere selfish desire for my own happiness. I went away," said he, "after you left the house, and prayed to God to take my life. I could not endure to have it known that I had always been deceived. I have been most intimate with our minister. I have journeyed with him, and slept with him, and conversed with him, and have been more intimate with him than any other member of the church; and yet I saw that I had always been a deceived hypocrite. The mortification was intolerable; and," said he, "I wanted to die, and prayed the Lord to take my life." However, he was all broken down then, and from that time became a new man.

That conversion did a great deal of good. I might relate many other interesting facts connected with this revival; but as there were so many things that pained me, in regard to the relation of the pastor to it, and especially of the pastor's wife, I will forbear.

Early in the spring, 1825, I left Brownville, with my horse and cutter, to go after my wife. I had been absent six months since our marriage; and as mails then were between us, we had seldom been able to exchange letters. I drove on some fifteen miles, and the roads were very slippery. My horse was smooth shod, and I found I must have his shoes reset. I stopped at Le Rayville, a small village about three miles south of Evans' Mills. While my horse was being shod, the people finding that I was there, ran to me, and wanted to know if I would not preach, at one o'clock, in the schoolhouse; for they had no meeting house.

At one o'clock the house was packed; and while I preached, the Spirit of God came down with great power upon the people. So great and manifest was the outpouring of the Spirit, that in compliance with their earnest entreaty I concluded to spend the night there, and preach again in the evening. But the work increased more and more; and in the evening I appointed another meeting in the morning, and in the morning I appointed another in the evening; and soon I saw that I should not be able to go any farther after my wife. I told a brother that if he would take my horse and cutter and go after my wife, I would remain. He did so, and I went on preaching, from day to day, and from night to night; and there was a powerful revival.

I should have said that, while I was at Brownville, God revealed to me, all at once, in a most unexpected manner, the fact that he was going to pour out his Spirit at Gouverneur, and that I must go there and preach. Of the place I knew absolutely nothing, except that, in that town there was so much opposition manifested to the revival in Antwerp, the year before. I can never tell how, or why, the Spirit of God made that revelation to me. But I knew then, and I have no doubt now, that it was a direct revelation from God to me. I had not thought of the place, that I know of, for months; but in prayer the thing was all shown to me, as clear as light, that I must go and preach in Gouverneur, and that God would pour out his Spirit there.

Very soon after this, I saw one of the members of the church from Gouverneur, who was passing through Brownville. I told him what God had revealed to me. He stared at me as if he supposed that I was insane. But I charged him to go home, and tell the brethren what I said, that they might prepare themselves for my coming, and for the outpouring of the Lord's Spirit. From him I learned that they had no minister; that there were two churches and two meeting houses, in the town, standing near together; that the Baptists had a minister, and the Presbyterians no minister; that an elderly minister lived there who had formerly been their pastor, but had been dismissed; and that they were having, in the Presbyterian church, no regular Sunday services. From what he said, I gathered that religion was in a very low state; and he himself was as cold as an iceberg.

But now I return to my labors in Le Rayville. After laboring there a few weeks, the great mass of the inhabitants was converted; and among the rest Judge C., a man in point of influence, standing head and shoulders above all the people around him. My wife arrived, of course, a few days after I sent for her; and we accepted the invitation of Judge C. and his wife, to become their guests. But after a few weeks, the people urged me to go and preach in a Baptist church in the town of Rutland, where Rutland joins Le Ray. I made an appointment to preach there one afternoon. The weather had become warm, and I walked over, through a pine grove, about three miles to their place of worship. I arrived early, and found the house open, but nobody there. I was warm from having walked so far, and went in and took my seat near the broad aisle, in the center of the house. Very soon people began to come in and take their seats here and there, scattered over the house. Soon the number increased so that they were coming continually. I sat still; and, being an entire stranger there, no person came in that I knew, and I presume that no person that came in knew me.

Presently a young woman came in, who had two or three tall plumes in her bonnet, and was rather gaily dressed. She was slender, tall, dignified, and decidedly handsome. I observed as soon as she came in, that she waved her head and gave a very graceful motion to her plumes. She came as it were sailing around, and up the broad aisle toward where I sat, mincing as she came, at every step, waving her great plumes most gracefully, looking around just enough to see the impression she was making. For such a place the whole thing was so peculiar that it struck me very much. She entered a slip directly behind me, in which, at the time, nobody was sitting. Thus we were near together but each occupying a separate slip. I turned partly around, and looked at her from head to foot. She saw that I was observing her critically, and looked a little abashed. In a low voice I said to her, very earnestly "Did you come in here to divide the worship of God's house, to make people worship you, to get their attention away from God and his worship?" This made her writhe; and I followed her up, in a voice so low that nobody else heard me, but I made her hear me distinctly. She quailed under the rebuke, and could not hold up her head. She began to tremble, and when I had said enough to fasten the thought of her insufferable vanity on her mind, I arose and went into the pulpit. As soon as she saw me go into the pulpit, and that I was the minister that was about to preach, her agitation began to increase — so much so as to attract the attention of those around her. The house was soon full, and I took a text and went on to preach.

The Spirit of the Lord was evidently poured out on the congregation; and at the close of the sermon, I did what I do not know I had ever done before, called upon any who would give their hearts to God, to come forward and take the front seat. The moment I made the call, this young woman was the first to arise. She burst out into the aisle, and came forward, like a person in a state of desperation. She seemed to have lost all sense of the presence of anybody but God. She came rushing forward to the front seats, until she finally fell in the aisle, and shrieked with agony. A large number arose in different parts of the house and came forward; and a goodly number appeared to give their hearts to God upon the spot, and among them this young woman. On inquiry I found that she was rather the beauty of the place; that she was an agreeable girl, but was regarded by everybody as very vain and dressy.

Many years afterwards, I saw a man who called my attention to that meeting. I inquired after this young woman. He informed me that he knew her well; that she still resided there, was married, and was a very useful woman; and had always, from that time, been a very earnest Christian.

I preached a few times at this place, and then the question of Gouverneur came up again; and God seemed to say to me, "Go to Gouverneur; the time has come." Brother Nash had come a few days before this, and was spending some time with me. At the time of this last call to Gouverneur. I had some two or three appointments ahead, in that part of Rutland. I said therefore to brother Nash, "You must go to Gouverneur and see what is there, and come back and make your report." He started the next morning, and after he had been gone two or three days, returned, saying, that he had found a good many professors of religion, under considerable exercise of mind, and that he was confident that there was a good deal of the Spirit of the Lord among the people; but that they were not aware what the state of things really was. I then informed the people where I was preaching, that I was called to Gouverneur, and could make no more appointments to preach in that place. I requested Brother Nash to return immediately, informing the people that they might expect me on a certain day that week.

CHAPTER 10

REVIVAL AT GOUVERNEUR

He said to them, "Now, mark me, young men!
God will break your ranks in less than one week,
either by converting some of you,
or by sending some of you to hell."

Brother Nash accordingly returned the next day, and made the appointment as I desired. I had to ride nearly thirty miles, I believe, to reach the place. In the morning it rained very hard; but the rain abated in time for me to ride to Antwerp. While I was getting dinner at that place, the rain came on again, and literally poured, until quite late in the afternoon. It seemed in the morning before I started, and at noon, that I should not be able to reach my appointment. However, the rain abated again, in time for me to ride rapidly to Gouverneur. I found that the people had given up expecting me that day, in consequence of the great rain.

Before I reached the village, I met a Mr. S., one of the principal members of the church, returning from the church meeting to his house, which I had just passed. He stopped his carriage, and, addressing me, said, "Is this Mr. Finney?" After my reply in the affirmative, he says, "Please to go back to my house, for I shall insist on your being my guest. You are fatigued with the long ride and the roads are so bad, you will not have any meeting tonight." I replied that I must fulfill my appointment, and asked him if the church meeting had adjourned. He said it had not, when he left; and he thought it possible I might reach the village before they would dismiss.

I rode rapidly on, alighted at the meeting house door, and hurried in. Brother Nash stood in front of the pulpit, having just risen up to dismiss the meeting. On seeing me enter, he held up his hands, and waited till I came near the pulpit, and then he took me right in his arms. After thus embracing me, he introduced me to the congregation. In a word I informed them that I had come to fulfill my appointment; and, the Lord willing, I would preach at a certain hour which I named.

When the hour arrived, the house was filled. The people had heard enough, for and against me, to have their curiosity excited, and there was a general turning out. The Lord gave me a text, and I went into the pulpit and let my heart out to the people. The word took powerful effect. That was very manifest to everybody, I think. I dismissed the meeting, and that night got some rest.

The village hotel was at that time kept by a Dr. S., an avowed Universalist. The next morning, I went out, as usual, to call on the people, and converse with them about their souls, and found the village excited. After making a few calls, I dropped into a tailor's shop, where I found a number of people discussing the subject of the sermon the night before.

Dr. S., at that time, I had never heard of; but I found him among the number at this tailor's shop, and defending his Universalist sentiments. As I went in, the remarks that were made immediately opened the conversation; and Dr. S. stepped forward, manifestly sustained by the whole influence of his comrades, to dispute the positions that I had advanced, and to maintain, as opposed to them, the doctrine of universal salvation. Somebody introduced him to me; and I said to him, "Doctor, I should be very happy to converse with you about your views; but if we are going to have a conversation, we must first agree upon the method upon which we are going to discuss." I was too much used to discussing with Universalists, to expect any good to come from it, unless certain terms were agreed upon and adhered to, in the discussion. I proposed, therefore, first that we should take up one point at a time, and discuss it till we had settled it, or had no more to say upon it, and then another, and another; confining ourselves the point immediately in debate; secondly, that we should not interrupt each other, but each one should be at liberty to give his views upon the point, without interruption; and thirdly, that there should be no caviling or mere banter, but that we should observe candor and courtesy, and give to every argument due weight, on whichever side it was presented. I knew they were all of one way of thinking; and I could easily see that they were banded together, and had come together that morning, for the sake of sustaining each other in their views.

Having settled the preliminaries, we commenced the argument. It did not take long to demolish every position that he assumed. He really knew but little of the Bible. He had a way of disposing of the principal passages, as he remembered them, that are generally arrayed against the doctrine of Universalism. But, as Universalists always do, he dwelt mainly on the utter injustice of endless punishment. I soon showed him, and those around him, that he had but slender ground to stand on, so far as the Bible was concerned; and he very soon took the position, that whatever the Bible said about its endless punishment was unjust; and that therefore, if the Bible threatened men with endless punishment, it could not be true. This settled the question, so far as the Bible was concerned. In fact, I could easily see that they were all skeptics, and would not at all give in because they saw that the Bible contradicted their views. I then closed in with him on the justice of endless punishment. I saw that his friends became agitated, and felt as if the foundations were giving away under them. Pretty soon one of them went out; and as I proceeded, another went out, and finally they all forsook him, seeing, as they must have done, one after the other, that he was utterly wrong. He had been their leader; and God gave me thus an opportunity to use him entirely up, in the presence of his followers. When he had nothing more to say, I urged upon him with warmth, the question of immediate attention to salvation, and very kindly bid him good morning, and went away, feeling sure that I should soon hear from that conversation again.

The doctor's wife was a Christian woman, and a member of the church. She told me a day or two after, that the Doctor came home from that conversation apparently greatly agitated, though she did not know where he had been. He would walk the room, and then sit down, but could not remain sitting. He would thus walk and sit alternately; and she could see in his countenance that he was greatly troubled. She said to him, "Doctor, what is the matter?" "Nothing," was his reply. But his agitation increased; and she inquired again, "Doctor, do tell me what is the matter." She suspected that he had somewhere fallen in with me; and she said to him, "Doctor, have you seen Mr. Finney this morning.?" This brought him to a stand; and he burst into tears and exclaimed, "Yes! and he has turned my weapons on my own head!" His agony became intense; and as soon as the way was opened for him to speak out, he surrendered himself up to his convictions, and soon after expressed hope in Christ. In a few days his companions were brought in, one after the other, till I believe, the revival made a clean sweep of them.

I have said that there was a Baptist church, and a Presbyterian, each having a meeting house standing upon the green, not far apart; and that the Baptist church had a pastor, but the Presbyterian had none. As soon as the revival broke out, and attracted general attention, the Baptist brethren began to oppose it. They spoke against it, and used very objectionable means indeed to arrest its progress. This encouraged a set of young men to join hand in hand, to strengthen each other in opposition to the work. The Baptist church was quite influential; and the stand that they took greatly emboldened the opposition, and seemed to give it a peculiar bitterness and strength, as might be expected. Those young men seemed to stand like a bulwark in the way of the progress of the work.

In this state of things, brother Nash and myself, after consultation, made up our minds that that thing must be overcome by prayer, and that it could not be reached in any other way. We therefore retired to a grove and gave ourselves up to prayer until we prevailed, and we felt confident that no power which earth or hell could interpose, would be allowed permanently to stop the revival. The next Sunday, after preaching morning and afternoon myself — for I did the preaching altogether, and brother Nash gave himself up almost continually to prayer — we met at five o'clock in the church, for a prayer meeting. The meeting house was filled. Near the close of the meeting, brother Nash arose, and addressed that company of young men who had joined hand in hand to resist the revival. I believe they were all there, and they sat braced up against the Spirit of God. It was too solemn for them really to make ridicule of what they heard and saw; and yet their brazen-facedness and stiff-neckedness were apparent to everybody.

Brother Nash addressed them very earnestly, and pointed out the guilt and danger of the course they were taking. Toward the close of his address, he waxed exceeding warm, and said to them, "Now, mark me, young men! God will break your ranks in less than one week, either by converting some of you, or by sending some of you to hell. He will do this as certainly as the Lord is my God!" He was standing where he brought his hand down on the top of the pew before him, so as to make it thoroughly jar. He sat immediately down, dropped his head, and groaned with pain.

The house was as still as death, and most of the people held down their heads. I could see that the young men were agitated. For myself, I regretted that brother Nash had gone so far. He had committed himself, that God would either take the life of some of them, and send them to hell, or convert some of them, within a week. However, on Tuesday morning of the same week, the leader of these young men came to me, in the greatest distress of mind. He was all prepared to submit; and as soon as I came to press him he broke down like a child, confessed, and manifestly gave himself to Christ. Then he said, "What shall I do, Mr. Finney?" I replied "Go immediately to all your young companions, and pray with them, and exhort them, at once to turn to the Lord." He did so; and before the week was out, nearly if not all of that class of young men, were hoping in Christ.

There was a merchant living in the village by the name of S.. He was a very amiable man, a gentleman, but a deist. His wife was the daughter of a Presbyterian minister. She was his second wife; and his first had also been the daughter of a Presbyterian minister. He had thus married into two ministers' families. His fathers-in-law had taken the greatest pains to secure his conversion to Christ. He was a reading, reflecting man. Both of his fathers-in-law were old school Presbyterians, and had put into his hands the class of books that presented their peculiar views. This had greatly stumbled him; and the more he had read, the more he was fixed in his convictions that the Bible was a fable.

His wife urgently entreated me to come and converse with her husband. She informed me of his views, and of the pains that had been taken to lead him to embrace the Christian religion. But she said he was so firmly settled in his views, she did not know that any conversation could meet the case. Nevertheless, I promised to call and see him, and did so. His store was in the front part of the building in which they resided. She went into the store, and requested him to come in. He declined. He said it would do no good; that he had talked with ministers enough; that he knew just what I would say, beforehand, and he could not spend the time; beside, it was very repulsive to his feelings. She replied to him, "Mr. S., you have never been in the habit of treating ministers, who called to see you, in this way. I have invited Mr. Finney to call and see you, to have a conversation on the subject of religion; and I shall be greatly grieved and mortified, if you decline to see him."

He greatly respected and loved his wife; and she was indeed a gem of a woman. To oblige her, he consented to come in. Mrs. S. introduced me to him, and left the room. I then said to him, "Mr. S., I have not come in here to have any dispute with you at all; but if you are willing to converse, it is possible that I may suggest something that may help you over some of your difficulties, in regard to the Christian religion, as I probably have felt them all myself." As I addressed him in great kindness, he immediately seemed to feel at home with me, and sat down near me and said, "Now, Mr. Finney, there is no need of our having a long conversation on this point. We are both of us so familiar with the arguments, on both sides, that I can state to you, in a very few minutes, just the objections to the Christian religion on which I rest, and which I find myself utterly unable to overcome. I suppose I know beforehand how you will answer them, and that the answer will be utterly unsatisfactory to me. But if you desire it, I will state them."

I begged him to do so; and he began, as nearly as I can recollect, in this way: "You and I agree in believing in the existence of God." "Yes." "Well, we agree that he is infinitely wise, and good, and powerful." "Yes." "We agree that he has, in our very creation, given us certain irresistible convictions of right and wrong, of justice and injustice." "Yes." "Well, we agree, then, that whatever contravenes our irresistible convictions of justice, cannot be from God." "Yes," I said, "What, according to our irresistible convictions, is neither wise nor good, cannot be from God." "Yes," I said, "we agree in that." "Well now," said he, "the Bible teaches us that God has created us with a sinful nature, or that we come into existence totally sinful and incapable of any good, and this in accordance with certain preestablished laws of which God is the author; that notwithstanding this sinful nature, which is utterly incapable of any good, God commands us to obey him, and to be good, when to do so is utterly impossible to us; and he commands this on pain of eternal death."

I replied, "Mr. S., have you a Bible? Will you not turn to the passage that teaches this?" "Why, there is no need of that," he says; "you admit that the Bible teaches it." "No," I said, "I do not believe any such thing." "Then," he continued, "the Bible teaches that God has imputed Adam's sin to all his posterity; that we inherit the guilt of that sin by nature, and are exposed to eternal damnation for the guilt of Adam's sin." "Now," said he, "I do not care who says it, or what book teaches such a thing, I know that such teaching cannot be from God. This is a direct contradiction of my irresistible convictions of right and justice." "Yes," I replied, "and so it is directly in contradiction of my own." "But now," said I, "where is this taught in the Bible?"

He began to quote the catechism, as he had done before. "But," I replied, "that is catechism, not Bible." "Why," said he, "you are a Presbyterian minister, are you not? I thought the catechism was good authority for you." "No," I said; "we are talking about the Bible now — whether the Bible is true. Can you say that this is the doctrine of the Bible?" "Oh," he said, "if you are going to deny that it is taught in the Bible — why, that is taking such ground as I never knew a Presbyterian minister to take." He then proceeded to say that the Bible commanded men to repent, but at the same time taught them that they could not repent; it commanded them to obey and believe, and yet at the same time taught them that this was impossible. I of course closed with him again, and asked him where these things were taught in the Bible. He quoted catechism; but I would not receive it.

He went on to say that the Bible taught also, that Christ died only for the elect; and yet it commanded all men everywhere, whether elect or non-elect, to believe, on pain of eternal death. "The fact is," said he, "the Bible, in its commands and teachings, contravenes my innate sense of justice at every step. I cannot, I will not receive it!" He became very positive and warm. But I said to him: "Mr. S., there is a mistake in this. These are not the teachings of the Bible. They are the traditions of men rather than the teachings of the Bible." "Well then," said he, "Mr. Finney, do tell me what you do believe!" This he said with a considerable degree of impatience. I said to him, "If you will give me a hearing for a few moments, I will tell you what I do believe."

I then began and told him what my views of both the law and the gospel were. He was intelligent enough to understand me easily and quickly. In the course of an hour, I should think, I took him over the whole ground of his objections. He became intensely interested; and I saw that the views that I was presenting, were new to him.

When I came to dwell upon the atonement, and showed that it was made for all men — dwelt upon its nature, its design, its extent, and the freeness of salvation through Christ, I saw his feelings rise, till at last he put both hands over his face, threw his head forward upon his knees, and trembled all over with emotion. I saw that the blood rushed to his head, and that the tears began to flow freely. I rose quickly and left the room without saying another word. I saw that an arrow had transfixed him, and I expected him to be converted immediately. It turned out that he was converted before he left the room.

Very soon after, the meeting house bell tolled for a prayer and conference meeting. I went into the meeting and soon after the meeting commenced, Mr. and Mrs. S. came in. His countenance showed that he had been greatly moved. The people looked around, and appeared surprised to see Mr. S. come into a prayer meeting. He had always been in the habit of attending worship on the Sunday, I believe; but to come into a prayer meeting, and that in the daytime, was something new. For his sake, I took up a good deal of the time, at that meeting, in remarks, to which he paid the utmost attention.

His wife afterward told me, that as he walked home when the prayer meeting was over, he said, "My dear, where has all my infidelity gone? I cannot recall it. I cannot make it look as if it had any sense in it. It appears to me as if it always had been perfect nonsense. And how I could ever have viewed the subject as I did, or respected my own arguments as I did, I cannot imagine. It seems to me," said he, "as if I had been called to pass judgment on some splendid piece of architecture, some magnificent temple; and that as soon as I came in view of one corner of the structure, I fell into disgust, and turned away and refused to inspect it farther. I condemned the whole, without at all regarding its proportions. Just so I have treated the government of God." She said he had always been particularly bitter against the doctrine of endless punishment. But on this occasion, as they were walking home, he said that, for the manner in which he had treated God, he deserved endless damnation. His conversion was very clear and decided. He warmly espoused the cause of Christ, and enlisted heartily in the promotion of the revival. He joined the church, and soon after became a deacon; and to the day of his death, as I have been told, was a very useful man.

After the conversion of Mr. S., and of that class of young men to whom I have alluded, I thought it was time, if possible, to put a stop to the opposition of the Baptist church and minister. I therefore had an interview first with a deacon of the Baptist church, who had been very bitter in his opposition; and said to him, "Now you have carried your opposition far enough. You must be satisfied that this is the work of God. I have made no allusion in public to your opposition, and I do not wish to do so, or to appear to know that there is any such thing; but you have gone far enough; and I shall feel it my duty, if you do not stop immediately, to take you in hand, and expose your opposition from the pulpit." Things had got into such a state that I was sure that both God and the public would sustain me in carrying out the measure that I proposed.

He confessed, and said that he was sorry; and promised that he would make confession, and that he would not oppose the work anymore. He said that he had made a great mistake, and had been deceived; but that he also had been very wicked about it. He then went after his minister; and I had a long conversation with them together. The minister confessed that he had been all wrong; that he had been deceived, and had been wicked; and that his sectarian feeling had carried him too far. He hoped that I would forgive him, and prayed God to forgive him. I told him that I should take no notice whatever of the opposition of his church, provided they stopped it; which they promised to do.

But I then said to him, "Now a considerable number of the young people, whose parents belong to your church, have been converted." If I recollect right, as many as forty of their young people had been converted in that revival. "Now," said I, "if you go to proselyting, that will create a sectarian feeling in both churches, and will be worse than any opposition which you have offered." I said to him, "In spite of your opposition, the work has gone on; because the Presbyterian brethren have kept clear of a sectarian Spirit, and have had the spirit of prayer. But if you go to proselyting, it will destroy the spirit of prayer, and will stop the revival immediately." He knew it, he said; and therefore he would say nothing about receiving any of the converts, and would not open the doors of the church for their reception, until the revival was over; and then, without any proselyting, let the converts all join which church they pleased.

This was on Friday. The next day, Saturday, was the day for their monthly covenant meeting. When they had gathered, instead of keeping his word, he threw the doors of the church open and invited the converts to come forward and tell their experience and join the church. As many as could be persuaded to do so, told their experience; and the next day there was a great parade in baptizing them. The minister sent off immediately, and secured the help of one of the most proselyting Baptist ministers that I ever knew. He came in and began to preach and lecture on baptism. They traversed the town for converts in every direction; and whenever they could find anyone to join, they would get up a procession, and march, and sing, and make a great parade in going to the water and baptizing them. This soon so grieved the Presbyterian church, as to destroy their spirit of prayer and faith, and the work came to a dead stand. For six weeks there was not a single conversion. All, both saints and sinners, were discussing the question of baptism.

There was a considerable number of men, and some of them prominent men, in the village, that had been under strong conviction, and appeared to be near conversion, who had been entirely diverted by this discussion of baptism; and indeed, this seemed to be the universal effect. Everybody could see that the revival had stopped; and that the Baptists, although they had opposed the revival from the beginning, were bent upon having all the converts join their church. However, I think that a majority of those converted, could not be persuaded to be immersed, although nothing had been said to them on the other side.

I finally said to the people on the Sunday, "You see how it is — that the work of conversion is suspended, and we do not know that a conversion has occurred now for six weeks; and you know the reason." I did not tell them, at all, how the pastor of the Baptist church had violated his word, nor did I allude to it; for I knew that it would do no good, but much hurt, to inform the people that he had been guilty of taking such a course.

Due to God's grace, soon afterwards, the spirit of prayer returned, and the revival was revived and went on again with great power. Not long after, the ordinances were administered, and a large number of the converts united with the church.

I have already intimated that I was a guest of Mr. S. He had a very interesting family. He and his wife, — called by everybody, "Aunt Lucy" — had no children of their own; but they had, from time to time, through the yearnings of their hearts, adopted one child after another, until they had ten; and they were so nearly of an age that, at this time, his family was composed of himself, and "Aunt Lucy," his wife, and ten young people, I think about equally divided, young men and young women. They were all soon converted, and their conversions were very striking. They were bright converts, and very intelligent young people; and a happier and more lovely family I never saw than they were when they were all converted.

But Aunt Lucy had been converted under other circumstances, when there was no revival; and she had never before seen the freshness, and strength, and joy of converts in a powerful revival. Their faith and love, their joy and peace, completely stumbled her. She began to think that she was never converted; and although she had given herself, heart and soul, to the promotion of the work, yet, right in the midst of it, she fell into despair, in spite of all that could be said or done. She concluded that she never had been converted, and of course that she never could be.

This introduced into the family a matter of great pain and concern. Her husband thought she would go deranged. The young people, who all regarded her as a mother, were filled with concern about her; and indeed the house was thrown into mourning. Mr. S. gave up his time to converse and to pray with her, and to try to revive her hope. I had several conversations with her; but in the great light which the experience of those young converts, to which she was daily listening, threw around her, she could not be persuaded to believe, either that she ever was converted, or ever could be. This state of things continued day after day, till I began myself to think that she would be deranged. The street on which they lived was a thickly settled street, almost a village, for some three miles in extent. The work had extended on that street until there was but one adult unconverted person left. He was a young man, by the name of B. H., and he was almost frantic in his opposition to the work. Almost the whole neighborhood gave themselves to prayer for this young man, and his case was in almost everybody's mouth.

One day I came in, and found Aunt Lucy taking on very much about this B. H.. "Oh dear!" she said; "what will become of him? Why, Mr. S.! he will certainly lose his soul. What will become of him?" She seemed to be in the greatest agony, lest that young man should lose his soul. I listened to her for a few moments, and then looked gravely at her, and said: "Aunt Lucy, when you and B. H. die, God will have to make a partition in hell, and give you a room by yourself." She opened her large blue eyes, and looked at me with a reproving look. "Why, Mr. Finney!" said she. "Just so," I said. "Do you think God will be guilty of so great an impropriety, as to put you and B. H. in the same place? Here he is, raving against God; and you are almost insane in feeling the abuse which he heaps upon God, and with the fear that he is going to hell. Now can two such persons, in two such opposite states of mind, do you think, be sent to the same place?" I calmly met her reproving gaze, and looked her steadily in the face. In a few moments her features relaxed, and she smiled, the first time for many days. "It is just so, my dear," said Mr. S., "just so. How can you and B. H. go to the same place?" She laughed and said, "We cannot." From that moment her despair cleared up; and she came out clear, and as happy as any of the young converts. This B. H. was afterward converted.

About three-quarters of a mile from Mr. S.'s lived a Mr. M., who was a strong Universalist, and, for a considerable time, kept away from our meetings. One morning, Father Nash, who was at the time with me at Mr. S.'s, rose up, as his custom was, at a very early hour; and went back to a grove some fifty rods, perhaps, from the road, to have a season of prayer alone. It was before sunrise; and brother Nash, as usual, became very much engaged in prayer. It was one of those clear mornings, on which it is possible to hear sounds a great distance. Mr. M. had risen, and was out of doors at that early hour in the morning, and heard the voice of prayer. He listened, and could distinctly hear Father Nash's voice. He knew it was prayer, he afterward said; though he could not distinguish much that was said. He, however, said that he knew what it was, and who it was. And it lodged an arrow in his heart. He said it brought a sense of the reality of religion over him, such as he never had experienced before. The arrow was fastened. He found no relief, till he found it in believing in Jesus.

I do not know the number of those converted in that revival. It was a large farming town, settled by well-to-do inhabitants. The great majority of them, I am confident, were, in that revival, converted to Christ. I have not been in that place for many years. But I have often heard from there; and have always understood that there has been a very healthful state of religion in that place, and that they have never had anything like a discussion on the subject of baptism since.

The doctrines preached in promoting that revival, were those that I have preached everywhere. The total moral, voluntary depravity of unregenerate man; the necessity of a radical change of heart, through the truth, by the agency of the Holy Ghost; the divinity and humanity of our Lord Jesus Christ; his vicarious atonement, equal to the wants of all mankind; the gift, divinity and agency of the Holy Ghost: repentance, faith, justification by faith, sanctification by faith; persistence in holiness as a condition of salvation; indeed all the distinctive doctrines of the Gospel, were stated and set forth with as much clearness, and point, and power, as were possible to me under the circumstances. A great spirit of prayer prevailed; and after the discussion on baptism, a spirit of most interesting unity, brotherly love, and Christian fellowship prevailed. I never had occasion finally, to rebuke the opposition of the Baptist brethren publicly. In my readings on the subject of baptism, the Lord enabled me to maintain such a spirit that no controversy was started, and no controversial spirit prevailed. The discussion produced no evil result, but great good, and, so far as I could see, only good.

CHAPTER 11

REVIVAL AT DE KALB

The spirit of prayer
that prevailed in those revivals was
a very marked feature of them.

FROM Gouverneur I went to De Kalb, another village still farther north, some sixteen miles, I think. Here were a Presbyterian church and minister; but the church was small, and the minister seemed not to have a very strong hold upon the people. However, I think he was decidedly a good man. I began to hold meetings in De Kalb, in different parts of the town. The village was small and the people were very much scattered. The country was new, and the roads were new and bad. But a revival commenced immediately, and went forward with a good deal of power, for a place where the inhabitants were so much scattered.

A few years before, there had been a revival there under the labors of the Methodists. It had been attended with a good deal of excitement; and many cases had occurred of, what the Methodists call, "Falling under the power of God." This the Presbyterians had resisted, and, in consequence, a bad state of feeling had arisen, between the Methodists and the Presbyterians; the Methodists accusing the Presbyterians of having opposed the revival among them because of these cases of falling. As nearly as I could learn, there was a good deal of truth in this, and the Presbyterians had been decidedly in error.

I had not preached long, before, one evening, just at the close of my sermon, I observed a man fall from his seat near the door; and the people gathered around him to take care of him. From what I saw, I was satisfied that it was a case of falling under the power of God, as the Methodists would express it, and supposed that it was a Methodist. I must say that I had a little fear that it might reproduce that state of division and alienation that had before existed. But on inquiry I learned that it was one of the principal members of the Presbyterian church, that had fallen. And it was remarkable that during this revival, there were several cases of this kind among the Presbyterians, and none among the Methodists. This led to such confessions and explanations among the members of the different churches, as to secure a state of great cordiality and good feeling among them.

While laboring at De Kalb, I first became acquainted with Mr. F., of Ogdensburgh. He heard of the revival in De Kalb, and came from Ogdensburgh, some sixteen miles, to see it. He was wealthy, and very benevolent. He proposed to employ me as his missionary, to work in the towns throughout that county, and he would pay me a salary. However, I declined to pledge myself to preach in any particular place, or to confine my labors within any given lines.

Mr. F. spent several days with me, in visiting from house to house, and in attending our meetings. He had been educated in Philadelphia, an old school Presbyterian, and was himself an elder in the Presbyterian church in Ogdensburgh. Departing, he left a letter for me, containing three ten dollar bills. A few days later he came up again, and spent two or three days, and attended our meetings, and became very much interested in the work. When he went away he left another letter, containing, as before, three ten dollar bills. Thus I found myself possessed of sixty dollars, with which I immediately purchased a buggy. Before this time, though I had a horse, I had no carriage; and my young wife and myself used to go a good deal on foot, to meeting.

The revival took a very strong hold of the church in this place; and among others, one of the elders of the church, by the name of B., was thoroughly broken up and broken down, and became quite another man. The impression deepened on the public mind from day to day.

One Saturday, just before evening, a German merchant tailor, from Ogdensburgh, by the name of F., called on me, and informed me that Squire F. had sent him from Ogdensburgh, to take my measure for a suit of clothes. I had begun to need clothes, and had once, not long before, spoken to the Lord about it, that my clothes were getting shabby; but it had not occurred to me again. Mr. F., however, had observed it; and sent this man, who was a Roman Catholic, to take my measure. I asked him if he would not stay over the Sunday, and take my measure Monday morning. I said, "It is too late for you to return tonight; and if I allow you to take my measure tonight, you will go home tomorrow." He admitted that he expected to do so. I said, "Then you shall not take it. If you will not stay till Monday morning, I will not be measured for a suit of clothes." He remained.

The same afternoon there were other arrivals from Ogdensburgh; and among them was an elder S., who was a brother elder in the same church with Mr. F.. Mr. S.'s son, an unconverted young man, came with him.

Elder S. attended meeting in the morning, and at the intermission was invited by elder B. to go home with him, and get some refreshment. Elder B. was full of the Holy Spirit; and on the way home he preached to elder S., who was at the time very cold and backward in religion. Elder S. was very much penetrated by his words. Soon after they entered the house the table was spread, and they were invited to sit down and take some refreshment. As they drew around the table, elder S. said to elder B., "How did you get this blessing?" Elder B. replied, "I stopped lying to God." Said he, "All my Christian life I have been making pretenses, and asking God for things that I was not, on the whole, willing to have; and I had gone on and prayed as other people prayed, and often had been insincere, and really lied to God." He continued: "As soon as I made up my mind that I never would say anything to God in prayer, that I did not really mean, God answered me; and the Spirit came down, and I was filled with the Holy Ghost." At this moment Mr. S., who had not commenced to eat, shoved his chair back from the table, and fell on his knees and began to confess how he had lied to God; and how he had played the hypocrite in his prayers, as well as in his life. The Holy Ghost fell upon him immediately, and filled him as full as he could hold.

In the afternoon the people had assembled for worship, and I was standing in the pulpit reading a hymn. I heard somebody talking very loud, and approaching the house, the door and windows being open. Directly two men came in. Elder B. I knew; the other man was a stranger. As soon as he came in at the door, he lifted his eyes to me, came straight into the desk, and took me up in his arms: — "God bless you!" said he

"God bless you!" He then began and told me, and told the congregation, what the Lord had just done for his soul. His countenance was all in a glow; and he was so changed in his appearance, that those that knew him were perfectly astonished at the change. His son who had not known of this change in his father, when he saw and heard him, rose up and was hastening out of the church. His father cried out, "Do not leave the house, my son; for I never loved you before." He went on to speak; and the power with which he spoke was perfectly astonishing. The people melted down on every side; and his son broke down almost immediately.

Very soon the Roman Catholic tailor, Mr. F., rose up, and said, "I must tell you what the Lord has done for my soul. I was brought up, a Roman Catholic; and I never dared to read my Bible. I was told that if I did, the devil would carry me off bodily. Sometimes when I dared to look into it, it seemed as if the devil was peering over my shoulder, and had come to carry me off." "But," said he, "I see it is all a delusion." And he went on to tell what the Lord had done for him, just there on the spot — what views the Lord had given him of the way of salvation by Jesus Christ. It was evident to everybody that he was converted.

This made a great impression on the congregation. I could not preach. The whole course of the meeting had taken on a type which the Lord had given it. I sat still, and saw the salvation of God. All that afternoon, conversions were multiplied in every part of the congregation. As they arose one after another, and told what the Lord had done, and was doing, for their souls, the impression increased; and so spontaneous a movement by the Holy Ghost, in convicting and converting sinners, I had scarcely ever seen.

The next day this elder S. returned to Ogdensburgh. But, as I understand he made many calls on the way, and conversed and prayed with many families; and thus the revival was extended to Ogdensburgh.

In the early part of October, the synod to which I belonged, met in Utica. I took my wife, and we went down to Utica to attend the synod, and to visit her father's family living near Utica. Mr. Gale, my theological teacher, had left Adams not long after I left it myself; and had removed to a farm in the town of Western Oneida county, where he was endeavoring to regain his health, and was employed in teaching some young men, who proposed to prepare themselves to preach the Gospel. I spent a few days at the synod at Utica, and then set out on my return to my former field of labor, in St. Lawrence county.

We had not gone more than a dozen miles when we met Mr. Gale in his carriage, on his way to Utica. He leaped from his carriage and said, "God bless you, Brother Finney! I was going down to the synod to see you. You must go home with me; I cannot be denied. I do not believe that I ever was converted; and I wrote the other day to Adams, to know where a letter would reach you, as I wanted to open my mind to you on the subject." He was so importunate that I consented; and we drove immediately to Western.

In reflecting upon what I have said of the revivals of religion, in Jefferson and St. Lawrence counties, I am not quite sure that I have laid as much stress as I intended upon the manifest agency of the Holy Spirit, in those revivals. I wish it to be distinctly understood, in all that I shall say, in my narrative of the revivals that I have witnessed, that I always in my own mind, and practically, laid the utmost stress upon this fact, underlying, directing, and giving efficiency to the means, without which nothing would be accomplished.

I have said, more than once, that the spirit of prayer that prevailed in those revivals was a very marked feature of them. It was common for young converts to be greatly exercised in prayer; and in some instances, so much so, that they were constrained to pray whole nights, and until their bodily strength was quite exhausted, for the conversion of souls around them. There was a great pressure of the Holy Spirit upon the minds of Christians; and they seemed to bear about with them the burden of immortal souls. They manifested the greatest solemnity of mind, and the greatest watchfulness in all their words and actions. It was very common to find Christians, whenever they met in any place, instead of engaging in conversation, to fall on their knees in prayer.

Not only were prayer meetings greatly multiplied and fully attended, not only was there great solemnity in those meetings; but *there was a mighty spirit of secret prayer.* Christians prayed a great deal, many of them spending many hours in private prayer. It was also the case that two, or more, would take the promise: "If two of you shall agree on earth as touching anything that they shall ask, it shall be done for them of my Father which is in heaven," and make some particular person a subject of prayer; and it was wonderful to what an extent they prevailed. Answers to prayer were so manifestly multiplied on every side, that no one could escape the conviction that

God was daily and hourly answering prayer. If anything occurred that threatened to mar the work, if there was any appearance of any root of bitterness springing up, or any tendency to fanaticism or disorder, Christians would take the alarm, and give themselves to prayer that God would direct and control all things; and it was surprising to see, to what extent, and by what means, God would remove obstacles out of the way, in answer to prayer.

In regard to my own experience, I will say that *unless I had the spirit of prayer I could do nothing. If even for a day or an hour I lost the spirit of grace and supplication, I found myself unable to preach with power and efficiency, or to win souls by personal conversation.* In this respect my experience was what it has always been.

For several weeks before I left De Kalb to go to the synod, I was very strongly exercised in prayer, and had an experience that was somewhat new to me. I found myself so much exercised, and so borne down with the weight of immortal souls, that I was constrained to pray without ceasing. Some of my experiences, indeed, alarmed me. A spirit of importunity sometimes came upon me so that I would say to God that he had made a promise to answer prayer, and I could not, and would not, be denied. I felt so certain that he would hear me, and that faithfulness to his promises, and to himself, rendered it impossible that he should not hear and answer, that frequently I found myself saying to him, "I hope thou dost not think that I can be denied. I come with thy faithful promises in my hand, and I cannot be denied." I cannot tell how absurd unbelief looked to me, and how certain it was, in my mind, that God would answer prayer — those prayers that, from day to day, and from hour to hour, I found myself offering in such agony and faith. I had no idea of the shape the answer would take, the locality in which the prayers would be answered, or the exact time of the answer. My impression was that the answer was near, even at the door; and I felt myself strengthened in the divine life, put on the harness for a mighty conflict with the powers of darkness, and expected soon to see a far more powerful outpouring of the Spirit of God, in that new country where I had been laboring.

CHAPTER 12

REVIVAL AT WESTERN

*I do not intend to leave this house until you
and your wife repent...
Now, my dear sir, will you get down here on your knees
and engage in prayer?*

I have spoken of my turning aside to Western, as I was returning from the synod at Utica. At this place, commenced that series of revivals, afterward called "The Western Revivals." So far as I know these revivals first attracted the notice, and excited the opposition of certain prominent ministers at the East, and raised the cry of "New Measures."

The churches in that region were mostly Presbyterian. There were in that county, however, three Congregational ministers who called themselves "The Oneida Association," who, at the time, published a pamphlet against those revivals. This much we knew; but as the pamphlet made no public impression that we could learn, no public notice, so far as I am aware, was ever taken of it. We thought it likely that that association had much to do with the opposition that was raised in the East. Their leader, Rev. William R. Weeks, as was well known, embraced and propagated the peculiar doctrines of Dr. Emmons, and insisted very much upon what he called "The divine efficiency scheme." His peculiar views on this subject naturally led him to be suspicious of whatever was not connected with those views, in preaching, and in the means that were used to promote a revival.

He seemed to have little or no confidence in any conversions that did not bring men to embrace his views of divine efficiency and divine sovereignty; and as those of us who labored in those revivals had no sympathy with his views in that respect, it was very natural for him to have but little confidence in the genuineness of the revivals. But we never supposed that the whole of the opposition could have originated in representations made by any of the members of that association.

No public replies were made to the letters that found their way into the public prints, nor to anything that was published in opposition to the revivals. Those of us who were engaged in them, had our hands too full, and our hearts too full, to turn aside, to reply to letters, or reports, or publications, that so manifestly misrepresented the character of the work.

The fact that no answers were made at the time, left the public abroad, and without the range of those revivals, and where the facts were not known, to misapprehend their character. So much misapprehension came to exist, that it has been common for good men, in referring to those revivals, to assume, that although they were, upon the whole, revivals of religion; yet, that they were so conducted that great disorders were manifest in them, and that there was much to deplore in their results.

Now all this is an entire mistake. I shall relate as fairly as I can, the characteristics of these revivals, the measures that were used in promoting them, and disclose, to the best of my ability, their real character and results; understanding well, as I do, that there are multitudes of living witnesses, who can attest the truth of what I say, or if, in anything, I am mistaking can correct me.

And now I will turn to Western, where these revivals commenced, in Oneida county. I have said, that Mr. Gale had settled upon a farm in Western; and was employing some young men, in helping to cultivate the farm, and was engaged in teaching them, and endeavoring to regain his health. I went directly to his house, and for several weeks was his guest. We arrived there Thursday, I think, and that afternoon there was a stated prayer meeting, in the schoolhouse, near the church. The church had no settled minister, and Mr. Gale was unable to preach; indeed, he did not go there to preach, but simply for his health. I believe they usually had a minister, only a part of the time; and for some time previously to my going there, I think, they had had no stated preaching at all, in the Presbyterian church. There were three elders in the church, and a few members; but the church was very small, and religion was at low water mark. There seemed to be no life, or courage, or enterprise, on the part of Christians; and nothing was doing to secure the conversion of sinners, or the sanctification of the church.

In the afternoon Mr. Gale invited me to go to the prayer meeting, and I went. They asked me to take the lead of the meeting; but I declined, expecting to be there only for that afternoon, and preferring rather to hear them pray and talk, than to take part in the meeting myself. The meeting was opened by one of the elders, who read a chapter in the Bible, then a hymn, which they sung. After this he made a long prayer, or perhaps I should say an exhortation, or gave a narrative — I hardly know what to call it. He told the Lord how many years they had been holding that prayer meeting weekly, and that no answer had been given to their prayers. He made such statements and confessions as greatly shocked me. After he had done, another elder took up the same theme. He read a hymn, and, after singing, engaged in a long prayer, in which he went over very nearly the same ground, making such statements as the first one had omitted. Then followed the third elder, in the same strain. By this time, I could say with Paul, that my Spirit was stirred within me. They had got through and were about to dismiss the meeting. But one of the elders asked me if I would not make a remark, before they dismissed. I arose and took their statements and confessions for a text; and it seemed to me, at the time, that God inspired me to give them a terrible searching.

When I arose, I had no idea what I should say; but the Spirit of God came upon me, and I took up their prayers, and statements and confessions, and dissected them. I showed them up, and asked if it had been understood that that prayer meeting was a mock prayer meeting — whether they had come together professedly to mock God, by implying that all the blame of what had been passing all this time, was to be ascribed to his sovereignty?

At first I observed that they all looked angry. Some of them afterward said, that they were on the point of getting up and going out. But I followed them up on the track of their prayers and confessions, until the elder, who was the principal man among them, and opened the meeting, bursting into tears, exclaimed, "Brother Finney, it is all true!" He fell upon his knees and wept aloud. This was the signal for a general breaking down. Every man and woman went down upon their knees. There were probably not more than a dozen present; but they were the leading members in the church. They all wept, and confessed, and broke their hearts before God. This scene continued, I presume, for an hour; and a more thorough breaking down and confession I have seldom witnessed.

As soon as they recovered themselves somewhat, they besought me to remain and preach to them on the Sunday. I regarded it as the voice of the Lord, and consented to do so. This was Thursday, at night. On Friday, my mind was greatly exercised. I went off frequently into the church, to engage secret prayer, and had a mighty hold upon God. The news was circulated, and on Sunday the church was full of hearers. I preached all day, and God came down with great power upon the people. It was manifest to everybody that the work of grace had begun. I made appointments to preach in different parts of the town, in schoolhouses, and at the center, during the week; and the work increased from day to day.

In the meantime, my own mind was much exercised in prayer; and I found that the spirit of prayer was prevailing, especially among the female members of the church. Mrs. B. and Mrs. H., the wives of two of the elders of the church, I found, were, almost immediately, greatly exercised in prayer. Each of them had families of unconverted children; and they laid hold in prayer with an earnestness that, to me, gave promise that their families must be converted. Mrs. H., however, was a woman of very feeble health, and had not ventured out much, to any meeting, for a long time. But, as the day was pleasant, she was out at the prayer meeting to which I have alluded, and seemed to catch the inspiration of that meeting, and took it home with her.

It was the next week, I think, that I called in at Mr. H.'s, and found him pale and agitated. He said to me "Brother Finney, I think my wife will die. She is so exercised in her mind that she cannot rest day or night, but is given up entirely to prayer. She has been all the morning," said he, "in her room, groaning and struggling in prayer; and I am afraid it will entirely overcome her strength." Hearing my voice in the sitting room, she came out from her bedroom, and upon her face was a most heavenly glow. Her countenance was lighted up with a hope and a joy that were plainly from heaven. She exclaimed,

"Brother Finney, the Lord has come! This work will spread over all this region! A cloud of mercy overhangs us all; and we shall see such a work of grace as we have never yet seen." Her husband looked surprised, confounded, and knew not what to say. It was new to him, but not to me. I had witnessed such scenes before, and believed that prayer had prevailed; nay, I felt sure of it in my own soul.

The work went on, spread, and prevailed, until it began to exhibit unmistakable indications of the direction in which the Spirit of God was leading from that place. The distance to home was nine miles, I believe. About half way, was a small village, called Elmer's Hill. There was a large schoolhouse, where I held a weekly lecture; and it soon became manifest that the work was spreading in the direction of Rome and Utica. There was a settlement northeast of Rome, about three miles, called Wright's settlement. Large numbers of persons came down to attend the meetings at Elmer's Hill, from Rome and from Wright's settlement; and the work soon began to take effect among them.

But I must relate a few of the incidents that occurred in the revival at Western. Mrs. B., to whom I have already alluded, had a large family of unconverted children. One of the sons was, I believe, a professor of religion, and lived at Utica; the rest of the family were at home. They were a very amiable family; and the eldest daughter, especially, had been manifestly regarded by the family as almost perfect. I went in several times to converse with her; but I found that the family were so tender of her feelings that I could not strip away her self-righteousness. She had evidently been made to believe that she was almost, if not quite a Christian. Her life had been so irreproachable, that it was very difficult to convict her of sin. The second daughter was also a very amiable girl; but she did not regard herself as worthy to be compared with the eldest, in respect to amiability and excellence of character.

One day when I was talking with S., the eldest, and trying to make her see herself as a great sinner, notwithstanding her morality, C., the second daughter said to me, "Mr. Finney I think that you are too hard upon S.. If you should talk so to me, I should feel that I deserved it; but I don't think that she does." After being defeated several times in my attempts to secure the conviction and conversion of S., I made up my mind to bide my time, and improve some opportunity when I should find her away from home, or alone. It was not long before the opportunity came. I entered into conversation with her, and by God's help stripped the covering from her heart, and she was brought under powerful conviction for sin. The Spirit pursued her with mighty power. The family were surprised and greatly distressed for S.; but God pushed the question home till, after a struggle of a few days, she broke thoroughly down, and came out into the kingdom, as beautiful a convert as, perhaps, I have ever seen. Her convictions were so thorough, that when she came out, she was strong in faith, clear in her apprehension of duty and of truth, and immediately became a host in her power for good among her friends and acquaintances.

In the meantime, C., the second daughter, became very much alarmed about herself, and very anxious for the salvation of her own soul. The mother seemed to be in real travail of soul day and night. I called in to see the family almost daily, and sometimes, two or three times a day. One of the children after another was converted; and we were expecting every day to see C. come out a bright convert. But for some reason she lingered. It was plain the Spirit was resisted; and one day I called to see her, and found her in the sitting room alone. I asked her how she was getting on, and she replied, "Mr. Finney, I am losing my conviction. I do not feel nearly as much concerned about myself as I have done." Just at this moment, a door was opened, and Mrs. B. came into the room, and I told her what C. had said. It shocked her so that she groaned aloud, and fell prostrate on the floor. She was unable to rise; and she struggled and groaned out her prayers, in a manner that immediately indicated to me that C. must be converted. She was unable to say much in words, but her groans and tears witnessed the extreme agony of her mind. As soon as this scene had occurred, the Spirit of God manifestly came upon her afresh. She fell upon her knees, and before she arose she broke down; and became to all appearance as thorough a convert as S. was. The B. children, sons and daughters, were all converted at that time, I believe, except the youngest, then a little child. One of the sons has preached the gospel for many years.

Among other incidents, I recollect the case of a young woman, in a distant part of the town, who came to the meeting at the center almost every day. I had conversed with her several times, and found her deeply convicted, and, indeed, almost in despair. I was expecting to hear, from day to day, that she had been converted; but she remained stationary, or rather despair increased upon her. This led me to suspect that something was wrong at home. I asked her if her parents were Christians. She said they were members of the church. I asked her if they attended meetings. She said, "Yes, on the Sunday." "Do not your parents attend meetings at other times?" "No," was the reply. "Do you have family prayers at home?" "No sir," she said. "We used to have; but we have not had family prayers for a long time." This revealed to me the stumbling block, at once. I inquired when I could probably find her father and mother at home. She said, almost any time, as they were seldom away from home. Feeling that it was infinitely dangerous to leave this case as it was, I went the next morning to see the family.

This daughter was, I think, an only child; at any rate, she was the only child at home. I found her bowed down, dejected, and sunken in despair. I said to the mother, "The Spirit of the Lord is striving with your daughter." "Yes," she said, "I don't know but he is." I asked her if she was praying for her. She gave me an answer that led me to understand that she did not know what it was to pray for her. I inquired for her husband. She said that he was in the field at work. I asked her to call him in. He came, and as he came in I said to him, "Do you see the state that your daughter is in?" He replied that he thought she felt very bad. "And are you awake, and engaged in prayer for her?" His answer revealed the fact that if he was ever converted he was a miserable backslider, and had no hold upon God whatever. "And," said I, "you do not have family prayers." "No sir." "Now," said I, "I have seen your daughter, day after day, bowed down with conviction, and I have learned that the difficulty is here at home. You have shut up the kingdom of heaven against your daughter. You neither enter yourself, nor will you suffer her to enter. Your unbelief and worldly-mindedness prevent the conversion of your daughter, and will ruin your own soul. Now you must repent. I do not intend to leave this house until you and your wife repent, and get out of the way of your daughter. You must establish family prayer, and build up the altar that has fallen down. Now, my dear sir, will you get down here on your knees, you and your wife, and engage in prayer? And will you promise, that from this time you will do your duty, set up your family altar, and return to God?"

I was so earnest with them, that they both began to weep. My faith was so strong, that I did not trifle when I told them that I would not leave the house, until they would repent, and establish their family altar. I felt that the work must be done, and done then. I cast myself down upon my knees and began to pray; and they knelt down and wept sorely. I confessed for them as well as I could, and tried to lead them to God, and to prevail with God in their behalf. It was a moving scene. They both broke down their hearts, and confessed their sins; and before we rose from our knees the daughter got into liberty, and was manifestly converted. She arose rejoicing in Christ. Many answers to prayer, and many scenes of great interest were presented in this revival.

There was one passage of my own experience that, for the honor of God, I must not omit to relate in this connection. I had paralleled and prayed almost continually during the time that I had been at Mr. Gale's. As I was accustomed to use my voice in private prayer, for convenience' sake, that I might not be heard, I had spread a buffalo robe on the hayloft; where I used to spend much of my time, when not abroad visiting, or engaged in preaching, in secret prayer to God. Mr. Gale had admonished me, several times, that, if I did not take care, I should go beyond my strength and break down. *But the Spirit of prayer was upon me, and I would not resist him*; but gave him scope, and let out my strength freely, in pouring my soul out to God. It was November, and the weather was becoming cold. Mr. Gale and I had been out visiting inquirers with his horse and buggy. We came home and went into the barn, and put out the horse. Instead of going into the house, I crept up into the hayloft to pour out my burdened song to God in prayer. I prayed until my burden left me. I was so far exhausted that I fell down, and lost myself in sleep. I must have fallen asleep almost instantly, I judge, from the fact that I had no recollection of any time elapsing, after the struggle in my soul was over. The first I knew, Mr. Gale came climbing up into the hayloft, and said, "Brother Finney, are you dead?" I awoke, and at first could give no account why I was there asleep, and could form no idea how long I had been there. But this I knew, that my mind was calm and my faith unwavering. The work would go on, of that I felt assured.

I have already said that I was ordained to the ministry by a presbytery. This was years before the division of the Presbyterian church into what is known as the Old and New School Assemblies. The well-known doctrine of natural and moral ability and inability, was held by the Presbyterian church, almost universally, in the region where I commenced my ministry. I must here repeat also that Mr. Gale, who, by direction of the presbytery, had attended somewhat to my theological studies, held firmly to the doctrine of the sinner's inability to obey God; and the subject as he presented it in his preaching, as was the case with most of the Presbyterian ministers of that day, left the impression upon the people that they must wait God's time. If they were elect, in due time the Spirit would convert them; if they were non-elect, nothing that they could do for themselves, or that anybody else could do for them, would ever benefit them.

They held the doctrine that moral depravity was constitutional, and belonged to the very nature; that the will, though free to do evil, was utterly impotent to all good; that the work of the Holy Spirit in changing the heart, was a physical operation on the substance or essence of the soul; that the sinner was passive in regeneration, till the Holy Spirit had implanted a new principle in his nature, and that all efforts on his part were utterly unavailing; that properly speaking there were no means of regeneration, this being a physical recreation of the soul by the direct agency of the Holy Ghost; that the atonement was limited to the elect, and that for the non-elect to be saved was an utter impossibility.

In my studies and controversies with Mr. Gale, I had maintained the opposite of this. I assumed that moral depravity is, and must be, a voluntary attitude of the mind; that it does, and must, consist in the committal of the will to the gratification of the desires, or as the Bible expresses it, of the lusts of the flesh, as opposed to that which the law of God requires. In consistency with this I maintained that the influence of the Spirit of God upon the soul of man is moral, that is persuasive; that Christ represented him as a teacher; that his work is to convict and convert the sinner, by divine teaching and persuasion.

I held also that there are means of regeneration, and that the truths of the Bible are, in their nature, calculated to lead the sinner to abandon his wickedness and turn to God. I held also that there must be an adaptation of means to the end to be secured; that is, that the intelligence must be enlightened, the unreasonableness of moral depravity must be set before the sinner, and its wickedness and ill-desert clearly revealed to him; that when this was done the mission of Christ could be strongly presented, and could be understood by him;

that taking this course with the sinner, had a tenderness to convert him to Christ; and that when this was faithfully and prayerfully done, we had a right to expect the Holy Spirit to cooperate with us, giving effect to our feeble effort.

Furthermore, I held that the Holy Spirit operates in the preacher, clearly revealing these truths in their proper order to him, and enabling him to set them before the people, in such proportion, and in such order as is calculated to convert them. I understood then, as I do now, the charge and promise which Christ gave to the apostles and to the church, to be applicable in the present day: "Go and disciple all nations, baptizing them in the name of the Father, and of the Son, and of the Holy Ghost; and lo, I am with you always, even unto the end of the world."

This I regarded as a charge committed to me, to all ministers, and to the church; with the express promise that when we go forth to this work, with a single eye, and with a prayerful heart, Christ will be with us by his Spirit, giving efficiency to our efforts to save souls. It appeared to me then, as it ever has since, that the great failure of the ministry and of the church, in promoting religion, consisted, in great measure, in the want of a suitable adaptation of means to that end. I had sat under Mr. Gale's preaching for years, and could never see any adaptation in his preaching to convert anybody. It did not appear to me as if that could have been his design. I found the same was true of all the sermons that I heard, anywhere. I had on one occasion spoken to Mr. Gale on this subject, and said to him, that of all the causes that were ever plead, the cause of religion, I thought, had the fewest able advocates; and that if advocates at the bar should pursue the same course in pleading the cause of their clients, that ministers do in pleading the cause of Christ with sinners, they would not gain a single case.

But at that time, Mr. Gale could not see it; for what connection was there between means and ends, upon his view of what regeneration consisted in, and the manner in which the Holy Spirit changed the heart?

As an illustration, soon after I began to preach, in the midst of a powerful revival, a young man from the theological seminary at Princeton, came into the place. The former pastor of the church, an elderly gentleman, lived there, and had a great curiosity to hear this young man preach. The church had no pastor at the time; I therefore had the sole charge of the pulpit, and was conducting things according to my own discretion. He said he had known the young man before he went to college, and he desired very much to see what proficiency he had made; and wanted I should let him preach. I said I was afraid to set him to preach, lest he should mar the work, by not preaching that which was needed at the time. "Oh," said the old gentleman, "he will preach the truth; and there is no connection in religion, you know, between means and ends, and therefore there is no danger of his marring the work." I replied, "That is not my doctrine. I believe there is as much connection between means and ends in religion as in nature; and therefore cannot consent to let him preach."

I have often found it necessary to take substantially the same course in revivals of religion; and sometimes, by doing so, I have found that I gave offense; but I dared not do otherwise. In the midst of a revival of religion, and when souls needed peculiar instruction, adapted to their present condition and their present wants, I dared not put a stranger into the pulpit, where I had the charge, to preach any of his great sermons, and generally too, a sermon not at all adapted to the wants of the people. For this course I have frequently been accused of supposing that I could preach better than others. And I confess I did suppose that I could meet the wants of the people, better than those that knew less about them, or than those that would preach their old written sermons to them; and I supposed that Christ had put the work into my hands in such a sense, that I was under obligation to adapt means to ends, and not call upon others who knew little of the state of things, to attempt to instruct the people. I did in these cases just as I would be done by. I would not allow myself to go in, where another man was laboring to promote a revival, and suffer myself to be put in his place, when I knew little or nothing about the state of the people.

I have said that at Western I was the guest of Mr. Gale, and that he had come to the conclusion that he was never converted. He told me the progress of his mind; that he had firmly believed, as he had so frequently urged upon me, that God would not bless my labors, because I would not preach what he regarded as the truths of the Gospel. But when he found that the Spirit of God did accompany my labors, it led him to the conclusion that he was wrong; and this led him to such an overhauling of his whole state of mind, and of his views as a preacher, as resulted in his coming to the conclusion that he had never been converted, and did not understand the Gospel himself. During the revival in Western, he attended nearly all the meetings; and before many weeks, he told me he had come into an entirely different state of mind in regard to his own soul, and had changed his views of the Gospel, and thought I was right. He said he thanked God that he had had no influence with me, to lead me to adopt his views; that I should have been ruined as a minister if he had prevailed. From this time, he became a very efficient worker, so far as his health would permit, in the revival in that region of country.

The doctrine upon which I insisted, that the command to obey God implied the power to do so, created in some places considerable opposition at first. Denying also, as I did, that moral depravity is physical, or the depravity of the nature, and maintaining, as I did, that it is altogether voluntary, and therefore that the Spirit's influences are those of teaching, persuading, convicting, and, of course, a moral influence, I was regarded by many as teaching new and strange doctrines. Indeed, as late as 1832, when I was laboring in Boston for the first time, Dr. Beecher said that he never had heard the doctrine preached before, that the Spirit's influences are moral, as opposed to physical. Therefore, to a considerable extent, ministers and Christians regarded that doctrine as virtually a denial of the Spirit's influence altogether; and hence, although I ever insisted very much, and incessantly, upon the divine agency in conviction and regeneration, and in every Christian exercise; yet it was a long time before the cry ceased to be heard that I denied the agency of the Holy Ghost, in regeneration and conversion. It was said that I taught self-conversion, self-regeneration; and not unfrequently was I rebuked for addressing the sinner, as if the blame of his impenitence all belonged to himself, and for urging him to immediate submission. However, I persisted in this course, and it was seen by ministers and Christians that God owned it as his truth, and blessed it to the salvation of thousands of souls.

I have spoken of the meetings at Elmer's Hill, and have said that people from Rome and Wright's settlement began to come in large numbers; and that the manifest effect of the word upon those that came, plainly indicated that the work was rapidly extending in that direction.

CHAPTER 13

REVIVAL AT ROME

*The work was with such power,
that even a few words of conversation would make
the stoutest men writhe on their seats,
as if a sword had been thrust into their hearts.*

At this time Rev. Moses Gillett, pastor of the Congregational Church in Rome, hearing what the Lord was doing in Western, came, in company with a Miss H., one of the prominent members of his church, to see the work that was going on. They were both greatly impressed with the work of God. I could see that the Spirit of God was stirring them up to the deepest foundations of their minds. After a few days, Mr. Gillett and Miss H. came up again. Miss H. was a very devout and earnest Christian girl. On their second coming up, Mr. Gillett says to me, "Brother Finney, it seems to me that I have a new Bible. I never before understood the promises as I do now; I never got hold of them before; I cannot rest," said he; "my mind is full of the subject, and the promises are new to me." This conversation, protracted as it was for some time, gave me to understand that the Lord was preparing him for a great work in his own congregation.

Soon after this, and when the revival was in its full strength at Western, Mr. Gillett persuaded me to exchange a day with him. I consented reluctantly. On the Saturday before the day of our exchange, on my way to Rome, I greatly regretted that I had consented to the exchange. I felt that it would greatly mar the work in Western, because Mr. Gillett would preach some of his old sermons, which I knew very well could not be adapted to the state of things. However, the people were praying; and it would not stop the work, although it might retard it. I went to Rome and preached three times on the Sunday. To me it was perfectly manifest that the word took great effect. I could see during the day that many heads were down, and that a great number of them were bowed down with deep conviction for sin. I preached in the morning on the text: "The carnal mind is enmity against God;" and followed it up with something in the same direction, in the afternoon and evening. I waited on Monday morning, till Mr. Gillett returned from Western. I told him what my impressions were in respect to the state of the people. He did not seem to realize that the work was beginning with such power as I supposed. But he wanted to call for inquirers, if there were any in the congregation, and wished me to be present at the meeting. I have said before, that the means that I had all along used, thus far, in promoting revivals, were much prayer, secret and social, public preaching, personal conversation, and visitation from house to house; and when inquirers became multiplied, I appointed meetings for them, and invited those that were inquiring to meet for instruction, suited to their necessities. These were the means and the only means, that I had thus far used, in attempting to secure the conversion of souls.

Mr. Gillett asked me to be present at the proposed meeting of inquiry. I told him I would; and that he might circulate information through the village, that there would be a meeting of inquiry, on Monday evening. I would go to Western, and return just at evening; it being understood that he was not to let the people know that he expected me to be present. The meeting was called at the house of one of his deacons. When we arrived, we found the large sitting room crowed to its utmost capacity. Mr. Gillett looked around with surprise, and manifest agitation; for he found that the meeting was composed of many of the most intelligent and influential members of his congregation; and especially was largely composed of the prominent young men in the town. We spent a little while in attempting to converse with them; and I soon saw that the feeling was so deep, that there was danger of an outburst of feeling, that would be almost uncontrollable. I therefore said to Mr. Gillett, "It will not do to continue the meeting in this shape. I will make some remarks, such as they need, and then dismiss them."

Nothing had been said or done to create any excitement in the meeting. The feeling was all spontaneous. The work was with such power, that even a few words of conversation would make the stoutest men writhe on their seats, as if a sword had been thrust into their hearts. It would probably not be possible for one who had never witnessed such a scene, to realize what the force of the truth sometimes is, under the power of the Holy Ghost. It was indeed a sword, and a two-edged sword. The pain that it produced when searchingly presented in a few words of conversation, would create a distress that seemed unendurable.

Mr. Gillett became very much agitated. He turned pale; and with a good deal of excitement he said, "What shall we do? What shall we do?" I put my hand on his shoulder, and in a whisper said, "Keep quiet, keep quiet, brother Gillett." I then addressed them in as gentle but plain a manner as I could; calling their attention at once to their only remedy, and assuring them that it was a present and all-sufficient remedy. I pointed them to Christ, as the Savior of the world; and kept on in this strain as long as they could well endure it, which, indeed, was but a few moments.

Mr. Gillett became so agitated that I stepped up to him, and taking him by the arm I said, "Let us pray." We knelt down in the middle of the room where we had been standing. I led in prayer, in a low, unimpassioned voice; but interceded with the Savior to interpose his blood, then and there, and to lead all these sinners to accept the salvation which he proffered, and to believe to the saving of their souls. The agitation deepened every moment; and as I could hear their sobs, and sighs, I closed my prayer and rose suddenly from my knees. They all arose, and I said, "Now please go home without speaking a word to each other. Try to keep silent, and do not break out into any boisterous manifestation of feeling; but go without saying a word, to your rooms."

At this moment a young man by the name of W., a clerk in Mr. H.'s store, being one of the first young men in the place, so nearly fainted, that he fell upon some young men that stood near him; and they all of them partially swooned away, and fell together. This had well-nigh produced a loud shrieking; but I hushed them down, and said to the young men, "Please set that door wide open, and go out, and let all retire in silence." They did as I requested. They did not shriek; but they went out sobbing and sighing, and their sobs and sighs could be heard till they got out into the street.

This Mr. W., to whom I have alluded, kept silence till he entered the door where he lived; but he could contain himself no longer. He shut the door, fell upon the floor, and burst out into a loud wailing, in view of his awful condition: This brought the family around him, and scattered conviction among the whole of them. I afterwards learned that similar scenes occurred in other families. Several, as it was afterwards ascertained, were converted at the meeting, and went home so full of joy, that they could hardly contain themselves.

The next morning, as soon as it was fairly day, people began to call at Mr. Gillett's, to have us go and visit members of their families, whom they represented as being under the greatest conviction. We took a hasty breakfast, and started out. As soon as we were in the streets, the people ran out from many houses, and begged us to go into their houses. As we could only visit but one place at a time, when we went into a house, the neighbors would rush in and fill the largest room. We would stay and give them instruction for a short time, and then go to another house, and the people would follow us.

We found a most extraordinary state of things. Convictions were so deep and universal, that we would sometimes go into a house, and find some in a kneeling posture, and some prostrate on the floor. We visited, and conversed, and prayed in this manner, from house to house, till noon. I then said to Mr. Gillett, "This will never do; we must have a meeting of inquiry. We cannot go from house to house, and we are not meeting the wants of the people at all." He agreed with me; but the question arose, where shall we have the meeting?

A Mr. F., a religious man, at that time kept a hotel, on the corner, at the center of the town. He had a large dining room; and Mr. Gillett said, "I will step in and see if I cannot be allowed to appoint the meeting of inquiry in his dining room." Without difficulty he obtained consent, and then went immediately to the public schools, and gave notice that at one o'clock there would be a meeting of inquiry at Mr. F.'s dining room. We went home, and took our dinner, and started for the meeting. We saw people hurrying, and some of them actually running to the meeting. They were coming from every direction. By the time we were there, the room, though a large one, was crammed to its utmost capacity. Men, women, and children crowded the apartment.

This meeting was very much like the one we had had the night before. The feeling was overwhelming. Some men of the strongest nerves were so cut down by the remarks which were made, that they were unable to help themselves, and had to be taken home by their friends. This meeting lasted till nearly night. It resulted in a great number of hopeful conversions, and was the means of greatly extending the work on every side.

I preached that evening, and Mr. Gillett appointed a meeting for inquiry, the next morning, in the courthouse. This was a much larger room than the dining hall, though it was not so central. However, at the hour, the court house was crowded; and we spent a good part of the day in giving instruction, and the work went on with wonderful power. I preached again in the evening, and Mr. Gillett appointed a meeting of inquiry, the next morning, at the church; as no other room in the village was then large enough to hold the inquirers.

At evening, if I rightly remember the order of things; we undertook to hold a prayer and conference meeting in a large schoolhouse. But the meeting was hardly begun before the feeling deepened so much that, to prevent an undesirable outburst of overwhelming feeling, I proposed to Mr. Gillett that we should dismiss the meeting, and request the people to go in silence, and Christians to spend the evening in secret prayer, or in family prayer, as might seem most desirable. Sinners we exhorted not to sleep, until they gave their hearts to God. After this the work became so general that I preached every night, I think, for twenty nights in succession, and twice on the Sunday. Our prayer meetings during this time were held in the church, in the daytime. The prayer meeting was held one part of the day, and a meeting for inquiry the other part. Every day, if I remember aright, after the work had thus commenced, we held a prayer meeting and a meeting for inquiry, with preaching in the evening. There was a solemnity throughout the whole place, and an awe that made everybody feel that God was there.

Ministers came in from neighboring towns, and expressed great astonishment at what they saw and heard, as well they might. Conversions multiplied so rapidly, that we had no way of learning who were converted. Therefore, every evening, at the close of my sermon, I requested all who had been converted that day, to come forward and report themselves in front of the pulpit, that we might have a little conversation with them. We were every night surprised by the number and the class of persons that came forward.

At one of our morning prayer meetings, the lower part of the church was full. I arose and was making some remarks to the people, when an unconverted man, a merchant, came into the meeting. He came along till he found a seat in front of me, and near where I stood speaking. He had sat but a few moments, when he fell from his seat as if he had been shot. He writhed and groaned in a terrible manner. I stepped to the pew door, and saw that it was altogether an agony of mind.

A skeptical physician sat near him. He stepped out of his slip, and came and examined this man who was thus distressed. He felt his pulse, and examined the case for a few moments. He said nothing, but turned away, and leaned his head against a post that supported the gallery, and manifested great agitation. He said afterward that he saw at once that it was distress of mind, and it took his skepticism entirely away. He was soon after hopefully converted. We engaged in prayer for the man who fell in the pew; and before he left the house, I believe, his anguish passed away, and he rejoiced in Christ.

Another physician, a very amiable man but a skeptic, had a little daughter and a praying wife. Little H., a girl perhaps eight or nine years old, was strongly convicted of sin, and her mother was greatly interested in her state of mind. But her father was, at first, quite indignant. He said to his wife, "The subject of religion is too high for me. I never could understand it. And do you tell me that that little child understands it so as to be intelligently convicted of sin? I do not believe it. I know better. I cannot endure it. It is fanaticism; it is madness." Nevertheless, the mother of the child held fast in prayer. The doctor made these remarks, as I learned, with a good deal of spirit. Immediately he took his horse, and went several miles to see a patient. On his way, as he afterward remarked, that subject took possession of his mind in such a manner, that it was all opened to his understanding; and the whole plan of salvation by Christ was so clear to him that he saw that a child could understand it. He wondered that it had ever seemed so mysterious to him. He regretted exceedingly that he had said what he had to his wife about little H., and felt in haste to get home that he might take it back. He soon came home, another man; told his wife what had passed in his own mind; encouraged dear little H. to come to Christ; and both father and daughter have since been earnest Christians, and have lived long and done much good.

But in this revival, as in others that I have known, God did some terrible things in righteousness. On one Sunday while I was there, as we came out of the pulpit, and were about to leave the church, a man came in haste to Mr. Gillett and myself, and requested us to go to a certain place, saying that a man had fallen down dead there. I was engaged in conversing with somebody, and Mr. Gillett went alone. When I was through with the conversation, I went to Mr. Gillett's house, and he soon returned and related this fact. Three men who had been opposing the work, had met that Sunday-day, and spent the day in drinking and ridiculing the work. They went on in this way until one of them suddenly fell dead. When Mr. Gillett arrived at the house, and the circumstances were related to him, he said, "There is no doubt that man has been stricken down by God, and has been sent to hell." His companions were speechless. They could say nothing; for it was evident to them that their conduct had brought upon him this awful stroke of divine indignation.

As the work proceeded, it gathered in nearly the whole population. Nearly every one of the lawyers, merchants, and physicians, and almost all the principal men, and indeed, nearly all the adult population of the village, were brought in, especially those who belonged to Mr. Gillett's congregation. He said to me before I left, "So far as my congregation is concerned, the millennium is come already. My people are all converted. Of all my past labors I have not a sermon that is suited at all to my congregation, for they are all Christians." Mr. Gillett afterward reported that, during the twenty days that I spent at Rome, there were five hundred conversions in that town.

During the progress of this work, a good deal of excitement sprung up in Utica, and some there, were disposed to ridicule the work at Rome. Mr. E., who lived at Rome, was a very prominent citizen, and was regarded as standing at the head of society there, in point of wealth and intelligence. But he was skeptical; or, perhaps I should say, he held Unitarian views. He was a very moral and respectable man, and held his peculiar views unobtrusively, saying very little to anybody about them. The first Sunday I preached there, Mr. H. was present; and he was so astonished, as he afterwards told me, at my preaching, that he made up his mind that he would not go again. He went home and said to his family: "That man is mad, and I should not be surprised if he set the town on fire." He stayed away from the meeting for some two weeks. In the meantime, the work became so great as to confound his skepticism, and he was in a state of great perplexity.

He was president of a bank in Utica, and used to go down to attend the weekly meeting of the directors. On one of these occasions, one of the directors began to rally him on the state of things in Rome, as if they were all running mad there. Mr. H. remarked, "Gentlemen, say what you will, there is something very remarkable in the state of things in Rome. Certainly no human power or eloquence has produced what we see there. I cannot understand it. You say it will soon subside. No doubt the intensity of feeling that is now in Rome, must soon subside, or the people will become insane." "But, gentlemen," said he, "there is no accounting for that state of feeling by any philosophy, unless there be something divine in it."

After Mr. H. had stayed away from the meeting about two weeks, a few of us assembled one afternoon, to make him a special subject of prayer. The Lord gave us strong faith in praying for him; and we felt the conviction that the Lord own working in his soul. That evening he came to meeting. When he came into the house, Mr. Gillett whispered to me as he sat in the pulpit, and said, "Brother Finney, Mr. H. has come. I hope you will not say anything that will offend him." "No," said I, "but I shall not spare him." In those days I was obliged to preach altogether without premeditation; for I had not an hour in a week, which I could take to arrange my thoughts beforehand.

I chose my subject and preached. The word took a powerful hold; and as I hoped and intended, it took a powerful hold of Mr. H. himself. I think it was that very night, when I requested, at the close of the meeting, all those who had been converted that day and evening to come forward and report themselves, Mr. H. was one who came deliberately, solemnly forward, and reported himself as having given his heart to God. He appeared humble and penitent, and I have always supposed, was truly converted to Christ.

The state of things in the village, and in the neighborhood round about, was such that no one could come into the village, without feeling awe-stricken with the impression that God was there, in a peculiar and wonderful manner. As an illustration of this, I will relate an incident. The sheriff of the county resided in Utica. There were two courthouses in the county, one at Rome, and the other at Utica; consequently, the sheriff B. by name, had much business at Rome. He afterwards told me that he had heard of the state of things at Rome; and he, together with others, had a good deal of laughing, in the hotel where he boarded, about what they had heard.

But one day it was necessary for him to go to Rome. He said that he was glad to have business there; for he wanted to see for himself what it was that people talked so much about, and what the state of things really was in Rome. He drove on in his one horse sleigh, as he told me, without any particular impression upon his mind at all, until he crossed what was called the old canal, a place about a mile, I think, from the town. He said as soon as he crossed the old canal, a strange impression came over him, an awe so deep that he could not shake it off. He felt as if God pervaded the whole atmosphere. He said that this increased the whole way, till he came to the village. He stopped at Mr. F.'s hotel, and the hostler came out and took his horse. He observed, he said, that the hostler looked just as he himself felt, as if he were afraid to speak. He went into the house, and found the gentleman there with whom he had business. He said they were manifestly all so much impressed, they could hardly attend to business. He said that several times, in the course of the short time he was there, he had to rise from the table abruptly, and go to the window and look out, and try to divert his attention, to keep from weeping. He observed, he said, that everybody else appeared to feel just as he did. Such an awe, such a solemnity, such a state of things, he had never had any conception of before. He hastened through with his business, and returned to Utica; but, as he said, never to speak lightly of the work at Rome again. A few weeks later, at Utica, he was hopefully converted; the circumstances of which I shall relate in the proper place.

I have spoken of Wright's settlement, a village northeast of Rome, some two or three miles. The revival took powerful effect there, and converted the great mass of the inhabitants.

The means that were used at Rome, were such as I had used before, and no others; preaching, public, social, and private prayer, exhortations, and personal conversation. It is difficult to conceive so deep and universal a state of religious feeling, with no instance of disorder, or tumult, or fanaticism, or anything that was objectionable, as was witnessed at Rome. There are many of the converts of that revival, scattered all through the land, living to this day; and they can testify that in those meetings the greatest order and solemnity prevailed, and the utmost pains were taken to guard against everything that was to be deplored.

The Spirit's work was so spontaneous, so powerful and so overwhelming, as to render it necessary to exercise the greatest caution and wisdom, in conducting all the meetings, in order to prevent an undesirable outburst of feeling, that soon would have exhausted the sensibility of the people, and brought about a reaction. But no reaction followed, as everybody knows who is acquainted with the facts. They kept up a sunrise prayer meeting for several months, and I believe for more than a year afterwards, at all seasons of the year, that was very fully attended, and was as full of interest as perhaps a prayer meeting could well be. The moral state of the people was so greatly changed, that Mr. Gillett often remarked that it did not seem like the same place. Whatever of sin was left, was obliged to hide its head. No open immorality could be tolerated there for a moment. I have given only a very faint outline of what passed at Rome. A faithful description of all the moving incidents that were crowded into that revival, would make a volume of itself.

I should say a few words in regard to the spirit of prayer which prevailed at Rome at this time. I think it was on the Saturday that I came down from Western to exchange with Mr. Gillett, that I met the church in the afternoon in a prayer meeting, in their house of worship. I endeavored to make them understand that God would immediately answer prayer, provided they fulfilled the conditions upon which he had promised to answer prayer; and especially if they believed, in the sense of expecting him to answer their requests. I observed that the church was greatly interested in my remarks, and their countenances manifested an intense desire to see an answer to their prayers. Near the close of the meeting I recollect making this remark. "I really believe, if you will unite this afternoon in the prayer of faith to God, for the immediate outpouring of his Spirit, that you will receive an answer from heaven, sooner than you would get a message from Albany, by the quickest post that could be sent."

I said this with great emphasis, and felt it; and I observed that the people were startled with my expression of earnestness and faith in respect to an immediate answer to prayer. The fact is, I had so often seen this result in answer to prayer, that I made the remark without any misgiving. Nothing was said by any of the members of the church at the time; but I learned after the work had begun, that three or four members of the church called in at Mr. Gillett's study, and felt so impressed with what had been said about speedy answers to prayer, that they determined to take God at his word, and see whether he would answer while they were yet speaking. One of them told me afterwards that they had wonderful faith given them by the Spirit of God, to pray for an immediate answer; and he added, "The answer did come quicker than we could have got an answer from Albany, by the quickest post we could have sent."

Indeed, the town was full of prayer. Go where you would, you heard the voice of prayer. Pass along the street, and if two or three Christians happened to be together, they were praying. Wherever they met they prayed. Wherever there was a sinner unconverted, especially if he manifested any opposition, you would find some two or three brethren or sisters agreeing to make him a particular subject of prayer.

There was the wife of an officer in the United States army residing at Rome, the daughter of a prominent citizen of that place. This lady manifested a good deal of opposition to the work, and, as was reported, said some strong things against it; and this led to her being made a particular subject of prayer. This had come to my knowledge but a short time before the event occurred, which I am about to relate. I believe, in this case, some of the principal women made this lady a particular subject of prayer, as she was a person of prominent influence in the place. She was an educated lady, of great force of character, and of strong will; and of course she made her opposition felt. But almost as soon as this was known, and the spirit of prayer was given for her in particular, the Spirit of God took her case in hand. One evening, almost immediately after I had heard of her case, and perhaps the evening of the very day that the facts came to my knowledge, after the meeting was dismissed, and the people had retired, Mr. Gillett and myself had remained to the very last, conversing with some persons who were deeply bowed down with conviction. As they went away, and we were about to retire, the sexton came hurriedly to us as we were going out, and said, "There is a lady in yonder pew that cannot get out; she is helpless. Will you not come and see her?" We returned, and lo! down in the pew, was this lady of whom I have spoken, perfectly overwhelmed with conviction. The pew had been full, and she had attempted to retire with the others that went out; but as she was the last to go out, she found herself unable to stand, and sunk down upon the floor, and did so without being noticed by those that preceded her. We had some conversation with her, and found that the Lord had stricken her with unutterable conviction of sin. After praying with her, and giving her the solemn charge to give her heart immediately to Christ, I left her; and Mr. Gillett, I believe, helped her home. It was but a few rods to her house. We afterwards learned, that when she got home she went into a chamber by herself and spent the night. It was a cold winter's night. She locked herself in, and spent the night alone. The next day she expressed hope in Christ, and so far as I have known, proved to be soundly converted.

I think I should mention also the conversion of Mrs. Gillett, during this revival. She was a sister of the missionary Mills, who was one of the young men whose zeal led to the organization of the American Board. She was a beautiful woman, considerably younger than her husband, and his second wife. She had been, before Mr. Gillett married her, under conviction for several weeks and had become almost deranged. She had the impression, if I recollect right, that she was not one of the elect, and that there was no salvation for her. Soon after the revival began in Rome, she was powerfully convicted again by the Spirit of the Lord.

She was a woman of refinement, and fond of dress; and as is very common, wore about her head and upon her person some trifling ornaments; nothing, however, that I should have thought of as being any stumbling block in her way, at all. Being her guest, I conversed repeatedly with her as her convictions increased; but it never occurred to me that her fondness for dress could stand in the way of her being converted to God. But as the work became so powerful, her distress became alarming; and Mr. Gillett, knowing what had formally occurred in her case, felt quite alarmed lest she should get into that state of despondency, in which she had been years before. She threw herself upon me for instruction. Every time I came into the house, almost, she would come to me and beg me to pray for her, and tell me that her distress was more than she could bear. She was evidently going fast to despair; but I could see that she was depending too much on me; therefore, I tried to avoid her.

It went on thus, until one day I came into the house, and turned into the study. In a few moments, as usual, she was before me, begging me to pray for her, and complaining that there was no salvation for her. I got up abruptly and left her, without praying with her, and saying to her that it was of no use for me to pray for her, that she was depending upon my prayers. When I did so, she sunk down as if she would faint. I left her alone, notwithstanding, and went abruptly from the study to the parlor. In the course of a few moments she came rushing across the hall into the parlor, with her face all in a glow, exclaiming, "O Mr. Finney! I have found the Savior! I have found the Savior! Don't you think that it was the ornaments in my hair that stood in the way of my conversion? I have found when I prayed that they would come up before me; and I would be tempted, as I supposed, to give them up." "But," said she, "I thought they were trifles, and that God did not care about such trifles. This was a temptation of Satan. But the ornaments that I wore, continually kept coming up before my mind, whenever I attempted to give my heart to God." "When you abruptly left me," she said, "I was driven to desperation. I cast myself down, and, lo! these ornaments came up again; and I said, I will not have these things come up again, I will put them away from me forever." Said she, "I renounced them, and hated them as things standing in the way of my salvation. As soon as I promised to give them up, the Lord revealed himself to my soul; and O!" said she, "I wonder I have never understood this before. This was really the great difficulty with me before, when I was under conviction, my fondness for dress; and I did not know it."

CHAPTER 14

REVIVAL AT UTICA, NEW YORK

Both in this place and in Rome,
it was a common remark that nobody could be
in the town, or pass through it, without being
aware of the presence of God.

When I had been at Rome about twenty days, one of the elders of Mr. Aiken's church in Utica, a very prominent and a very useful man, died; and I went down to attend his funeral. Mr. Aiken conducted the funeral exercises; and I learned from him that the spirit of prayer was already manifest in his congregation, and in that city. He told me that one of his principal women had been so deeply exercised in her soul about the state of the church, and of the ungodly in that city, that she had prayed for two days and nights, almost incessantly, until her strength was quite overcome; that she had literal travail of soul, to such an extent that when her own strength was exhausted, she could not endure the burden of her mind, unless somebody was engaged in prayer with her, upon whose prayer she could lean — someone who could express her desires to God.

I understood this, and told Mr. Aiken that the work had already begun in her heart. He recognized it, of course; and wished me to commence labor with him and his people immediately. I soon did so, and, be sure, the work began at once. The word took immediate effect, and the place became filled with the manifested influence of the Holy Spirit. Our meetings were crowded every night and the work spread and went on powerfully, especially in the two Presbyterian congregations; of one of which Mr. Aiken was pastor, and Mr. Brace of the other. I divided my labors between the two congregations.

Soon after I commenced in Utica, I observed to Mr. Aiken, that Mr. B., the sheriff of whom I have made mention, did not attend the meetings, as I saw. But a few evenings afterward, just as I was about to begin to preach, Mr. Aiken whispered to me that Mr. B. had come in. He pointed him out to me, as he made his way up the aisle to his seat. I took my text, and proceeded to address the congregation. I had spoken but a few moments, when I observed Mr. B. rise up in the slip, turn deliberately around, wrap his great coat about him, and kneel down. I observed that it excited the attention of those that sat near, who knew him, and produced a considerable sensation in that part of the house. The sheriff continued on his knees during the whole service. He then retired to his room at the hotel in which he boarded. He was a man, perhaps fifty years old, and unmarried.

He afterwards told me that his mind was greatly burdened when he went home, and brought up the subject to which he had been listening. I had pressed the congregation to accept Christ, just as he was presented in the gospel. The question of the present acceptance of Christ, and the whole situation in regard to the sinner's relation to him, and his relation to the sinner, had been the subject of discourse. He said that he had treasured up in his mind the points that had been made, and that he presented them solemnly before himself, and said, "My soul, will you consent to this? Will you accept of Christ, and give up sin, and give up yourself? And will you do it now?" He said he had thrown himself, in the agony of his mind, upon his bed. He made this point with himself, and conjured his soul, to accept "now, and here." Right there, he said, his distress left him so suddenly that he fell asleep, and did not wake for several hours. When he did awake, he found his mind full of peace and rest in Christ; and from this moment he became an earnest worker for Christ among his acquaintances.

The hotel at which he boarded, was at that time kept by a Mr. S.. The Spirit took powerful hold in that house. Mr. S. himself, was soon made a subject of prayer, and became converted; and a large number of his family and of his boarders. Indeed, that largest hotel in the town became a center of spiritual influence, and many were converted there. The stages, as they passed through, stopped at the hotel; and so powerful was the impression in the community, that I heard of several cases of persons that just stopped for a meal, or to spend a night, being powerfully convicted and converted before they left the town. Indeed, both in this place and in Rome, it was a common remark that nobody could be in the town, or pass through it, without being aware of the presence of God; that a divine influence seemed to pervade the place, and the whole atmosphere to be instinct with a divine life.

A merchant from Lowville came to Utica, to do some business in his line. He stopped at the hotel where Mr. B. boarded. He found the whole conversation in the town was such as greatly to annoy him, for he was an unconverted man. He was vexed, and said he could do no business there; it was all religion; and he resolved to go home. He could not go into a store, but religion was intruded upon him, and he could do no business with them. That evening he would go home.

These remarks had been made in the presence of some of the young converts who boarded at the hotel, and I think especially in the presence of Mr. B.. As the stage was expected to leave late at night, he was observed to go to the bar, just before he retired, to pay his bill; saying that Mr. S. would not probably be up when the stage passed through, and he wished therefore to settle his bill before he retired. Mr. S. said that he observed, while he was settling his bill, that his mind was very much exercised, and he suggested to several of the gentleman boarders that they should make him a subject of prayer. They took him, I believe, to Mr. B.'s room, and conversed with him, and prayed with him and before the stage came, he was a converted man. And so concerned did he feel immediately about the people of his own place, that when the stage came he took passage, and went immediately home. As soon as he arrived at home, he told his family his experience, and called them together and prayed with them. As he was a very prominent citizen, and very outspoken, and everywhere proclaiming what the Lord had done for his soul, it immediately produced a very solemn impression in Lowville, and soon resulted in a great revival in that place.

It was in the midst of the revival in Utica, that we first heard of the opposition to those revivals, that was springing up in the East. Mr. Nettleton wrote some letters to Mr. Aiken, with whom I was laboring; in which it was manifest that he was very much mistaken with regard to the character of those revivals. Mr. Aiken showed me those letters; and they were handed around among the ministers in the neighborhood, as they were intended to be. Among them was one in which Mr. Nettleton stated fully what he regarded as objectionable in the conduct of these revivals; but as no such thing as he complained of were done in those revivals, or had been known at all, we took no other notice of the letters than to read them, and let them pass. Mr. Aiken, however, replied privately to one or two of them, assuring Mr. Nettleton that no such things were done. I do not recollect now whether Mr. Nettleton complained of the fact, that women would sometimes pray in the social meetings. It was true, however, that in a few instances women, and some very prominent women, who were strongly pressed in spirit, would lead in prayer, in the social meetings which we held daily from house to house. No opposition, that I know of, was manifested to this, either at Utica or at Rome. I had no agency in introducing the practice among the people, and do not know whether it had existed there before or not. Indeed, it was not a subject of much conversation or thought, so far as I know, in the neighborhood where it occurred.

I have already said that Mr. Weeks, who maintained the most offensive doctrines on the subject of divine efficiency, was known to be opposed to those revivals. For the information of those who may not know that any such doctrines were ever held, I would say, that Mr. Weeks, and those that agreed with him, held that both sin and holiness were produced in the mind by a direct act of almighty power; that God made men sinners or holy, at his sovereign discretion, but in both cases by a direct act of almighty power, an act as irresistible as that of creation itself; that in fact God was the only proper agent in the universe, and that all creatures acted only as they were moved and compelled to act, by his irresistible power; that every sin in the universe, both of men and of devils, was the result of a direct, irresistible act on the part of God. This they attempted to prove from the Bible.

Mr. Weeks' idea of conversion, or regeneration, was that God, who had made men sinners, brought them also, in regenerating them, to admit that he had a right to make them sinners, for his glory, and to send them to hell for the sins which he had directly created in them, or compelled them to commit, by the force of omnipotence. In conversion; that did not bring sinners to accept this view of the subject, he had no confidence. Those that have read Mr. Weeks' nine sermons on the subject, will see that I have not misrepresented his views. And as this view of Mr. Weeks, was embraced, to a considerable extent, by ministers and professors of religion in that region, his known opposition, together with that of some other ministers, greatly emboldened and increased the opposition of others.

The work, however, went on with great power, converting all classes, until Mr. Aiken reported the hopeful conversion of five hundred, in the course of a few weeks, most of them, I believe, belonging to his own congregation. Revivals were comparatively a new thing in that region; and the great mass of the people had not become convinced that they were the work of God. They were not awed by them, as they afterwards became. It seemed to be extensively the impression that those revivals would soon pass away, and would prove to have been but a mere excitement of animal feeling. I do not mean that those that were interested in the work, had any such idea.

One circumstance occurred, in the midst of that revival, that made a powerful impression. The Oneida presbytery met there, while the revival was going on in its full strength. Among others there was an aged clergyman, a stranger to me, who was very much annoyed by the heat and fervor of the revival. He found the public mind all absorbed on the subject of religion; that there was prayer and religious conversation everywhere, even in the stores and other public places. He had never seen a revival, and had never heard what he heard there. He was a Scotchman, and, I believe, had not been very long in this country.

On Friday afternoon, before presbytery adjourned, he arose and made a violent speech against the revival, as it was going on. What he said, greatly shocked and grieved the Christian people who were present. They felt like falling on their faces before God, and crying to him to prevent what he had said from doing any mischief.

The presbytery adjourned just at evening. Some of the members went home, and others remained overnight. Christians gave themselves to prayer. There was a great crying to God that night, that he would counteract any evil influence that might result from that speech. The next morning, this man was found dead in his bed.

In the course of these revivals, persons from a distance, in almost every direction, hearing what the Lord was doing, or being attracted by curiosity and wonder at what they heard, came to see for themselves; and many of them were converted to Christ. Among these visitors, Dr. Garnet Judd, who soon after went to the Sandwich Islands as a missionary, and has been well-known to lovers of missions for many years, was one. He belonged to the congregation of Mr. Weeks, to whom I have referred. His father, old Dr. Judd, was an earnest Christian man. He came down to Utica and sympathized greatly with the revival.

About the same time a young woman, Miss F. T., from some part of New England, came to Utica under the following circumstances: she was teaching a high school, in the neighborhood of Newburgh, New York. As much was said in the newspapers about the revival in Utica, Miss T., among others, became filled with wonder and astonishment, and with a desire to go and see for herself what it meant. She dismissed her school for ten days, and took the stage for Utica. As she passed through Genesee street to the hotel, she observed on one of the signs, the name of B. T.. She was an entire stranger in Utica, and did not know that she had an acquaintance or relative there. But after stopping a day or two at her hotel, and inquiring who B. T. was, she dropped him a note, saying that the daughter of a Mr. T., naming her father, was at the hotel, and would be pleased to see him. Mr. T. waited upon her and found that she was a distant relative of his, and invited her immediately to his house. She accepted his invitation, and he being an earnest Christian man, immediately took her to all the meetings, and tried to interest her in religion. She was greatly surprised at all that she saw, and a good deal annoyed.

She was an energetic, highly cultivated, and proud young lady; and the manner in which people conversed with her, and pressed upon her the necessity of immediately giving her heart to God, very much disturbed her. The preaching which she heard, from night to night, took a deep hold upon her. The guilt of sinners was largely insisted upon; and their desert and danger of eternal damnation, were made prominent in what she heard. This aroused her opposition; but still the work of conviction went powerfully on in her heart.

In the meantime, I had not seen her, to converse with her; but had heard from Mr. T. of her state of mind. After writhing under the truth for a few days, she called at my lodging. She sat down upon the sofa in the parlor. I drew up my chair in front of her, and began to press her with the claims of God. She referred to my preaching that sinners deserved to be sent to an eternal hell; and said that she could not receive it, that she did not believe that God was such a being. I replied, "Nor do you yet understand what sin is, in its true nature and ill desert; if you did, you would not complain of God for sending the sinner to an eternal hell." I then spread out that subject before her in conversation, as plainly as I could. Much as she hated to believe it, still the conviction of its truth was becoming irresistible. I conversed in this strain for some time, until I saw that she was ready to sink under the ripened conviction; and then I turned and said a few words about the place which Jesus holds, and what is the real situation of things, in regard to the salvation of those who thus deserved to be damned.

Her countenance waxed pale, in a moment after she threw up her hands and shrieked, and then fell forward upon the arm of the sofa, and let her heart break. I think she had not wept at all before. Her eyes were dry, her countenance haggard and pale, her sensibility all locked up; but now the flood gates were opened, she let her whole gushing heart out before God. I had no occasion to say any more to her. She soon arose and went to her own lodgings. She almost immediately gave up her school, offered herself as a foreign missionary, was married to a Mr. Gulick, and went out to the Sandwich Islands, I think, at the same time that Dr. Judd went out. Her history, as a missionary, is well known. She has been a very efficient missionary, and has raised several sons, who also are missionaries.

While making my home in Utica, I preached frequently in New Hartford, a village four miles south of Utica. There was a precious and powerful work of grace, a Mr. Coe being at the time pastor of the Presbyterian church. I preached also at Whitesboro', another beautiful village, four miles west of Utica; where also was a powerful revival. The pastor, Mr. John Frost, was a most efficient laborer in the work.

A circumstance occurred in this neighborhood, which I must not fail to notice. There was a cotton manufactory on the Oriskany creek, a little above Whitesboro', a place now called New York Mills. It was owned by a Mr. W., an unconverted man, but a gentleman of high standing and good morals. My brother-in-law, Mr. G. A., was at that time superintendent of the factory. I was invited to go and preach at that place, and went up one evening, and preached in the village schoolhouse, which was large, and was crowded with hearers. The word, I could see, took powerful effect among the people, especially among the young people who were at work in the factory.

The next morning, after breakfast, I went into the factory, to look through it. As I went through, I observed there was a good deal of agitation among those who were busy at their looms, and their mules, and other implements of work. On passing through one of the apartments, where a great number of young women were attending to their weaving, I observed a couple of them eyeing me, and speaking very earnestly to each other; and I could see that they were a good deal agitated, although they both laughed. I went slowly toward them. They saw me coming, and were evidently much excited. One of them was trying to mend a broken thread, and I observed that her hands trembled so that she could not mend it. I approached slowly, looking on each side at the machinery, as I passed; but observed that this girl grew more and more agitated, and could not proceed with her work. When I came within eight or ten feet of her, I looked solemnly at her. She observed it, and was quite overcome, and sunk down, and burst into tears. The impression caught almost like powder, and in a few moments nearly all in the room were in tears. This feeling spread through the factory. Mr. W., the owner of the establishment, was present, and seeing the state of things, he said to the superintendent, "Stop the mill, and let the people attend to religion; for it is more important that our souls should be saved than that this factory run." The gate was immediately shut down, and the factory stopped; but where should we assemble? The superintendent suggested that the mule room was large; and, the mules being run up, we could assemble there. We did so, and a more powerful meeting I scarcely ever attended. It went on with great power. The building was large, and had many people in it, from the garret to the cellar. The revival went through the mill with astonishing power, and in the course of a few days nearly all in the mill were hopefully converted.

As much has been said about the hopeful conversion of Theodore D. Weld, at Utica, it may be well for me to give a correct report of the facts. He had an aunt, Mrs. C., living in Utica, who was a very praying, godly woman. He was the son of an eminent clergyman in New England, and his aunt thought he was a Christian. He used to lead her family in its worship. Before the commencement of the revival, he had become a member of Hamilton College, at Clinton. The work at Utica had attracted so much attention, that many persons from Clinton, and among the rest some of the professors of the college, had been down to Utica, and had reported what was doing there, and a good deal of excitement had resulted. Weld held a very prominent place among the students of Hamilton College, and had a very great influence. Hearing what was going on at Utica, he became very much excited, and his opposition was greatly aroused. He became quite outrageous in his expressions of opposition to the work, as I understood.

This fact became known in Utica; and his aunt, with whom he had boarded, became very anxious about him. To me he was an entire stranger. His aunt wrote him, and asked him to come home and spend a Sunday, hear the preaching, and become interested in the work. He at first declined, but finally got some of the students together, and told them that he had made up his mind to go down to Utica; that he knew it must be fanaticism or enthusiasm; that he knew it would not move him, they would see that it would not. He came full of opposition, and his aunt soon learned that he did not intend to hear me preach. Mr. Aiken had usually occupied the pulpit in the morning, and I, in the afternoon and evening. His aunt learned that he intended to go to Mr. Aiken's church in the morning, when he expected Mr. Aiken to preach; but that he would not go in the afternoon or evening, because he was determined not to hear me.

In view of this, Mr. Aiken suggested that I should preach in the morning. I consented, and we went to meeting. Mr. Aiken took the introductory exercises, as usual. Mrs. C. came to meeting with her family, and among them Mr. Weld. She took pains to have him so seated in the slip that he could not well get out, without herself, and one or two other members of the family, stepping out before him; for she feared, as she said, that he would go out when he saw that I was going to preach. I knew that his influence among the young men of Utica was very great, and that his coming there would have a powerful influence to make them band together in opposition to the work. Mr. Aiken pointed him out to me, as he came in and took his seat.

After the introductory exercises, I arose and named this text: "One sinner destroys much good." I had never preached from it, or heard it preached from; but it came home with great power to my mind, and this fact decided the selection of the text. I began to preach, and to show in a great many instances, how one sinner might destroy much good, and how the influence of one man might destroy a great many souls. I suppose that I drew a pretty vivid picture of Weld, and of what his influence was, and what mischief he might do. Once or twice he made an effort to get out; but his aunt perceiving it, would throw herself forward, and lean on the slip in front, and engage in silent prayer, and he could not get out without arousing and annoying her; and therefore he remained in his seat till meeting was out.

The next day I called at a store in Genesee street, to converse with some people there, as it was my custom to go from place to place for conversation; and whom should I find there but Weld? He fell upon me very unceremoniously, and I should think, for nearly or quite an hour, talked to me in a most abusive manner. I had never heard anything like it. I got an opportunity to say but very little to him myself, for his tongue ran incessantly. He was very gifted in language. It soon attracted the attention of all that were in the store and the news ran along the streets, and the clerks gathered in from the neighboring stores, and stood to hear what he had to say. All business ceased in the store, and all gave themselves up to listening to his vituperation. But finally I appealed to him and said, "Mr. Weld, are you the son of a minister of Christ, and is this the way for you to behave?" I said a few words in that direction, and I saw that it stung him; and throwing out something very severe, he immediately left the store.

I went out also, and returned to Mr. Aiken's, where for the time I was lodging. I had been there but a few moments when somebody called at the door, and as no servant was at hand I went to the door myself. And who should come in but Mr. Weld? He looked as if he would sink. He began immediately to make the humblest confession and apology for the manner in which he had treated me; and expressed himself in the strongest terms of self-condemnation. I took him kindly by the hand and had a little conversation with him, assured him that I had laid up nothing against him, and exhorted him earnestly, to give his heart to God. I believe I prayed with him before he went. He left, and I heard no more of him that day.

That evening I preached, I think, at New Hartford, and returned late in the evening. The next morning, I heard that he went to his aunt's, greatly impressed and subdued. She asked him to pray in the family. He said that he was at first shocked at the idea. But his enmity arose so much, that he thought that that was one way in which he had not yet expressed his opposition, and therefore he would comply with her request. He knelt down, and began and went on with what his aunt intended should be a prayer; but from his own account of it, it was the most blasphemous strain of vituperation that could well be uttered. He kept on in a most wonderful way, until they all became convulsed with feeling and astonishment; and he kept on so long, that the light went out before he closed. His aunt attempted to converse with him, and to pray with him; but the opposition of his heart was terrible. She became frightened at the state of mind which he manifested. After praying with him, and entreating him to give his heart to God, she retired.

He went to his room; and walked his room by turns, and by turns he lay upon the floor. He continued the whole night in that terrible state of mind, angry, rebellious, and yet so convicted that he could scarcely live. Just at daylight, while walking back and forth in his room, he said, a pressure came upon him that crushed him down to the floor; and with it came a voice that seemed to command him to repent, to repent now. He said it broke him down to the floor, and there he lay, until, late in the morning, his aunt coming up, found him upon the floor calling himself a thousand fools; and to all human appearance, with his heart all broken to pieces.

The next night he rose in meeting, and asked if he might make confession. I answered, yes; and he made public confession before the whole congregation. He said it became him to remove the stumbling block which he had cast before the whole people; and he wanted opportunity to make the most public confession he could. He did make a very humble, earnest, broken-hearted confession.

From that time, he became a very efficient helper in the work. He labored diligently; and being a powerful speaker, and much-gifted in prayer and labor, he was instrumental, for several years, in doing a great deal of good, and in the hopeful conversion of a great many souls. At length his health became enfeebled by his great labor. He was obliged to leave college, and he went on a fishing excursion to the coast of Labrador. He returned, the same earnest laborer as before he went away, with health renewed. I found him, for a considerable time, an efficient helper, where I was attempting to labor.

I have said that no public replies were made to the things that found their way into print, in opposition to these revivals; that is, to nothing that was written by Dr. Beecher or Mr. Nettleton. I have also said, that a pamphlet was published by the ministers that composed the Oneida Association, in opposition to the work. To this, I believe, no public answer was given. I recollect that a Unitarian minister, residing at Trenton, in that county, published an abusive pamphlet, in which he greatly misrepresented the work, and made a personal attack upon myself. To this the Rev. Mr. Wetmore, one of the members of the Oneida Presbytery, published a reply.

This revival occurred in the winter and spring of 1826. When the converts had been received into the churches throughout the county, Rev. John Frost, pastor of the Presbyterian Church at Whitesboro', published a pamphlet giving some account of the revival, and stated, if I remember right, that within the bounds of that presbytery, the converts numbered three thousand. I have no copy of any of these pamphlets. I have said that the work spread from Rome and Utica, as from a center, in every direction. Ministers came from a considerable distance, and spent more or less time in attending the meetings, and in various ways helping forward the work. I spread my own labors over as large a field as I could, and labored more or less throughout the bounds of the presbytery. I cannot now remember all the places where I spent more or less time. The pastors of all those churches sympathized deeply with the work; and like good and true men, laid themselves upon the altar, and did all they could to forward the great and glorious movement; and God gave them a rich reward.

The doctrines preached in these revivals were the same that have been already presented. Instead of telling sinners to use the means of grace and pray for a new heart, we called on them to make themselves a new heart and a new spirit, and pressed the duty of instant surrender to God. We told them the Spirit was striving with them to induce them now to give him their hearts, now to believe, and to enter at once upon a life of devotion to Christ, of faith, and love, and Christian obedience. We taught them that while they were praying for the Holy Spirit, they were constantly resisting him; and that if they would at once yield to their own convictions of duty, they would be Christians. We tried to show them that everything they did or said before they had submitted, believed, given their hearts to God, was all sin, was not that which God required them to do, but was simply deferring repentance and resisting the Holy Ghost.

Such teaching as this was of course opposed by many; nevertheless, it was greatly blessed by the Spirit of God. Formerly it had been supposed necessary that a sinner should remain under conviction a long time; and it was not uncommon to hear old professors of religion, say that they were under conviction many months, or years, before they found relief; and they evidently had the impression that the longer they were under conviction, the greater was the evidence that they were truly converted. We taught the opposite of this. I insisted that if they remained long under conviction, they were in danger of becoming self-righteous, in the sense that they would think that they had prayed a great deal, and done a great deal to persuade God to save them; and that finally they would settle down with a false hope. We told them that under this protracted conviction, they were in danger of grieving the Spirit of God away, and when their distress of mind ceased, a reaction would naturally take place; they would feel less distress, and perhaps obtain a degree of comfort, from which they were in danger of inferring that they were converted; that the bare thought that they were possibly converted, might create a degree of joy, which they might mistake for Christian joy and peace; and that this state of mind might still farther delude them, by being taken as evidence that they were converted.

We tried thoroughly to dispose of this false teaching. We insisted then, as I have ever done since, on immediate submission, as the only thing that God could accept at their hands; and that all delay, under any pretext whatever, was rebellion against God. It became very common under this teaching, for persons to be convicted and converted, in the course of a few hours, and sometimes in the course of a few minutes. Such sudden conversions were alarming to many good people; and of course they predicted that the converts would fall away, and prove not to be soundly converted. But the event proved, that among those sudden conversions, were some of the most influential Christians that ever have been known in that region of country; and this has been in accordance with my own experience, through all my ministry.

I have said that Mr. Aiken privately replied to some of Mr. Nettleton's and Dr. Beecher's letters. Some of Dr. Beecher's letters at the time, found their way into print; but no public notice was taken of them. Mr. Aiken's replies, which he sent through the mail, seemed to make no difference with the opposition of either Mr. Nettleton or Dr. Beecher. From a letter which Dr. Beecher wrote, about this time, to Dr. Taylor of New Haven, it appeared that someone had made the impression upon him, that the brethren engaged in promoting those revivals were untruthful. In that letter, he asserted that the spirit of lying was so predominant in those revivals, that the brethren engaged in promoting them, could not be at all believed. This letter of Dr. Beecher to Dr. Taylor, found its way into print. If it should be republished at this day, the people of the region where those revivals prevailed, would think it very strange that Dr. Beecher should, even in a private letter, ever have written such things, of the ministers and Christians engaged in promoting those great and wonderful revivals.

CHAPTER 15

REVIVAL AT AUBURN
IN 1826

---

*God assured me that he would be with me and uphold me;
that no opposition should prevail against me;
that I had nothing to do, in regard to all this matter,
but to keep about my work, and wait for the salvation of God.*

Dr. Lansing, pastor of the First Presbyterian Church at Auburn, came to Utica, to witness the revival there, and urged me to go out and labor for a time with him. In the summer of 1826, I complied with his request, and went there and labored with him for a season. Soon after I went to Auburn, I found that some of the professors in the theological seminary in that place, were taking an attitude hostile to the revival. I had before known that ministers east of Utica were, a considerable number of them, holding correspondence with reference to these revivals, and taking an attitude of hostility to them.

However, until I arrived at Auburn, I was not fully aware of the amount of opposition I was destined to meet, from the ministry; not the ministry in the region where I had labored; but from ministers where I had not labored, and who knew personally nothing of me, but were influenced by the false reports which they heard. But soon after I arrived at Auburn, I learned from various sources that a system of espionage was being carried on, that was destined to result, and intended to result, in an extensive union of ministers and churches to hedge me in, and prevent the spread of the revivals in connection with my labors.

About this time, I was informed that Mr. Nettleton had said that I could go no farther East; that all the New England churches especially were closed against me. Mr. Nettleton came and made a stand at Albany; and a letter from Dr. Beecher fell into my possession, in which he exhorted Mr. Nettleton to make a manful stand against me and the revivals in central New York; promising that when the judicatures, as he called them, of New England met, they would all speak out, and sustain him in his opposition.

But for the present I must return to what passed at Auburn. My mind became, soon after I went there, very much impressed with the extensive working of that system of espionage of which I have spoken. Mr. Frost, of Whitesboro', had come to a knowledge of the facts to a considerable extent, and communicated them to me. I said nothing publicly, or as I recollect privately, to anybody on the subject; but gave myself to prayer. I looked to God with great earnestness day after day, to be directed; asking him to show me the path of duty, and give me grace to ride out the storm.

I shall never forget what a scene I passed through one day in my room at Dr. Lansing's. The Lord showed me as in a vision what was before me. He drew so near to me, while I was engaged in prayer, that my flesh literally trembled on my bones. I shook from head to foot, under a full sense of the presence of God. At first, and for some time, it seemed more like being on the top of Sinai, amidst its full thundering, than in the presence of the cross of Christ. Never in my life, that I recollect, was I so awed and humbled before God as then. Nevertheless, instead of feeling like fleeing, I seemed drawn nearer and nearer to God — seemed to draw nearer and nearer to that Presence that filled me with such unutterable awe and trembling. After a season of great humiliation before him, there came a great lifting up. God assured me that he would be with me and uphold me; that no opposition should prevail against me; that I had nothing to do, in regard to all this matter, but to keep about my work, and wait for the salvation of God.

The sense of God's presence, and all that passed between God and my soul at that time, I can never describe. It led me to be perfectly trustful, perfectly calm, and to have nothing but the most perfectly kind feelings toward all the brethren that were misled, and were arraying themselves against me. I felt assured that all would come out right; that my true course was to leave everything to God, and to keep about my work; and as the storm gathered and the opposition increased, I never for one moment doubted how it would result. I was never disturbed by it, I never spent a waking hour in thinking of it; when to all outward appearance, it seemed as if all the churches of the land, except where I had labored, would unite to shut me out of their pulpits. This was indeed the avowed determination, as I understood, of the men that led in the opposition. They were so deceived that they thought there was no effectual way but to unite, and, as they expressed it, "put him down." But God assured me that they could not put me down.

A passage in the twentieth chapter of Jeremiah was repeatedly set home upon me with great power. It reads thus: *"O Lord, thou hast deceived me and I was deceived. Thou art stronger than I, and hast prevailed. I am in derision daily, everyone mocks me. For since I spoke, I cried out, I cried violence and spoil; because the word of the Lord was made a reproach unto me, and a derision daily." Then I said, "I will not make mention of him nor speak any more in his name." But his word was in my heart as a burning fire shut up in my bones, and I was weary with forbearing, and I could not stay. For I heard the defaming of many, and fear was on every side. Report, say they, and we will report it. All my familiars watched for my halting, saying, peradventure he will be enticed, and we shall prevail against him, and we shall take our revenge on him. But the Lord is with me as a mighty, terrible one; therefore, my persecutors shall stumble, and they shall not prevail. They shall be greatly ashamed, for they shall not prosper; their everlasting confusion shall never be forgotten. But O Lord of hosts that tries the righteous, and sees the reins and the heart, let me see thy vengeance on them; for unto thee have I opened my cause." Jeremiah 20:7-12.*

I do not mean that this passage literally described my case, or expressed my feelings; but there was so much similarity in the case, that this passage was often a support to my soul. The Lord did not allow me to lay the opposition to heart; and I can truly say, so far as I can recollect, I never had an unkind feeling toward Mr. Nettleton or Dr. Beecher, or any leading opposer of the work, during the whole of their opposition.

I recollect having had a peculiar feeling of horror in respect to the pamphlet published, and the course taken by William R. Weeks, to whom I have made allusion. Those who are acquainted with the history of Mr. Weeks, recollect that soon after this, he began to write a book which he called "The pilgrim's progress in the nineteenth century." This was published in members, and finally bound up in a volume, with which many of the readers of this narrative may be familiar. He was a man of considerable talent, and I must hope a good man; but as I think much deluded in his philosophy, and exceedingly out of the way in his theology. I do not mention him because I wish to say any evil of him, or of his book; but merely to say that he never ceased, so far as I can learn, to offer more or less opposition, direct and indirect, to revivals that did not favor his peculiar views. He took much pains, without naming him, to defend the course which Mr. Nettleton took, in putting himself at the head of the opposition to those revivals. But God has disposed of all that influence. I have heard nothing of it now for many years.

Notwithstanding the attitude that some of the professors at Auburn were taking, in connection with so many ministers abroad, the Lord soon revived his work in Auburn. Mr. Lansing had a large congregation, and a very intelligent one. The revival soon took effect among the people, and became powerful.

It was at that time that Dr. S of Auburn, who still resides there, was so greatly blessed in his soul, as to become quite another man. Dr. S. was an elder in the Presbyterian church when I arrived there. He was a very timid and doting kind of Christian; and had but little Christian efficiency, because he had but little faith. He soon, however, became deeply convicted of sin; and descended into the depths of humiliation and distress, almost to despair. He continued in this state for weeks, until one night, in a prayer meeting, he was quite overcome with his feelings, and sunk down helpless on the floor. Then God opened his eyes to the reality of his salvation in Christ. This occurred just after I had left Auburn, and gone to Troy, New York, to labor. Dr. S. soon followed me to Troy, and the first time I saw him there he exclaimed with an emphasis peculiarly his own, "Brother Finney, they have buried the Savior, but Christ is risen." He received such a wonderful baptism of the Holy Ghost, that he has been ever since the rejoicing and the wonder of God's people.

Partly in consequence of the known disapproval of my labors on the part of many ministers, a good deal of opposition sprung up in Auburn; and a number of the leading men, in that large village, took strong ground against the work. But the Spirit of the Lord was among the people with great power.

I recollect that one Sunday morning, while I was preaching, I was describing the manner in which some men would oppose their families, and if possible, prevent their being converted. I gave so vivid a description of a case of this kind, that I said, "Probably if I were acquainted with you, I could call some of you by name, who treat your families in this manner." At this instant a man cried out in the congregation, "Name me!" and then threw his head forward on the seat before him; and it was plain that he trembled with great emotion. It turned out that he was treating his family in this manner; and that morning had done the same things that I had named. He said, his crying out, "Name me!" was so spontaneous and irresistible that he could not help it. But I fear he was never converted to Christ.

There was a hatter, by the name of H., residing at this time in Auburn. His wife was a Christian woman; but he was a Universalist, and an opposer of the revival. He carried his opposition so far, as to forbid his wife attending our meetings; and, for several successive evenings, she remained at home. One night, as the warning bell rang for meeting, half an hour before the assembly met, Mrs. H. was so much exercised in mind about her husband, that she retired for prayer, and spent the half hour in pouring out her soul to God. She told him how her husband behaved, and that he would not let her attend meeting; and she drew very near to God.

As the bell was tolling for the people to assemble, she came out of her closet, as I learned, and found that her husband had come in from the shop; and, as she entered the sitting room, he asked her if she would not go to meeting; and said that if she would go, he would accompany her. He afterwards informed me that he had made up his mind to attend meeting that night, to see if he could not get something to justify his opposition to his wife; or at least, something to laugh about, and sustain him in ridiculing the whole work. When he proposed to accompany his wife, she was very much surprised, but prepared herself, and they came to meeting.

Of all this, I knew nothing at the time, of course. I had been visiting and laboring with inquirers the whole day, and had had no time whatever, to arrange my thoughts, or even settle upon a text. During the introductory services, a text occurred to my mind. It was the words of the man with the unclean spirit, who cried out, "Let us alone." I took those words and went on to preach, and endeavored to show up the conduct of those sinners that wanted to let be alone, that did not want to have anything to do with Christ. The Lord gave me power to give a very vivid description of the course that class of men were pursuing. In the midst of my discourse, I observed a person fall from his seat near the broad aisle, who cried out in a most terrific manner. The congregation were very much shocked; and the outcry of the man was so great, that I stopped preaching and stood still. After a few moments, I requested the congregation to sit still, while I should go down and speak with the man. I found him to be this Mr. E., of whom I have been speaking. The Spirit of the Lord had so powerfully convicted him, that he was unable to sit on his seat. When I reached him, he had so far recovered his strength as to be on his knees, with his head on his wife's lap. He was weeping aloud like a child confessing his sins, and accusing himself in a terrible manner. I said a few words to him, to which he seemed to pay but little attention. The Spirit of God had his attention so thoroughly, that I soon desisted from all efforts to make him attend to what I said. When I told the congregation who it was, they all knew him and his character; and it produced tears and sobs in every part of the house. I stood for some little time, to see if he would be quiet enough for me to go on with my sermon; but his loud weeping rendered it impossible. I can never forget the appearance of his wife, as she sat and held his face in her hands upon her lap. There appeared in her face a holy joy and triumph that words cannot express.

We had several prayers, and then I dismissed the meeting, and some persons helped Mr. H. to his house. He immediately wished them to send for certain of his companions, with whom he had been in the habit of ridiculing the work of the Lord in that place. He could not rest until he had sent for a great number of them, and had made confession to them; which he did with a very broken heart. He was so overcome that for two or three days he could not get about town, and continued to send for such men as he wished to see, that he might confess to them, and warn them to flee from the wrath to come. As soon as he was able to get about, he took hold of the work with the utmost humility and simplicity of character, but with great earnestness. Soon after, he was made an elder, or deacon, and he has ever since been a very exemplary and useful Christian. His conversion was so marked and so powerful, and the results were so manifest, that it did very much to silence opposition.

There were several wealthy men in the town who took offense at Dr. Lansing and myself, and the laborers in that revival; and after I left, they got together and formed a new congregation. Most of them were, at the time, unconverted men. Let the reader bear this in mind; for in its proper place, I shall have occasion to notice the results of this opposition and the formation of a new congregation, and the subsequent conversion of nearly every one of those opposers.

While at Auburn, I preached more or less in the neighboring churches round about; and the revival spread in various directions, to Cayuga, and to Skeneateles. This was in the summer and autumn of 1826.

Soon after my arrival at Auburn, a circumstance occurred, of so striking a character, that I must give a brief relation of it. My wife and myself were guests of Dr. Lansing, the pastor of the church. The church was much conformed to the world, and were accused by the unconverted of being leaders in dress, and fashion, and worldliness. As usual I directed my preaching to secure the reformation of the church, and to get them into a revival state. One Sunday I had preached, as searchingly as I was able, to the church, in regard to their attitude before the world. The word took deep hold of the people.

At the close of my address, I called, as usual, upon the pastor to pray. He was much impressed with the sermon, and instead of immediately engaging in prayer, he made a short but very earnest address to the church, confirming what I had said to them. At this moment a man arose in the gallery, and said in a very deliberate and distinct manner, "Mr. Lansing, I do not believe that such remarks from you can do any good, while you wear a ruffled shirt and a gold ring, and while your wife and the ladies of your family sit, as they do, before the congregation, dressed as front-runners in the fashions of the day." It seemed as if this would kill Dr. Lansing outright. He made no reply, but cast himself across the side of the pulpit, and wept like a child. The congregation was almost as much shocked and affected as himself. They almost universally dropped their heads upon the seat in front of them, and many of them wept on every side. With the exception of the sobs and sighs, the house was profoundly silent. I waited a few moments, and as Dr. Lansing did not move, I arose and offered a short prayer and dismissed the congregation.

I went home with the dear, wounded pastor, and when all the family were returned from church, he took the ring from his finger — it was a slender gold ring that could hardly attract notice — and said, his first wife, when upon her dying bed, took it from her finger, and placed it upon his, with a request that he should wear it for her sake. He had done so, without a thought of its being a stumbling block. Of his ruffles he said, he had worn them from his childhood, and did not think of them as anything improper. Indeed, he could not remember when he began to wear them, and of course thought nothing about them. "But," said he "if these things are an occasion of offense to any, I will not wear them." He was a precious Christian man, and an excellent pastor.

Almost immediately after this, the church was disposed to make to the world a public confession of their backsliding, and want of a Christian spirit. Accordingly, a confession was drawn up, covering the whole ground. It was submitted to the church for their approval, and then read before the congregation. The church arose and stood, many of them weeping while the confession was read. From this point the work went forward, with greatly increased power. The confession was evidently a heart work and no sham; and God most graciously and manifestly accepted it, and the mouths of gainsayers were shut. The fact is that, to a great extent, the churches and ministers were in a low state of grace, and those powerful revivals took them by surprise. I did not much wonder then, nor have I since, that those wonderful works of God were not well understood and received by those who were not in a revival state.

There were a great many interesting conversions in Auburn and its vicinity, and also in all the neighboring towns, throughout that part of the state, as the work spread in every direction. In the Spring of 1831, I was again in Auburn and saw another powerful revival there. The circumstances were peculiar, and deeply interesting, and will be related in their appropriate place in this narrative.

CHAPTER 16

REVIVAL AT TROY
AND AT NEW LEBANON

"Finney, I know your plan… you mean to come to Connecticut…
But if you attempt it, as the Lord lives,
I'll meet you at the state line, and call out all the artillerymen,
and fight every inch of the way to Boston,
and then I'll fight you there."

Early in the autumn of this year, 1826, I accepted an invitation from the Rev. Dr. Beman and his session, to labor with them in Troy, for the revival of religion. At Troy, I spent the fall and winter, and the revival was powerful in that city. I have already said that Mr. Nettleton had been sent by Dr. Beecher, as I understood, to Albany, to make a stand against the revivals that were spreading in central New York. I had had the greatest confidence in Mr. Nettleton, though I had never seen him. I had had the greatest desire to see him; so much so that I had frequently dreamed of visiting him, and obtaining information from him in regard to the best means of promoting a revival. I felt like sitting at his feet, almost as I would at the feet of an apostle, from what I had heard of his success in promoting revivals. At that time my confidence in him was so great that I think he could have led me, almost or quite, at his discretion.

Soon after my arrival at Troy, I went down to Albany to see him. He was the guest of a family with which I was acquainted. I spent part of an afternoon with him, and conversed with him in regard to his doctrinal views; especially of the views held by the Dutch and Presbyterian churches in regard to the nature of moral depravity. I found that he entirely agreed with me, so far as I had opportunity to converse with him, on all the points of theology upon which we conversed. Indeed, there had been no complaint, by Dr. Beecher, or Mr. Nettleton, of our teaching in those revivals. They did not complain at all that we did not teach what they regarded as the true Gospel. What they complained of was something that they supposed was highly objectionable in the measures that we used.

Our conversation was brief, upon every point upon which we touched. I observed that he avoided the subject of promoting revivals. When I told him that I intended to remain in Albany, and hear him preach in the evening, he manifested uneasiness, and remarked that I must not be seen with him. Hence Judge C., who accompanied me from Troy, and who had been in college with Mr. Nettleton, went with me to the meeting, and we sat in the gallery together. I saw enough to satisfy me that I could expect no advice or instruction from him, and that he was there to take a stand against me. I soon found I was not mistaken.

Since writing the last paragraph, my attention has been called to a statement in the biography of Mr. Nettleton, to the effect that he tried in vain to change my views and practices in promoting revivals of religion. I cannot think that Mr. Nettleton ever authorized such a statement, for certainly he never attempted to do it. As I have said, at that time he could have molded me at discretion; but he said not a word to me about my manner of conducting revivals, nor did he ever write a word to me upon the subject. He kept me at arm's length; and although, as I have said, we conversed on some points of theology then much discussed, it was plain that he was unwilling to say anything regarding revivals, and would not allow me to accompany him to meeting. This was the only time I saw him, until I met him in the convention at New Lebanon. At no time did Mr. Nettleton try to correct my views in relation to revivals.

We soon began to feel, in Troy, the influence of Dr. Beecher's letters, over some of the leading members of Dr. Beman's church. This opposition increased, and was doubtless fomented by an outside influence, until finally it was determined to complain of Dr. Beman, and bring his case before the presbytery. This was done; and for several weeks the presbytery sat, and examined the charges against him.

In the meantime, I went on in my labors in the revival. Christian people continued praying mightily to God. I kept up preaching and praying incessantly, and the revival went on with increasing power; Dr. Beman, in the meantime, being under the necessity of giving almost his entire attention to his case before the presbytery. When the presbytery had examined the charges and specifications, I think they were nearly or quite unanimous in dismissing the whole subject, and justifying the course which he had taken. The charge was not for heresy nor were the specifications for heresy, I believe; but for things conjured up by the enemies of the revival, and by those who were misled by an outside influence.

In the midst of the revival it became necessary that I should leave Troy for a week or two, and visit my family at Whitesboro'. While I was gone, Rev. Horatio Foote was invited by Dr. Beman to preach. I do not know how often he preached; but this I recollect, that he gave great offense to the already disaffected members of the church. He bore down upon them with the most searching discourses, as I learned. A few of them finally made up their minds to withdraw from the congregation. They did so, and established another congregation; but this was after I had left Troy, I do not recollect how long.

The failure of this effort to break Dr. Beman down, considerably discomfited the outside movement, in opposition to the revival. A great many very interesting incidents occurred during this revival, that I must pass in silence, lest they should appear to reflect too severely on those who opposed the work.

In this revival, as in those that had preceded, there was a very earnest spirit of prayer. We had a prayer meeting from house to house, daily, at eleven o'clock. At one of those meetings I recollect that a Mr. S., cashier of a bank in that city, was so pressed by the spirit of prayer, that when the meeting was dismissed he was unable to rise from his knees, as we had all just been kneeling in prayer. He remained upon his knees, and writhed and groaned in agony. He said, "Pray for Mr. __," president of the bank of which he was cashier. This president was a wealthy, unconverted man. When it was seen that his soul was in travail for that man, the praying people knelt down, and wrestled in prayer for his conversion. As soon as the mind of Mr. S. was so relieved that he could go home, we all retired; and soon after the president of the bank, for whom we prayed, expressed hope in Christ.

He had not before this, I believe, attended any of the meetings; and it was not known that he was concerned about his salvation. But prayer prevailed, and God soon took his case in hand.

The father of Judge C. who was at Albany with me, was living with his son whose guest I was at the time. The old gentleman had been a judge in Vermont. He was remarkably correct in his outward life, a venerable man, whose house, in Vermont, had been the home of ministers who visited the place; and he was to all appearance quite satisfied with his amiable and self-righteous life. His wife had told me of her anxiety for his conversion, and his son had repeatedly expressed fear that his father's self-righteousness would never be overcome, and that his natural amiability would ruin his soul.

One Sunday morning, the Holy Spirit opened the case to my apprehension, and showed me how to reach it. In a few moments I had the whole subject in my mind. I went down stairs, and told the old lady and her son what I was about to do, and exhorted them to pray earnestly for him. I followed out the divine showing, and the word took such powerful hold of him that he spent a sleepless night. His wife informed me that he had spent a night of anguish, that his self-righteousness was thoroughly annihilated, and that he was almost in despair. His son had told me that he had long prided himself, as being better than members of the church. He soon became clearly converted, and lived a Christian life to the end.

Before I left Troy, a young lady, a Miss S., from New Lebanon, in Columbia county, who was an only daughter of one of the deacons or elders of the church in New Lebanon, came to Troy, as I understood, to purchase a dress for a ball which she wished to attend. She had a young lady relative in Troy, who was numbered among the young converts, and was a zealous Christian. She invited Miss S. to attend with her all the meetings. This aroused the enmity of her heart. She was very restive; but her cousin plead with her to stay from day to day, and to attend the meetings, until, before she left, she was thoroughly converted to Christ.

As soon as her eyes were opened, and her peace was made with God, she went immediately home, and began her labors for a revival in that place. Religion in New Lebanon was, at that time, in a very low state. The young people were nearly all unconverted; and the old members of the church were in a very cold and inefficient state.

Miss S.'s father had become very formal; and for a long time religious matters had been in a great measure neglected in the place. They had an aged minister, a good man, I trust, but a man that did not seem to know how to perform revival work.

Miss S. first began at home, and besought her father to give up his "old prayer," as she expressed it, and wake up, and be engaged in religion. As she was a great favorite in the family, and especially with her father, her conversion and conversation greatly affected him. He was very soon aroused, and became quite another man, and felt deeply that they must have a revival of religion. The daughter went also to the house of her pastor, and began with a daughter of his who was in her sins. She was soon converted; and they two united in prayer for a revival of religion, and went to work, from house to house, in stirring up the people.

In the course of a week or two, there was so much interest excited that Miss S. came out herself to Troy, to beg me to go there to preach. She was requested to do so by the pastor and by members of the church. I went out and preached. The Spirit of the Lord was poured out, and the revival soon went forward with great power. Very interesting incidents occurred almost every day. Striking conversions were multiplied, and a great and blessed change came over the religious aspect of the whole place.

Here we were out of the region poisoned by the influence of the opposition raised by Dr. Beecher and Mr. Nettleton; consequently, we heard but little of opposition at this place during the revival, especially from professors of religion. Everything seemed to go on harmoniously, so far as I know, in the church. They were soon led to feel that they greatly needed a revival, and seemed to be very thankful that God had visited them. Most of the prominent men in the community were converted.

Among these was a Dr. W., who was said to be an infidel. He at first manifested a good deal of hostility to the revival, and declared that the people were mad. But he was made a particular subject of prayer by Miss S., and some others who laid hold upon his case, and who had great faith that, notwithstanding his fiery opposition, he would soon be converted. One Sunday morning he came to meeting, and I could see that those who felt for him were burdened. Their heads were down, and they were in a prayerful state during nearly the whole sermon. It was plain, however, before night, that the doctor's opposition began to give way. He listened through the day, and that night he spent in a deeply exercised state of mind. The next morning, he called on me, subdued like a little child, and confessed that he had been all wrong. He was very frank in opening his heart, and declaring the change that had come over him. It was plain that he was another man; and from that day he took hold of the work and went forward with all his might.

There was also a Mr. T., a merchant, probably the most prominent and wealthy citizen of the town at that time, but a skeptic. I recollect one evening I preached on the text, "The carnal mind is enmity against God" He was present. He had been a very moral man, in the common acceptation of that term; and it had been very difficult to fasten anything upon his mind that would convict him of sin. His wife was a Christian woman, and the Lord had converted his daughter. The state of things in the town and in his family, had so far interested him, that he would come to meeting and hear what was said. The next day after this sermon on moral depravity, he confessed himself convinced. He told me it came home to him with restless power. He saw it was all true, and assured me his mind was made up to serve the Lord the rest of his life.

I recollect also that John T. Avery, a noted evangelist, who has labored in many places for many years, was present at that meeting. His family lived in New Lebanon. He was born and brought up there; and was at this time a lad, perhaps fifteen or sixteen years of age. The next morning after that sermon was preached, he came to me, one of the most interesting youthful converts that I have ever seen. He began and told me what had been passing in his mind for several days; and then he added, "I was completely rolled up in the sermon, and it carried me right along. I could understand it. I gave up; I gave all to Christ." This he said in a manner not to be forgotten. But why should I multiply cases? I might spend hours in relating incidents, and the conversion of particular individuals. But I must not enter too much into particulars.

But I must mention a little incident, connected somewhat with the opposition that had been manifested at Troy. The presbytery of Columbia had a meeting, somewhere within its bounds, while I was at New Lebanon; and being informed that I was laboring in one of their churches, they appointed a committee to visit the place, and inquire into the state of things; for they had been led to believe, from Troy and other places, and from the opposition of Mr. Nettleton and the letters of Dr. Beecher, that my method of conducting revivals was so very objectionable, that it was the duty of presbytery to inquire into it. They appointed two of their number, as I afterward understood, to visit the place; and they attempted to do so. As I afterward learned, though I do not recollect to have heard it at the time, the news reached New Lebanon, of this action of the presbytery, and it was feared that it might create some division, and make some disturbance, if this committee came. Some of the most engaged Christians made this a particular subject of prayer; and for a day or two before the time when they were expected, they prayed much that the Lord would overrule this thing, and not suffer it to divide the church, or introduce any element of discord. The committee were expected to be there on the Sunday, and attend the meetings. But the day before, a violent snowstorm set in; and the snow fell so deep that they found it impossible to get through, were detained over the Sunday, and on Monday, found their way back to their own congregations. Those brethren were the Rev. J. B. and the Rev. Mr. C.. Mr. C. was pastor of the Presbyterian church at Hudson, New York; and Mr. B. was pastor of the Presbyterian church in Chatham, a village some fifteen or sixteen miles below Albany.

Soon after this, I received a letter from Mr. B., informing me that the presbytery had appointed him one of a committee to visit me, and make some inquiry in regard to my mode of conducting revivals, and inviting me to come and spend a Sunday with him, and preach for him. I did so. As I understood afterward, his report to the presbytery was, that it was unnecessary and useless for them to take any farther action in the case; that the Lord was in the work, and they should take heed lest they be found fighting against God. I heard no more of opposition from that source. I have never doubted that the presbytery of Columbia was honestly alarmed at what they had heard. I have never called in question the propriety of the course which they took; and I ever admired their manifest honesty, in receiving testimony from proper sources. So far as I know, they thereafter sympathized with the work that was going on.

About this time, a proposition was made by somebody, I know not who, to hold a convention or consultation on the subject of conducting revivals. Correspondence was entered into between the Western brethren who had been engaged in those revivals, and the Eastern brethren who had been opposing them. It was finally agreed to hold the convention on a certain day, I think in July, 1827, in New Lebanon, where I had been laboring. I had left New Lebanon, and had been spending a short time at the village of Little Falls, on the Mohawk, near Utica. Some very interesting incidents occurred there during my short stay; but nothing so marked as naturally to find a place in this narrative, as I was obliged to leave after a very short stay in that place, and return to New Lebanon to attend the convention.

It would seem that the design of this meeting has since been, by many, very much misunderstood. I find there is an impression in the public mind, that some complaint had been alleged against myself; and that this meeting was for the trial of myself, as complained of, before a council. But this was by no means the case. I had nothing to do with getting up the convention. Nor was I any more particularly concerned in its results, than any of the members that attended. The design was to get at the facts of those revivals that had been so much opposed, to consult in reference to them, compare views, and see if we could not come to a better understanding than had existed, between the Eastern opposers of the revivals, and the brethren who had been instrumental in promoting them.

I arrived in New Lebanon a day or two before the convention met. On the appointed day, the invited members arrived. They were not men that had been appointed by any ecclesiastical bodies; but they had been invited by the brethren most concerned, East and West, to come together for consultation. None of us were men representing any churches or ecclesiastical bodies whatever. We came together with no authority to act for the church, or any branch of it; but simply, as I have said, to consult, to compare views, to see if anything was wrong in fact; and if so, to agree to correct what was wrong, on either side. For myself, I supposed that as soon as the brethren came together, and exchanged views, and the facts were understood, that the brethren from the East who had opposed the revivals, especially Dr. Beecher and Mr. Nettleton, would see their error, and that they had been misled; and that the thing would be disposed of; for I was certain that the things of which they complained in their letters, had no foundation in fact.

Of the brethren that composed this convention I can remember the following: from the East there were Dr. Beecher and Mr. Nettleton, Dr. Joel Hawes from Hartford, Dr. Dutton from New Haven, Dr. Humphrey, president of Amherst College, Rev. Justin Edwards of Andover, and a considerable number of other brethren whose names I do not recollect. From the West, that is from central New York where those revivals had been in progress, there were, Dr. Beman of Troy, Dr. Lansing of Auburn, Mr. Aiken of Utica, Mr. Frost of Whitesboro, Mr. Gillett of Rome, Mr. Coe of New Hartford, Mr. Gale of Western, Mr. Weeks of Paris Hill, and perhaps some others whose names I do not now recollect, and myself.

We soon discovered that some policy was on foot in organizing the convention, on the part of Dr. Beecher. However, we regarded it not. The convention was organized, and I believe Dr. Humphrey presided as moderator. There was not the least unkindness of feeling, that I know of, existing among the members of the convention toward each other. It is true that the members from the West regarded with suspicion Mr. Weeks, as I have already intimated, as being the man who was responsible, in a considerable degree for the misapprehension of the Eastern brethren. As soon as the convention was duly organized, and the business before us was stated and understood, the inquiry was raised by the brethren from the West in regard to the source whence Dr. Beecher and Mr. Nettleton had received their information. We had been particularly solicitous to find out who it was that was misleading those brethren, and giving them such a view of the revivals, as to make them feel justified in the course they were taking. We wanted to know whence all this mysterious opposition had proceeded. We therefore raised the inquiry at once; and wished to know of those brethren from what source they had received their information, as touching those revivals. It was discovered at once that this was an embarrassing question.

I should have observed before, and now wish to be distinctly understood to say, that no opposition had been manifested by any of the ministers from the East, who attended the convention, except Dr. Beecher and Mr. Nettleton. It was not difficult to see from the outset that Dr. Beecher felt himself committed, and that his reputation was at stake; that as his letters, some of them, had found their way into the public prints, he would be held responsible for them, should they not prove to have been called for. It was very plain that he and Mr. Nettleton were both very sensitive. It was also very apparent, that Dr. Beecher had secured the attendance of these most influential of the New England ministers, in order to sustain himself before the public, and justify himself in the course he had taken. As for Mr. Nettleton, Dr. Beecher had assured him that he would be sustained by New England; and that all the New England church judicatories would seek out in his favor, and sustain him.

When the question was raised as to the sources of the information, Dr. Beecher replied: "We have not come here to be catechized; and our spiritual dignity forbids us to answer any such questions." For myself I thought this was strange, that when such letters had been written and published as had appeared in opposition to those revivals; when such things had been affirmed as facts, which were no facts at all; and when such a storm of opposition had been raised throughout the length and breadth of the land; and we had come together to consider the whole question, that we were not allowed to know the source from which their information had been obtained. But we found ourselves utterly unable to learn anything about it. The convention sat several days; but as the facts came out in regard to the revivals, Mr. Nettleton became so very nervous that he was unable to attend several of our sessions. He plainly saw that he was losing ground, and that nothing could be ascertained that could justify the course that he was taking. This must have been very visible also to Dr. Beecher.

I should have said before, that when the question came up, how the facts were to be learned about those revivals, Dr. Beecher took the ground that the testimony of those brethren from the West, who had been engaged in promoting them, should not be received; that as we were, in a sense, parties to the question, and had been ourselves, the objects of his censure, it was like testifying in our own case; that we were therefore not admissible as witnesses, and the facts should not be received from us. But to this, the Brethren from the East would not listen for a moment. Dr. Humphrey very firmly remarked, that we were the best witnesses that could be produced; that we knew what we had done, and what had been done, in those revivals of religion; that we were therefore the most competent and the most credible witnesses; and that our statements were to be received without hesitation, by the convention. To this, so far as I know, there was a universal agreement, with the exception of Dr. Beecher and Mr. Nettleton.

This decision, however, it was very plain at the time, greatly affected both Dr. Beecher and Mr. Nettleton. They saw that if the facts came out, from the brethren who had witnessed the revivals, who had been on the ground, and knew all about them, they might entirely overrule all the misapprehensions and all the misstatements that had been made and entertained upon the subject. Our meeting was very fraternal throughout; there was no sparring or bitterness manifested; but, with the exception of the two brethren whom I have named, Dr. Beecher and Mr. Nettleton, the brethren from the East appeared candid, and desirous to know the truth, and glad to learn the particulars of the Western revivals.

There were several points of discussion during the convention, especially one on the propriety of women taking any part in social meetings. Dr. Beecher brought up that objection, and argued it at length, insisting upon it, that the practice was unscriptural and inadmissible. To this Dr. Beman replied in a very short address, showing conclusively, that this practice was familiar to the apostles; and that in the eleventh chapter of Corinthians, the apostle called the attention of the church to the fact that Christian women had given a shock to Eastern ideas, by their practice of taking part, and praying in their religious meetings, without their veils. He showed clearly that the apostle did not complain of their taking part in the meeting, but of the fact that they did so, laying aside their veils; which had given a shock to the prevalent sentiment, and occasion of reproach to heathen opposers. The apostle did not reprove the practice of their praying, but simply admonished them to wear their veils when they did so. To this reply of Dr. Beman, no answer was made or attempted. It was manifestly too conclusive to admit of any refutation.

Near the close of the convention, Mr. Nettleton came in, manifestly very much agitated; and said that he would now give the convention to understand the reasons he had for the course he had taken. He had what he called "a historical letter," in which he professed to give the reasons, and state the facts, upon which he had founded his opposition. I was glad to hear the announcement that he wished to read this letter to the convention. A copy of it had been sent to Mr. Aiken, when I was laboring with him in Utica, and Mr. Aiken had given it to me. I had it in my possession at the convention, and should have called it up in due time, had not Mr. Nettleton done so.

He went on to read the letter. It was a statement, under distinct heads, of the things of which he complained; and which he had been informed, were practiced in those revivals, and especially by myself. It is evident that the letter was aimed at me particularly, though, perhaps, I was seldom mentioned in it, by name. Yet the things complained of were so presented, that there was no mistaking the design. The convention listened attentively to the whole letter, which was as long as a sermon. Mr. Nettleton then observed, that the convention had before them the facts upon which he had acted, and which he supposed had called for and justified his proceedings.

When he sat down I arose, and expressed my satisfaction that that letter had been read; and remarked that I had a copy of it, and should have read it in due time, if Mr. Nettleton had not done so. I then affirmed that so far as I was personally concerned, not one of those facts mentioned there, and complained of, was true. And I added, "All the brethren are here, with whom I have performed all these labors and they know whether I am chargeable with any of these things, in any of their congregations. If they know or believe that any of these things are true of me, let them say so now and here."

They all at once affirmed, either by expressly saying so, or by their manifest acquiescence, that they knew of no such thing. Mr. Weeks was present; and I expected, therefore, that if anything was said in reply to my explicit denial of all the facts charged in Mr. Nettleton's letter, with respect to myself, that it would come from Mr. Weeks. I supposed that if he had written to Dr. Beecher or Mr. Nettleton, affirming those facts, that he would feel called upon, then and there, to speak out, and justify what he had written. But he said not a word. No one there pretended to justify a single sentence in Mr. Nettleton's historical letter, that related to myself. This of course was astounding to Mr. Nettleton and Dr. Beecher. If any of their supposed facts had been received from Mr. Weeks, no doubt they expected him to speak out, and justify what he had written. But he said nothing intimating that he had any knowledge of any of the facts that Mr. Nettleton had presented in his letter. The reading of this letter, and what immediately followed, prepared the way for closing up the convention.

And now follow some things that I am sorry to be obliged to mention. Mr. Justin Edwards had been present during all the discussions; and had attended, I believe, all the sessions of the convention. He was a very intimate friend of Dr. Beecher and Mr. Nettleton, and he must have seen clearly how the whole thing stood. At whose suggestion, I do not know, near the close of the convention, he brought in a string of resolutions, in which, from step to step, he resolved to disapprove of such, and such, and such measures in the promotion of revivals. He went over, in his resolutions, nearly, if not quite, every specification contained in Mr. Nettleton's historical letter, disapproving of all the things of which Mr. Nettleton had complained.

When he had read his resolutions, it was said immediately by several of the brethren from the West, "We approve of these resolutions, but what is their purpose? It is manifest that their design is to make the public impression that such things have been practiced; and that this convention, condemning those practices, condemns the brethren that have been engaged in those revivals; and that this convention justifies, therefore, the opposition that has been made." Dr. Beecher insisted that the design of the resolutions was entirely prospective; that nothing was asserted or implied with respect to the past, but that they were merely to serve as landmarks, and to let it be known that the convention disapproved of such things, if they ever should exist, with no implication whatever that any such things had been done.

It was immediately replied, that from the fact that such complaints had gone abroad, and it was publicly known that such charges had been made, it was evident that these resolutions were designed to sustain the brethren who had made the opposition, and to make the impression that such things had been done in those revivals, as were condemned in the resolutions. It was indeed perfectly plain that such was the meaning of those resolutions on the part of Mr. Beecher and Mr. Nettleton. The brethren from the West said, "Of course we shall vote for these resolutions. We believe in these things as much as you do; and we as much disapprove of the practices condemned in these resolutions as you do yourselves; therefore, we cannot help voting for them. But we believe that they are intended to justify this opposition, to have a retrospective rather than a prospective application." However, we passed the resolutions, I believe unanimously; and I recollect saying that, for my part, I was willing that these resolutions should go forth, and that all the facts should be left to the publication and adjudication of the solemn judgment. I then proposed that, before we dismissed, we should pass a resolution against lukewarmness in religion, and condemning it as strongly as any of the practices mentioned in the resolutions. Dr. Beecher declared that there was no danger of lukewarmness at all; whereupon the convention adjourned sine die.

How the publication of the whole proceedings was received by the public, I need not say, in the second volume of the biography of Dr. Beecher, page 101, I find the following note by the editor. He says, "A careful perusal of the minutes of this convention has satisfied us, that there was no radical difference of views between the Western brethren and those from New England, and that but for the influence of one individual, the same settlement might have been made there, which was afterward effected at Philadelphia." This is no doubt true. The fact is that had not Mr. Nettleton listened to false reports, and got committed against those revivals, no convention would have been held upon this subject, or thought of. It was all the more wonderful that he should have credited such reports since he had so often been made the subject of manifold misrepresentations. But he was nearly worn out, had become exceedingly nervous, and was of course fearful, and easily excited, and withal had the infirmity, attributed to him by Dr. Beecher in his biography, of never giving up his own will. I am sure that I say this with entirely kind feelings toward Mr. Nettleton. I never entertained or had any other.

After this convention, the reaction of public feeling was overwhelming. Late in the fall of the same year I met Mr. Nettleton in the city of New York. He told me he was there, to give his letters against the Western revivals to the public, in pamphlet form. I asked him if he would publish his "historical letter" which he read before the convention. He said he must publish his letters to justify what he had done. I told him if he published that letter it would react against himself, as all who were acquainted with those revivals would see that he was acting without a valid reason. He replied that he should publish his letters, and would risk the reaction. He published several other letters, but that one he did not publish, so far as I could learn. If it had been true, the publication of it would have made the impression that his opposition had been called for. But as it was not true, it was well for him that he did not publish it.

Here I must take a slight notice of some things I find in Dr. Beecher's biography, about which I think there must have been some misunderstanding. The biography represents him as having justified his opposition to those revivals — that is to the manner in which they were conducted — until the day of his death; and as having maintained that the evils complained of were real and were corrected by the opposition. If this was his opinion after that convention, he must still have believed that the brethren who testified that no such things had been done, were a set of liars; and he must have wholly rejected our united testimony. But as he and Mr. Nettleton were exceedingly anxious to justify their opposition, if they still believed those statements in the "historical letter" to be true, why did they not publish it, and appeal to those who were on the ground and witnessed the revivals? Had the letter been true, its publication would have been their justification. If they still believed it true, why was it not published with Mr. Nettleton's other letters? That the developments made at that convention, had shaken the confidence of Dr., Beecher in the wisdom and justice of Mr. Nettleton's opposition, I had inferred from the fact that during my labors in Boston, a year and a half after the convention, and after Mr. Nettleton's letters were published, Dr. Beecher, speaking of that convention, remarked, that after that, he "would not have had Mr. Nettleton come to Boston for a thousand dollars." Is it possible that, until his death, Dr. Beecher continued to believe that the pastors of those churches where those revivals occurred, were liars, and not to be believed in regard to facts which must have been within their personal knowledge?

I find in the biographies of Dr. Beecher and Mr. Nettleton, much complaint of the bad spirit that prevailed in those revivals. Their mistake lies in their attributing a spirit of denunciation to the wrong side. I never heard the name of Dr. Beecher or Mr. Nettleton mentioned, during those revivals, in public, that I recollect, and certainly not censoriously. They were never, even in private conversation, spoken of, to my knowledge, with the least bitterness. The friends and promoters of those revivals were in a sweet, Christian spirit, and as far as possible from being denunciatory. If they had been in a denunciatory spirit, those blessed revivals could never have been promoted by them, and the revivals could never have turned out as gloriously as they did. No, the denunciation was on the side of the opposition. A quotation from Dr. Beecher's biography will illustrate the animus of the opposition. In the second volume, page

101, Dr. Beecher is represented as saying to me, at the convention at New Lebanon, "Finney, I know your plan, and you know I do; you mean to come to Connecticut, and carry a streak of fire to Boston. But if you attempt it, as the Lord lives, I'll meet you at the state line, and call out all the artillerymen, and fight every inch of the way to Boston, and then I'll fight you there." I do not remember this; but, as Dr. Beecher does, let it illustrate the spirit of his opposition. The fact is, he was grossly deceived at every step. I had no design nor desire to go to Connecticut, nor to Boston. The above, and many other things which I find in his biography, show how completely he was deceived, and how utterly ignorant he was of the character, and motives, and doings, of those who had labored in those glorious revivals. I write these things with no pleasure. I find much in this biography that surprises me, and leads me to the conclusion that, by some mistake, Dr. Beecher has been misunderstood and misrepresented. But I pass by other matters.

After this convention I heard no more of the opposition of Dr. Beecher and Mr. Nettleton. Opposition in that form had spent itself. The results of the revivals were such as to shut the mouths of gainsayers, and convince everybody that they were indeed pure and glorious revivals of religion, and as far from anything objectionable as any revivals that ever were witnessed in this world. Let anyone read the Acts of the Apostles, and the record of the revivals of their day; and then read what they say, in their epistles, of the reaction, backsliding, and apostasies that followed. Then let them find out the truth respecting the glorious revivals of which I have been writing, their commencement, progress, and results, which have been more and more manifest for nearly forty years, and they cannot fail to see that these revivals were as truly from God as those.

Revivals should increase in purity and power, as intelligence increases. The converts in apostolic times were either Jews, with all their prejudice and ignorance, or degraded heathen. The art of printing had not been discovered. Copies of the Old Testament, and of the written word of God, were not to be had, except by the rich who were able to purchase manuscript copies. Christianity had no literature that was accessible to the masses. The means of instruction were not at hand. With so much darkness and ignorance, with so many false notions of religion, with so much to mislead and debase, and so few facilities for sustaining a religious reformation, it was not to be expected that revivals of religion should be pure and free from errors.

We have, and preach, the same Gospel that the apostles preached. We have every facility for guarding against error in doctrine and practice, and for securing a sound Gospel religion. The people among whom these great revivals prevailed, were an intelligent, cultivated people. They had not only the means of secular, but also of religious education, abounding in their midst. Nearly every church had an educated, able, and faithful pastor. These pastors were well able to judge of the soundness, and discretion of an evangelist, whose labors they wished to enjoy. They were well able to judge of the propriety of the measures employed. God set his seal to the doctrines that were preached, and to the means that were used to carry forward that great work, in a most striking and remarkable manner. The results are now found in all parts of the land. The converts of those revivals are still living, and laboring for Christ and for souls, in almost or quite every state in this Union. It is but just to say that they are among the most intelligent and useful Christians in this, or any other country.

As I have since labored extensively in this country, and in Great Britain, and no exceptions have been taken to my measures, it has been assumed and asserted that since the opposition made by Mr. Nettleton and Dr. Beecher, I have been reformed, and have given up the measures they complained of. This is an entire mistake. I have always and everywhere, used all the measures I used in those revivals and have often added other measures, whenever I have deemed it expedient. I have never seen the necessity of reformation in this respect. Were I to live my life over again, I think that, with the experience of more than forty years in revival labors, I should, under the same circumstances, use substantially the same measures that I did then.

And let me not be understood to take credit to myself. No indeed. It was no wisdom of my own that directed me. I was made to feel my ignorance and dependence, and led to look to God continually for his guidance. I had no doubt then, nor have I ever had, that God led me by his Spirit, to take the course I did. So clearly did he lead me from day to day, that I never did or could doubt that I was divinely directed.

That the brethren who opposed those revivals were good men, I do not doubt. That they were misled, and grossly and most injuriously deceived, I have just as little doubt. If they died under the belief that they had just reasons for what they did, and wrote, and said, and that they corrected the evils of which they complained, they died grossly deceived in this respect. It is not for the safety of the church, the honor of revivals, or the glory of Christ, that posterity should believe that those evils existed, and were corrected, by such a spirit, and in such a manner as has been represented. I should have remained silent had not so marked an effort been made to perpetuate and confirm the delusion, that the opposition to those revivals was justifiable and successful. The fact is, it was neither.

I have no doubt that Dr. Beecher was led, by somebody, to believe that his opposition was called for. From his biography, it appears that at Philadelphia, the next spring after the convention, it was agreed by himself, Dr. Beman and others, to drop the subject and publish no more in regard to those revivals. The truth is, that all the controversy and all the publishing had been on the side of the opposition. Previously to the meeting at Philadelphia, Mr. Nettleton had published his letters, and I saw nothing farther in print upon the subject.

I was not a party to the agreement entered into at Philadelphia; nevertheless, had not Dr. Beecher's biography reopened this subject, with the manifest design to justify the course that he took, and rivet the impression upon the public mind, that in making that opposition to those revivals he performed a great and good work, I should not feel called upon to say, what I cannot now be justified in withholding. I write from personal knowledge, and to me it matters not who may have given to Dr. Beecher the supposed facts upon which he acted. Those asserted facts were no facts, as I stated before the convention; to which statement every brother with whom I had labored assented. This was proof, if anything can be proven by human testimony. This testimony, it would seem, Dr. Beecher did not believe, if his biographer has not misrepresented him. And what will the churches in Oneida county say to this? Will they, can they believe that such men as Rev. Dr. Aiken, Rev. John Frost, Rev. Moses Gillett, Rev. Mr. Coe, and the other men from that county, who attended that convention, deliberately falsified upon a subject which was within their own personal knowledge? It matters not who Dr. Beecher's informants were; certainly none of the pastors where those revivals prevailed, ever gave him any information that justified his course; and no other men understood the matter as well as they did. I submit that, as the convention decided; they were the best possible witnesses of what was said and done in their own congregations; and their testimony was unanimous that no such things were done us were charged.

I had read the strong, and even terrible charges against the brethren who labored in those revivals, contained in Dr. Beecher's letter to Dr. Taylor, in which he states that his correspondence will justify what he was doing and writing against those brethren. When I learned that this matter was to be spread before the public in Dr. Beecher's biography, I hoped that, at last, we should get at the authors of those reports, through the publication of his correspondence. But I see nothing in his correspondence to justify his course. Are these charges to be virtually repeated and stereotyped, and the correspondence, by which they are said to be justified, concealed? If, as it seems, Dr. Beecher, until the day of his death, continued to reject our united testimony, may we not know by whose counter testimony ours is impeached?

On page 103, of the second volume of Dr. Beecher's autobiography, we have the following: "In the spring of 1828," said Dr. Beecher in conversation on the subject, "I found out that Mr. Finney's friends were laying their plans to make an impression on the general assembly, that held its session at Philadelphia, and to get one of their men into Mr. Skinner's place. Skinner's church had just asked me to preach for them; and I wrote back that I would supply, if they wished, while the assembly was in session. That blocked somebody's wheels. I stayed till the close, when Beman preached half a day. That defeated their plans. They failed." What this means I cannot say. In reading the above, and what follows to the end of the chapter, together with what I find elsewhere on this subject, in this biography, I stand amazed in view of the suspicions and delusions under which Dr. Beecher's mind was laboring. If any of my friends were trying to get into Dr. Skinner's pulpit which he had vacated, I have no recollection of ever having heard of it. I was, at that time, a minister in the Presbyterian church, and was preaching in Philadelphia when the assembly was in session and while Dr. Beecher was there. I was as ignorant as a child of all this management revealed in the biography. I shared none of the terrors and distractions, that seem to have so much distressed Dr. Beecher and Mr. Nettleton. If any of my friends were sharing in the state of mind in which these brethren were, I knew it not.

The truthful record of my labors up to the time of the convention, and from that time onward, will show how little I knew or cared what Dr. Beecher and Mr. Nettleton were saying or doing about me. I bless the Lord that I was kept from being diverted from my work by their opposition, and that I never gave myself any uneasiness about it. When at Auburn, as I have related, God had given me the assurance that he would overrule all opposition, without my turning aside to answer my opposers. This I never forgot. Under this divine assurance I went forward with a single eye, and a trustful spirit; and now when I read what agitations, suspicions, and misapprehensions possessed the minds of these brethren, I stand amazed at their delusion and consequent anxiety, respecting myself and my labors. At the very time that Dr. Beecher was in Philadelphia, managing with members of the general assembly, as related in his biography, I was laboring in that city, and had been for several months, in different churches, in the midst of a powerful revival of religion, perfectly ignorant of Dr. Beecher's errand there. I cannot be too thankful that God kept me from being agitated, and changed in my spirit, or views of labor, by all the opposition of those days.

CHAPTER 17

REVIVAL
IN STEPHENTOWN

...if the Lord wants me to go to Stephentown,
the devil will prevent it if he can;
and if you have not a steady horse,
he will try to make him kill me.

After this convention, I remained a short time in New Lebanon. I do not think the convention injured the religious state of the people in that place. It would have done so, had any facts come out to justify the opposition which they knew had been made to the revivals that had been the subject of discussion. But, as it resulted, the church in New Lebanon were, I believe, edified and strengthened by what they knew of the convention. Indeed, everything had been conducted in a spirit tending to edify rather than stumble the people.

Soon after the convention, on the Sunday, as I came out of the pulpit, a young lady by the name of S., from Stephentown, was introduced to me. She asked me if I could not go up to their town and preach. I replied, that my hands were full, and that I did not see that I could. I saw her utterance was choked with deep feeling; but as I had not time to converse with her then, I went to my lodging.

Afterward I made inquiry about Stephentown, a place north of, and adjoining New Lebanon. Many years before, a wealthy individual had died, and given to the Presbyterian church in that place, a fund, the interest of which was sufficient to support a pastor. Soon after this, a Mr. B., who had been a chaplain in the Revolutionary army, was settled there as pastor of the church. He remained until the church ran down, and he finally became an open infidel. This had produced a most disastrous influence in that town. He remained among them, openly hostile to the Christian religion. After he had ceased to be pastor of the church, they had had one or two ministers settled. Nevertheless, the church declined, and the state of religion grew worse and worse; until, finally, they had left their meeting house, as so few attended meeting, and held their services on the Sunday, in a small schoolhouse, which stood near the church.

The last minister they had had, affirmed that he stayed until not more than half-a-dozen people in the town would attend on the Sunday; and although there was a fund for his support, and his salary was regularly paid, yet he could not think it his duty to spend his time in laboring in such a field. He had, therefore, been dismissed. No other denomination had taken possession of the field, so as to excite any public interest, and the whole town was a complete moral waste. Three elders of the Presbyterian church remained, and about twenty members. The only unmarried person in the church, was this Miss S., of whom I have spoken. Nearly the whole town was in a state of impenitence. It was a large, rich, farming town, with no considerable village in it.

On the next Sunday, Miss S. met me again, as I came out of the pulpit, and begged me to go up there and preach; and asked me if I knew anything of the state of things there. I informed her that I did; but I told her I did not know how I could go. She appeared greatly affected, too much so to converse, for she could not control her feelings. These facts, with what I had heard, began to take hold of me; and my mind began to be profoundly stirred in respect to the state of things in Stephentown. I finally told her that if the elders of the church desired me to come, she might have a notice given out that I would come up, the Lord willing, and preach in their church, the next Sunday at five o'clock in the afternoon. This would allow me to preach twice in New Lebanon, after which I could ride up to Stephentown and preach at five o'clock. This seemed to light up her countenance and lift the load from her heart. She went home and had the notice given.

Accordingly, the next Sunday, after preaching the second time, one of the young converts at New Lebanon offered to take me up to Stephentown in his carriage. When he came in his buggy to take me, I asked him, "Have you a steady horse?" "O yes!" he replied, "perfectly so;" and smiling, asked, "What made you ask the question?" "Because," I replied, "if the Lord wants me to go to Stephentown, the devil will prevent it if he can; and if you have not a steady horse, he will try to make him kill me." He smiled, and we rode on; and, strange to tell, before we got there, that horse ran away twice, and came near killing us. His owner expressed the greatest astonishment, and said he had never known such a thing before.

However, in due time we arrived in safety at Mr. S.'s, the father of Miss S. whom I have mentioned. He lived about half a mile from the church, in the direction of New Lebanon. As we went in, we met Maria — for that was her name — who tearfully, yet joyfully received us, and showed me to a room where I could be alone, as it was not quite time for meeting. Soon after I heard her praying in a room over my head. When it was time for meeting, we all went, and found a very large gathering. The congregation was solemn and attentive, but nothing very particular occurred that evening. I spent the night at Mr. S.'s, and this Maria seemed to be praying over my room nearly all night. I could hear her low, trembling voice, interrupted often by sobs and manifest weeping. I had made no appointment to come again; but before I left in the morning, she plead so hard, that I consented to have an appointment made for me for five o'clock the next Sunday. When I came up on the next Sunday, nearly the same things occurred as before; but the congregation was more crowded; and as the house was old, for fear the galleries would break down, they had been strongly propped during the week. I could see a manifest increase of solemnity and interest, the second time I preached there. I then left an appointment to preach again. At the third service the Spirit of God was poured out on the congregation.

There was a Judge P., that lived in a small village in one part of the town, who had a large family of unconverted children. At the close of the service as I came out of the pulpit, Miss S. stepped up to me, and pointed me to a pew — the house had then the old square pews — in which sat a young woman greatly overcome with her feelings. I went in to speak to her, and found her to be one of the daughters of this Judge P.. Her convictions were very deep. I sat down by her and gave her instructions; and I think, before she left the house she was converted. She was a very intelligent, earnest young woman, and became a very useful Christian. She was afterwards the wife of the evangelist Underwood, who has been so well known in many of the churches, in New Jersey especially, and in New England. She and Miss S. seemed immediately to unite their prayers. But I could not see as yet, much movement among the older members of the church. They stood in such relations to each other, that a good deal of repentance and confession had to pass among them, as a condition of their getting into the work.

The state of things in Stephentown, now demanded that I should leave New Lebanon, and take up my quarters there. I did so. The spirit of prayer in the meantime had come powerfully upon me, as had been the case for some time with Miss S.. The praying power so manifestly spreading and increasing, the work soon took on a very powerful type; so much so that the word of the Lord would cut the strongest men down, and render them entirely helpless. I could name many cases of this kind.

One of the first that I recollect was on Sunday, when I was preaching on the text, "God is love." There was a man by the name of J., a man of strong nerves, and of considerable prominence as a farmer, in the town. He sat almost immediately before me, near the pulpit. The first that I observed was that he fell, and writhed in agony for a few moments; but afterwards became still, and nearly motionless, but entirely helpless. He remained in this state until the meeting was out, when he was taken home. He was very soon converted, and became an effective worker, in bringing his friends to Christ.

In the course of this revival, Zebulon R. Shipherd, a celebrated lawyer from Washington county, New York, being in attendance upon the court at Albany, and hearing of the revival at Stephentown, so disposed of his business as to come out and labor with me in the revival. He was an earnest Christian man, attended all the meetings, and enjoyed them greatly. He was there when the November elections occurred through the State. I looked forward to the election day with considerable solicitude, fearing that the excitement of that day would greatly retard the work. I exhorted Christians to watch and pray greatly, that the work might not be arrested by any excitement that should occur on that day.

On the evening of election day, I preached. When I came out of the pulpits after preaching, Mr. Shipherd — who, by the way was the father of Rev. J. J. Shipherd who afterward established Oberlin — beckoned to me from a pew where he sat, to come to him. It was a pew in the corner of the house, at the left hand of the pulpit. I went to him, and found one of the gentlemen who had sat at the table to receive votes during the day, so overcome with conviction of sin as to be unable to leave his seat. I went in and had some conversation with him, and prayed with him, and he was manifestly converted. A considerable portion of the congregation had, in the meantime, sat down. As I came out of the pew, and was about to retire, my attention was called to another pew, at the right hand side of the pulpit, where was another of those men that had been prominent at the election, and had been receiving votes, precisely in the same condition of mind. He was too much overpowered by the state of his feelings to leave the house. I went and conversed with him also; and, if I recollect, he was converted before he left the house. I mention these cases as specimens of the type of the work in that place.

I have mentioned the family of Mr. P. as being large. I recollect there were sixteen members of that family, children and grandchildren, hopefully converted; all of whom I think, united with the church before I left. There was another family in the town by the name of M.; which was also a large and very influential family, one of the most so of any in town. Most of the people lived scattered along on a street which, if I recollect right, was about five miles in length. On inquiry I found there was not a religious family on that whole street, and not a single house in which family prayer was maintained.

I made an appointment to preach in a schoolhouse, on that street, and when I arrived the house was very much crowded. I took for my text: "The curse of the Lord is in the house of the wicked." The Lord gave me a very clear view of the subject, and I was enabled to bring out the truth effectively. I told them that I understood that there was not a praying family in that whole district. The fact is, the town was in an awful state. The influence of Mr. B., their former minister, now an infidel, had borne its legitimate fruit; and there was but very little conviction of the truth and reality of religion left, among the impenitent in that town. This meeting that I have spoken of, resulted in the conviction of nearly all that were present, I believe, at the meeting. The revival spread in that neighborhood; and I recollect that in this M. family, there were seventeen hopeful conversions.

But there were several families in the town who were quite prominent in influence, who did not attend the meetings. It seemed that they were so much under the influence of Mr. B., that they were determined not to attend. However, in the midst of the revival, this Mr. B. died a horrible death; and this put an end to his opposition.

I have said there were several families in town that did not attend meeting; and I could devise no means by which they could be induced to attend. The Miss S. of New Lebanon, who was converted at Troy, heard that these families did not attend, and came up to Stephentown; and as her father was a man very well-known and very much respected, she was received with respect and deference in any family that she wished to visit. She went and called on one of these families. I believe she was acquainted with their daughters, and induced them to accompany her to meeting. They soon became so interested that they needed no influence to persuade them to attend. She then went to another, with the same result, and to another; and finally, I believe, secured the attendance of all those families that had stayed away. These families were nearly or quite all converted before I left the town. Indeed, nearly all the principal inhabitants of the town were gathered into the church, and the town was morally renovated. I have never been there since that time, which was in the fall of 1827. But I have often heard from there, and the revival produced permanent results. The converts turned out to be sound; and the church has maintained a good degree of spiritual vigor.

As elsewhere, the striking characteristics of this revival, were a mighty spirit of prevailing prayer; overwhelming conviction of sin; sudden and powerful conversions to Christ; great love and abounding joy of the converts, and their great earnestness, activity, and usefulness in their prayers and labors for others. This revival occurred in the town adjoining New Lebanon, and immediately after the Convention. The opposition had, at that convention, received its death-blow. I have seldom labored in a revival with greater comfort to myself, or with less opposition, than in Stephentown. At first the people chafed a little under the preaching, but with such power was it set home by the Holy Spirit, that I soon heard no more complaint.

CHAPTER 18

REVIVALS AT WILMINGTON
AND AT PHILADELPHIA

*Lord you have got me down
and I hope you will keep me down.
And since you have had so good luck with me,
I hope you will try other sinners.*

While I was laboring at New Lebanon, the preceding summer, Rev. Mr. Gilbert of Wilmington, Delaware, whose father resided in New Lebanon, came there on a visit. Mr. Gilbert was very old-school in his theological views, but a good and earnest man. His love of souls overruled all difficulty on nice questions of theological difference, between him and myself. He heard me preach in New Lebanon, and saw the results; and he was very earnest that I should come, and aid him in Wilmington.

As soon as I could see my way clear to leave Stephentown, therefore, I went to Wilmington, and engaged in labors with Mr. Gilbert. I soon found that his teaching had placed the church in a position that rendered it impossible to promote a revival among them, till their views could be corrected. They seemed to be afraid to make any effort, lest they should take the work out of the hands of God. They had the oldest of the old-school views of doctrine; and consequently their theory was that God would convert sinners in his own time; and that therefore to urge them to immediate repentance, and in short to attempt to promote a revival, was to attempt to make men Christians by human agency, and human strength, and thus to dishonor God by taking the work out of his hands. I observed also, that in their prayers there was no urgency for an immediate outpouring of the Spirit, and that this was all in accordance with the views in which they had been educated.

It was plain that nothing could be done, unless Mr. Gilbert's view could be changed upon this subject. I therefore spent hours each day in conversing with him on his peculiar views. We talked the subject all over in a brotherly manner; and after laboring with him in this way for two or three weeks, I saw that his mind was prepared to have my own views brought before his people. The next Sunday, I took for my text: "Make to yourselves a new heart and a new spirit; for why will ye die?" I went thoroughly into the subject of the sinner's responsibility; and showed what a new heart is not, and what it is. I preached about two hours; and did not sit down till I had gone as thoroughly over the whole subject, as very rapid speaking would enable me to do, in that length of time. The congregation became intensely interested, and great numbers rose and stood on their feet, in every part of the house. The house was completely filled, and there were strange looks in the assembly. Some looked distressed and offended, others intensely interested. Not unfrequently, when I brought out strongly the contrast between my own views, and the views in which they had been instructed, some laughed, some wept, some were manifestly angry; but I do not recollect that anyone left the house. It was a strange excitement.

In the meantime, Mr. Gilbert moved himself from one end of the sofa to the other, in the pulpit behind me. I could hear him breathe and sigh, and could not help observing that he was himself in the greatest anxiety. However, I knew I had him, in his convictions, fast; but whether he would make up his mind to withstand what would be said by his people, I did not know. But I was preaching to please the Lord, and not man. I thought that it might be the last time I should ever preach there; but purposed, at all events, to tell them the truth, and the whole truth, on that subject, whatever the result might be.

I tried to show that if man were as helpless as their views represented him to be, he was not to blame for his sins. If he had lost in Adam all power of obedience, so that obedience had become impossible to him, and that not by his own act or consent, but by the act of Adam, it was mere nonsense to say that he could be blamed for what he could not help. I had endeavored also to show that, in that case, the atonement was no grace, but really a debt due to mankind, on the part of God, for having placed them in a condition so deplorable and so unfortunate.

When I was through, I did not call upon Mr. Gilbert to pray, for I dared not; but prayed myself that the Lord would set home the word, make it understood, and give a candid mind to weigh what had been said, and to receive the truth, and to reject what might be erroneous. I then dismissed the assembly, and went down the pulpit stairs, Mr. Gilbert following me. The congregation withdrew very slowly, and many seemed to be standing and waiting for something, in almost every part of the house. The aisles were cleared pretty nearly; and the rest of the congregation seemed to remain in a waiting position, as if they supposed they should hear from Mr. Gilbert, upon what had been said. Mrs. Gilbert, however went immediately out.

As I came down the pulpit stairs, I observed two ladies sitting on the left hand of the aisle through which we must pass, to whom I had been introduced, and who, I knew, were particular friends and supporters of Mr. Gilbert. I saw that they looked partly grieved, and partly offended, and greatly astonished. The first we reached, who was near the pulpit stairs, took hold of Mr. Gilbert as he was following behind me, and said to him, "Mr. Gilbert, what do you think of that?" She spoke in a loud whisper. He replied in the same manner, "It is worth five hundred dollars." That greatly gratified me, and affected me very much. She replied, "Then you have never preached the Gospel." "Well," said he, "I am sorry to say I never have." We passed along, and then the other lady said to him about the same things, and received a similar reply. That was enough for me; I made my way to the door and went out. Those that had gone out were standing, many of them, in front of the house, discussing vehemently the things that had been said. As I passed along the streets going to Mr. Gilbert's, where I lodged, I found the streets full of excitement and discussion. The people were comparing views; and from the few words that escaped from those that did not observe me as I passed along, I saw that the impression was decidedly in favor of what had been said.

When I arrived at Mr. Gilbert's, his wife accosted me as soon as I entered, by saying, "Mr. Finney, how dared you preach any such thing in our pulpit?" I replied, "Mrs. Gilbert, I did not dare to preach anything else; it is the truth of God." She replied, "Well, it is true that God was in justice bound to make an atonement for mankind. I have always felt it, though I never dared say it. I believed that if the doctrine preached by Mr. Gilbert was true, God was under obligation, as a matter of justice, to make an atonement, and to save me from those circumstances in which it was impossible for me to help myself, and from a condemnation which I did not deserve."

Just at this moment Mr. Gilbert entered. "There," said I, "Brother Gilbert, you see the results of your preaching, here in your own family;" and then repeated to him what his wife had just said. He replied, "I have sometimes thought that my wife was one of the most pious women that I ever knew; and at other times I have thought that she had no religion at all." "Why!" I exclaimed, "she has always thought that God owed her, as a matter of justice, the salvation provided in Christ; how can she be a Christian?" This was all said, by each of us, with the greatest solemnity and earnestness. Upon my making the last remark, she got up and left the room. The house was very solemn; and for two days, I believe, I did not see her. She then came out clear, not only in the truth, but in the state of her own mind; having passed through a complete revolution of views and experience.

From this point the work went forward. The truth was worked out admirably by the Holy Spirit. Mr. Gilbert's views became greatly changed; and also his style of preaching, and manner of presenting the Gospel. So far as I know, until the day of his death, his views remained corrected, new school as opposed to the old school views which he had before maintained.

The effect of this sermon upon many of Mr. Gilbert's church members was very peculiar. I have spoken of the lady who asked him what he thought of it. She afterwards told me that she was so offended, to think that all her views of religion were so overthrown, that she promised herself she never would pray again. She had been in the habit of so far justifying herself because of her sinful nature, and had taken, in her own mind, such an opposition as Mrs. Gilbert had held, that my preaching on that subject had completely subverted her views, her religion, and all. She remained in this state of rebellion, if I recollect right, for some six weeks, before she would pray again. She then broke down, and became thoroughly changed in her views and religious experience. And this, I believe, was the case with a large number of that church.

In the meantime, I had been induced to go up and preach for Mr. Patterson, at Philadelphia, twice each week. I went up on the steamboat and preached in the evening, and returned the next day and preached at Wilmington; thus alternating my evening services between Wilmington and Philadelphia. The distance was about forty miles The word took so much effect in Philadelphia as to convince me that it was my duty to leave Mr. Gilbert to carry on the work in Wilmington, while I gave my whole time to labor in Philadelphia.

Rev. James Patterson, with whom I first labored in Philadelphia, held the views of theology then held at Princeton, since known as the theology of the old school Presbyterians. But he was a godly man, and cared a great deal more for the salvation of souls, than for nice questions about ability and inability, or any of those points of doctrine upon which the old and new school Presbyterians differ. His wife held the New England views of theology; that is, she believed in a general, as opposed to a restricted atonement, and agreed with what was called New England orthodoxy, as distinguished from Princeton orthodoxy.

It will be remembered that at this time I belonged to the Presbyterian church myself. I had been licensed and ordained by a presbytery, composed mostly of men educated at Princeton. I have also said that when I was licensed to preach the gospel, I was asked whether I received the Presbyterian confession of faith, as containing the substance of Christian doctrine. I replied that I did, so far as I understood it. But not expecting to be asked any such question, I had never examined it with any attention, and I think I had never read it through. But when I came to read the confession of faith and ponder it, I saw that although I could receive it, as I now know multitudes of Presbyterians do, as containing the substance of Christian doctrine, yet there were several points upon which I could not put the same construction that was put on them at Princeton; and I accordingly, everywhere, gave the people to understand that I did not accept that construction; or if that was the true construction, then I entirely differed from the confession of faith. I suppose that Mr. Patterson understood this before I went to labor with him; as when I took that course in his pulpit he expressed no surprise. Indeed, he did not at all object to it.

The revival took such hold in his congregation as greatly to interest him; and as he saw that God was blessing the word as I presented it, he stood firmly by me, and never, in any case, objected to anything that I advanced. Sometimes when we returned from meeting, Mrs. Patterson would smilingly remark, "Now you see Mr. Patterson, that Mr. Finney does not agree with you on those points upon which we have so often conversed." He would always, in the greatness of his Christian faith and love, reply, "Well, the Lord blesses it."

The interest became so great that our congregations were packed at every meeting. One day Mr. Patterson said to me, "Brother Finney, if the Presbyterian ministers in this city find out your views, and what you are preaching to the people, they will hunt you out of the city as they would a wolf." I replied, "I cannot help it. I can preach no other doctrine; and if they must drive me out of the city, let them do it, and take the responsibility. But I do not believe that they can get me out." However, the ministers did not take the course that he predicted, by any means; but nearly all received me to their pulpits. When they learned what was going on at Mr. Patterson's church and that many of their own church members were greatly interested, they invited me to preach for them; and if I recollect right, I preached in all of the Presbyterian churches except that of Arch street.

Philadelphia was at that time a unit, almost, in regard to the views of theology held at Princeton. Dr. Skinner held to some extent, what have since been known as new school viewers; and differed enough from the tone of theology round about him, to be suspected as not altogether sound, according to the prevailing orthodoxy. I have ever regarded it as a most remarkable thing, that, so far as I know, my doctrinal views did not prove a stumbling block in that city; so was my orthodoxy openly called in question, by any of the ministers or churches. I preached in the Dutch church to Dr. Livingston's congregation; and I found that he sympathized with my views, and encouraged me, with all his influence, to go on and preach the preaching that the Lord had bidden me. I did not hesitate everywhere, and on all occasions, to present my own views of theology, and those which I had everywhere presented, to the churches.

Mr. Patterson was himself, I believe, greatly surprised that I met no open opposition from the ministers or churches, on account of my theological views. Indeed, I did not present them at all in a controversial way; but simply employed them in my instructions to saints; and sinners, in a way so natural as not, perhaps, to excite very much attention, except with discriminating theologians. But many things that I said were new to the people. For example, one night I preached on this text: "There is one God, and one Mediator between God and men, the man Christ Jesus; who gave himself a ransom for all, to be testified in due time." This was a sermon on the atonement, in which I took the view that I have always held, of its nature and of its universality; and stated, as strongly as I could, those points of difference between my own views and those that were held by limited atonement theologians. This sermon attracted so much attention, and excited so much interest, that I was urged to preach on the same subject in other churches. The more I preached upon it, the more desirous people were to hear; and the excitement became so general, that I preached on that subject seven different evenings in succession, in as many different churches.

It would seem that the people had heard much said against what was called Hopkinsianism[1]; the two great points of which were understood to be, that man ought to be willing to be damned for the glory of God, and that God was the author of sin. In preaching, I sometimes noticed these points, and took occasion to denounce Hopkinsianism; and said that they appeared to have too much of it in Philadelphia; that their great neglect in attending to the salvation of their souls looked very much as if they were willing to be damned; and that they must hold that God was the author of sin, for they maintained that their nature was sinful. This I turned over and over, and these two points I dwelt upon. I heard again and again that the people said, "Well, he is no Hopkinsian." Indeed, I felt it my duty to expose all the hiding places of sinners, and to hunt them out from under those peculiar views of orthodoxy, in which I found them entrenched.

The revival spread, and took a powerful hold. All our meetings for preaching, for prayer, and for inquiry, were crowded. There were a great many more inquirers than we could well attend to. It was late in the fall when I took my lodgings in Philadelphia, and I continued to labor there without any intermission until the following August, 1828.

As in other places, there were some cases of very bitter opposition on the part of individuals. In one case, a man whose wife was very deeply convicted, was so enraged that he came in, and took his wife

---

1 - Hopkinsianism – a modified Calvinism taught by Samuel Hopkins, that emphasized the sovereignty of God, necessity of submitting to His will, accepting even damnation, if required, for His glory.

out of meeting by force. Another case I recollect as a very striking one, of a German whose name I cannot now recall. He was a tobacconist. He had a very amiable and intelligent wife; and was himself, as I afterwards found, when I became acquainted with him, an intelligent man. He was, however, a skeptic, and had no confidence in religion at all. His wife, however, came to our meetings, and became very much concerned about her soul; and after a severe struggle of many days, she was thoroughly converted. As she attended meetings frequently, and became very much interested, it soon attracted the attention of her husband, and he began to oppose her being a Christian. He had, as I learned, a hasty temper, and was a man of athletic frame, and of great resolution and fixedness of purpose. As his wife became more and more interested, his opposition increased, till finally he forbade her attending meetings any more.

She then called to see me, and asked my advice with regard to what course she should take. I told her that her first obligation was to God; that she was undoubtedly under obligation to obey his commands, even if they conflicted with the commands of her husband; and that, while I advised her to avoid giving him offense if she could, and do her duty to God, still in no case to omit, what she regarded as her duty to God, for the sake of complying with his wishes. I told her that, as he was an infidel, his opinions on religious subjects were not to be respected, and that she could not safely follow his advice. She was well aware of this. He was a man that paid no attention to religion at all, except to oppose it.

In accordance with my advice; she attended the meetings as she had opportunity, and received instructions; and she soon came into the liberty of the Gospel, had great faith and peace of mind, and enjoyed much of the presence of God. This highly displeased her husband; and he finally went so far as to threaten her life, if she went to meeting again. She had so frequently seen him angry, that she had no confidence that he would fulfill his threat. She told him calmly that whatever it cost her, her mind was made up to do her duty to God; that she felt it her duty to avail herself of the opportunity to get the instruction she needed; and that she must attend those meetings, whenever she could do it without neglecting her duty to her family.

One Sunday evening, when he found she was going to meeting, he renewed his threat that if she went he would take her life. She told me afterward that she had no thought that it was anything but a vain threat. She calmly replied to him that her duty was plain; that there was no reason why she should remain at home at that time, but simply to comply with his unreasonable wishes; and that to stay at home, under such circumstances; would be entirely inconsistent with her duty to God and to herself. She therefore went to meeting. When she returned from meeting, she found him in a great rage. As soon as she entered the door he locked it after her, and took out the key, and then drew a dagger and swore he would take her life. She ran upstairs. He caught a light to follow her. The servant girl blew out the light as he passed by her. This left them both in the dark. She ran up and through the rooms in the second story, found her way down into the kitchen, and then to the cellar. He could not follow her in the dark; and she got out of the cellar window, and went to a friend's house and spent the night.

Taking it for granted that he would be ashamed of his rage before morning, she went home early, and entered the house, and found things in the greatest disorder. He had broken some of the furniture, and acted like a man distracted. He again locked the door, as soon as she was fairly in the house; and drawing a dagger, he threw himself upon his knees and held up his hands, and took the most horrible oath that he would there take her life. She looked at him with astonishment and fled. She ran upstairs, but it was light, and he followed her. She ran from room to room, till finally, she entered the last, from which there was no escape. She turned around and faced him. She threw herself upon her knees, as he was about to strike her with his dagger, and lifted up her hands to heaven, and cried for mercy upon herself and upon him. At this point God arrested him. She said he looked at her for a moment, dropped his dagger, and fell upon the floor and cried for mercy himself. He then and there broke down confessed his sins to God and to her; and begged God, and begged her, to forgive him.

From that moment he was a wonderfully changed man. He became one of the most earnest Christian converts. He was greatly attached to myself; and some year or two after this, as he heard that I was to come to Philadelphia, in a certain steamboat, he was the first man in Philadelphia that met and greeted me. I received him and his wife into the church, before I left Philadelphia, and baptized their children. I have not seen or heard from them for many years.

But while there were individual cases of singular bitterness and opposition to religion, still I was not annoyed or hindered by anything like public opposition. The ministers received me kindly; and in no instance that I recollect, did they speak publicly, if indeed they did privately, against the work that was going on.

After preaching in Mr. Patterson's church for several months, and, more or less, in clearly all the Presbyterian churches in the city, it was thought best that I should take up a central position, and preach steadily in one place. In Race street there was a large German church, the pastor of which was a Mr. Helfenstein. The elders of the congregation, together with their pastor, requested me to occupy their pulpit. Their house was then, I think, the largest house of worship in the city. It was always crowded; and it was said, it seated three thousand people, when the house was packed and the aisles were filled. There I preached for many months. I had an opportunity to preach to a great many Sunday-school teachers. Indeed, it was said that the Sunday-school teachers throughout the city generally attended my ministry.

About midsummer of 1829, I left for a short time, and visited my wife's parents in Oneida county, and then returned to Philadelphia, and labored there until about midwinter. I do not recollect exact dates, but think that in all, I labored in Philadelphia about a year and a half. In all this time there was no abatement of the revival, that I could see. The converts became numerous in every part of the city; but I never had any knowledge, nor could I form any estimate of their exact number. I never had labored anywhere where I was received more cordially; and where Christians, and especially converts, appeared better than they did there. There was no jar or schism among them, that I ever knew of; and I never heard of any disastrous influence resulting from that revival.

There were a great many interesting facts connected with this revival. I recollect that a young woman who was the daughter of a minister of the old school stamp, attended my ministry at Mr. Patterson's church, and became awfully convicted. Her convictions were so deep, that she finally fell into a most distressing despair. She told me she had been taught from her childhood by her father, that if she was one of the elect, she would be converted in due time; and that until she was converted, and her nature changed by the Spirit of God, she could do nothing for herself, but to read her Bible, and pray for a new heart.

When she was quite young she had been greatly convicted of sin, but had followed her father's instruction, had read her Bible, and prayed for a new heart, and thought that was all that was required of her. She waited to be converted, and thus for evidence that she was one of the elect. In the midst of her great struggle of soul on the subject of her salvation, something had come up relative to the question of marriage; and she promised God that she never would give her hand to any man till she was a Christian. When she made the promise, she said that she expected God would very soon convert her. But her convictions passed away. She was not converted; and still that promise to God was upon her soul, and she dared not break it.

When she was about eighteen years of age, a young man proposed to make her his wife. She approved, but as that vow was upon her, she could not consent to be married until she was a Christian. She said they greatly loved each other, and he urged her to be married without delay. But without telling him her real reason, she kept deferring it from time to time, for some five years, if I recollect right, waiting for God to convert her. Finally, in riding one day, the young man was thrown from the carriage, and instantly killed. This aroused the enmity of her heart against God. She accused God of dealing hardly with her. She said that she had been waiting for him to convert her, and had been faithful to her promise, not to get married until she was converted; that she had kept her lover for years waiting for her to get ready; and now, behold! God had cut him off, and she was still unconverted. She had learned that the young man was a Universalist; and now she was greatly interested to believe that Universalism was true, and would not believe that God had sent him to hell; and if he had sent him to hell, she could not be reconciled to it at all. Thus she had been warring with God, for a considerable time, before she came to our meetings, supposing that the blame of her not being converted, was chargeable upon God, and not upon herself.

When she heard my preaching, and found that all her refuges of lies were torn away, and saw that she should have given her heart to God long before, and all would have been well; she saw that she herself had been entirely to blame, and that the instructions of her father on all those points had been entirely wrong; and remembering, as she did, how she had blamed God, and what a blasphemous attitude she had maintained before him, she very naturally despaired of mercy. I reasoned with her, and tried to show her the long suffering of God, and encouraged her to hope, to believe, and to lay hold upon eternal life. But her sense of sin was so great, that she seemed unable to grasp the promise, and sunk down deeper and deeper into despair, from day to day.

After laboring with her a great deal, I became greatly distressed about her case. At the close of every meeting she would follow me home, with her despairing complaints, and would exhaust me by appeals to my sympathy and Christian compassion for her soul. After this state of things had continued for many weeks, one morning she called upon me in company with an aunt of hers, who had become greatly concerned about her, and who thought her on the very verge of a desperate insanity. I was myself of the opinion that it would result in that, if she would not believe. Catharine — for that was her name — came into my room in her usually despairing way; but with a look of wildness in her face that indicated a state of mind that was unendurable; and at the moment, I think it was the Spirit of God that suggested to my mind, to take an entirely different course with her from what I had ever taken.

I said to her, "Catharine, you profess to believe that God is good." "O yes!" she said, "I believe that." "Well, you have often told me that his goodness forbids him to have mercy on you — that your sins have been so great that it would be a dishonor to him to forgive you and save you. You have often confessed to me that you believed that God would forgive you if he wisely could; but that your forgiveness would be an injury to him, to his government, and to his universe, and therefore he cannot forgive you." "Yes," she said, "I believe that." I replied, "Then your difficulty is that you want God to sin, to act unwisely and injure himself and the universe for the sake of saving you." She opened and set her large blue eyes upon me, and looked partly surprised and partly indignant. But I proceeded: "Yes! you are in great trouble and anguish of mind, because God will not do wrong, because he will persist in being good, whatever may become of you. You go about in the greatest distress of mind, because God will not be persuaded to violate his own sense of propriety and duty, and save you to his own injury, and that of the entire universe. You think yourself of more consequence than God and all the universe; and cannot be happy unless God makes himself and everybody else unhappy, in making you happy."

I pressed this upon her. She looked with the utmost astonishment at me, and after a few moments she submitted. She seemed to be almost instantly subdued, like a little child. She said, "I accept it. Let God send me to hell, if he thinks that is the best thing to be done. I do not want him to save me at his own expense, and at the expense of the universe. Let him do what seems good to him." I got up instantly and left the room; and to get entirely away from her, I went out and got into a carriage and rode away. When I returned she had gone of course; but in the afternoon she and her aunt returned, to declare what God had done for her soul. She was filled with joy and peace, and became one of the most submissive, humble, beautiful converts that I have known.

Another young woman, I recollect, a very beautiful girl, perhaps twenty years old, called to see me under great conviction of sin. I asked her, among other things, if she was convinced that she had been so wicked, that God might in justice send her to hell. She replied in the strongest language, "Yes! I deserve a thousand hells." She was gaily, and I think, richly dressed. I had a very thorough conversation with her, and she broke down in heart, and gave herself to Christ. She was a very humble, broken-hearted convert. I learned that she went home and gathered up a great many of her artificial flowers and ornaments, with which she had decked herself, and of which she was very vain, and passed through the room with them in her hands. They asked her what she was going to do with them. She said she was going to burn them up. Said she, "I will never wear them again." "Well," they said to her, "if you will not wear them, you can sell them; don't burn them." But she said, "If I sell them, somebody else will be as vain of them, as I have been myself; I will burn them up." And she actually put them into the fire.

A few days after this she called on me, and said that she had, in passing through the market, I think that morning, observed a very richly dressed lady, in the market. Her compassions were so stirred, that she went up to her and asked if she might speak to her. The lady replied that she might. She said to her, "My dear madam, are you not proud of your dress, and are you not vain, and neglecting the salvation of your soul?" She said that she herself burst into tears as she said it, and told the lady a little of her own experience, how she had been attached to dress, and how it had well-nigh ruined her soul. "Now," said she, "you are a beautiful lady, and are finely dressed; are you not in the same state of mind that I was in myself?" She said the lady wept, and confessed that that had been her snare; and she was afraid that her love of dress and society would ruin her soul. She confessed that she had been neglecting the salvation of her soul, because she did not know how to break away from the circle in which she moved. The young lady wanted to know if I thought she had done wrong, in what she said to the lady. I told her, no! that I wished all Christians were as faithful as she; and that I hoped she would never cease to warn other women, against that which had so nearly ruined her own soul.

In the spring of 1829, when the Delaware was high, the lumber men came down with their rafts from the region of the high land, where they had been getting the lumber out, during the winter. At that time there was a large tract of country, along the northern region of Pennsylvania, called by many "the lumber region," that extended up toward the head waters of the Delaware river. Many persons were engaged in getting out lumber there, summer and winter. Much of this lumber was floated down in the spring of the year, when the water was high, to Philadelphia. They would get out their lumber when the river was low; and when the snow went off, and the spring rains came on, they would throw it into the river and float it down to where they could build rafts, or otherwise embark it for the Philadelphia market. Many of the lumber men were raising families in that region, and there was a large tract of country there unsettled and unoccupied, except by these lumber men. They had no schools, and at that time, had no churches or religious privileges at all. I knew a minister who told me he was born in that lumber region; and that when he was twenty years old, he had never attended a religious meeting, and did not know his alphabet.

These men that came down with lumber, attended our meetings, and quite a number of them were hopefully converted. They went back into the wilderness, and began to pray for the outpouring of the Holy Spirit, and to tell the people around them what they had seen in Philadelphia, and to exhort them to attend to their salvation. Their efforts were immediately blessed, and the revival began to take hold, and to spread among those lumber men. It went on in a most powerful and remarkable manner. It spread to such an extent that in many cases persons would be convicted and converted, who had not attended any meetings, and who were almost as ignorant as heathen. Men who were getting out lumber, and were living in little shanties alone, or where two or three or more were together, would be seized with such conviction that it would lead them to wander off and inquire what they should do; and they would be converted, and thus the revival spread. There was the greatest simplicity manifested by the converts.

An aged minister who had been somewhat acquainted with the state of things, related to me as an instance of what was going on there, the following fact. He said one man in a certain place, had a little shanty by himself where he slept nights, and was getting out his shingles during the day. He began to feel that he was a sinner, and his convictions increased upon him until he broke down, confessed his sins, and repented; and the Spirit of God revealed to him so much of the way of salvation, that he evidently knew the Savior. But he had never attended a prayer meeting, or heard a prayer, that he recollected, in his life. His feelings became such, that he finally felt constrained to go and tell some of his acquaintances, that were getting out lumber in another place, how he felt. But when he arrived, he found that they felt, a good many of them, just as he did; and that they were holding prayer meetings. He attended their prayer meetings, and heard them pray, and finally prayed himself; and this was the form of his prayer: "Lord you have got me down and I hope you will keep me down. And since you have had so good luck with me, I hope you will try other sinners."

I have said that this work began in the spring of 1829. In the spring of 1831, I was at Auburn again. Two or three men from this lumber region, came there to see me, and to inquire how they could get some ministers to go in there. They said that not less than five thousand people had been converted in that lumber region; that the revival had extended itself along for eighty miles, and there was not a single minister of the gospel there.

I have never been in that region; but from all I have ever heard about it, I have regarded that as one of the most remarkable revivals that have occurred in this country. It was carried on almost independently of the ministry, among a class of people very ignorant, in regard to all ordinary instruction; and yet so clear and wonderful were the teachings of God, that I have always understood the revival was remarkably free from fanaticism, or wildness, or anything that was objectionable. I may have been misinformed in some respects, but report the matter as I have understood it. "Behold how great a matter a little fire kindles!" The spark that was struck into the hearts of those few lumber men that came to Philadelphia, spread over that forest, and resulted in the salvation of a multitude of souls.

I found Mr. Patterson to be one of the truest and holiest men that I have ever labored with. His preaching was quite remarkable. He preached with great earnestness; but there was often no connection in what he said, and very little relation to his text. He has often said to me, "When I preach, I preach from Genesis to Revelation." He would take a text, and after making a few remarks upon it, or perhaps none at all, some other text would be suggested to him, upon which he would make some very pertinent and striking remarks, and then another text; and thus his sermons were made up of pithy and striking remarks upon a great number of texts, as they arose in his mind. He was a tall man, of striking figure and powerful voice. He would preach with the tears rolling down his cheeks, and with an earnestness and pathos that were very striking. It was impossible to hear him preach without being impressed with a sense of his intense earnestness and his great honesty. I only heard him preach occasionally; and when I first did so, was pained, thinking that such was the rambling nature of his preaching that it could not take effect. However, I found myself mistaken. I found that notwithstanding the rambling nature of his preaching, his great earnestness and unction fastened the truth on the hearts of his hearers; and I think I never heard him preach without finding that some persons were deeply convicted by what he said.

He always used to have a revival of religion every winter; and at the time when I labored with him, I think he told me he had had a revival for fourteen winters in succession. He had a praying people. When I was laboring with him I recollect that for two or three days, at one time, there seemed to be something in the way. The work seemed to be in a measure suspended; and I began to feel alarmed lest something had grieved the Holy Spirit. One evening at prayer meeting, while this state of things was becoming manifest, one of his elders arose and made a confession. He said, "Brethren, the Spirit of God has been grieved, and I have grieved him. I have been in the habit," said he, "of praying for brother Patterson, and for the preaching, on Saturday night, until midnight. This has been my habit for many years, to spend Saturday night, till midnight, in imploring the blessing of God upon the labors of the Sunday." "Last Saturday night," he continued, "I was fatigued, and omitted it. I thought the work was going on so pleasantly and so powerfully, that I might indulge myself, and go to bed without looking to God for a blessing on the labors of the Sunday." "On the Sunday," said he, "I was impressed with the conviction that I had grieved the Spirit; and I saw that there was not the usual manifestation of the influence of the Spirit upon the congregation. I have felt convicted ever since; and have felt that it was my duty to make this public confession." "I do not know," said he, "who beside myself has grieved the Spirit of God; but I am sure that I have done so."

CHAPTER 19

REVIVAL AT READING

"O yes!" he said, "O yes! I see and feel all this.
But am I not given up of God?
Is not my day of grace past?"

As I found myself in Philadelphia, in the heart of the Presbyterian church, and where Princeton views were almost universally embraced, I must say still more emphatically than I have done, if possible, that the greatest difficulty I met with in promoting revivals of religion, was the false instruction given to the people, and especially to inquiring sinners. Indeed, in all my ministerial life, in every place and country where I have labored, I have found this difficulty to a greater or less extent; and I am satisfied that multitudes are living in sin, who would immediately be converted if they were truly instructed. The foundation of the error of which I speak, is the dogma that human nature is sinful in itself; and that, therefore, sinners are entirely unable to become Christians. It is admitted, either expressly or virtually, that sinners may want to be Christians, and that they really do want to be Christians, and often try to be Christians, and yet somehow fail.

It had been the practice, and still is to some extent, when ministers were preaching repentance, and urging the people to repent, to save their orthodoxy by telling them that they could not repent, any more than they could make a world. But the sinner must be set to do something; and with all their orthodoxy, they could not bear to tell him that he had nothing to do. They must therefore, set him self-righteously to pray for a new heart. They would sometimes tell him to do his duty, to press forward in duty, to read his Bible, to use the means of grace; in short, they would tell him to do anything and everything, but the very thing which God commands him to do. God commands him to repent now, to believe now, to make to him a new heart now. But they were afraid to urge God's claims in this form, because they were continually telling the sinner that he had no ability whatever to do these things.

As an illustration of what I have found in this and other countries, more or less, ever since I have been in the ministry, I will refer to a sermon that I heard from the Rev. Baptist Noel, in England, a good man, and orthodox in the common acceptation of the term. His text was: "Repent and be converted, that your sins may be blotted out, when the times of refreshing shall come from the presence of the Lord." In the first place he represented repentance not as a voluntary, but as an involuntary change, as consisting in sorrow for sin, a mere state of the sensibility. He then insisted upon its being the sinner's duty to repent, and urged the claims of God upon him. But he was preaching to an orthodox congregation; and he must not, and did not, fail to remind them that they could not repent; that although God required it of them, still he knew that it was impossible for them to repent, only as he gave them repentance. "You ask, then," he said, "what you shall do." "Go home," said he, in reply, "and pray for repentance; and if it does not come, pray again for repentance; and still if it does not come, keep praying till it does come." Here he left them. The congregation was large, and the people very attentive; and I actually found it difficult to keep from screaming to the people, to repent, and not to think that they were doing their duty in merely praying for repentance.

Such instructions always pained me exceedingly; and much of my labor in the ministry has consisted in correcting these views, and in pressing the sinner immediately to do just what God commands him to do. When he has inquired of me, if the Spirit of God has nothing to do with it, I have said, "Yes; as a matter of fact, you will not do it of yourself. But the Spirit of God is now striving with you to lead you to do just what he would have you do. He is striving to lead you to repentance, to lead you to believe; and is striving with you, not to secure the performance of mere outward acts, but to change your heart." The church, to a very great extent, have instructed sinners to begin on the outside in religion; and by what they have called an outward performance of duty, to secure an inward change of their will and affections.

But I have ever treated this as totally wrong, unorthodox, and in the highest degree dangerous. Almost innumerable instances have occurred, in which I have found the results of this teaching, of which I have complained, to be a misapprehension of duty on the part of sinners; and I think I may say I have found thousands of sinners, of all ages, who are living under this delusion, and would never think themselves called upon to do anything more than merely to pray for a new heart, live a moral life, read their Bibles, attend meeting, use the means of grace, and leave all the responsibility of their conversion and salvation with God.

From Philadelphia in the winter of 1829-1830, I went to Reading, a city about forty miles west of Philadelphia. At this place an incident occurred, which I shall mention in its place, that was a striking illustration of the kind of teaching to which I have alluded, and of its natural results. In Reading there were several German churches, and one Presbyterian church. The pastor of the latter was the Rev. Dr. Greer. At his request, and that of the elders of the church, I went out to labor there for a time.

I soon found, however, that neither Dr. Greer, nor any of his people, had any just idea of what they needed, or what a revival really was. None of them had ever seen a revival, so far as I could learn. Besides, all revival efforts, for that winter, had been forestalled, by an arrangement to have a ball every alternate week, which was attended by many of the members of the church, one of the leading elders in Dr. Greer's church being one of the managers. I could not learn that Dr. Greer had ever said anything against this. They had no preaching during the week, and I believe no religious meetings of any kind.

When I found what the state of things was, I thought it my duty to tell Dr. Greer that those balls would very soon be given up, or I should not be allowed to occupy his pulpit; that those balls, attended by his church members, and headed by one of his elders, would not long consist with my preaching. But he said, "Go on; take your own course." I did so; and preached three times on the Sunday, and four times, I think, during the week, for about three weeks, before I said anything about any other meetings. We had no prayer meetings, I believe, for the reason that the lay members had never been in the habit of taking part in such meetings.

However, on the third Sunday, I think, I gave notice that a meeting for inquiry would be held in the lecture room, in the basement of the church, on Monday evening. I stated as clearly as possible the object of the meeting, and mentioned the class of persons that I desired to attend; inviting those, and those only, that were seriously impressed with the state of their souls, and had made up their minds to attend immediately to the subject, and desired to receive instruction on the particular question of what they should do to be saved. Dr. Greer made no objection to this, as he had left everything to my judgment. But I do not think he had an idea that many, if any, would attend such a meeting, under such an invitation; as to do so would be, to make an open acknowledgment that they were anxious for the salvation of their souls, and had made up their minds to attend to the subject at once.

Monday was rather a snowy, cold day. I think I observed that conviction was taking hold of the congregation; yet I felt doubtful how many would attend a meeting of inquirers. However, when evening came, I went to the meeting. Dr. Greer came in, and behold! the lecture room, a large one — I think nearly as large as the body of the church above, full; and on looking around Dr. Greer observed that most of the impenitent persons in his congregation were present; and among them, those who were regarded as the most respectable and influential.

He said nothing publicly. But he said to me, "I know nothing about such a meeting as this; take it into your own hands, and manage it in your own way." I opened the meeting by a short address, in which I explained to them what I wished; that is to have a few moments of conversation with each of them, and to have them state to me frankly how they felt on the subject, what their convictions were, what their determinations were, what their difficulties were. I told them that if they were sick and called a physician, he would wish to know their symptoms, and that they should tell him how they were, and how they had been. I said to them, "I cannot adapt instruction to your present state of mind, unless you reveal it to me. The thing, therefore, that I want, is that you reveal, in as few words as you can, your exact state of mind at the present time. I will now pass around among you, and give each of you an opportunity to say in the fewest words, what your state of mind is." Dr. Greer said not a word, but followed me around, and stood or sat by me and heard all that I had to say. He kept near me, for I spoke to each one in a low voice, so as not to be heard by others than those in the immediate vicinity. I found a great deal of conviction and feeling in the meeting. They were greatly pressed with conviction. Conviction had taken hold of all classes, the high and the low, the rich and the poor.

Dr. Greer was greatly moved. Though he said nothing, still it was evident to me that his interest was intense. To see his congregation in such a state as that, was what he had never had any conception of. I saw that with difficulty, at times, he controlled his emotions.

When I had spent as much time as was allowed me in personal conversation, I then went back to the desk, and gave them an address; in which, according to my custom, I summed up the results of what I had found that was interesting, in the communications that they had made to me. Avoiding all personalities, I took up the representative cases, and dissected, and corrected, and taught them. I tried to strip away their misapprehensions and mistakes, to correct the impression that they had, that they must simply use means and wait for God to convert them; and in an address of perhaps a half or three-quarters of an hour, I set before them the whole situation, as clearly as I possibly could. After praying with them I called on those that felt prepared to submit, and who were willing then and there to pledge themselves to live wholly to God, who were willing to commit themselves to the sovereign mercy of God in Christ Jesus, who were willing to give up all sin, and to renounce it forever, to kneel down, and while I prayed, to commit themselves to Christ, and inwardly to do what I exhorted them to do. I called on those only to kneel down, who were willing to do what God required of them, and what I presented before them. Dr. Greer looked very much surprised at the test I put, and the manner in which I pressed them to instant submission.

As soon as I saw that they thoroughly understood me, I called on them to kneel, and knelt myself. Dr. Greer knelt by my side, but said nothing. I presented the case in prayer to God, and held right to the point of now submitting, believing, and consecrating themselves to God. There was an awful solemnity pervading the congregation, and the stillness of death, with the exception of my own voice in prayer, and the sobs, and sighs, and weeping that were heard more or less throughout the congregation.

After spreading the case before God we rose from our knees, and without saying anything farther I pronounced the blessing and dismissed them. Dr. Greer took me cordially by the hand, and smiling said, "I will see you in the morning." He went his way, and I went to my lodgings. At about eleven o'clock, I should judge, a messenger came running over to my lodgings, and called me, and said that Dr. Greer was dead. I inquired what it meant. He said Dr. Greer had just retired, and was taken with a fit of apoplexy, and died immediately. He was greatly respected and beloved by his people, and I am persuaded he deserved to be. He was a man of thorough education, and I trust of earnest piety. But his theological education had not at all fitted him for the work of the ministry, that is to win souls to Christ. He was besides rather a timid man. He did not like to face his people, and resist the encroachments of sin as he needed to do. His sudden death was a great shock, and became the subject of constant conversation throughout the town.

Although I found a goodly number had, to all human appearance, submitted at the meeting on Monday evening, still the death of Dr. Greer, under such extraordinary circumstances, proved a great diversion of the public mind for a week or more. But after his funeral was over, and the usual evening services got into their proper channel, the work took on a powerful type, and went forward in a most encouraging manner.

Many very interesting incidents occurred in this revival. I recollect on one very snowy night, when the snow had already fallen deep, and was drifting in a terrible manner under a fierce gale of wind, I was called up about midnight, to go and visit a man who, they informed me, was under such awful conviction that he could not live, unless something could be done for him. The man's name was B. He was a stalwart man, very muscular, a man of great force of will and strength of nerve, physically a fine specimen of humanity. His wife was a professor of religion; but he had "cared for none of these things." He had been at the meeting that evening, and the sermon had torn him to pieces. He went home in a terrible state of mind, his convictions and distress increasing till it overcame his bodily strength; and his family feared he would die. Although it was in the midst of such a terrific storm, they dispatched a messenger for me. I heard his moanings, or rather howlings, before I got near the house. When I entered I found him sitting on the floor, his wife, I believe, supporting his head — and what a look in his face! It was indescribable. Accustomed as I was to seeing persons under great convictions, I must confess that his appearance gave me a tremendous shock. He was writhing in agony, grinding his teeth, and literally gnawing his tongue for pain. He cried out to me, "O, Mr. Finney! I am lost! I am a lost soul!" I was greatly shocked and exclaimed, "If this is conviction, what is hell?" However, I recovered myself as soon as I could, and sat down by his side. At first he found it difficult to attend; but I soon led his thoughts to the way of salvation through Christ. I pressed the Savior upon his attention and upon his acceptance. His burden was soon removed. He was persuaded to trust the Savior, and he came out free and joyful in hope.

Of course, from day to day, I had my hands, my head, and my heart entirely full. There was no pastor to help me, and the work spread on every hand. The elder of the church to whom I have alluded as being one of the managers of their stated balls soon broke down his heart before the Lord, and entered into the work; and, as a consequence, his family were soon converted. The revival made a thorough sweep in the families of those members of the church that entered into the work.

I said that in this place a circumstance occurred, that illustrated the influence of that old school teaching of which I have complained. Very early one morning a lawyer, belonging to one of the most respectable families in the town, called at my room, in the greatest agitation of mind. I saw he was a man of first-rate intelligence, and a gentleman; but I had nowhere seen him, to know him. He came in and introduced himself, and said he was a lost sinner — that he had made up his mind that there was no hope for him. He then informed me that when he was in Princeton College, he and two of his classmates became very anxious about their souls. They went together to Dr. Ashbel Green, who was then president of the college, and asked him what they should do to be saved. He said the doctor told them he was very glad to have them come and make the inquiry; and then told them to keep out of all bad company, to read their Bible statedly, and to pray God to give them a new heart. "Continue this," he said, "and press forward in duty; and the Spirit of God will convert you; or else he will leave you, and you will return back to your sins again." "Well," I inquired, "how did it terminate?" "O," said he, "we did just as he told us to do. We kept out of bad company, and prayed that God would make us a new heart. But after a little while our convictions wore away, and we did not care to pray any longer. We lost all interest in the subject;" and then bursting into tears he said, "My two companions are in drunkards' graves, and if I cannot repent I shall soon be in one myself." This remark led me to observe that he had indications of being a man that made too free use of ardent spirits. However, this was early in the morning; and he was entirely free from drink, and in terrible anxiety about his soul.

I tried to instruct him, and to show him the error that he had fallen into, under such instructions as he had received, and that he had resisted and grieved the Spirit, by waiting for God to do what he had commanded him to do. I tried to show him that, in the very nature of the case, God could not do for him what he required him to do. God required him to repent, and God could not repent for him; required him to believe, but God could not believe for him; God required him to submit, but could not submit for him. I then tried to make him understand the agency that the Spirit of God has in giving the sinner repentance and a new heart; that it is a divine persuasion; that the Spirit leads him to see his sins, urges him to give them up and to flee from the wrath to come. He presents to him the Savior, the atonement, the plan of salvation, and urges him to accept it.

I asked him if he did not feel this urgency upon himself, in these truths revealed in his own mind; and a call, now to submit, to believe, to make himself a new heart. "O yes!" he said, "O yes! I see and feel all this. But am I not given up of God? Is not my day of grace past?" I said to him, "No! It is plain the Spirit of God is still calling you, still urging you to repentance; you acknowledge that you feel this urgency in your own mind." He inquired, "Is this, then, what the Spirit of God is doing, to show me all this?" I assured him that it was; and that he was to understand this as a divine call, and as evidence conclusive that he was not abandoned, and had not sinned away the day of grace, but that God was striving to save him still. I then asked him if he would respond to the call, if he would come to Jesus, if he would lay hold upon eternal life then and there.

He was an intelligent man, and the Spirit of God was upon and teaching him, and making him understand every word that I said. When I saw that the way was fully prepared, I called on him to kneel down and submit; and he did so, and to all human appearance, became a thorough convert right upon the spot. "Oh!" he afterwards said, "if Dr. Green had only told us this that you have told me, we should all have been converted immediately. But my friends and companions are lost; and what a wonder of mercy it is that I am saved!"

I recollect a very interesting incident in the case of a merchant in Reading, one branch of whose business was the making of whiskey. He had just been fitting up a very large distillery at a good deal of expense. He had constructed it with all the latest improvements, on a large scale, and was going deeply into the business. But as soon as he was converted, he gave up all thought of going any farther with that business. It was a spontaneous conclusion of his own mind. He said at once, "I shall have nothing to do with that. I shall tear my distillery down. I will neither work it, nor sell it to be worked."

His wife was a good woman, and a sister to Mr. B., whose conversion I have mentioned as occurring on that stormy night. The merchant's name was O'B.. The revival took a powerful hold in his family, and several of them were converted. I do not recollect now how many there were; but I think every impenitent person in his household was converted. His brother also, and his brother's wife, and, I know not how many, but quite a large circle of relatives was among the converts. But Mr. O'B. himself was in feeble health, and was rapidly passing away with the consumption. I visited him frequently, and found him full of joy.

We had been examining candidates for admission to the church, and a large number were to be admitted on a certain Sunday. Among them were those members of his own family, and those relatives of his that had been converted Sunday morning came. It was soon found Mr. O'B. could not live through the day. He called his wife to his bedside and said to her, "My dear, I am going to spend the Sunday in heaven. Let all the family go, and all the friends, and unite with the church below; and I will join the church above." Before meeting time, he was dead. Friends were called in to lay him in his shroud; his family and relatives gathered around his corpse, and then turned away and came to meeting; and, as he had desired, united with the church militant, while he went to unite with the church triumphant.

Their pastor had but just gone before; and I think it was that morning, I had said to Mr. O'B., "Give my love to brother Greer, when you get to heaven." He smiled with holy joy and said to me, "Do you think I shall know him?" I said, "Yes, undoubtedly you will know him. Give him my love, and tell him the work is going on gloriously." "I will, I will," said he. His wife and family sat at the communion table, showing in their countenance mingled joy and sorrow. There was a kind of holy triumph manifested, as their attention was called to the fact that the husband, and father; and brother, and friend, was sitting that day at the table of Jesus on high, while they were gathered around his table on earth.

There was much that was moving and interesting in that revival, in a great many respects. It was among a population that had had no conception of revivals of religion. The German population supposed themselves to have been made Christians by baptism, and especially by receiving the communion. Nearly every one of them, if asked when they became Christians, would reply that they took their communion at such a time of Dr. M., or some other German divine. And when I asked them if they thought that was religion, they would say, yes, they supposed it was. Indeed, that was the idea of Dr. M. himself. In walking with him to the grave of Dr. Greer, on the occasion of his funeral, he told me he had made sixteen hundred Christians by baptism, and giving them the communion, since he had been pastor of that church. He seemed himself to have no other idea of becoming a Christian than simply to learn the catechism, and to be baptized and partake of the communion.

The revival had to encounter that view of things; and the influence was at first, almost altogether in that direction. It was held, as I was informed, and I have no doubt of it, that for them to begin to think of being religious, by being converted, and to establish family prayer, or to give themselves to secret prayer, was not only fanaticism, but was virtually saying that their ancestors had all gone to hell; for they had done no such thing. The German ministers would preach against all those things, as I was informed by those that heard them, and speak severely of those that forsook the ways of their fathers, and thought necessary to be converted, and to maintain family and secret prayer.

The great majorities I think, of Dr. Greer's congregation were converted in this revival. At first I had considerable difficulty in getting rid of the influence of the daily press. I think there were two or more daily newspapers published there at the time. I learned that the editors were drinking men; and were not infrequently carried home, on public occasions, in a state of intoxication. The people were a good deal under the influence of the daily press. I mean the German population particularly. These editors began to give the people religious advice, and to speak against the revival, and the preaching. This threw the people into a state of perplexity. It went on from day to day, and from week to week, till finally the state of things became such that I thought it my duty to notice it. I therefore went into the pulpit when the house was crowded, and took for my text: "Ye are of your father the devil, and the lusts of your father ye will do." I then went on to show in what way sinners would fulfill the desires of the devil, pointing out a great many ways in which they would perform his dirty work, and do for him what he could not do for himself.

After I had got the subject well before the people, I applied it to the course pursued by the editors of those daily papers. I asked the people if they did not think that those editors were fulfilling the desires of the devil; if they did not believe the devil desired them to do just what they did? I then asked them if it was suitable and decent, for men of their character, to attempt to give religious instruction to the people? I told the people what I understood their character to be, and turned my hand upon them pretty heavily, that such men should attempt to instruct the people, in regard to their duties to God and their neighbors. I said, "If I had a family in the place I would not have such a paper in the house; I should fear to have it under my roof; I should consider it too filthy to be touched with my fingers, and would take the tongs and throw it into the street." In some way the papers got into the street the next morning, pretty plentifully, and I neither saw nor heard any more of their opposition.

I continued in Reading until late in the spring. There were many very striking conversions; and so far as I know, Dr. Greer's congregation was left entirely united, greatly encouraged and strengthened, and with large additions made to their number. I have never been in that place since.

From Reading I went to Lancaster, Pennsylvania, at that time and until his death, the home of the late President Buchanan. The Presbyterian church at Lancaster had no pastor, and I found religion in a very low state. They had never had a revival of religion, and manifestly had no just conception of what it was, or of the appropriate means of securing it. I remained at Lancaster but a very short time. However, the work of God was immediately revived, the Spirit of God being poured out almost at once upon the people. I was the guest of an aged gentleman by the name of K., who was one of the elders of the church, and indeed the leading man in the church.

A fact occurred in relation to him, while I was in his family, that revealed the real state of things in a religious point of view, in that church. A former pastor of the church had invited Mr. K. to join the church and hold the office of elder. I should say that the facts I am about to communicate respecting this event, were related to me by himself. One Sunday evening after hearing a couple of very searching sermons, the old gentleman could not sleep. He was so greatly exercised in his mind, that he could not endure it until morning. He called me up in the middle of the night, stated what his convictions were, and then said that he knew he had never been converted. He said that when he was requested to join the church and become an elder, he knew that he was not a converted man. But the subject was pressed upon him till he finally consulted Rev. Dr. C., an aged minister of a Presbyterian church not far from Lancaster. He stated to him the fact that he had never been converted, and yet that he was desired to join the church that he might become an elder. Dr. C., in view of all the circumstances, advised him to join and accept the office, which he did.

His convictions at the time I speak of, were very deep. I gave him such instructions as I thought he needed, pressed him to accept the Savior; and dealt with him just as I would with any other inquiring sinner. It was a very solemn time. He professed at the time to submit and accept the Savior. Of his subsequent history I know nothing. He was certainly a gentleman of high character, and never to my knowledge did anything outwardly, to disgrace the position which he held. Those who are acquainted with the state of the church of which Dr. C. was pastor, in regard to the eldership at that time, will not wonder at the advice which he gave to Mr. K..

Among the incidents that occurred, during my short stay at Lancaster, I recall the following. One evening I preached on a subject that led me to insist upon the immediate acceptance of Christ. The house was very much crowded, literally packed. At the close of my sermon I made a strong appeal to the people to decide at once; and I think I called on those whose minds were made up, and who would then accept the Savior, to rise up, that we might know who they were, and that we might make them subjects of prayer. As I learned the next day; there were two men sitting near one of the doors of the church, one of whom was very much affected under the appeal that was made, and could not avoid manifesting very strong emotion, which was observed by his neighbor. However, the man did not rise up, nor give his heart to God. I had pressed the thought upon them, that might be the last opportunity that some of them would ever have, to meet and decide this question; that in so large a congregation it was not unlikely that there were those there who would then decide their everlasting destiny, one way or the other. It was not unlikely that God would hold some of them to the decision that they then made.

After the meeting was dismissed, as I learned the next day, these two men went out together, and one said to the other, "I saw you felt very deeply under the appeals Mr. Finney made." "I did," he replied. "I never felt so before in my life; and especially when he reminded us that might be the last time we should ever have an opportunity to accept the offer of mercy." They went on conversing in this way, for some distance, and then separated, each one going to his own home. It was a dark night, and the one who had felt so deeply, and was so pressed with the conviction that he might then be rejecting his last offer, fell over the curbstone, and broke his neck. This was reported to me the next day.

I established prayer meetings in Lancaster, and insisted upon the elders of the church taking part in them. This they did at my earnest request, although, as I learned, they had never been accustomed to do it before. The interest seemed to increase from day to day, and hopeful conversions multiplied. I do not recollect now why I did not remain longer than I did; but I left at so early a period as not to be able to give anything like a detailed account of the work there.

CHAPTER 20

REVIVAL IN COLUMBIA
AND NEW YORK CITY

*Brother Finney, I have a great deal of business pressing me
during the day, and have but little time for secret devotion;
and my custom is, after having a nap at night,
to arise and have a season of communion with God.*

From Lancaster, about mid-summer, 1830, I returned to Oneida county, New York, and spent a short time at my father-in-law's. I think it was at that time, during my stay in Whitestown, that a circumstance occurred of great interest, and which I will relate. A messenger came from the town of Columbia, in Herkimer county, requesting me to go down and assist in a work of grace there, which was already commenced. Such representations were made to me as induced me to go. However, I did not expect to remain there, as I had other more pressing calls for labor. I went down, however, to see; and to lend such aid as I was able for a short time.

At Columbia was a large German church, the membership of which had been received, according to their custom, upon examination of their doctrinal knowledge, instead of their Christian experience. Consequently, the church had been composed mostly, as I was informed, of unconverted persons. Both the church and congregation were large. Their pastor was a young man by the name of H.. He was of German descent, and from Pennsylvania.

He gave me the following account of himself, and of the state of things in Columbia. He said he studied theology with a German doctor of divinity, at the place where he lived, who did not encourage experimental religion at all. He said that one of his fellow students was religiously inclined, and used to pray in his closet. Their teacher suspected this, and in some way came to a knowledge of the fact. He warned the young man against it, as a very dangerous practice, and said he would become insane if he persisted in it, and he should be blamed himself for allowing a student to take such a course. Mr. H. said that he himself had no religion. He had joined the church in the common way, and had no thought that anything else was requisite, so far as piety was concerned, to become a minister. But his mother was a pious woman. She knew better, and was greatly distressed that a son of hers should enter the sacred ministry, who had never been converted. When he had received a call to the church in Columbia, and was about to leave home, his mother had a very serious talk with him, impressed upon him the fact of his responsibility, and said some things that bore powerfully upon his conscience. He said that this conversation of his mother he could not get rid of; that it bore upon his mind heavily, and his convictions of sin deepened until he was nearly in despair.

This continued for many months. He had no one to consult, and did not open his mind to anybody. But after a severe and protracted struggle he was converted, came into the light, saw where he was, and where he had been, and saw the condition of his church, and of all those churches which had admitted their members in the way in which he had been admitted. His wife was unconverted. He immediately gave himself to labor for her conversion, and, under God, he soon secured it. His soul was full of the subject; and he read his Bible, and prayed and preached with all his might. But he was a young convert, and had had no instruction such as he needed, and he felt at a loss what to do. He rode about the town, and conversed with the elders of the church, and with the principal members, and satisfied himself that one or two of his leading elders, and several of his female members, knew what it was to be converted.

After much prayer and consideration, he made up his mind what to do. On the Sunday he gave them notice that there would be a meeting of the church, on a certain day during the week, for the transaction of business, and wished all the church, especially, to be present. His own conversion, and preaching, and visiting, and conversing around the town had already created a good deal of excitement, so that religion came to be the common topic of conversation; and his call for a church meeting was responded to, so that, on the day appointed, nearly the whole church was present. He then addressed them in regard to the real state of the church, and the error they had fallen into in regard to the conditions on which members had been received. He made a speech to them, partly in German, and partly in English, so as to have all classes understand as far as he could; and after talking until they were a good deal moved, he proposed to disband the church and form a new one, insisting upon it that this was essential to the prosperity of religion. He had an understanding with those members of the church that he was satisfied were truly converted, that they should lead in voting for the disbanding of the church. The motion was put; whereupon the converted members arose as requested. They were very influential members, and the people looking around and seeing these on their feet, rose up, and finally they kept rising till the vote was nearly or quite unanimous. The pastor then said, "There is now no church in Columbia; and we propose to form one of Christians, of people who have been converted."

He then, before the congregation, related his own experience, and called on his wife, and she did the same. Then the converted elders and members followed, one after another, as long as any could come forward, and relate a Christian experience. These, they proceeded to form into a church. He then said to the others, "Your church relations are dissolved. You are out in the world; and until you are converted, and in the church, you cannot have your children baptized, and you cannot partake of the ordinances of the church." This created a great panic; for according to their views, it was an awful thing not to partake of the sacrament, and not to have their children baptized; for this was the way in which they themselves had been made Christians.

Mr. H. then labored with all his might. He visited, and preached, and prayed, and held meetings, and the interest increased. Thus the work had been going on for some time, when he heard that I was in Oneida county, and sent the messenger for me. I found him a warm-hearted young convert. He listened to my preaching with almost irrepressible joy. I found the congregation large and interested; and so far as I could judge, the work was in a very prosperous, healthful state. That revival continued to spread until it reached and converted nearly all the inhabitants of the town. Galesburg, in Illinois, was settled by a colony from Columbia, who were nearly all converts, I believe, of the revival. The founder of the colony and of Knox College, located there, was Mr. Gale, my former pastor at Adams.

I have told facts, as I remember them, as related to me by Mr. H.. I found his views evangelical, and his heart warm; and he was surrounded by a congregation as thoroughly interested in religion as could well be desired. They would hang on my lips, as I explained them the Gospel of Christ, with an interest, an attention, and a patience, that was in the highest degree interesting and affecting. Mr. H. himself, was like a little child — teachable, and humble, and earnest. That work continued for over a year, as I understood, spreading throughout that large and interesting population of farmers.

After I returned to Whitestown, I was invited to visit the city of New York. Anson G. Phelps, since well-known as a great contributor, by will, to the leading benevolent institutions of our country, hearing that I had not been invited to the pulpits of that city, hired a vacant church in Vandewater street, and sent me an urgent request to come there and preach. I did so, and there we had a powerful revival. I found Dr. Phelps very much engaged in the work, and not hesitating at any expense that was necessary to promote it. The church which he hired, could be had only for three months. Accordingly, Mr. Phelps, before the three months were out, purchased a church in Prince street, near Broadway. This church had been built by the Universalists, and was sold to Mr. Phelps, who bought and paid for it himself. From Vandewater street, we went therefore, to Prince street, and there formed a church, mostly of persons that had been converted during our meetings in Vandewater street. I continued my labors in Prince street for some months, I think until quite the latter part of summer.

I was very much struck, during my labors there, with the piety of Mr. Phelps. While we continued at Vandewater street, myself and wife, with our only child, were guests in his family. I had observed that, while Mr. Phelps was a man literally loaded with business, somehow he preserved a highly spiritual frame of mind; and that he would come directly from his business to our prayer meetings, and enter into them with such spirit, as to show clearly that his mind was not absorbed in business, to the exclusion of spiritual things. As I watched him from day to day, I became more and more interested in his interior life, as it was manifested in his outward life. One night I had occasion to go downstairs, I should think about twelve or one o'clock at night, to get something for our little child. I supposed the family were all asleep, but to my surprise I found Mr. Phelps sitting by his fire, in his nightdress, and saw that I had broken in upon his secret devotions. I apologized by saying that I supposed he was in bed. He replied, "Brother Finney, I have a great deal of business pressing me during the day, and have but little time for secret devotion; and my custom is, after having a nap at night, to arise and have a season of communion with God." After his death, which occurred not many years ago, it was found that he had kept a journal during these hours in the night, comprising several transcript volumes. This journal revealed the secret workings of his mind, and the real progress of his interior life.

I never knew the number converted while I was in Prince and Vandewater streets; but it must have been large. There was one case of conversion that I must not omit to mention. A young woman visited me one day, under great conviction of sin. On conversing with her, I found that she had many things upon her conscience. She had been in the habit of stealing, as she told me, from her very childhood. She was the daughter, and the only child, I think, of a widow lady; and she had been in the habit of taking from her schoolmates and others, handkerchiefs, and breastpins, and pencils, and whatever she had an opportunity to steal. She made confession respecting some of these things to me, and asked me what she should do about it. I told her she must go and return them, and make confession to those from whom she had taken them.

This of course greatly tried her; yet her convictions were so deep that she dared not keep them, and she began the work of making confession and restitution. But as she went forward with it, she continued to recall more and more instances of the kind, and kept visiting me frequently, and confessing to me her thefts of almost every kind of articles that a young woman could use. I asked her if her mother knew that she had these things. She said, yes; but that she had always told her mother that they were given her. She said to me on one occasion, "Mr. Finney, I suppose I have stolen a million of times. I find I have many things that I know I stole, but I cannot recollect from whom." I refused altogether to compromise with her, and insisted on her making restitution in every case, in which she could, by any means, recall the facts. From time to time she would come to me, and report what she had done. I asked her, what the people said when she returned the articles. She replied, "Some of them say that I am crazy; some of them say that I am a fool; and some of them are very much affected." "Do they all forgive you?" I asked. "O yes!" said she, "they all forgive me; but some of them think that I had better not do as I am doing."

One day she informed me that she had a shawl which she had stolen from a daughter of Bishop Hobart, then bishop of New York, whose residence was on St. John's square, and near St. John's church. As usual, I told her she must restore it. A few days after, she called and related to me the result. She said she folded up the shawl in a paper, and went with it, and rung the bell at the Bishop's door; and when the servant can, she handed him the bundle directed to the Bishop. She made no explanation, but turned immediately away, and ran around the corner into another street, lest someone should look out and see which way she went, and find out who she was. But after she got around the corner, her conscience smote her, and she said to herself, "I have not done this thing right. Somebody else may be suspected of having stolen the shawl, unless I make known to the Bishop who did it."

She turned around, went immediately back, and inquired if she could see the Bishop. Being informed that she could, she was conducted to his study. She then confessed to him, told him about the shawl, and all that had passed. "Well," said I, "and how did the Bishop receive you?" "Oh," said she, "when I told him, he wept, laid his hand on my head, and said he forgave me, and prayed God to forgive me." "And have you been at peace in your mind," said I, "about that transaction since?" "O yes!" said she. This process continued for weeks, and I think for months. This girl was going from place to place in all parts of the city, restoring things that she had stolen, and making confession. Sometimes her convictions would be so awful, that it seemed as if she would be deranged.

One morning she sent for me to come to her mother's residence. I did so, and when I arrived I was introduced to her room, and found her with her hair hanging over her shoulders, and her clothes in disorder, walking the room in an agony of despair, and with a look that was frightful, because it indicated that she was well-nigh deranged. Said I, "My dear child, what is the matter?" She held in her hand, as she was walking, a little Testament. She turned to me and said, "Mr. Finney, I stole this Testament. I have stolen God's word; and will God ever forgive me? I cannot recollect which of the girls it was that I stole it from. I stole it from one of my schoolmates, and it was so long ago that I had really forgotten that I had stolen it. It occurred to me this morning; and it seems to me that God can never forgive me for stealing his word." I assured her that there was no reason for her despair. "But," said she, "what shall I do? I cannot remember where I got it." I told her, "Keep it as a constant remembrance of your former sins, and use it for the good you may now get from it." "Oh," said she, "if I could only remember where I got it, I would instantly restore it." "Well," said I, "if you can ever recollect where you got it, make an instant restitution, either by restoring that, or giving another as good." "I will," said she.

All this process was exceedingly affecting to me; but as it proceeded, the state of mind that resulted from these transactions was truly wonderful. A depth of humility, a deep knowledge of herself and her own depravity, a brokenness of heart, and contrition of spirit, and finally, a faith, and joy, and love, and peace, like a river, succeeded; and she became one of the most delightful young Christians that I have known.

When the time drew near that I expected to leave New York, I thought that someone in the church ought to be acquainted with her, who could watch over her. Up to this time, whatever had passed between us had been a secret, secretly kept to myself. But as I was about to leave, I narrated the fact to Mr. Phelps and the narration affected him greatly. He said, "Brother Finney, introduce me to her. I will be her friend; I will watch over her for her good." He did so, as I afterwards learned. I have not seen the young woman for many years, and I think not since I related the fact to Mr. Phelps. But when I returned from England the last time, in visiting one of Mr. Phelps' daughters, in the coupe of the conversation, this case was alluded to. I then inquired, "Did your father introduce you to that young woman?" "O yes!" she replied, "we all knew her;" meaning, as I supposed, all the daughters of the family. "Well, what do you know of her?" said I. "O," said she, "she is a very earnest Christian woman. She is married, and her husband is in business in this city. She is a member of the church, and lives in street," pointing to the place, not far from where we then were. I inquired, "Has she always maintained a consistent Christian character?" "O yes!" was the reply; "she is an excellent, praying woman." In some way, I have been informed, and I cannot recollect now the source of the information, that the woman said that she never had had a temptation to pilfer, from the time of her conversion; that she had never known what it was to have the desire to do so.

This revival prepared the way, in New York, for the organization of the Free Presbyterian churches in the city. Those churches were composed afterward, largely, of the converts of that revival. Many of them had belonged to the church in Prince street.

At this point of my narrative, in order to render intelligible many things that I shall have to say hereafter, I must give a little account of the circumstances connected with the conversion of Mr. Lewis Tappan, and his connection afterward with my own labors. This account I received from himself. His conversion occurred before I was personally acquainted with him, under the following circumstances: He was a Unitarian, and lived in Boston. His brother Arthur, then a very extensive dry goods merchant in New York, was orthodox, and an earnest Christian man. The revivals through central New York had created a good deal of excitement among the Unitarians; and their newspapers had a good deal to say against them. Especially were there strange stories in circulation about myself, representing me as a half-crazed fanatic. These stories had been related to Lewis Tappan by Mr. W., a leading Unitarian minister of Boston, and he believed them. They were credited by many of the Unitarians in New England, and throughout the State of New York.

While these stories were in circulation, Lewis Tappan visited his brother Arthur in New York, and they fell into conversation in regard to those revivals. Lewis called Arthur's attention to the strange fanaticism connected with these revivals, especially to what was said of myself. He asserted that I gave out publicly that I was "the brigadier general of Jesus Christ." This, and like reports were in circulation, and Lewis insisted upon their truth. Arthur utterly discredited them and told Lewis that they were all nonsense and false, and that he ought not to believe any of them. Lewis, relying upon the statements of Mr. W., proposed to bet five hundred dollars that he could prove these reports to be true; especially the one already referred to. Arthur replied, "Lewis, you know that I do not bet; but I will tell you what I will do. If you can prove by credible testimony, that that is true, and that the reports about Mr. Finney are true, I will give you five hundred dollars. I make this offer to lead you to investigate. I want you to know that these stories are false, and that the source whence they come is utterly unreliable." Lewis, not doubting that he could bring the proof, inasmuch as these things had been so confidently asserted by the Unitarians, wrote to Rev. Mr. P., Unitarian ministry in Trenton Falls, New York, to whom Mr. W. had referred him, and authorized him to expend five hundred dollars, if need be, in procuring sufficient testimony that the story was true; such testimony as would lead to the conviction of a party in a court of justice. Mr. P., accordingly, undertook to procure the testimony, but after great painstaking, was unable to furnish any, except what was contained in a small Universalist newspaper, printed in Buffalo, in which it had been asserted that Mr. Finney claimed that he was a brigadier general of Jesus Christ. Nowhere could he get the least proof that the report was true. Many persons had heard, and believed, that I had said these things somewhere; but as he followed up the reports from town to town, by his correspondence, he could not learn that these things had been said, anywhere.

This in connection with other matters, he said, led him to reflect seriously upon the nature of the opposition, and upon the source whence it had come. Knowing as he did what stress had been laid upon these stories by the Unitarians, and the use they had made of them to oppose the revivals in New York and other places, his confidence in them was greatly shaken. Thus his prejudices against the revivals and orthodox people became softened. He was led to review the theological writings of the Orthodox and the Unitarians with great seriousness, and the result was that he embraced orthodox views. The mother of the Tappans was a very godly, praying woman. She had never had any sympathy with Unitarianism. She had lived a very praying life, and had left a strong impression upon her children.

As soon as Lewis Tappan was converted, he became as firm and zealous in his support of orthodox views and revivals of religion, as he had been in his opposition to them. About the time that I left New York, after my first labors there in Vandewater and Prince streets, Mr.

Tappan and some other good brethren, became dissatisfied with the state of things in New York, and after much prayer and consideration, concluded to organize a new congregation, and introduce new measures for the conversion of men. They obtained a place to hold worship, and called the Rev. Joel Parker, who was then pastor of the Third Presbyterian church in Rochester, to come to their aid. Mr. Parker arrived in New York, and began his labors, I think about the time that I closed my labors in Prince street. The First Free Presbyterian church was formed in New York, about this time, and Mr. Parker became its pastor. They labored especially among that class of the population that had not been in the habit of attending meeting anywhere, and were very successful. They finally fitted up the upper story of some warehouses in Dey street, that would hold a good congregation, and there they continued their labors.

CHAPTER 21

REVIVAL IN
ROCHESTER, 1830

---

*The spirit of prayer was poured out powerfully,
so much so, that some persons stayed away from
the public services to pray, being unable
to restrain their feelings under preaching.*

Leaving New York, I spent a few weeks in Whitestown; and, as was common, being pressed to go in many directions, I was greatly at a loss what was my duty. But among others, an urgent invitation was received from the Third Presbyterian church in Rochester, of which Mr. Parker had been pastor, to go there and supply them for a season.

I inquired into the circumstances, and found that on several accounts it was a very unpromising field of labor. There were but three Presbyterian churches in Rochester. The Third church, that extended the invitation, had no minister, and religion was in a low state. The Second church, or "the Brick Church," as it was called, had a pastor, an excellent man; but in regard to his preaching there was considerable division in the church, and he was restive and about to leave. There was a controversy existing between an elder of the Third church and the pastor of the First church, that was about to be tried before the presbytery. This and other matters had aroused unchristian feeling, to some extent, in both churches; and altogether it seemed a forbidding field of labor at that time. The friends at Rochester were exceedingly anxious to have me go there — I mean the members of the Third church. Being left without a pastor, they felt as if there was great danger that they would be scattered, and perhaps annihilated as a church, unless something could be done to revive religion among them.

With these pressing invitations before me, I felt, as I have often done, greatly perplexed. I remained at my father-in-law's, and considered the subject, until I felt that I must take hold and work somewhere. Accordingly, we packed our trunks and went down to Utica, about seven miles distant, where I had many praying friends. We arrived there in the afternoon, and in the evening quite a number of the leading brethren, in whose prayers and wisdom I had a great deal of confidence, at my request met for consultation and prayer, in regard to my next field of labor. I laid all the facts before them in regard to Rochester; and so far as I was acquainted with them, the leading facts in respect to the other fields to which I was invited at that time. Rochester seemed to be the least inviting of them all.

After talking the matter all over, and having several seasons of prayer, interspersed with conversation, the brethren gave their opinions one after another, in relation to what they thought it wise for me to do. They were unanimous in the opinion that Rochester was too uninviting a field of labor, to be put at all in competition with New York, or Philadelphia, and some other fields to which I was then invited. They were firm in the conviction that I should go east from Utica, and not west. At the time, this was my own impression and conviction; and I retired from this meeting, as I supposed, settled not to go to Rochester, but to New York or Philadelphia. This was before railroads existed; and when we parted that evening I expected to take the canal boat, which was the most convenient way for a family to travel, and start in the morning for New York.

But after I retired to my lodging the question was presented to my mind under a different aspect. Something seemed to question me: "What are the reasons that deter you from going to Rochester?" I could readily enumerate them, but then the question returned: "Ah! but are these good reasons? Certainly you are needed at Rochester all the more because of these difficulties. Do you shun the field because there are so many things that need to be corrected, because there is so much that is wrong? But if all was right, you would not be needed." I soon came to the conclusion that we were all wrong;

and that the reasons that had determined us against my going to Rochester, were the most cogent reasons for my going. I felt ashamed to shrink from undertaking the work because of its difficulties; and it was strongly impressed upon me, that the Lord would be with me, and that was my field. My mind became entirely decided, before I retired to rest, that Rochester was the place to which the Lord would have me go. I informed my wife of my decision; and accordingly, early in the morning, before the people were generally moving in the city, the packet boat came along, and we embarked and went westward instead of eastward.

The brethren in Utica were greatly surprised when they learned of this change in our destination, and awaited the result with a good deal of solicitude.

We arrived in Rochester early in the morning, and were invited to take up our lodgings for the time with Mr. Josiah Bissell, who was the leading elder in the Third church, and who was the person that had complained to the presbytery respecting Dr. Penny. On my arrival I met my cousin, Mr. S., in the street, who invited me to his house. He was an elder in the First church, and hearing that I was expected at Rochester, was very anxious to have his pastor, Dr. Penny, meet and converse with me, and be prepared to cooperate with me in my labors. I declined his kind invitation, informing him that I was to be the guest of Mr. Bissell. But he called on me again after breakfast, and informed me that he had arranged an interview between myself and Dr. Penny, at his house. I hastened to meet the doctor, and we had a cheering Christian interview. When I commenced my labors, Dr. Penny attended our meetings, and soon invited me to his pulpit. Mr. S. exerted himself to bring about a good understanding between the pastors and churches and a great change soon manifested itself in the attitude and spiritual state of the churches.

There were very soon some very marked conversions. The wife of a prominent lawyer in that city, was one of the first converts. She was a woman of high standing, a lady of culture and extensive influence. Her conversion was a very marked one. The first that I saw her, a friend of hers came with her to my room, and introduced her. The lady who introduced her was a Christian woman, who had found that she was very much exercised in her mind, and persuaded her to come and see me.

Mrs. M. had been a cheerful worldly woman, and very fond of society. She afterward told me that when I first came there, she greatly regretted it, and feared there would be a revival; and a revival would greatly interfere with the pleasures and amusements that she had promised herself that winter. On conversing with her I found that the Spirit of the Lord was indeed dealing with her, in an unsparing manner. She was bowed down with great conviction of sin. After considerable conversation with her, I pressed her earnestly to renounce sin, and the world, and self, and everything for Christ. I saw that she was a very proud woman, and this struck me as rather the most marked feature of her character. At the conclusion of our conversation we knelt down to pray; and my mind being full of the subject of the pride of her heart, as it was manifested, I very soon introduced the text: "Except you be converted and become as little children, you shall in no wise enter into the kingdom of heaven." I turned this subject over in prayer; and almost immediately I heard Mrs. M., as she was kneeling by my side, repeating that text: "Except you be converted and become as little children — as little children — Except you be converted and become as little children." I observed that her mind was taken with that, and the Spirit of God was pressing it upon her heart. I therefore continued to pray, holding that subject before her mind, and holding her up before God as needing that very thing, to be converted — to become as a little child.

I felt that the Lord was answering prayer. I felt sure that he was doing the very work that I asked him to do. Her heart broke down, her sensibility gashed forth, and before we rose from our knees, she was indeed a little child. When I stopped praying, and opened my eyes and looked at her, her face was turned up toward heaven, and the tears streaming down; and she was in the attitude of praying that she might be made a little child. She rose up, became peaceful, settled into a joyous faith, and retired. From that moment she was outspoken in her religious convictions, and zealous for the conversion of her friends. Her conversion, of course, produced much excitement among that class of people to which she belonged.

I had never, I believe, except in rare instances, until I went to Rochester, used as a means of promoting revivals, what has since been called "the anxious seat." I had sometimes asked persons in the congregation to stand up; but this I had not frequently done.

However, in studying upon the subject, I had often felt the necessity of some measure that would bring sinners to a stand. From my own experience and observation, I had found, that with the higher classes especially, the greatest obstacle to be overcome was their fear of being known as anxious inquirers. They were too proud to take any position that would reveal them to others as anxious for their souls.

I had found also that something was needed, to make the impression on them that they were expected at once to give up their hearts; something that would call them to act, and act as publicly before the world, as they had in their sins; something that would commit them publicly to the service of Christ. When I had called them simply to stand up in the public congregations I found that this had a very good effect; and so far as it went, it answered the purpose for which it was intended. But after all, I had felt for some time, that something more was necessary to bring them out from among the mass of the ungodly, to a public renunciation of their sinful ways, and a public committal of themselves to God.

At Rochester, if I recollect right, I first introduced this measure; This was years after the cry had been raised of "new measures." A few days after the conversion of Mrs. M., I made a call, I think for the first time, upon all that class of persons whose convictions were so ripe that they were willing to renounce their sins and give themselves to God, to come forward to certain seats which I requested to be vacated, and offer themselves up to God, while we made them subjects of prayer. A much larger number came forward than I expected, and among them was another prominent lady; and several others of her acquaintance, and belonging to the same circle of society, came forward. This increased the interest among that class of people; and it was soon seen that the Lord was aiming at the conversion of the highest classes of society. My meetings soon became thronged with that class. The lawyers, physicians, merchants, and indeed all the most intelligent people, became more and more interested, and more and more easily influenced.

Very soon the work took effect, extensively, among the lawyers in that city. There has always been a large number of the leading lawyers of the state, resident at Rochester. The work soon got hold of numbers of these. They became very anxious, and came freely to our meetings of inquiry; and numbers of them came forward to the anxious seat, as it has since been called, and publicly gave their hearts to God. I recollect one evening after preaching, three of them followed me to my room, all of them deeply convicted; and all of them had been, I believe, on the anxious seat, but were not clear in their minds, and felt that they could not go home until they were convinced their peace was made with God. I conversed with them, and prayed with them; and I believe, before they left, they all found peace in believing in the Lord Jesus Christ.

I should have said that very soon after the work commenced, the difficulties between Mr. Bissell and Dr. Penny were healed; and all the distractions and collisions that had existed there were adjusted; so that a spirit of universal kindness and fellowship pervaded all the churches.

On one occasion I had an appointment in the First church. There had been a military parade in the city that day. The militia had been called out, and I had feared that the excitement of the parade, might divert the attention of the people, and mar the work of the Lord. The house was filled in every part. Dr. Penny had introduced the services, and was engaged in the first prayer, when I heard something which I supposed to be the report of a gun, and the jingling of glass, as if a window had been broken. My thought was that some careless person from the military parade on the outside, had fired so near the window as to break a pane of glass. But before I had time to think again, Dr. Penny leaped from the pulpit almost over me, for I was kneeling by the sofa behind him. The pulpit was in the front of the church, between the two doors. The rear wall of the church stood upon the brink of the canal. The congregation, in a moment, fell into a perfect panic, and rushed for the doors and the windows, as if they were all distracted. One elderly woman held up a window in the rear of the church, where several, as I was informed, leaped out into the canal. The rush was terrific. Some jumped over the galleries into the aisles below; they ran over each other in the aisles.

I stood up in the pulpit, and not knowing what had happened, put up my hands, and cried at the top of my voice, "Be quiet! Be quiet!" Directly a couple of women rushing up into the pulpit, one on the one side, and the other on the other side, caught hold of me, in a state of distraction. Dr. Penny ran out into the streets, and they were getting out in every direction, as fast as possible. As I did not know that there was any danger, the scene looked so ludicrous to me, that I could scarcely refrain from laughing. They rushed over each other in the aisles, so that in several instances I observed men that had been crushed down, rising up and throwing off others that had rushed upon them. All at length got out. Several were considerably hurt, but no one killed. But the house was strewn with all sorts of women's apparel. Bonnets, shawls, gloves, handkerchiefs, and parts of dresses, were scattered in every direction. The men had very generally gone out without their hats, I believe; and many persons had been seriously bruised in the awful rush.

I afterwards learned that the walls of the church had been settling for some time, the ground being very damp from its proximity to the canal. It had been spoken of, in the congregation, as not in a satisfactory state; and some were afraid that either the tower would fall, or the roof, or the walls of the building would come down. Of this I had heard nothing myself. The original alarm was created by a timber from the roof, falling end downwards, and breaking through the ceiling, above the lamp in front of the organ.

On examining the house, it was found that the walls had spread in such a manner, that there was indeed danger of the roof falling in. The pressure that night in the gallery was so great as to spread the walls on each side, until there was real danger. At the time this occurred, I greatly feared, as I suppose others did, that the public attention would be diverted, and the work greatly hindered. But the Spirit of the Lord had taken hold of the work in earnest, and nothing seemed to stay it.

The Brick church was thrown open to us, and from that time our meetings alternated between the Second and Third churches, the people of the First church and congregation attending as far as they could get into the house. The three churches, and indeed Christians of every denomination generally, seemed to make common cause, and went to work with a will, to pull sinners out of the fire. We were obliged to hold meetings almost continually. I preached nearly every night, and three times on the Sunday. We held our meetings of inquiry, after the work took on such a powerful type, very frequently in the morning.

One morning I recollect we had been holding a meeting of inquiry, and a gentleman was present and was converted there, who was the son-in-law of a very praying, godly woman belonging to the

Third church. She had been very anxious about him, and had been spending much time in prayer for him. When he returned from the meeting of inquiry, he was full of joy and peace and hope. She had been spending the time in earnest prayer that God would convert him at that meeting. As soon as she met him and he declared his conversion to her, and from his countenance she saw that it was really so, it overcame her, and she swooned away and fell dead.

There was at that time a high school in Rochester, presided over by a Mr. B., the son of A. B., then pastor of the church at Brighton, near Rochester. Mr. B. was a skeptic, but was at the head of a very large and flourishing school. As the school was made up of both sexes, a Miss A. was his assistant and associate in the school, at that time. Miss A. was a Christian woman. The students attended the religious services, and many of them soon became deeply anxious about their souls. One morning Mr. B. found that his classes could not recite. When he came to have them before him, they were so anxious about their souls that they wept, and he saw that they were in such a state, that it very much confounded him. He called his associate, Miss A., and told her that the young people were so exercised about their souls that they could not recite; and asked if they had not better send for Mr. Finney to give them instruction. She afterwards informed me of this, and said that she was very glad to have him make the inquiry, and most cordially advised him to send for me. He did so, and the revival took tremendous hold of that school. Mr. B. himself was soon hopefully converted, and nearly every person in the school. A few years since, Miss A. informed me that more than forty persons, that were then converted in that school, had become ministers. That was a fact that I had not known before. She named many of them to me at the time. A large number of them had become foreign missionaries.

After remaining a few weeks at Josiah Bissell's, we took lodgings in a more central position, at the house of Mr. B., a lawyer of the city, who was a professedly Christian man. His wife's sister was with them, and was an impenitent girl. She was a young woman of fine appearance, an exquisite singer, and a cultivated lady; and, as we soon learned, was engaged in marriage to a man, who was then judge of the supreme court of the state. He was a very proud man, and resisted the anxious seat, and spoke against it. He was absent a good deal from the city, in holding court, and was not that winter converted. A large number of the lawyers, however, were converted; and the young lady to whom he was engaged was converted. I mention this because the Judge afterwards married her; which no doubt led to his own conversion in a revival which occurred some ten years later, the leading particulars of which I shall mention in another part of my narrative.

This revival made a great change in the moral state and subsequent history of Rochester. The great majority of the leading men and women in the city, were converted. A great number of very striking incidents occurred, that I shall not soon forget. One day the lady who first visited me and whose conversion I have mentioned, called on me in company with a friend of hers with whom she wished me to converse. I did so, but found her to all appearance very much hardened, and rather disposed to trifle with the subject. Her husband was a merchant, and they were persons of high standing in the community. When I pressed her to attend to the subject, she said she would not do it, because her husband would not attend to it, and she was not going to leave him. I asked her if she was willing to be lost because her husband would not attend to it; and if it was not folly to neglect her soul because he did his. She replied very promptly, "If he goes to hell, I want to go. I want to go where he does. I do not want to be separated from him, at any rate." It seemed that I could make very little, if any, impression upon her. But from night to night I had been making appeals to the congregation, and calling forward those that were prepared to give their hearts to God; and large numbers were converted every evening.

As I learned afterwards, when this woman went home, her husband said to her, "My dear, I mean to go forward tonight, and give my heart to God." "What!" said she; "I have today told Mr. Finney that I would not become a Christian, or have anything to do with it; that you did not become a Christian, and I would not; and that if you went to hell, I should go with you." "Well," said he, "I do not mean to go to hell. I have made up my mind to go forward tonight, and give my heart to Christ." "Well," said she, "then I will not go to meeting, I do not want to see it. And if you have a mind after all, to become a Christian, you may; I won't." When the time came, he went to meeting alone. The pulpit was between the doors, in the front of the church. The house was a good deal crowded; but he finally got a seat near one of the aisles, in quite the back path of the church. At the close of the meeting, as I had done at other times, I called for those that were anxious and whose minds were made up, to come forward, and take certain seats and occupy a certain space about the pulpit, where we could commend them to God in prayer. It afterward appeared that the wife herself had come to the meeting, had passed up the other aisle, and taken a seat almost opposite him, in the extreme part of the house. When I made the call, he started immediately. She was watching, and as soon as she saw him on his feet, and making his way along the crowded aisle, she also started down the other aisle, and they met in front of the pulpit, and knelt down together as subjects of prayer.

A large number obtained hope on the spot; but this husband and wife did not. They went home, too proud to say much to each other about what they had done, and spent a very restless night. The next day, about ten o'clock, he called to see me, and was shown into my room. My wife occupied a front room on the second floor; and I a room in the rear on the same floor. While I was conversing with him, the servant informed me that a lady was waiting in Mrs. Finney's room to see me I excused myself for a few moments, and requested him to wait, while I went in to see her. I found that it was the woman who but the day before had been so stubborn, and the wife of the man who was then in my room. Neither of them knew that the other had called to see me. I conversed with her, and found that she was on the very verge of submitting to Christ. I had learned that he was also, to all appearance, in the same state. I then returned to him and said, "I am going to pray with a lady in Mrs. Finney's room, and we will go in there, if you please, and all join in prayer, together." He followed me, and found his own wife. They looked at each other with surprise, but we were both greatly affected, each to find the other there. We knelt down to pray. I had not proceeded far in prayer before she began to weep, and to pray audibly for her husband. I stopped and listened, and found that she had lost all concern for herself, and was struggling in an agony of prayer for his conversion. His heart seemed to break and give way, and just at this time the bell rang for our dinner. I thought it would be well to leave them together alone. I therefore touched my wife, and we rose silently and went down to dinner, leaving them in prayer. We took a hasty dinner and returned, and found them as mellow, and as humble, and as loving as could be desired.

I have not said much, as yet, of the spirit of prayer that prevailed in this revival, which I must not omit to mention. When I was on my way to Rochester, as we passed through a village, some thirty miles east of Rochester, a brother minister whom I knew, seeing me on the canal boat, jumped aboard to have a little conversation with me, intending to ride but a little way and return. He, however, became interested in conversation, and upon finding where I was going, he made up his mind to keep on and go with me to Rochester. We had been there but a few days when this minister became so convicted that he could not help weeping aloud, at one time, as he passed along the street. The Lord gave him a powerful spirit of prayer, and his heart was broken. As he and I prayed much together, I was struck with his faith in regard to what the Lord was going to do there. I recollect he would say, "Lord, I do not know how it is; but I seem to know that thou art going to do a great work in this city." The spirit of prayer was poured out powerfully, so much so, that some persons stayed away from the public services to pray, being unable to restrain their feelings under preaching.

And here I must introduce the name of a man, whom I shall have occasion to mention frequently, Mr. Abel Clary. He was the son of a very excellent man, and an elder of the church where I was converted. He was converted in the same revival in which I was. He had been licensed to preach; but *his spirit of prayer was such, he was so burdened with the souls of men, that he was not able to preach much, his whole time and strength being given to prayer.* The burden of his soul would frequently be so great that he was unable to stand, and he would writhe and groan in agony. I was well acquainted with him, and knew something of the wonderful spirit of prayer that was upon him. He was a very silent man, as almost all are who have that powerful spirit of prayer.

The first I knew of his being at Rochester, a gentleman who lived about a mile west of the city, called on me one day, and asked me if I knew a Mr. Abel Clary, a minister. I told him that I knew him well. "Well," said he, "he is at my house, and has been there for some time, and I don't know what to think of him." I said, "I have not seen him at any of our meetings." "No," he replied, "he cannot go to meeting," he says. "He prays nearly all the time, day and night, and in such an agony of mind that I do not know what to make of it. Sometimes he cannot even stand on his knees, but will lie prostrate on the floor, and groan and pray in a manner that quite astonishes me." I said to the brother, "I understand it; please keep still. It will all come out right; he will surely prevail."

I knew at the time a considerable number of men who were exercised in the same way. A Deacon P., of Camden, Oneida county; a Deacon T., of Rodman, Jefferson county; a Deacon B., of Adams, in the same country; this Mr. Clary, and many others among the men, and a large number of women, partook of the same spirit, and spent a great part of their time in prayer. Father Nash, as we called him, who in several of my fields of labor came to me and aided me, was another of those men that had such a powerful spirit of prevailing prayer. This Mr. Clary continued in Rochester as long as I did, and did not leave it until after I had left. He never, that I could learn, appeared in public, but gave himself wholly to prayer.

I have said that the moral aspect of things was greatly changed by this revival. It was a young city, full of thrift and enterprise, and full of sin. The inhabitants were intelligent and enterprising, in the highest degree; but as the revival swept through the town, and converted the great mass of the most influential people, both men and women, the change in the order, sobriety, and morality of the city was wonderful.

At a subsequent period, which I shall mention in its place, I was conversing with a lawyer, who was converted at this revival of who I have been speaking, and who soon after had been made district attorney of the city. His business was to superintend the prosecution of criminals. From his position he was made thoroughly acquainted with the history of crime in that city. In speaking of the revival in which he was converted, he said to me, many years afterward: "I have been examining the records of the criminal courts, and I find this striking fact, that whereas our city has increased since that revival, threefold, there are not one third as many prosecutions for crime, as there had been up to that time." "This is," he said, "the wonderful influence that revival had upon the community." Indeed, by the power of that revival, public sentiment has been molded. The public affairs of the city have been, in a great measure in the hands of Christian men; and the controlling influences in the community have been on the side of Christ.

Among other conversions I must not forget to mention that of Mr. P., a prominent citizen of that place, a bookseller. Mr. P. was an infidel; not an atheist, but a disbeliever in the divine authority of the Bible. He was a reader and a thinker, a man of keen, shrewd mind, strong will, and most decided character. He was, I believe, a man of good outward morals, and a gentleman highly respected. He came to my room early one morning, and said to me, "Mr. Finney, there is a great movement here on the subject of religion, but I am a skeptic, and I want you to prove to me that the Bible is true." The Lord enabled me at once to discern his state of mind, so far as to decide the course I should take with him. I said to him, "Do you believe in the existence of God?" "O yes!" he said, "I am not an atheist." "Well, do you believe that you have treated God as you ought? Have you respected his authority? Have you loved him? Have you done that which you thought would please him, and with the design to please him? Don't you admit that you ought to love him, and ought to worship him, and ought to obey him, according to the best light you have?" "O yes!" he said, "I admit all this." "But have you done so?" I asked. "Why, no," he answered, "I cannot say that I have." "Well then," I replied, "why should I give you farther information, and farther light, if you will not do your duty and obey the light you already have?" "Now," said I, "when you will make up your mind to live up to your convictions, to obey God according to the best light you have; when you will make up your mind to repent of your neglect thus far, and to please God just as well as you know how, the rest of your life, I will try to show you that the Bible is from God. Until then it is of no use for me to do any such thing." I did not sit down, and I think had not asked him to sit down. He replied, "I do not know but that is fair;" and retired.

I heard no more of him until the next morning. Soon after I arose, he came to my room again; and as soon as he entered, he clapped his hands and said, "Mr. Finney, God has wrought a miracle!" "I went down to the store," he continued, "after I left your room, thinking of what you had said; and I made up my mind that I would repent of what I knew was wrong in my relations to God, and that hereafter I would live according to the best light I had. And when I made up my mind to this," said he, "my feelings so overcame me that I fell; and I do not know but I should have died, if it had not been for Mr.__, who was with me in the store." From this time, he has been, as all who know him are aware, a praying, earnest Christian man. For many years he has been one of the trustees of Oberlin College, has stood by us through all our trials, and has aided us with his means and his whole influence.

During this great revival, persons wrote letters from Rochester, to their friends abroad, giving an account of the work, which were read in different churches throughout several states, and were instrumental in producing great revision of religion. Many persons came in from abroad to witness the great work of God, and were converted. I recollect that a physician was so attracted by what he heard of the work that he came from Newark, New Jersey, to Rochester, to see what the Lord was doing, and was himself converted there. He was a man of talents and high culture, and has been for years an ardent Christian laborer for immortal souls.

One evening, I recollect, when I made a call for the anxious to come forward and submit, a man of influence in a neighboring town came forward himself, and several members of his family, and gave themselves to God. Indeed, the work spread like waves in every direction. I preached in as many places round about, as I had time and strength to do, while my main labors were in Rochester. I went to Canandaigua and preached several times. There the word took effect, and many were converted. The pastor, Rev. Ansel Eddy, entered heartily into the work. A former pastor, an elderly man, an Englishmen by birth, also did what he could to forward the work. Wherever I went, the word of God took immediate effect; and it seemed only necessary to present the law of God, and the claims of Christ, in such relations and proportions as were calculated to secure the conversion of men, and they would be converted by scores.

The greatness of the work at Rochester, at that time, attracted so much of the attention of ministers and Christians throughout the State of New York, throughout New England, and in many parts of the United States, that the very fame of it was an efficient instrument in the hands of the Spirit of God in promoting the greatest revival of religion throughout the land, that this country had then ever witnessed. Years after this, in conversing with Dr. Beecher about this powerful revival and its results, he remarked: *"That was the greatest work of God, and the greatest revival of religion, that the world has ever seen, in so short a time." "One hundred thousand,"* he remarked, *"were reported as having connected themselves with churches, as the results of that great revival." "This,"* he said, *"is unparalleled in the history of the church, and of the progress of religion." He spoke of this having been done in one year; and said that in no year during the Christian era, had we any account of so great a revival of religion.*

From the time of the New Lebanon convention, of which I have spoken, open and public opposition to revivals of religion was less and less manifested, and especially did I meet with much less personal opposition than I had met with before. It gradually but greatly subsided. At Rochester I felt nothing of it. Indeed, the waters of salvation had risen so high, revivals had become so powerful and extensive, and people had time to become acquainted with them and their results, in such measure, that men were afraid to oppose them as they had done. Ministers had come to understand them better, and the most ungodly sinners had been convinced that they were indeed the work of God. So manifestly were the great mass of the conversions sound, the converts really regenerated and made new creatures, so thoroughly were individuals and whole communities reformed, and so permanent and unquestionable were the results, that the conviction became nearly universal, that they were the work of God.

CHAPTER 22

REVIVAL IN AUBURN, BUFFALO, PROVIDENCE, AND BOSTON

*I saw the Spirit of prayer was upon him,
and I felt his influence upon myself,
and took it for granted that
the work would move on powerfully*

During the latter part of the time that I was at Rochester, my health was poor. I was overdone; and some of the leading physicians, I learned, had made up their minds that I never would preach any more. My labors in Rochester at that time, had continued through six months; and near their close, Rev. Dr. Wisner, of Ithaca, came down and spent some time, witnessing and helping forward the work. In the meantime, I was invited to many fields; and among others I was urged by Dr. Nott, president of Union College, at Schenectady, to go and labor with him, and if possible secure the conversion of his numerous students. I made up my mind to comply with his request.

In company with Dr. Wisner and Josiah Bissell, I started in the stage, in the spring of the year 1831, when the going was exceedingly bad. I left my wife and children for the time at Rochester; as the traveling was too dangerous, and the journey too fatiguing for them. When we arrived at Geneva, Dr. Wisner insisted on my going home with him, to rest awhile. I declined, and said I must keep about my work. He pressed me very hard to go; and finally told me that the physicians in Rochester had told him to take me home with him, for I was going to die; that I would never labor anymore in revivals, for I had the consumption, and could live but a little while. I replied that I had been told this before, but that it was a mistake; that the doctors did not understand my case; that I was only fatigued, and a little rest would bring me up.

Dr. Wisner finally gave up his importunity, and I passed on in the stage to Auburn. The going was so very bad, that sometimes we could not get on more than two miles an hour, and we had been two or three days in going from Rochester to Auburn. As I had many dear friends in Auburn, and was very much fatigued, I made up my mind to stop there, and rest till the next stage. I had paid my fare quite through to Schenectady; but could stop over, if I chose, for one or more days. I stopped at the house of Mr. T.S., a son of Chief-Justice S.. He was an earnest Christian man, and a very dear friend of mine; consequently, I went to his house, instead of stopping at the hotel, and concluded to rest there till the next stage.

In the morning, after sleeping quietly at Mr. S.'s, I had risen, and was preparing to take the stage, which was to arrive in the early part of the day, when a gentleman came in with the request for me to remain — a request in writing, signed by that large number of influential men, of whom I have spoken before, as resting the revival in that place in 1826. These men had set themselves against the revival, on the former occasion, and carried their opposition so far as to break from Dr. Lansing's congregation, and form a new one. In the meantime, Dr. Lansing had been called to another field of labor; and Rev. Josiah Hopkins, of Vermont, was settled as pastor of the First church. The paper to which I have alluded, contained at earnest appeal to me to stop and labor for their salvation, signed at a long list of unconverted men, most of them among the most prominent citizens in the city. This was very striking to me. In this paper they alluded to the opposition they had formerly made to my labors, and besought me to overlook it, and stop and preach the Gospel to them.

This request did not come from the pastor, nor from his church, but from those who had formerly led in the opposition to the work.

But the pastor and the members of his church pressed me with all their influence, to remain and preach, and comply with the request of these men. They appeared as much surprised as I was myself, at the change in the attitude of those men. I went to my room, and spread the subject before God, and soon made up my mind what to do. I told the pastor and his elders that I was very much fatigued, and nearly worn out; but that upon certain conditions I would remain. I would preach twice upon the Sunday, and two evenings during the week; but that they should take all the rest of the labor upon their own hands; that they must not expect me to attend any other meetings than those at which I preached; and that they must take upon themselves the labor of instructing inquirers, and conducting the prayer and other meetings. I knew that they understood how to labor with sinners, and could well trust them to perform that part of the work. I furthermore stipulated that neither they nor their people should visit me, except in extreme cases, at my lodgings; for that I must have my days, Sundays excepted, that I might rest, and also my evenings, except those when I preached. There were three preaching services on the Sunday, one of which was filled by Mr. Hopkins. I preached in the morning and evening, I think, of each Sunday, and he in the afternoon.

The word took immediate effect. On the first or second Sunday evening that I preached, I saw that the word was taking such powerful hold that at the close I called for those whose minds were made up, to come forward, publicly renounce their sins, and give themselves to Christ. Much to my own surprise, and very much to the surprise of the pastor and many members of the church, the first man that I observed as coming forward and leading the way, was the man that had led, and exerted more influence than any other one man, in the opposition to the former revival. He came forward promptly, followed by a large number of the persons who had signed that paper; and that evening there was such a demonstration made, as to produce a general interest throughout the place.

I have spoken of Mr. Clary as the praying man, who was at Rochester. He had a brother, a physician, living in Auburn. I think it was the second Sunday that I was at Auburn at this time, I observed in the congregation the solemn face of this Mr. Clary. He looked as if he was borne down with an agony of prayer. Being well acquainted with him, and knowing the great gift of God that was upon him, the spirit of prayer, I was very glad to see him there. He sat in the pew with his brother, the Doctor, who was also a professor of religion, but who knew nothing by experience, I should think, of his Brother Abel's great power with God.

At intermission, as soon as I came down from the pulpit, Mr. Clary, with his brother, met me at the pulpit stairs, and the Doctor invited me to go home with him and spend the intermission and get some refreshments. I did so. After arriving at his house we were soon summoned to the dinner table. We gathered about the table, and Dr. Clary turned to his brother and said, "Brother Abel, will you ask a blessing?" Brother Abel bowed his head and began, audibly, to ask a blessing. He had uttered but a sentence or two when he broke instantly down, moved suddenly back from the table, and fled to his chamber. The Doctor supposed he had been taken suddenly ill, and rose up and followed him. In a few moments he came down and said, "Mr. Finney, brother Abel wants to see you." Said I, "What ails him?" Said he, "I do not know; but he says you know. He appears in great distress, but I think it is the state of his mind." I understood it in a moment, and went to his room. He lay groaning upon the bed, the Spirit making intercession for him, and in him, with groanings that could not be uttered. I had hardly entered the room, when he made out to say; "Pray, Brother Finney." I knelt down and helped him in prayer, by leading his soul out for the conversion of sinners. I continued to pray until his distress passed away, and then I returned to the dinner table.

I understood that this was the voice of God. I saw the Spirit of prayer was upon him, and I felt his influence upon myself, and took it for granted that the work would move on powerfully. It did so. I believe, but am not quite sure, that every one of those men that signed that paper, making a long list of names, was converted during that revival. But a few years since, Dr. S., of Auburn, wrote to me to know if I had preserved that paper, wishing, as he said, to ascertain whether every one of the men that signed it, was not at that time converted. The paper has been mislaid; and although it is probably among my numerous papers and letters, and may sometime be found, yet I could not, at the time, answer his inquiry.

I stayed, at this time, at Auburn, six Sundays, preaching, as I have said, twice on the Sunday, and twice during the week, and leaving all the rest of the labor for the pastor and members of the church. Here, as at Rochester, there was, at this time, little or no open opposition. Ministers and Christians took hold of the work, and everybody that had a mind to work found enough to do, and good success in labor. The pastor told me afterward, that he found that in the six weeks that I was there, five hundred souls had been converted. The means that were used, were the same that had been used at Rochester. This revival seemed to be only a wave of divine power, reaching Auburn from the center at Rochester, whence such a mighty influence had gone out over the length and breadth of the land.

Near the close of my labor here, a messenger arrived from Buffalo, with an earnest request that I should visit that city. The revival in Rochester had prepared the way in Auburn, as in every other place round about, and had also prepared the way in Buffalo. At Buffalo, the messenger informed me, the work had begun, and a few souls had been hopefully converted; but they felt that other means needed to be used, and they urged me so hard, that from Auburn I turned back through Rochester to Buffalo. I spent but about one month, I think, at Buffalo; during which time a large number of persons were hopefully converted.

The work at Buffalo, as at Auburn and Rochester, took effect very generally among the more influential classes. Rev. Dr. Lord, then a lawyer, was converted at that time, I think; also Mr. H., the father of Rev. Dr. H., of Buffalo. There were many circumstances connected with his conversion, that I have never forgotten. He was one of the wealthiest and influential men in Buffalo, and a man of outwardly good morals, fair character, and high standing as a citizen, but an impenitent sinner. His wife was a Christian woman, and had long been praying for him, and hoping that he would be converted. But when I began to preach there, and insisted that the sinner's "cannot" is his "will not," that the difficulty to be overcome was the voluntary wickedness of sinners, and that they were wholly unwilling to be Christians, Mr. H. rebelled very decidedly against such teaching. He insisted upon it that it was false in his case; for he was conscious of being willing to be a Christian, and that he had long been willing.

As his wife informed me of the position that he occupied, I did not spare him; but from day to day, I hunted him from his refuges, and answered all his objections, and met all his excuses. He became more and more excited. He was a man of strong will; and he declared that he did not, and would not, believe such teaching. He said so much in opposition to the teaching, as to draw around him some men with whom he had no sympathy at all, except in their opposition to the work. But I did not hesitate to press him in every sermon, in one shape or another, with his unwillingness to be a Christian.

After his conversion, he told me that he was shocked and ashamed, when he found that some scoffers had taken refuge behind him. One evening, he said, he sat directly across the aisle from a notorious scoffer. He said that repeatedly while I was preaching, this man, with whom he had no sympathy at all on other subjects, would look toward him and smile, and give great indications of his fellowship with Mr. H.'s opposition to the revival. He said that on discovering this, his heart rose up with indignation; and he said to himself, "I am not going to be in sympathy with that class of men; I will have nothing to do with them."

However, that very night, at the close of my sermon, I pressed the consciences of sinners so hard, and made so strong an appeal to them to give up their voluntary opposition and come to Christ, that he could not contain himself. As soon as meeting was out, altogether contrary to his custom, he began to resist, and to speak against what had been said, before he got out of the house. The aisles were full, and people were crowding around him on every side. Indeed, he made some profane expression, as his wife informed me, which very much disturbed her, as she felt that by his opposition he was very likely to grieve the Spirit of God away, and lose his soul.

That night he could not sleep. His mind was so exercised that he rose as soon as there was any light, left his house and went off to a considerable distance, where there was then a grove, near a place where he had some waterworks which he called "the hydraulics." There in the grove he knelt down to pray. He said he had felt, during the night, as if he must get away by himself, so that he could speak aloud and let out his voice and his heart, as he was pressed beyond endurance with the sense of his sins, and with the necessity of immediately making his peace with God. But to his surprise and mortification, when he knelt down and attempted to pray, he found that his heart would not pray. He had no words; he had no desires that he could express in words. He said that it appeared to him that his heart was as hard as marble, and that he had not the least feeling on the subject. He stood upon his knees disappointed and confounded, and found that if he opened his mouth to pray, he had nothing in the form of prayer that he could sincerely utter.

In this state it occurred to him that he could say the Lord's prayer. So he began, "Our Father which art in heaven." He said as soon as he uttered the words, he was convicted of his hypocrisy in calling God his Father. When he added the petition, "Hallowed be thy name," he said it almost shocked him. He saw that he was not sincere, that his words did not at all express the state of his mind. He did not care to have God's name hallowed. Then he uttered the next petition, "Thy kingdom come." Upon this, he said, he almost choked. He saw that he did not want the kingdom of God to come; that it was hypocritical in him to say so, and that he could not say it, as really expressing the sincere desire of his heart. And then came the petition, "Thy will be done on earth as it is done in heaven." He said his heart rose up against that, and he could not say it. Here he was brought face to face with the will of God. He had been told from day to day that he was opposed to this will; that he was not willing to accept it; that it was his voluntary opposition to God, to his law, and his will, that was the only obstacle in the way of his conversion. This consideration he had resisted and fought with desperation. But here on his knees, with the Lord's prayer in his mouth, he was brought face to face with that question; and he saw with perfect clearness that what he had been told, was true: that he was not willing that God's will should be done; and that he did not do it himself, because he would not.

Here the whole question of his rebellion, in its nature and its extent, was brought so strongly before him, that he saw it would cost him a mighty struggle, to give up that voluntary opposition to God. And then, he said, he gathered up all the strength of his will and cried aloud, "Thy will be done on earth as it is done in heaven." He said he was perfectly conscious that his will went with his words; that he accepted the will of God, and the whole will of God; that he made a full surrender to God, and accepted Christ just as he was offered in the Gospel. He gave up his sins, and embraced the will of God as his universal rule of life. The language of his heart was, "Lord, do with me as seems good to you. Let your will be done with me, and with all creatures on earth, as it is done in heaven." He said he prayed freely, as soon as his will surrendered; and his heart poured itself out like a flood. His rebellion all passed away, his feelings subsided into a great calm, and a sweet peace seemed to fill all his soul.

He rose from his knees and went to his house, and told his anxious wife, who had been praying for him so earnestly, what the Lord had done for his soul; and confessed that he had been all wrong in his opposition, and entirely deceived as it respected his willingness to be a Christian. From that time, he became an earnest laborer for the promotion of the work of God. His subsequent life attested the reality of the change, and he lived and died a useful, Christian man. From Buffalo I went, in June, I think, to my father-in-law's, in Whitestown. I spent a part of the summer in journeying for recreation, and for the restoration of my health and strength.

Early in the autumn of 1831, I accepted an invitation to hold what was then called "a protracted meeting," or a series of meetings, in Providence. I labored mostly in the church of which Rev. Dr. Wilson was at that time pastor. I think I remained there about three weeks, holding meetings every evening, and preaching three times on the Sunday. The Lord poured out his Spirit immediately upon the people, and the work of grace commenced and went forward in a most interesting manner. However, my stay was too short to secure so general a work of grace in that place, as occurred afterwards in 1842, when I spent some two months there; the particulars of which I shall relate in its proper connection.

There were many interesting conversions at that time; and several of the men who have had a leading Christian influence in that city, from that time to the present day, were converted. This was also true of the women; many very interesting cases of conversion among them occurred. I remember with great distinctness the conversion of one young lady, which I will in brief relate. I had observed in the congregation, on the Sunday, a young woman of great personal beauty, sitting in a pew with a young man who I afterwards learned was her brother. She had a very intellectual, and a very earnest look, and seemed to listen to every word I said, with the utmost attention and seriousness.

I was the guest of Mr. Josiah Chapin; and in going from the church with him to his own house, I observed this young brother and sister going up the same street. I pointed them out to Mr. Chapin, and asked him who they were. He informed me that they were a Mr. and a Miss A., brother and sister, and remarked that she was considered the most beautiful girl in Providence. I asked him if she was a professor of religion; and he said, no. I told him I thought her very seriously impressed, and asked him if he did not think it would be well for me to call and see her. He spoke discouragingly in regard to that, and thought it would be a waste of time, and that possibly I might not be cordially received. He thought that she was a girl so much caressed and flattered, and that her surroundings were such, that she probably entertained but little serious thought in regard to the salvation of her soul. But he was mistaken; and I was right in supposing that the Spirit of the Lord was striving with her.

I did not call upon her; but a few days after this, she called to see me. I knew her at once, and inquired of her in regard to the state of her soul. She was very thoroughly awakened; but her real convictions of sin, were not ripened into that state that I wished to see and which I thought was necessary, before she could be really brought intelligently to accept the righteousness of Christ. I therefore spent an hour or two — for her call was considerably protracted, in trying to show her the depravity of her heart. She at first recoiled from my searching questions. But her convictions seemed to ripen as I conversed with her; and she became more and more profoundly serious. When I had said to her what I thought was necessary to secure a ripened and thorough conviction, under the influence of the Spirit of God, she got up with a manifest feeling of dissatisfaction, and left me. I was confident the Spirit of God had so thoroughly taken hold of her case, that what I had said to her would not be shaken off, but on the contrary that it would work the conviction that I sought to produce.

Two or three days afterwards she called on me again. I could see at once that she was greatly bowed down in her spirit. As soon as she came in she sat down, and threw her heart open to me. With the utmost candor she said to me, "Mr. Finney, I thought when I was here before, that your questions and treatment of me were pretty severe." "But," said she, "I see now that I am all that you represented me to be." "Indeed," said she, "had it not been for my pride and regard for my reputation, I should have been as wicked a girl as there is in Providence." "I can see," said she, "clearly that my life has been restrained by pride, and a regard to my reputation, and not from any regard to God, or his law or Gospel. I can see that God has made use of my pride and ambition, to restrain me from disgraceful iniquities. I have been petted and flattered, and have stood upon my dignity; and have maintained my reputation, from purely selfish motives." She went on spontaneously, and owned up, and showed that her convictions were thorough and permanent. She did not appear to be excited, but calm, and in the highest degree rational, in everything that she said. It was evident, however, that she had a fervent nature, a strong will, and an uncommonly well-balanced and cultivated intellect.

After conversing with her for some time, and giving her as thorough instruction as I could, we bowed before the Lord in prayer; and she, to all human appearance, gave herself unreservedly to Christ. She was in a state of mind, at this time, that seemed to render it easy for her to renounce the world. She has always been a very interesting Christian. Not many years after her conversion, she was married to a wealthy gentleman in the city of New York. For several years I had no direct correspondence with her. Her husband took her into a circle of society with which I had no particular acquaintance; and, until after he died, I did not renew my acquaintance with her. Since then I have had much Christian correspondence with her, and have never ceased to be greatly interested in her religious life. I mention this case, because I have ever regarded it as a wonderful triumph of the grace of God over the fascinations of the world. *The grace of God was too strong for the world, even in a case like this, in which every worldly fascination was surrounding her.*

While I was at Providence, the question of my going to Boston was agitated by the ministers and deacons of the several Congregational churches of that city. I was not myself aware of what they were doing there; but Dr. Wisner, then pastor of the Old South church, came over to Providence and attended our meetings. I afterward learned that he was sent over by the ministers, "to spy out the land and bring back a report." I had several conversations with him, and he manifested an almost enthusiastic interest in what he saw and heard in Providence. About the time he was there, some very striking conversions took place.

The work at Providence was of a peculiarly searching character, as it respected professors of religion. Old hopes were terribly shaken, and there was a great shaking among the dry bones in the different churches. So terribly was a deacon of one of the churches searched on one occasion, that he said to me, as I came out of the pulpit, "Mr. Finney, I do not believe there are ten real Christians in Providence." "We are all wrong," said he; "we have been deceived." Dr. Wisner, I believe, was thoroughly convinced that the work was genuine, and for the time, extensive; and that there was no indication of influences or results that were to be deplored.

After Dr. Wisner returned to Boston, I soon received a request from the Congregational ministers and churches, to go to that city and labor. Dr. Lyman Beecher was at that time pastor of the Bowdoin street church; his son, Edward Beecher, was either pastor or stated supply at Park street; a Mr. Green was pastor of the Essex street church, but had gone to Europe for his health, and that church was without any stated supply at the time. Dr. Fay was pastor of the Congregational church in Charlestown; and Dr. Jenks was pastor of the Congregational church in Green street. I do not recollect who were the pastors of the other churches at the time.

I began my labors by preaching around in the different churches on the Sunday, and on week evenings I preached in Park street. I soon saw that the word of God was taking effect, and that the interest was increasing from day to day. But I perceived also that there needed to be a great searching among professed Christians. I could not learn that there was among them anything like the spirit of prayer that had prevailed in the revivals at the West and in New York City. There seemed to be a peculiar type of religion there, not exhibiting that freedom and strength of faith which I had been in the habit of seeing in New York.

I therefore began to preach some searching sermons to Christians. Indeed, I gave out on the Sunday, that I would preach a series of sermons to Christians, in Park street, on certain evenings of the week. But I soon found that these sermons were not at all palatable to the Christians of Boston. It was something they never had been used to, and the attendance at Park street became less and less, especially on those evenings when I preached to professed Christians. This was new to me. I had never before seen professed Christians shrink back, as they did at that time in Boston, from searching sermons. But I heard, again and again, of speeches like these: "What will the Unitarians say, if such things are true of us who are orthodox?" "If Mr. Finney preaches to us in this way, the Unitarians will triumph over us, and say, that at least the orthodox are no better Christians than Unitarians." It was evident that they somewhat resented my plain dealing, and that my searching sermons astonished, and even offended, very many of them. However, as the work went forward, this state of things changed greatly; and after a few weeks they would listen to searching preaching, and came to appreciate it.

I found in Boston, as I had everywhere else, that there was a method of dealing with inquiring sinners, that was very trying to me. I used sometimes to hold meetings of inquiry with Dr. Beecher, in the basement of his church. One evening when there was a large attendance, and a feeling of great searching and solemnity among the inquirers, at the close, as was my custom, I made an address in which I tried to point out to them exactly what the Lord required of them. My object was to bring them to renounce themselves and their all, and give themselves and all they possessed to Christ. I tried to show them that they were not their own, but were bought with a price; and pointed out to them the sense in which they were expected to forsake all that they had, and deliver everything to Christ as belonging to him.

I made this point as clear as I possibly could, and saw that the impression upon the inquirers seemed to be very deep. I was about to call on them to kneel down, while we presented them to God in prayer; when Dr. Beecher arose, and said to them, "You need not be afraid to give up all to Christ, your property and all, for he will give it right back to you." Without making any just discriminations at all, as to the sense in which they were to give up their possessions, and the sense in which the Lord would allow them to retain them, he simply exhorted them not to be afraid to give up all, as they had been urged to do, as the Lord would give it right back to them. I saw that he was making a false impression, and I felt in an agony. I saw that his language was calculated to make an impression, the direct opposite of the truth.

After he had finished his remarks, as wisely and carefully as I could, I led them to see that, in the sense of which God required them to give up their possessions, he would never give them back, and they must not entertain such a thought. I tried to say what I said, in such a way as not to appear to contradict Dr. Beecher, but yet thoroughly to correct the impression that I saw he had made. I told them that the Lord did not require them to relinquish all their possessions, to quit their business, and houses, and possessions, and never to have possession of them again; but he did require them to renounce the ownership of them, to understand and realize that these things were not theirs, but the Lord's; that his claim was absolute, and his property in themselves and in everything else, so entirely above the right of every other being in the universe, that what he required of them was to use themselves and everything else as belonging to him; and never to think that they had a right to use their time, their strength, their substance, their influence, or anything else which they possessed, as if it were their own, and not the Lord's. Dr. Beecher made no objection to what I said, either at the time, or ever, so far as I know; and it is not probable that he intended anything inconsistent with this, in what he said. Yet his language was calculated to make the impression that God would restore their possessions to them, in the sense in which they had relinquished them, and given them up to him.

The members of the orthodox churches of Boston, at this time, generally, I believe, received my views of doctrine without question. I know that Dr. Beecher did; for he told me that he had never seen a man with whose theological views he so entirely accorded, as he did with mine. There was one point of my orthodoxy, however, to which many of them at the time objected. There was a Mr. Rand, who published, I think, a periodical in Boston at that time, who wrote an earnest article against my views on the subject of the divine agency in regeneration. I preached that the divine agency was that of teaching and persuasion, that the influence was a moral, and not a physical one. President Edwards had held the contrary; and Mr. Rand held with President Edwards, that the divine agency exercised in regeneration, was a physical one; that it produced a change of nature, instead of a change in the voluntary attitude and preference of the soul. Mr. Rand regarded my views on this subject as quite out of the way.

Dr. Wisner wrote a reply, and justified my views, with the exception of those that I maintained on the persuasive or moral influence of the Holy Spirit. He was not then prepared to take the ground, against President Edwards, and the general orthodox view of New England, that the Spirit's agency was not physical, but only moral. Dr. Woods, of Andover, also published an article in one of the periodicals, I believe the one published at Andover, under this title: "The Holy Ghost the author of regeneration." This was, I think, the title; at any rate the design was to prove that regeneration was the work of God. He quoted of course, that class of scriptures that assert the divine agency, in the work of changing the heart.

To this, I made no reply in writing; but in my preaching I said that was only a half-truth; that the Bible just as plainly asserts that regeneration is the work of man; and I quoted those passages that affirm it. Paul said to one of the churches, that he had begotten them, that is regenerated them; for the same word is used as in other passages, where regeneration is ascribed to God. It is easy, therefore, to show that God has an agency in regeneration, and that his agony is that of teaching or persuasion. It is also easy to show that the subject has an agency; that the acts of repentance, faith, and love are his own; and that the Spirit persuades him to put forth these acts, by presenting to him the truth. As the truth is the instrument, the Holy Spirit must be one of the agents; and a preacher, or some human, intelligent agent, generally, also cooperates in the work. There was nothing at all unchristian, that I recollect, in any of the discussions that we had, at that time; nothing that grieved the Spirit or produced any unkind feelings among the brethren.

After I had spent some weeks, in preaching about in the different congregations, I consented to supply Mr. Green's church in Essex street statedly, for a time. I therefore concentrated my labors upon that field. We had a blessed work of grace; and a large number of persons were converted in different parts of the city.

I had become fatigued, as I had labored about ten years as an evangelist, without anything more than a few days or weeks of rest, during the whole period. The ministerial brethren were true men, had taken hold of the work as well as they knew how, and labored faithfully and efficiently in securing good results.

By this time, a second free church had been formed in New York City. Mr. Joel Parker's church, the first free church, had grown so large, that a colony had gone off, and formed a second church; to which Rev.

Mr. Barrows had been preaching. Some earnest brethren wrote to me from New York, proposing to lease a theater, and fit it up for a church, upon condition that I would come there and preach. They proposed to get what was called the "Chatham street theater," in the heart of the most irreligious population of New York. It was owned by men who were very willing to have it transformed into a church. At this time, we had three children, and I could not well take my family with me, while laboring as an evangelist. My strength, too, had become a good deal exhausted; and on praying and looking the matter over, I concluded that I would accept the call from the Second Free church, and labor, for a time at least, in New York.

CHAPTER 23

LABORS IN NEW YORK CITY.
IN 1832, AND ONWARD

The spirit of prayer came upon me
as a sovereign grace, bestowed upon me
without the least merit,
and in despite of all my sinfulness.

Mr. Lewis Tappan, with other Christian brethren, leased the Chatham street theatre, and fitted it up for a church, and as a suitable place to accommodate the various charitable societies, in holding their anniversaries. They called me, and I accepted the pastorate of the second Free Presbyterian church. I left Boston in April, 1832, and commenced labors in that theatre, at that time. The Spirit of the Lord was immediately poured out upon us, and we had an extensive revival that spring and summer.

About midsummer the cholera appeared in New York, for the first time. The panic became great, and a great many Christian people fled into the country. The cholera was very severe in the city that summer, more so than it ever has been since; and it was especially fatal in the part of the city where I resided. I recollect counting, from the door of our house five hearses drawn up at the same time, at different doors within sight. I remained in New York until quite the latter part of summer, not being willing to leave the city while the mortality was so great. But I found that the influence was undermining my health, and in the latter part of summer I went into the country, for two or three weeks. On my return, I was installed as pastor of the church. During the installation services, I was taken ill; and soon after I got home, it was plain that I was seized with the cholera. The gentleman at the next door, was seized about the same time, and before morning he was dead. The means used for my recovery, gave my system a terrible shock from which it took me long to recover. However, toward spring I was able to preach again. I invited two ministerial brethren to help me in holding a series of meetings. We preached in turn for two or three weeks, but very little was accomplished. I saw that it was not the way to promote a revival there, and I drew the meeting, in that form, to a close.

On the next Sunday, I made appointments to preach every evening during the week and a revival immediately commenced, and became very powerful. I continued to preach for twenty evenings in succession, beside preaching on the Sunday. My health was not yet vigorous, and after preaching twenty evenings, I suspended that form of my labors. The converts known to us numbered five hundred, and our church became so large, that very soon a colony was sent off to form another church; and a suitable building was erected for that purpose, on the corner of Madison and Catharine streets.

The work continued to go forward, in a very interesting manner. We held meetings of inquiry once or twice a week, and sometimes oftener, and found that every week, a goodly number of conversions was reported. The church consisted of praying, working people. They were thoroughly united, were well trained in regard to labors for the conversion of sinners, and were a most devoted and efficient church of Christ. They would go out into the highways and hedges, and bring people to hear preaching, whenever they were called upon to do so. Both men and women would undertake this work. When we wished to give notice of any extra meetings, little slips of paper, on which was printed an invitation to attend the services, would be carried from house to house, in every direction, by the members of the church; especially in that part of the city in which Chatham street chapel, as we called it, was located. By the distribution of these slips, and by oral invitations, the house could be filled, any evening in the week. Our ladies were not afraid to go and gather in all classes, from the neighborhood round about. It was something new to have religious services in that theatre, instead of such scenes as had formerly been enacted there.

There were three rooms, connected with the front part of the theatre, long, large rooms, which were fitted up for prayer meetings, and for a lecture room. These rooms had been used for very different purposes, while the main building was occupied as a theatre. But, when fitted up for our purpose, they were exceedingly convenient. There were three tiers of galleries; and those rooms were connected with the galleries respectively, one above the other.

I instructed my church members to scatter themselves over the whole house, and to keep their eyes open, in regard to any that were seriously affected under preaching, and if possible, to detain them after preaching, for conversation and prayer. They were true to their teaching, and were on the lookout at every meeting to see, with whom the word of God was taking effect; and they had faith enough to dismiss their fears, and to speak to any whom they saw to be affected by the word. In this way the conversion of a great many souls was secured. They would invite them into those rooms, and there we could converse and pray with them, and thus gather up the results of every sermon.

A case which I this moment recollect, will illustrate the manner in which the members would work. The firm of Naylor and Company, who were at that time the great cutlery manufacturers in Sheffield, England, had a house in New York, and a partner by the name of H.. Mr. H. was a worldly man, had traveled a great deal, and had resided in several of the principal cities of Europe. One of the clerks of that establishment had come to our meetings and been converted, and felt very anxious for the conversion of Mr. H.. The young man, for some time, hesitated about asking him to attend our meetings, but he finally ventured to do so; and in compliance with his earnest entreaty, Mr. H. came one evening to meeting.

As it happened, he sat near the broad aisle, over against where Mr. Tappan sat. Mr. Tappan saw that, during the sermon, he manifested a good deal of emotion; and seemed uneasy at times, as if he were on the point of going out. Mr. H. afterwards acknowledged to me, that he was several times on the point of leaving, because he was so affected by the sermon. But he remained till the blessing was pronounced. Mr. Tappan kept his eye upon him, and as soon as the blessing was pronounced, introduced himself as Mr. Tappan, a partner of Arthur Tappan and Company, a firm well known to everybody in New York.

I have heard Mr. H. himself relate the facts, with great emotion. He said that Mr. Tappan stepped up to him, and took him gently by the button of his coat, and spoke very kindly to him, and asked him if he would not remain for prayer and conversation. He tried to excuse himself and to get away; but Mr. Tappan was so gentlemanly and so kind, that he could not even get away from him. He was importunate, and, as Mr. H. expressed it, "he held fast to my button, so that," said he, "an ounce weight at my button was the means of saving my soul." The people retired, and Mr. H. among others, was persuaded to remain. According to our custom we had a thorough conversation; and Mr. H. was either then, or very soon after, hopefully converted.

When I first went to Chatham street chapel, I informed the brethren that I did not wish to fill up the house with Christians from other churches as my object was to gather from the world. I wanted to become the conversion of the ungodly, to the utmost possible extent. We therefore gave ourselves to labor for that class of persons, and by the blessing of God, with good success. Conversions were multiplied so much, that our church would soon become so large, that we would send off a colony; and when I left New York, I think, we had seven free churches, whose members were laboring with all their might to secure the salvation of souls. They were supported mostly by collections, that were taken up from Sunday to Sunday. If at any time there was a deficiency in the treasury, there were a number of brethren of property, who would at once supply the deficiency from their own purses; so that we never had the least difficulty in meeting the pecuniary demands. A more harmonious, prayerful, and efficient people, I never knew, than were the members of those free churches. They were not among the rich, although there were several men of property belonging to them. In general, they were gathered from the middle and lower classes of the people. This was what we aimed to accomplish, to preach the Gospel especially to the poor.

When I first went to New York, I had made up my mind on the question of slavery, and was exceedingly anxious to arouse public attention to the subject. I did not, however, turn aside to make it a hobby, or divert the attention of the people from the work of converting souls. Nevertheless, in my prayers and preaching, I so often alluded to slavery, and denounced it, that a considerable excitement came to exist among the people.

Soon after this, the question came up of building the Tabernacle in Broadway. The men that built it, and the leading members who formed the church there, built it with the understanding that I should be its pastor, and they formed a Congregational church. I then took my dismission from the presbytery, and became pastor of that Congregational church.

But I should have said that in January, 1834, I was obliged to leave on account of my health, and take a sea voyage. I went up the Mediterranean, therefore, in a small brig, in the midst of winter. We had a very stormy passage. My stateroom was small, and I was on the whole, very uncomfortable; and the voyage did not much improve my health. I spent some weeks at Malta, and also in Sicily. I was gone about six months. On my return, I found that there was a great excitement in New York. The members of my church, together with other abolitionists in New York, had held a meeting on the fourth of July[1], and had an address on the subject of slave-holding. A mob was stirred up, and this was the beginning of that series of mobs that spread in many directions, whenever and wherever there was an anti-slavery gathering, or a voice lifted up against the abominable institution of slavery.

However, I went forward in my labors in Chatham street. The work of God immediately revived and went forward with great interest, numbers being converted at almost or quite every meeting. I continued to labor thus in Chatham street, and the church continued to flourish, and to extend its influence and its labors, in every direction, until the Tabernacle in Broadway was completed. The plan of the interior of that house was my own. I had observed the defects of churches in regard to sound; and was sure that I could give the plan of a church, in which I could easily speak to a much larger congregation than any house would hold, that I had ever seen. An architect was consulted, and I gave him my plan. But he objected to it, that it would not appear well, and feared that it would injure his reputation, to build a church with such an interior as that. I told him that if he would not build it on that plan, he was not the man to superintend its construction at all. It was finally built in accordance with my ideas; and it was a most commodious, and comfortable place to speak in.

In this connection I must relate the origin of the New York Evangelist. When I first went to the city of New York, and before I

1 - Independence Day of the United States

went there, the New York Observer, in the hands of Mr. Morse, had gone into the controversy originating in Mr. Nettleton's opposition to the revivals in central New York. The Observer had sustained Mr. Nettleton's course, and refused to publish anything on the other side. The writings of Mr. Nettleton and his friends, Mr. Morse would publish in the Observer; but if any reply was made, by any of the friends of those revivals, he would not publish it. In this state of things, our friends had no organ through which they could communicate with the public to correct misapprehensions.

Judge Jonas Platt, of the supreme court, was then living in New York, and was a friend of mine. His son and daughter had been hopefully converted in the revival at Utica. Considerable effort was made, by the friends of those revivals, to get a hearing on the question in debate, but all in vain. Judge Platt found one day, pasted on the inside of the cover of one of his old law books, a letter written by one of the pastors in New York, against Whitefield, at the time he was in this country. That letter of the New York pastor struck Judge Platt, as so strongly resembling the opposition made by Mr. Nettleton, that he sent it to the New York Observer, and wished it to be published as a literary curiosity, it having been written nearly a hundred years before. Mr. Morse refused to publish it, assigning as a reason, that the people would regard it as applying to the opposition of Mr. Nettleton.

At length, some of the friends of the revivals in New York, assembled and talked the matter over, of establishing a new paper that should deal fairly with those questions. They finally commenced the enterprise. I assisted them in getting out the first number, in which I invited ministers and laymen to consider, and discuss several questions in theology, and also questions relating to the best means of promoting revivals of religion.

The first editor of the paper was a Mr. Saxton, a young man who had formerly labored a good deal with Mr. Nettleton, but who strongly disapproved of the course he had been taking, in opposing what he then called "the western revivals." This young man continued in the editorial chair about a year, and discussed, with considerable ability, many of the questions that had been proposed for discussion. The paper changed editors two or three times, perhaps, in the course of as many years; and finally Rev. Joshua Leavitt was called, and accepted the editorial chair. He, as everybody knows, was an able editor. The paper soon went into extensive circulation, and proved itself a medium through which the friends of revivals, as they then existed, could communicate their thoughts to the public.

I have spoken of the building of the Tabernacle, and of the excitement in New York on the subject of slavery. When the Tabernacle was in the process of completion, its walls being up, and the roof on, a story was set in circulation that it was going to be "an amalgamation church," in which colored and white people were to be compelled to sit promiscuously, over the house. Such was the state of the public mind in New York, at that time, that this report created a great excitement, and somebody set the building on fire. The firemen were in such a state of mind that they refused to put it out, and left the interior and roof to be consumed. However, the gentlemen who had undertaken to build it, went forward and completed it.

As the excitement increased on the subject of slavery, Mr. Leavitt espoused the cause of the slave, and advocated it in the New York Evangelist. I watched the discussion with a good deal of attention and anxiety, and when I was about to leave, on the sea voyage to which I have referred, I admonished Mr. Leavitt to be careful and not go too fast, in the discussion of the anti-slavery question, lest he should destroy his paper. On my homeward passage my mind became exceedingly exercised on the question of revivals. I feared that they would decline throughout the country. I feared that the opposition that had been made to them, had grieved the Holy Spirit. My own health, it appeared to me, had nearly or quite broken down; and I knew of no other evangelist that would take the field, and aid pastors in revival work. This view of the subject distressed me so much that one day I found myself unable to rest. My soul was in an utter agony. I spent almost the entire day in prayer in my stateroom, or walking the deck in intense agony, in view of the state of things. In fact, I felt crushed with the burden that was on my soul. There was no one on board to whom I could open my mind, or say a word.

It was the spirit of prayer that was upon me; that which I had often before experienced in kind, but perhaps never before to such a degree, for so long a time. I besought the Lord to go on with his work, and to provide himself with such instrumentalities as were necessary. It was a long summer day, in the early part of July. After a day of unspeakable wrestling and agony in my soul, just at night, the subject cleared up to my mind. The Spirit led me to believe that all would come out right, and that God had yet a work for me to do; that I might be at rest; that the Lord would go forward with his work and give me strength to take any part in it that he desired. But I had not the least idea what the course of his providence would be.

On arriving at New York I found, as I have said, the mob excitement, on the subject of slavery, very intense. I remained but a day or two in New York, and went into the country, to the place where my family were spending the summer. On my return to New York, in the fall, Mr. Leavitt came to me and said, "Brother Finney, I have ruined the Evangelist. I have not been as prudent as you cautioned me to be, and I have gone so far ahead of public intelligence and feeling on the subject, that my subscription list is rapidly failing; and we shall not be able to continue its publication beyond the first of January, unless you can do something to bring the paper back to public favor again." I told him my health was such that I did not know what I could do; but I would make it a subject of prayer. He said if I could write a series of articles on revivals, he had no doubt it would restore the paper immediately to public favor. After considering it a day or two, I proposed to preach a course of lectures to my people, on revivals of religion, which he might report for his paper. He caught at this at once. Says he, "That is the very thing;" and in the next number of his paper he advertised the course of lectures. This had the effect he desired, and he soon after told me that the subscription list was very rapidly increasing; and, stretching out his long arms, he said, "I have as many new subscribers every day, as would fill my arms with papers, to supply them each a single number." He had told me before, that his subscription list had fallen off at the rate of sixty a day. But now he said it was increasing more rapidly than it ever had decreased.

I began the course of lectures immediately, and continued them through the winter, preaching one each week. Mr. Leavitt could not write shorthand, but would sit and take notes, abridging what he wrote, in such a way that he could understand it himself; and then the next day he would sit down and fill out his notes, and send them to the press. I did not see what he had reported, until I saw it published in his paper. I did not myself write the lectures, of course; they were wholly extemporaneous. I did not make up my mind, from time to time, what the next lecture should be, until I saw his report of my last. Then I could see what was the next question that would naturally need discussion. Brother Leavitt's reports were meager, as it respects the matter contained in the lectures. The lectures averaged, if I remember right, not less than an hour and three quarters, in their delivery. But all that he could catch and report, could be read, probably in thirty minutes.

These lectures were afterward published in a book, and called, "Finney's Lectures on Revivals." Twelve thousand copies of them were sold, as fast as they could be printed. And here, for the glory of Christ, I would say, that they have been reprinted in England and France; they were translated into Welsh; and on the continent were translated into French and, I believe, into German; and were very extensively circulated throughout Europe, and the colonies of Great Britain. They were, I presume, to be found wherever the English language is spoken. After they had been printed in Welsh, the Congregational ministers of the Principality of Wales, at one of their public meetings, appointed a committee to inform me of the great revival that had resulted from the translation of those lectures into the Welsh language. This they did by letter. One publisher in London informed me, that his father had published eighty thousand volumes of them. These revival lectures, meager as was the report of them, and feeble as they were in themselves, have been instrumental, as I have learned, in promoting revivals in England, and Scotland, and Wales, on the continent in various places, in Canada East and West, in Nova Scotia[2], and in some of the islands of the sea.

In England and Scotland, I have often been refreshed by meeting with ministers and laymen, in great numbers, that had been converted, directly or indirectly, through the instrumentality of those lectures. I recollect the last time that I was abroad, one evening, three very prominent ministers of the Gospel introduced themselves to me, after the sermon, and said that when they were in college they got hold of my revival lectures, which had resulted in their becoming ministers. I found persons in England, in all the different denominations, who had not only read those revival lectures, but had been greatly blessed in reading them. When they were first published in the New York Evangelist, the reading of them resulted in revivals of religion, in multitudes of places throughout this country.

But this was not of man's wisdom. Let the reader remember that long day of agony and prayer at sea, that God would do something

---

2 - Nova Scotia – one of the Atlantic provinces in Canada

to forward the work of revivals, and enable me, if he desired to do it, to take such a course as to help forward the work. I felt certain then that my prayers would be answered; and I have regarded all that I have since been able to accomplish, as, in a very important sense, an answer to the prayers of that day. The spirit of prayer came upon me as a sovereign grace, bestowed upon me without the least merit, and in despite of all my sinfulness. He pressed my soul in prayer, until I was enabled to prevail; and through infinite riches of grace in Christ Jesus, I have been many years witnessing the wonderful results of that day of wrestling with God. In answer to that day's agony, he has continued to give me the spirit of prayer.

Soon after I returned to New York, I commenced my labors in the Tabernacle. The Spirit of the Lord was poured out upon us, and we had a precious revival, as long as I continued to be pastor of that church. While in New York, I had many applications from young men, to take them as students in theology. I, however, had too much on my hands, to undertake such a work. But the brethren who built the Tabernacle had this in view; and prepared a room under the choir, which we expected to use for prayer meetings, but more especially for a theological lecture room. The number of applications had been so large, that I had made up my mind to deliver a course of theological lectures in that room each year, and let such students as chose, attend them gratuitously.

But about this time, and before I had opened my lectures in New York, the breaking up at Lane Seminary took place, on account of the prohibition by the trustees, of the discussion of the question of slavery among the students. When this occurred, Mr. Arthur Tappan proposed to me, that if I would go to some point in Ohio, and take rooms where I could gather those young men, and give them my views in theology, and prepare them for the work of preaching throughout the West, he would be at the entire expense of the undertaking. He was very earnest in this proposal. But I did not know how to leave New York; and I did not see how I could accomplish the wishes of Mr. Tappan, although I strongly sympathized with him in regard to helping those young men. They were most of them converts in those great revivals, in which I had taken more or less part.

While this subject was under consideration, I think, in January, 1835, Rev. John Jay Shipherd, of Oberlin, and Rev. Asa Mahan, of

Cincinnati, arrived in New York, to persuade me to go to Oberlin, as professor of theology. Mr. Mahan had been one of the trustees of Lane Seminary — the only one, I think, that had resisted the prohibition of free discussion. Mr. Shipherd had founded a colony, and organized a school at Oberlin, about a year before this time, and had obtained a charter broad enough for a university. Mr. Mahan had never been in Oberlin. The trees had been removed from the college square, some dwelling-houses and one college building had been erected, and about a hundred pupils had been gathered, in the preparatory or academic department of the institution.

The proposal they laid before me was, to come on, and take those students that had left Lane Seminary, and teach them theology. These students had themselves proposed to go to Oberlin, in case I would accept the call. This proposal met the views of Arthur and Lewis Tappan, and many of the friends of the slave, who sympathized with Mr. Tappan, in his wish to have those young men instructed, and brought into the ministry. We had several consultations on the subject. The brethren in New York who were interested in the question, offered, if I would go and spend half of each year in Oberlin, to endow the institution, so far as the professorships were concerned, and to do it immediately.

I had understood that the trustees of Lane Seminary had acted "over the heads" of the faculty; and, in the absence of several of them, had passed the obnoxious resolution that had caused the students to leave. I said, therefore, to Mr. Shipherd, that I would not go at any rate, unless two points were conceded by the trustees. One was, that they should never interfere with the internal regulation of the school, but should leave that entirely to the discretion of the faculty. The other was, that we should be allowed to receive colored people on the same conditions that we did white people; that there should be no discrimination made on account of color.

When these conditions were forwarded to Oberlin, the trustees were called together, and after a great struggle to overcome their own prejudices, and the prejudices of the community, they passed resolutions complying with the conditions proposed. This difficulty being removed, the friends in New York were called together, to see what they could do about endowing the institution. In the course of an hour or two, they had a subscription filled for the endowment of eight professorships; as many, it was supposed, as the institution would need for several years. But after this endowment fund was subscribed, I felt a great difficulty in giving up that admirable place for preaching the Gospel, where such crowds were gathered within the sound of my voice. I felt, too, assured that in this new enterprise, we should have great opposition from many sources. I therefore told Arthur Tappan that my mind did not feel at rest upon the subject; that we should meet with great opposition because of our anti-slavery principles; and that we could expect to get but very scanty funds to put up our buildings, and to procure all the requisite apparatus of a college; that therefore I did not see my way clear, after all, to commit myself, unless something could be done that should guarantee us the funds that were indispensable.

Arthur Tappan's heart was as large as all New York, and I might say, as large as the world. When I laid the case thus before him, he said, "Brother Finney, my own income averages about a hundred thousand dollars a year. Now if you will go to Oberlin, take hold of that work, and go on, and see that the buildings are put up, and a library and everything provided, I will pledge you my entire income, except what I need to provide for my family, till you are beyond pecuniary want." Having perfect confidence in brother Tappan I said, "That will do. Thus far the difficulties are out of the way."

But still there was a great difficulty in leaving my church in New York. I had never thought of having my labors at Oberlin interfere with my revival labors and preaching. It was therefore agreed between myself and the church, that I should spend my winters in New York, and my summers at Oberlin; and that the church would be at the expense of my going and coming.

When this was arranged, I took my family, and arrived in Oberlin at the beginning of summer, 1835.

CHAPTER 24

EARLY LABORS IN OBERLIN

*The opposers of Oberlin have been unfounded,
and God has stood by you, and sustained you,
through all this opposition,
so that you have hardly felt it.*

The students from Lane Seminary came to Oberlin, and the trustees put up "barracks," in which they were lodged, and other students thronged to us from every direction. After I was engaged to come, the brethren at Oberlin wrote, requesting me to bring a large tent, to hold meetings in; as there was no room in the place, large enough to accommodate the people. I made this request known to some of my brethren, who told me to go and get a tent made, and they would furnish the money. I went and engaged the tent, and they handed me the money to pay for it. It was a circular tent, a hundred feet in diameter, furnished with all the equipment for putting it up. At the top of the center pole which supported the tent, was a streamer, upon which was written in very large characters, "Holiness to the Lord." This tent was of great service to us. When the weather would permit, we spread it upon the square every Sunday, and held public services in it; and several of our earliest commencements were held in it. It was used, to some extent also, for holding protracted meetings in the region round about, where there were no churches large enough to meet the necessities.

I have spoken of the promise of Arthur Tappan to supply us with funds, to the extent of his whole income, till we were beyond pecuniary want. Upon this understanding with him, I entered upon the work. But it was farther understood between us, that his pledge should not be known to the trustees, lest they should fail to make due efforts, as he desired, not merely to collect funds, but to make the wants and objects of the institution known throughout the land. In accordance with this understanding, the work here was pushed as fast as it could well be, considering that we were in the heart of a great forest, and in a location, at that time in many respects undesirable.

We had only fairly entered upon the work of putting up our buildings, and had arranged to need a large amount of money, when the great commercial crash prostrated Mr. Tappan, and nearly all the men who had subscribed for the fund for the support of the faculty. The commercial crash went over the country, and prostrated the great mass of wealthy men. It left us, not only without funds for the support of the faculty, but thirty thousand dollars in debt; without any prospect, that we could see, of obtaining funds from the friends of the college in this country. Mr. Tappan wrote me at this time, acknowledging expressly the promise he had made me, and expressing the deepest regret that he was prostrated, and wholly unable to fulfill his pledge. Our necessities were then great, and to human view it would seem that the college must be a failure. The great mass of the people of Ohio were utterly opposed to our enterprise, because of its abolition character. The towns around us were hostile to our movement, and in some places threats were made to come and tear down our buildings. A democratic legislature was, in the meantime, endeavoring to get some hold of us, that would enable them to abrogate our charter. In this state of things there was, of course, a great crying to God among the people here.

In the meantime, my revival lectures had been very extensively circulated in England; and we were aware that the British public would strongly sympathize with us, if they knew our objects, our prospects, and our condition. We therefore sent an agency to England, composed of Rev. John Keep and Mr. William Dawes, having obtained for them letters of recommendation, and expressions of confidence in our enterprise, from some of the leading anti-slavery men of the country. They went to England, and laid our objects and our wants before the

British public. They generously responded, and gave us six thousand pounds sterling. This very nearly canceled our indebtedness.

Our friends, scattered throughout the northern states, who were abolitionists and friends of revivals, generously aided us to the extent of their ability. But we had to struggle with poverty and many trials, for a course of years. Sometimes we did not know, from day to day, how we were to be provided for. But with the blessing of God we helped ourselves, as best we could.

At one time, I saw no means of providing for my family through the winter. Thanksgiving day came, and found us so poor that I had been obliged to sell my traveling trunk, which I had used in my evangelistic labors, to supply the place of a cow which I had lost. I rose on the morning of Thanksgiving[1], and spread our necessities before the Lord. I finally concluded by saying that, if help did not come, I should assume that it was best that it should not; and would be entirely satisfied with any course that the Lord would see it wise to take. I went and preached, and enjoyed my own preaching as well, I think, as I ever did. I had a blessed day to my own soul; and I could see that the people enjoyed it exceedingly.

After the meeting, I was detained a little while in conversation with some brethren, and my wife returned home. When I reached the gate, she was standing in the open door, with a letter in her hand. As I approached she smilingly said, "The answer has come, my dear;" and handed me the letter containing a check from Mr. Josiah Chapin of Providence, for two hundred dollars. He had been here the previous summer, with his wife. I had said nothing about my wants at all, as I never was in the habit of mentioning them to anybody. But in the letter containing the check, he said he had learned that the endowment fund had failed, and that I was in want of help. He intimated that I might expect more, from time to time. He continued to send me six hundred dollars a year, for several years; and on this I managed to live.

I should have said that, agreeably to my arrangement in New York, I spent my summers at Oberlin, and my winters at New York, for two or three years. We had a blessed reviving, whenever I returned to preach there. We also had a revival here continually. Very few students came here then without being converted. But my health soon became such that I found, I must relinquish one of these

---

1- *Thanksgiving Day is a national holiday celebrated in the United States. It was originally celebrated as a day of giving thanks for the blessing of the harvest and of the preceding year.*

fields of labor. But the interests connected with the college, seemed to forbid utterly that I should leave it. I therefore took a dismission from my church in New York, and the winter months which I was to have spent in New York, I spent in laboring, in various places, to promote revivals of religion.

The lectures on revivals of religion were preached while I was still pastor of the Presbyterian church in Chatham street chapel. The two following winters, I gave lectures to Christians in the Broadway Tabernacle which were also reported by Mr. Leavitt, and published in the New York Evangelist. These also have been printed in a volume in this country and in Europe. Those sermons to Christians were very much the result of a searching that was going on in my own mind. I mean that the Spirit of God was showing me many things, in regard to the question of sanctification, that led me to preach those sermons to Christians. Many Christians regarded those lectures as rather an exhibition of the Law, than of the Gospel. But I did not, and do not, so regard them. For me the Law and Gospel have but one rule of life; and every violation of the spirit of the Law, is also a violation of the spirit of the Gospel. I am persuaded that the higher forms of Christian experience are attained only as a result of a terribly searching application of God's Law to the human conscience and heart. The result of my labors up to that time had shown me more clearly than I had known before, the great weakness of Christians, and that the older members of the church, as a general thing, were making very little progress in grace. I found that they would fall back from a revival state, even sooner than young converts. It had been so in the revival in which I myself was converted. I saw clearly that this was owing to their early teaching; that is, to the views which they had been led to entertain, when they were young converts.

I was also led into a state of great dissatisfaction with my own want of stability in faith and love. To be candid, and tell the truth, I must say, to the praise of God's grace, he did not suffer me to backslide, to anything like the same extent, to which manifestly many Christians did backslide. But *I often felt myself weak in the presence of temptation; and needed frequently to hold days of fasting and prayer, and to spend much time in overhauling my own religious life, in order to retain that communion with God, and that hold upon the divine strength, that would enable me efficiently to labor for the promotion of revivals of religion.*

In looking at the state of the Christian church, as it had been revealed to me in my revival labors I was led earnestly to inquire whether there was not something higher and more enduring than the Christian church was aware of; whether there were not promises, and means provided in the Gospel, for the establishment of Christians in altogether a higher form of Christian life. I had known somewhat of the view of sanctification entertained by our Methodist brethren. But as their idea of sanctification seemed to me to relate almost altogether to states of the sensibility, I could not receive their teaching. However, I gave myself earnestly to search the Scriptures, and to read whatever came to hand upon the subject, until my mind was satisfied that an altogether higher and more stable form of Christian life was attainable, and was the privilege of all Christians.

This led me to preach in the Broadway Tabernacle, two sermons on Christian perfection. Those sermons are now included in the volume of lectures preached to Christians. In those sermons I defined what Christian perfection is, and endeavored to show that it is attainable in this life, and the sense in which it is attainable. But about this time, the question of Christian perfection, in the antinomian sense of the term, came to be agitated a good deal at New Haven, at Albany, and somewhat in New York City. I examined these views, as published in the periodical entitled "The Perfectionist." But I could not accept them. Yet I was satisfied that the doctrine of sanctification in this life, and entire sanctification, in the sense that it was the privilege of Christians to live without known sin, was a doctrine taught in the Bible, and that abundant means were provided for the securing of that attainment.

The last winter that I spent in New York, the Lord was pleased to visit my soul with a great refreshing After a season of great searching of heart, he brought me, as he has often done, into a large place, and gave me much of that divine sweetness in my soul, of which President Edwards speaks as attained in his own experience. That winter I had a thorough breaking up; so much so that sometimes, for a considerable period, I could not refrain from loud weeping in view of my own sins, and of the love of God in Christ. Such seasons were frequent that winter, and resulted in the great renewal of my spiritual strength, and enlargement of my views in regard to the privileges of Christians, and the abundance of the grace of God.

It is well known that my views on the question of sanctification have been the subject of a good deal of criticism. To be faithful to history, I must say some things that I would otherwise pass by in silence. Oberlin College was established by Mr. Shipherd, very much against the feelings and wishes of the men most concerned in building up Western Reserve College, at Hudson. Mr. Shipherd once informed me that the principal financial agent of that college, asserted to him that he would do all he could to put this college down. As soon as they heard, at Hudson, that I had received a call to Oberlin, as professor of theology, the trustees elected me as professor of "pastoral theology and sacred eloquence," at Western Reserve College; so that I held the two invitations at the same time. I did not, in writing, commit myself to either, but came on to survey the ground, and then decide upon the path of duty.

That spring, the general assembly of the Presbyterian church held their meeting at Pittsburgh. When I arrived at Cleveland, I was informed that two of the professors from Hudson, had been waiting at Cleveland for my arrival, designing to have me go first, at any rate, to Hudson. But I had been delayed on Lake Erie by adverse winds; and the brethren who had been waiting for me at Cleveland, had gone to be at the opening of the general assembly; and had left word with a brother, to see me immediately on my arrival, and by all means to get me to go to Hudson. But in Cleveland I found a letter awaiting me, from Arthur Tappan, of New York. He had in some way become acquainted with the fact, that strong efforts were making to induce me to go to Hudson, rather than to Oberlin.

The college at Hudson, at that time, had its buildings and apparatus, reputation and influence, and was already an established college. Oberlin had nothing. It had no permanent buildings, and was composed of a little colony settled in the woods; and just beginning to put up their own houses, and clear away the immense forest, and make a place for a college. It had, to be sure, its charter, and perhaps a hundred students on the ground; but everything was still to be done. This letter of brother Tappan was written to put me on my guard against supposing that I could be instrumental in securing, at Hudson, what we desired to secure at Oberlin.

I left my family at Cleveland, hired a horse and buggy, and came out to Oberlin, without going to Hudson. I thought at least that I would see Oberlin first. When I arrived at Elyria, I found some old acquaintances there, whom I had known in central New York. They informed me that the trustees of Western Reserve College thought that, if they could secure my presence at Hudson, it would, at least in a great measure, defeat Oberlin; and that at Hudson there was an old school influence, of sufficient power to compel me to fall in with their views and course of action. This was in precise accordance with the information which I had received from Mr. Tappan.

I came to Oberlin, and saw that there was nothing to prevent the building up of a college, on the principles that seemed to me, not only to lie at the foundation of all success in establishing a college here at the West; but on principles of reform, such as I knew were dear to the hearts of those who had undertaken the support and building up of Oberlin College. The brethren that were here on the ground, were heartily in favor of building up a school on radical principles of reform. I therefore wrote to the trustees of Hudson, declining to accept their invitation, and took up my abode at Oberlin. I had nothing ill to say of Hudson, and I knew no ill of it.

After a year or two, the cry of antinomian[2] perfectionism was heard, and this charge brought against us. Letters were written, and ecclesiastical bodies were visited, and much pains taken to represent our views here, as entirely heretical. Such representations were made to ecclesiastical bodies, throughout the length and breadth of the land, as to lead many of them to pass resolutions, warning the churches against the influence of Oberlin theology. There seemed to be a general union of ministerial influence against us. We understood very well here, what had set this on foot, and by what means all this excitement was raised. But we said nothing. We had no controversy with those Brethren that, we were aware, were taking pains to raise such a powerful public sentiment against us. I may not enter into particulars; but suffice it to say, that the weapons that were thus formed against us, reacted most disastrously upon those who used them, until at length there was a change of nearly all the members of the board of trustees and the faculty, at Hudson, and the general management of the college fell into other hands.

I scarcely ever heard anything said at Oberlin, at that time, against Hudson, or at any time. We kept about our own business, and felt that in respect to opposition from that quarter, our strength was to sit still;

---

2 - Antinomianism − (from Greek "against the law") is the belief that there are no moral laws God expects Christians to obey.

and we were not mistaken. We felt confident that it was not God's plan to suffer such opposition to prevail. I wish to be distinctly understood, that I am not at all aware that any of the present leaders and managers of that college, have sympathized with what was at that time done, or that they so much as know the course that was then taken.

The ministers, far and near, carried their opposition to a great extreme. At that time a convention was called to meet at Cleveland, to consider the subject of Western education, and the support of Western colleges. The call had been so worded that we went out from Oberlin, expecting to take part in the proceedings of the convention. When we arrived there, we found Dr. Beecher on the ground; and soon saw that a course of proceedings was on foot, to shut out Oberlin brethren, and those that sympathized with Oberlin, from the convention. I was therefore not allowed a seat in the convention as a member; yet I attended several of its sessions. I recollect hearing it distinctly said, by one of the ministers from the neighborhood, who was there, that he regarded Oberlin doctrines and influence as worse than those of Roman Catholicism.

That speech was a representative one, and seemed to be about the view that was entertained by that body. I do not mean by all of them, by any means. Some who had been educated in theology at Oberlin, were so related to the churches and the convention, that they were admitted to seats, having come there from different parts of the country. These were very outspoken upon the principles and practices of Oberlin, so far as they were called in question. The object of the convention evidently was, to hedge in Oberlin on every side, and crush us, by a public sentiment that would refuse us all support. But let me be distinctly understood to say, that I do not in the least degree blame the members of that convention, or but very few of them; for I knew that they had been misled, and were acting under an entire misapprehension of the facts. Dr. Lyman Beecher was the leading spirit in that convention. The policy that we pursued was to let opposition alone. We kept about our own business, and always had as many students as we knew what to do with. Our hands were always full of labor, and we were always greatly encouraged in our efforts.

A few years after the meeting of this convention, one of the leading ministers who was there, came and spent a day or two at our house. He said to me among other things: "Brother Finney, Oberlin is to us a great wonder." Said he, "I have, for many years been connected with a college as one of its professors. College life and principles, and the conditions upon which colleges are built up, are very familiar to me." "We have always thought," said he, "that colleges could not exist unless they were patronized by the ministry. We knew that young men who were about to go to college, would generally consult their pastors, in regard to what colleges they should select, and be guided by their judgment." "Now," said he, "the ministers almost universally arrayed themselves against Oberlin. They were deceived by the cry of antinomian perfectionism, and in respect to your views of reform; and ecclesiastical bodies united, far and near, Congregational, and Presbyterian, and of all denominations. They warned their churches against you, they discouraged young men universally from coming to Oberlin, and still the Lord has built you up. You have been supported with funds, better than almost any college in the West; you have had by far more students, and the blessing of God has been upon you, so that your success has been wonderful." "Now," said he, "this is a perfect anomaly in the history of colleges. The opposers of Oberlin have been unfounded, and God has stood by you, and sustained you, through all this opposition, so that you have hardly felt it."

It is difficult now for people to realize the opposition that we met with, when we first established this college. As an illustration of it, and as a representative case, I will relate a laughable fact that occurred about the time of which I am speaking. I had occasion to go to Akron, to preach on the Sunday. I went with a horse and buggy. On my way, beyond the village of Medina, I observed, in the road before me, a woman walking with a little bundle in her hand. As I drew near her, I observed she was an elderly woman, nicely dressed, but walking, as I thought, with some difficulty, on account of her age. As I came up to her I reined up my horse, and asked her, how far she was going on that road. She told me; and I then asked if she would accept a seat in my buggy, and ride. "O," she replied, "I should be very thankful for a ride, for I find I have undertaken too long a walk." I helped her into my buggy, and drove on. I found her a very intelligent lady, and very free and homelike in her conversation.

After riding for some distance, she said, "May I ask to whom I am indebted for this ride?" I told her who I was. She then inquired from whence I came. I told her I was from Oberlin. This announcement startled her. She made a motion as if she would sit as far from me as she could; and turning and looking earnestly at me, she said, "From Oberlin! why," said she, "our minister said he would just as soon send a son to state prison as to Oberlin!" Of course I smiled and soothed the old lady's fears, if she had any; and made her understand she was in no danger from me. I relate this simply as an illustration of the spirit that prevailed very extensively when this college was first established. Misrepresentations and misapprehensions abounded on every side; and these misapprehensions extended into almost every corner of the United States.

However, there was a great number of laymen, and no inconsiderable number of ministers, on the whole, in different parts of the country, who had no confidence in this opposition; who sympathized with our aims, our views, our efforts, and who stood firmly by us through thick and thin; and gave their money and their influence freely to help us forward. I have spoken of Mr. Chapin, of Providence, as having for several years, sent me six hundred dollars a year, on which to support my family. When he had done it as long as he thought it his duty, which he did, indeed, until financial difficulties rendered it inconvenient for him longer to do so; Mr. Willard Sears of Boston took his place, and for several years suffered me to draw on him for the same amount, annually, that Mr. Chapin had paid. In the meantime, efforts were constantly made to sustain the other members of the faculty; and by the grace of God we rode out the gale. After a few years the panic, in a measure, subsided.

President Mahan, Professor Cowles, Professor Morgan, and myself, published on the subject of sanctification. We established a periodical, "The Oberlin Evangelist," and afterwards, "The Oberlin Quarterly," in which we disabused the public, in a great measure, in regard to what our real views were. In 1846, I published two volumes on systematic theology; and in this work I discussed the subject of entire sanctification, more at large. After this work was published, it was reviewed by a committee of the Presbytery of Troy, New York. Then Dr. Hodge of Princeton, published, in the Biblical Repertory, a lengthy criticism upon my theology. This was from the old school standpoint. Then Dr. Duffield, of the New School Presbyterian church, living at Detroit, reviewed me, professedly from the new school standpoint, though his review was far enough from consistent newschoolism. To these different reviews, as they appeared, I published replies; and for many years past, so far as I am aware, no disposition has been shown to challenge our views.

I have thus far narrated the principal facts connected with the establishment and struggles of the school at Oberlin, so far as I have been concerned with them. And being the professor of theology, the theological opposition was directed, of course, principally toward myself; which has led me, of necessity, to speak more freely of my relations to it all, than I otherwise should have done. But let me not be misunderstood. I am not contending that the brethren who thus opposed, were wicked in their opposition. No doubt the great mass of them were really misled, and acted according to their views of right, as they then understood it.

I must say, for the honor of the grace of God, that none of the opposition that we met with, ruffled our spirits here, or disturbed us, in such a sense as to provoke us into a spirit of controversy or ill feeling. We were well aware of the pains that had been taken to lead to these misapprehensions, and could easily understand how it was, that we were opposed in the spirit and manner in which we were assailed. During these years of smoke and dust, of misapprehension and opposition from without, the Lord was blessing us richly within. We not only prospered in our own souls here, as a church, but we had a continuous revival, or were, in what might properly be regarded as a revival state. Our students were converted by scores; and the Lord overshadowed us continually with the cloud of his mercy. Gales of divine influence swept over us from year to year, producing abundantly the fruits of the Spirit "love, joy, peace, long-suffering, gentleness, goodness, faith, meekness, temperance."

I have always attributed our success in this good work entirely to the grace of God. It was no wisdom or goodness of our own that has achieved this success. Nothing but continued divine influence, pervading the community, sustained us under our trials, and kept us in an attitude of mind in which we could be efficient in the work we had undertaken. *We have always felt that if the Lord withheld his Spirit, no outward circumstances could make us truly prosperous.*

We have had trials among ourselves. Frequent subjects of public discussion have come up; and we have sometimes spent days, and even weeks, in discussing great questions of duty and expediency, on which we have not thought alike. But these questions have none of them permanently divided us. Our principle has been to accord to each other the right of private judgment. We have generally come to a substantial agreement on subjects upon which we had differed; and when we have found ourselves unable to see alike, the minority have submitted themselves to the judgment of the majority, and the idea of rending the church to pieces, because in some things we could not see alike, has never been entertained by us. We have to a very great extent preserved "the unity of the Spirit in the bond of peace;" and perhaps no community has existed for such a length of time, and passed through such trials and changes as we have, that has on the whole maintained a greater spirit of harmony, Christian forbearance, and brotherly love.

When the question of entire sanctification first came up here for public discussion, and when the subject first attracted the general attention of the church, we were in the midst of a powerful revival. When the revival was going on, one day, President Mahan had been preaching a searching discourse. I observed in the course of his preaching that he had left one point untouched, that appeared to me of great importance in that connection. He would often ask me, when he closed his sermon, if I had any remarks to make, and thus he did on this occasion. I arose and pressed the point that he had omitted. It was the distinction between desire and will. From the course of thought he had presented, and from the attitude in which I saw that the congregation was at the time, I saw, or thought I saw, that the pressing of that distinction, just at that point, upon the people, would throw much light upon the question whether they were really Christians or not, whether they were really consecrated persons, or whether they merely had desires without being in fact willing to obey God.

When this distinction was made clear, just in that connection, I recollect the Holy Spirit fell upon the congregation in a most remarkable manner. A large number of persons dropped down their heads, and some groaned so that they could be heard throughout the house. It cut up the false hopes of deceived professors on every side. Several arose on the spot, and said that they had been deceived, and that they could see wherein; and this was carried to such an extent as greatly astonished me, and indeed produced a general feeling of astonishment, I think, in the congregation.

The work went on with power; and old professors obtained new hopes, or were reconverted, in such numbers, that a very great and important change came over the whole community. President Mahan had been greatly blessed, among others, with some of our professors. He came manifestly into an entirely new form of Christian experience, at that time.

In a meeting a few days after this, one of our theological students arose, and put the inquiry, whether the Gospel did not provide for Christians, all the conditions of an established faith, and hope, and love; whether there was not something better and higher than Christians had generally experienced; in short, whether sanctification was not attainable in this life; that is, sanctification in such a sense that Christians could have unbroken peace, and not come into condemnation, or have the feeling of condemnation or a consciousness of sin. Brother Mahan immediately answered, "Yes." What occurred at this meeting, brought the question of sanctification prominently before us, as a practical question. We had no theories on the subject, no philosophy to maintain, but simply took it up as a Bible question. In this form it existed among us, as an experimental truth, which we did not attempt to reduce to a theological formula; nor did we attempt to explain its philosophy, until years afterwards. But the discussion of this question was a great blessing to us, and to a great number of our students, who are now scattered in various parts of the country, or have gone abroad as missionaries to different parts of the world.

CHAPTER 25

LABORS IN BOSTON
AND PROVIDENCE

*The Spirit of the Lord was immediately poured out,
and there was a general awakening
among the dry bones.*

Before I return to my revival record, in order to give some idea of the relation of things, I must dwell a little more upon the progress of the anti-slavery, or abolition movement, not only at Oberlin, but elsewhere, as connected with my own labors. I have spoken of the state of public feeling, on this subject, all around us, and have mentioned that even the legislature of the state, at that time democratic, endeavored to find some pretext for repealing our charter, because of our anti-slavery sentiments and action. It was at first reported on every side of us, that we intended to encourage marriage between colored and white students, and even to compel them to intermarry; and that our object was to introduce a universal system of miscegenation. A little fact will illustrate the feeling that existed among many people in the neighborhood. I had occasion to ride out a few miles, soon after we came, and called upon a farmer on some errand. He looked very sullen and suspicious, when he found who I was, and from whence I came; and intimated to me that he did not want to have anything to do with the people of Oberlin; that our object was to introduce amalgamation of the races, and compel the white and colored students to intermarry; that we also intended to bring about the union of church and state, and that our ideas and projects were altogether revolutionary and abominable. He was quite in earnest about this. But the thing was so ridiculous, that I knew that if I attempted a serious answer, I should laugh him in the face.

We had reason, at an early day, for apprehension that a mob from a neighboring town would come and destroy our buildings. But we had not been here long, before circumstances occurred that created a reaction in the public mind. This place became one of the points on "the underground railroad," as it has since been called, where escaped slaves, on their way to Canada, would take refuge for a day or two, until the way was open for them to proceed. Several cases occurred in which these fugitives were pursued by slave holders; and a hue and cry was raised, not only in this neighborhood, but in the neighboring towns, by their attempting to carry the slaves back into slavery. Slave catchers found no practical sympathy among the people; and scenes like these soon aroused public feeling in the towns around about, and began to produce a reaction. It set the farmers and people around us, to study more particularly into our aims and views, and our school soon became known and appreciated; and it has resulted in a state of universal confidence and good feeling, between Oberlin and the surrounding region.

In the meantime, the excitement on the subject of slavery was greatly agitating the Eastern cities, as well as the West and the South. Our friend, Mr. Willard Sears, of Boston, was braving a tempest of opposition there. And in order to open the way for a free discussion on that subject in Boston, and for the establishment of religious worship, where a pulpit should be open to the free discussion of all great questions of reform, he had purchased the Marlborough hotel on Washington street, and had connected with it a large chapel for public worship, and for reform meetings, that could not find an entrance anywhere else. This he had done at great expense. In 1842, I was strongly urged to go and occupy the Marlborough chapel, and preach for a few months. I went and began my labors, and preached with all my might for two months. The Spirit of the Lord was immediately poured out, and there was a general awakening among the dry bones. I was visited at my room almost constantly, during every day of the week, by inquirers from all parts of the city, and many were obtaining hopes from day to day.

At the same time, Mr. Josiah Chapin and many others, were insisting very strongly upon my coming and holding meetings in

Providence. I felt very much indebted to Mr. Chapin for what he had done for Oberlin, and for myself personally. It was a great trial for me to leave Boston, at this time. This was the time of the great revival in Boston. It prevailed wonderfully, especially among the Baptists, and more or less throughout the city. The Baptist ministers took hold with brother Knapp, and many Congregational brethren were greatly blessed, and the work was very extensive.

In the meantime, I commenced my labors in Providence. The work began almost immediately, and the interest visibly increased from day to day. There were many striking cases of conversion; among them was an elderly gentleman whose name I do not recollect. His father had been a Judge of the supreme court in Massachusetts, if I mistake not, many years before. This old gentleman lived not far from the church where I was holding my meetings, in High street. After the work had gone on for some time, I observed a very venerable looking gentleman come into meeting, who paid very strict attention to the preaching. My friend, Mr. Chapin, immediately noticed him; and informed me who he was, and what his religious views were. He said he had never been in the habit of attending religious meetings; and he expressed a very great interest in the man, and in the fact that he had been drawn out to meeting. I observed that he continued, night after night, to come; and could easily perceive, as I thought, that his mind was very much agitated, and deeply interested on the question of religion.

One evening as I came to the close of my sermon, this venerable looking man rose up, and asked if he might address a few words to the people. I replied in the affirmative. He then spoke in substance as follows: "My friends and neighbors, you are probably surprised to see me attend these meetings. You have known my skeptical views, and that I have not been in the habit of attending religious meetings, for a long time. But hearing of the state of things in this congregation, I came in here; and I wish to have my friends and neighbors know that I believe that the preaching we are hearing, from night to night, is the Gospel. I have altered my mind," said he. "I believe this is the truth, and the true way of salvation. I say this," he added, "that you may understand my real motive for coming here; that it is not to criticize and find fault, but to attend to the great question of salvation, and to encourage others to attend to it." He said this with much emotion, and sat down.

There was a very large Sunday school room in the basement of the church. The number of inquirers had become too large, and the congregation too much crowded, to call the inquirers forward, as I had done in some places; and I therefore requested them to go down, after the blessing was pronounced, to the lecture room below. The room was nearly as large as the whole audience room of the church, and would seat nearly as many, aside from the gallery. The work increased, and spread in every part of the city, until the number of inquirers became so great, together with the young converts, who were always ready to go below with them, as nearly or quite to fill that large room. From night to night, after preaching, that room would be filled with rejoicing young converts, and trembling, inquiring sinners. This state of things continued for two months. I was then, as I thought, completely tired out; having labored incessantly for four months, two in Boston, and two in Providence. Besides, the time of year had come, or nearly come, for opening of our spring term in Oberlin. I therefore took my leave of Providence, and started for home.

CHAPTER 26

THE REVIVAL IN ROCHESTER, IN 1842

...to pray for a new heart,
while not giving yourself up to God,
is to tempt God;
to pray for forgiveness
without truly repenting, is to insult God,
and to pray in unbelief,
is to charge God with lying.

After resting a day or two in Boston, I left for home. Being very weary with labor and travel, I called on a friend at Rochester, to take a day's rest before proceeding farther. As soon as it was known that I was in Rochester, Judge G. called on me, and with much earnestness, requested me to stop and preach. Some of the ministers also, insisted upon my stopping, and preaching for them. I informed them that I was worn out, and the time had come for me to be at home. However, they were very urgent, and especially one of the ministers, whose wife was one of my spiritual daughters, the Sarah B., of whom I have spoken, as having been converted in Western. I finally consented to stop, and preach a sermon or two, and did so. But this brought upon me a more importunate invitation, to remain and hold a series of meetings. I decided to remain and, though wearied, went on with the work.

Mr. George S. Boardman was pastor of what was then called, the Bethel, or Washington street church; and Mr. Shaw, of the Second or Brick church. Mr. Shaw was very anxious to unite with Mr. Boardman, and have the meetings at their churches alternately. Mr. Boardman was indisposed to take this course, saying that his congregation was weak, and needed the concentration of my labors at that point. I regretted this; but still I could not overrule it, and went on with my labors at the Bethel, or Washington street church. Soon after, Dr. Shaw secured the labors of Rev. Jedediah Burchard in his church, and undertook a protracted effort there.

In the meantime, Judge G. had united with other members of the bar, in a written request to me, to preach a course of sermons to lawyers, adapted to their ways of thinking. Judge G. was then one of the judges of the court of appeals in the state, and held a very high place in the estimation of the whole profession. I consented to deliver the course of lectures. I was aware of the half skeptical state of mind in which those members of the bar were, many of them at least, who were still unconverted. There was still left in the city, a goodly number of pious lawyers, who had been converted in the revival of 1830 and 1831.

I began my course of lectures to lawyers, by asking this question: "Do we know anything?" and followed up the inquiry by lecturing, evening after evening. My congregation became very select. Brother Burchard's meetings opened an interesting place for one class of the community, and made more room for the lawyers, and those especially attracted by my course of lectures, in the house where I was preaching. It was completely filled, every night. As I proceeded in my lectures, from night to night, I observed the interest constantly deepening. As Judge G.'s wife was a particular friend of mine, I had occasion to see him not unfrequently, and was very sure that the word was getting a strong hold of him. He remarked to me after I had delivered several lectures, "Mr. Finney, you have cleared the ground to my satisfaction, thus far; but when you come to the question of the endless punishment of the wicked, you will slip up; you will fail to convince us on that question." I replied, "Wait and see, Judge." This hint made me the more careful, when I came to that point, to discuss it with all thoroughness. The next day I met him, and he volunteered the remark at once, "Mr. Finney, I am convinced. Your dealing with that subject was a success; nothing can be said against it." The manner in which he said this, indicated that the subject had not merely convinced his intellect, but had deeply impressed him.

I was going on from night to night, but had not thought my somewhat new and select audience yet prepared for me to call for any decision, on the part of inquirers. But I had arrived at a point where I thought it was time to draw the net ashore. I had been carefully laying it around the whole mass of lawyers, and hedging them in, as I supposed, by a train of reasoning that they could not resist. I was aware that lawyers are accustomed to listen to argument, to feel the weight of a logically presented truth; and had no doubt that the great majority of them were thoroughly convinced, as far as I had gone; consequently, I had prepared a discourse, which I intended should bring them to the point, and if it appeared to take effect, I intended to call on them to commit themselves.

Judge G., at the time I was there before, when his wife was converted, had opposed the anxious seat. I expected he would do so again, as I knew he had strongly committed himself, in what he had said, against the use of the anxious seat. When I came to preach the sermon of which I have spoken, I observed that Judge G. was not in the seat he had usually occupied; and on looking around I could not see him anywhere among the members of the bar or the judges. I felt concerned about this, for I had prepared myself with reference to his case. I knew his influence was great, and that if he would take a decided stand, it would have a very great influence upon all the legal profession in the city. However, I soon observed that he had come into the gallery, and had found a seat just at the head of the gallery stairs, where he sat wrapped in his cloak. I went on with my discourse; but near the close of what I designed to say, I observed that Judge G. had gone from his seat. I felt distressed, for I concluded that, as it was cold where he sat, and perhaps there was some confusion, it being near the head of the stairs, he had gone home; and hence that the sermon which I had prepared with my eye upon him, had failed of its effect.

From the basement room of the church, there was a narrow stairway into the audience room above, coming up just by the side of, and partly behind, the pulpit. Just as I was drawing my sermon to a close, and with my heart almost sinking with the fear that I was to fail, in what I had hoped to secure that night, I felt some one pulling at the skirt of my coat. I looked around, and there was Judge G.. He had gone down through the basement room, and up those narrow stairs, and crept up the pulpit steps, far enough to reach me, and pull me by the coat. When I turned around to him, and beheld him with great surprise, he said to me, "Mr. Finney, won't you pray for me by name and I will take the anxious seat." I had said nothing about an anxious seat at all. The congregation had observed this movement on the part of Judge G., as he came up on the pulpit stairs; and when I announced to them what he said, it produced a wonderful shock. There was a great gush of feeling, in every part of the house. Many held down their heads and wept; others seemed to be engaged in earnest prayer. He crowded around in front of the pulpit, and knelt immediately down. The lawyers arose in great number, and crowded into the aisles, and filled the open space in front, wherever they could get a place to kneel. The movement had begun without my requesting it; but I then publicly invited any, who were prepared to renounce their sins, and give their hearts to God, and to accept Christ and his salvation, to come forward, into the aisles, or wherever they could, and kneel down. There was a mighty movement. We prayed, and then I dismissed the meeting.

As I had been preaching every night, and could not give up an evening to a meeting of inquiry, I appointed a meeting for the instruction of inquirers, the next day at two o'clock, in the basement of the church. When I went, I was surprised to find the room nearly full, and that the audience was composed almost exclusively of the more prominent citizens. This meeting I continued from day to day, having an opportunity to converse freely, with great numbers; and they were as teachable as children. I never attended a more interesting and affecting meeting of inquiry, I think, than that. A large number of the lawyers were converted, Judge G., I might say, at their head; as he had taken the lead in coming out on the side of Christ.

I remained there, at that time, two months. The revival became wonderfully interesting and powerful, and resulted in the conversion of great numbers. It took a powerful hold in one of the Episcopal churches, St. Luke's, of which Dr. Whitehouse, the present bishop of Illinois, was pastor. When I was in Reading, Pa., several years before, Dr. Whitehouse was preaching to an Episcopal congregation in that city; and, as one of his most intelligent ladies informed me, was greatly blessed in his soul, in that revival. When I came to Rochester, in 1830, he was the pastor of St. Luke's; and, as I was informed, encouraged his people to attend our meetings, and I was told that many of them, were at that time, converted. So also in this revival, in 1842, I was informed that he encouraged his people, and advised them to attend the meetings. He was himself a very successful pastor, and had great influence in Rochester. I have been informed that in this revival, in 1842, not less than seventy, and those almost all among the principal people of his congregation, were converted, and confirmed in his church.

One striking incident I must mention. I had insisted much, in my instructions, upon entire consecration to God, giving up all to him, body, and soul, and possessions, and everything, to be forever thereafter used for his glory, as a condition of acceptance with God. As was my custom in revivals, I made this as prominent as I well could. One day as I went into meeting, one of the lawyers with whom I had formed some acquaintance and who had been in deep anxiety of mind, I found waiting at the door of the church. As I went in, he took out of his pocket a paper, and handed me, remarking, "I deliver this to you as the servant of the Lord Jesus Christ." I put it in my pocket until after meeting. On examining it, I found it to be a quitclaim deed, made out in regular order, and executed ready for delivery, in which he quitclaimed to the Lord Jesus Christ, all ownership of himself, and of everything he possessed. The deed was in due form, with all the peculiarities and formalities of such conveyances. I think I have it still among my papers. He appeared to be in solemn earnest, and so far as I could see, was entirely intelligent in what he did. But I must not go farther into particulars.

As it regards the means used in this revival, I would say, that the doctrines preached were those that I always preached, everywhere. The moral government of God was made prominent; and the necessity of an unqualified and universal acceptance of God's will, as a rule of life; the acceptance by faith, of the Lord Jesus Christ as the Savior of the world, and in all his official relations and work; and the sanctification of the soul through or by the truth, these and kindred doctrines were dwelt upon as time would permit, and as the necessities of the people seemed to require.

The measures were simply preaching the gospel, and abundant prayer, in private, in social circles, and in public prayer meetings; much stress being always laid upon prayer as an essential means of promoting the revival. Sinners were not encouraged to expect the Holy Ghost to convert them, while they were passive; and never told to wait God's time, but were taught, unequivocally, that their first and immediate duty was, to submit themselves to God, to renounce their own will, their own way, and themselves, and instantly to deliver up all that they were, and all that they had, to their rightful owner, the Lord Jesus Christ. They were taught here, as everywhere in those revivals, that the only obstacle in the way was their own stubborn will; that God was trying to gain their unqualified consent to give up their sins, and accept the Lord Jesus Christ as their righteousness and salvation. The point was frequently urged upon them to give their consent; and they were told that the only difficulty was, to get their own honest and earnest consent to the terms upon which Christ would save them, and the lowest terms upon which they possibly could be saved.

Meetings of inquiry were held, for the purpose of adapting instruction to those who were in different stages of conviction; and after conversing with them, as long as I had time and strength, I was in the habit of summing up at last, and taking up representative cases, and meeting all their objections, answering all their questions, correcting their errors, and pursuing such a course of remark, as was calculated to strip them of every excuse, and bring them face to face with the great question of present, unqualified, universal acceptance of the will of God in Christ Jesus. Faith in God, and God in Christ, was ever made prominent. They were informed that this faith is not a mere intellectual assent, but is the consent or trust of the heart, a voluntary, intelligent trust in God, as he is revealed in the Lord Jesus Christ.

The doctrine of the justice of endless punishment was fully insisted upon; and not only its justice, but the certainty that sinners will be endlessly punished, if they die in their sins, was strongly held forth. On all these points the Gospel was so presented as to give forth no uncertain sound. This was at least my constant aim, and the aim of all who gave instructions. The nature of the sinner's dependence upon divine influence, was explained, and enforced, and made prominent. Sinners were taught that, without the divine teaching and influence, it is certain, from their depraved state, that they never would be reconciled to God; and yet that their want of reconciliation was simply their own hardness of heart, or the stubbornness of their own wills, so that their dependence upon the Spirit of God is no excuse for their not being Christians at once. These points that I have noticed, and others which logically flow from them, were held forth in every aspect, so far as time would permit. Sinners were never taught, in those revivals, that they needed to expect conversion, in answer to their own prayers. They were told that if they regarded iniquity in their hearts, the Lord would not hear them; and that while they remained impenitent, they did regard iniquity in their hearts. I do not mean that they were exhorted not to pray. They were informed that God required them to pray, but to pray in faith, to pray in the spirit of repentance; and that when they asked God to forgive them, they were to commit themselves unalterably to his will. They were taught, expressly, that unrepentant and unbelieving prayer, is an abomination to God; but that if they were truly disposed to offer acceptable prayer to God, they could do it; for that there was nothing but their own obstinacy in the way of their offering acceptable prayer at once. They were never left to think that they could do their duty in any respect, could perform any duty whatever, unless they gave their hearts to God. To repent, to believe, to submit, as inward acts of the mind, were the first duties to be performed; and until these were performed, no outward act whatever was doing their duty. That for them to pray for a new heart, while they did not give themselves up to God, was to tempt God; that to pray for forgiveness until they truly repented, was to insult God, and to ask him to do what he had no right to do; that to pray in unbelief, was to charge God with lying, instead of doing their duty; and that all their unbelief was nothing but a blasphemous charging of God with lying. In short, pains were taken to shut the sinner up to accepting Christ, his whole will, atonement, official work and official relations, cordially, and with fixed purpose of heart, renouncing all sin, all excuse-making, all unbelief, all hardness of heart, and every wicked thing, in heart, and life, here, and now, and forever.

I have always been particularly interested in the salvation of lawyers, and of all men of the legal profession. To that profession I was myself educated. I understood pretty well their habits of reading and thinking, and knew that they were more certainly controlled by argument, by evidence, and by logical statements, than any other class of men. I have always found, wherever I have labored, that when the Gospel was properly presented, they were the most accessible class of men; and I believe it is true that, in proportion to their relative number, in any community, more have been converted, than of any other class. I have been particularly struck with this, in the manner in which a clear presentation of the Law and of the Gospel of God, will carry the intelligence of judges, men who are in the habit of sitting and hearing testimony, and weighing arguments on both sides. I have never, to my recollection, seen a case, in which judges were not convinced of the truth of the gospel, where they have attended meetings, in the revivals which I have witnessed. I have often been very much affected, in conversing with members of the legal profession, by the manner in which they would consent to propositions, to which persons of ill-disciplined minds would have objected.

There was one of the judges of the court of appeals, living in Rochester, who seemed to be possessed of a chronic skepticism. He was a reader and a thinker, a man of great refinement, and of great intellectual honesty. His wife, having experienced religion under my ministry, was a particular friend of mine. I have had very thorough conversation with that man. He always freely confessed to me that the arguments were conclusive, and that his intellect was worried, by the preaching and the conversation. He said to me, "Mr. Finney, you always in your public discourses carry me right along with you; but while I assent to the truth of all that you say, I do not feel right; somehow my heart does not respond." He was one of the loveliest of unconverted men, and it was both a grief and a pleasure to converse with him. His candor and intelligence made conversation with him, on religious subjects, a great pleasure; but his chronic unbelief rendered it exceedingly painful. I have conversed with him more than once, when his whole mind seemed to be agitated to its lowest depths. And yet, so far as I know, he has never been converted. His praying and idolized wife has gone to her grave. His only child, a son, was drowned before his eyes. After these calamities had befallen him, I wrote him a letter, referring to some conversations I had with him, and trying to win him to a source from which he could get consolation. He replied in all kindness; but dwelling upon his loss, he said, there could be no consolation that could meet a case like that. He was truly blind to all the consolation he could find in Christ. He could not conceive how he could ever accept this dispensation, and be happy. He has lived in Rochester, through one great revival after another; and although his mouth was shut, so that he had no excuse to make, and no refuge to which he could betake himself, still so far as I know, he has mysteriously remained in unbelief. I have mentioned his case, as an illustration of the manner in which the intelligence of the legal profession can be carried, by the force of truth. When I come to speak of the next revival in Rochester, in which I had a share, I shall have occasion to mention other instances that will illustrate the same point.

Several of the lawyers that were at this time converted in Rochester, gave up their profession and went into the ministry. Among these was one of Chancellor W.'s sons, at that time a young lawyer in Rochester, and who appeared at the time to be soundly converted. For some reason, with which I am not acquainted, he went to Europe and to Rome, and finally became a Roman Catholic priest. He has been for years laboring zealously to promote revivals of religion among them, holding protracted meetings; and, as he told me himself, when I met him in England, trying to accomplish in the Roman Catholic church what I was endeavoring to accomplish in the Protestant church. Mr. W. seems to be an earnest minister of Christ, given up, heart and soul, to the salvation of Roman Catholics. How far he agrees with all their views, I cannot say. When I was in England, he was there, and sought me out, and came very affectionately to see me; and we had just as pleasant an interview, so far as I know, as we should have had, if we had both been Protestants. He said nothing of his peculiar views, but only that he was laboring among the Roman Catholics, to promote revivals of religion. Many ministers have been the fruits of the great revivals in Rochester.

It was a fact that often greatly interested me, when laboring in that city, that lawyers would come to my room, when they were pressed hard, and were on the point of submission, for conversation and light, on some point which they did not clearly apprehend; and I observed, again and again, that when those points were cleared up, they were ready at once to submit. Indeed, as a general thing, they take a more intelligent view of the whole plan of salvation, than any other class of men to whom I have ever preached, or with whom I have ever conversed.

Very many physicians have also been converted, in the great revivals which I have witnessed. I think their studies incline them to skepticism, or to a form of materialism. Yet they are intelligent; and if the Gospel is thoroughly set before them, stripped of those peculiar features which are embodied in hyper-Calvinism, they are easily convinced, and as readily converted, as any other class of the people. Their studies, as a general thing, have not prepared them so readily to apprehend the moral government of God, as those of the legal profession. But still I have found them open to conviction, and by no means a difficult class of persons to deal with, upon the great question of salvation.

I have everywhere found, that the teachings of hyper-Calvinism have been a great stumbling block, both of the church and of the world. A nature sinful in itself, a total inability to accept Christ, and to obey God, condemnation to eternal death for the sin of Adam, and for a sinful nature, and all the kindred and resultant dogmas of that peculiar school, have been the stumbling block of believers and the ruin of sinners. Universalism, Unitarianism, and indeed all forms of fundamental error, have given way and fallen out of sight in the presence of great revivals. I have learned, again and again, that a man needs only to be thoroughly convicted of sin by the Holy Ghost, to give up at once and forever, and gladly give up, Universalism and Unitarianism. When I speak of the next great revival in Rochester, I shall have occasion to speak more fully of the manner in which skeptics, if a right course is taken with them, are sometimes shut up to condemnation, by their own irresistible convictions; so that they will rejoice to find a door of mercy opened through the revelations that are made in the Scriptures. But this I leave to be introduced in the proper order.

CHAPTER 27

ANOTHER WINTER IN BOSTON

I had oftentimes experienced inexpressible joy,
and very deep communion with God;
but all this had fallen so into the shade,
under my enlarged experience.

In the fall of 1843, I was called again to Boston. I have found that to be true of Boston, of which Dr. Beecher assured me, the first winter that I labored there. He said to me, "Mr. Finney, you cannot labor here as you do anywhere else. You have got to pursue a different course of instruction, and begin at the foundation; for Unitarianism is a system of denials, and under its teaching, the foundations of Christianity are fallen away. You cannot take anything for granted; for the Unitarians and the Universalists have destroyed the foundations, and the people are all confused. You can find here almost any conceivable form of error."

I have since found this to be true, to a greater extent than in any other field, in which I have ever labored. The mass of the people in Boston, are more unsettled in their religious convictions, than in any other place that I have ever labored in, notwithstanding their intelligence; for they are surely a very intelligent people, on all questions but that of religion. It is extremely difficult to make religious truths lodge in their minds, because the influence of Unitarian teaching has been, to lead them to call in question all the principal doctrines of the Bible. Their system is one of denials. Their theology is negative. They deny almost everything, and affirm al-most nothing. In such a field, error finds the ears of the people open; and the most irrational views, on religious subjects, come to be held by a great many people.

I began my labors in the Marlborough chapel at this time, and found there a very singular state of things. A church had been formed, composed greatly of radicals; and most of the members held extreme views, on various subjects. They had come out from other orthodox churches, and united in a church of their own, at Marlborough chapel. They were steadfast, and many of them con-sistent, reformers; they were good people; but I cannot say that they were a united people. Their extreme views seemed to be an element of mutual repellence among them. Some of them were ex-treme non-resistance, and held it to be wrong to use any physical force, or any physical means whatever, even in controlling their own children. Everything must be done by moral suasion. Upon the whole, however, they were a praying, earnest, Christian people. I found no particular difficulty in getting along with them; but at that time the Miller excitement, and various other causes, had been operating to beget a good deal of confusion among them. They were not at all in a prosperous state, as a church.

A young man by the name of S. had risen up among them, who professed to be a prophet. I had many conversations with him, and tried to convince him that he was all wrong; and I labored with his followers, to try to make them see that he was wrong. However, I found it impossible to do anything with him, or with them, until he finally committed himself on several points, and predicted that certain things would happen, at certain dates. One was that his fa-ther would die on a certain day. I then said to him: "Now we shall prove you. Now the truthfulness of your pretensions will be tested. If these things that you predict come to pass, and come to pass, as you say they will, at certain times, then we shall have reason to believe that you are a prophet. But if they do not come to pass, it will prove that you are deceived." This he could not deny. As the good providence of God would have it, these predictions related to events, but a few weeks from the time the predictions were uttered. He had staked his reputation as a prophet, upon the truth of these predictions, and awaited their fulfillment. Of course they every one of them failed, and he failed with them; I never heard anything more of his predictions.

But he had confused a good many minds, and really neutralized their efforts; and I am not aware that those who were his followers, ever regained their former influence as Christians.

During this winter, the Lord gave my own soul a very thorough overhauling, and a fresh baptism of his Spirit. I boarded at the Marlborough hotel, and my study and bedroom were in one corner of the chapel building. My mind was greatly drawn out in prayer, for a long time; as indeed it always has been, when I have labored in Boston. I have been favored there, uniformly, with a great deal of the spirit of prayer. But this winter, in particular, my mind was ex-ceedingly exercised on the question of personal holiness; and in re-spect to the state of the church, their want of power with God; the weakness of the orthodox churches in Boston, the weakness of their faith, and their want of power in the midst of such a community. The fact that they were making little or no progress in overcoming the errors of city, greatly affected my mind.

I gave myself to a great deal of prayer. After my evening services, I would retire as early as I well could; but rose at four o'clock in the morning, because I could sleep no longer, and immediately went to the study, and engaged in prayer. And so deeply was my mind exercised, and so absorbed in prayer, that I frequently continued from the time I arose, at four o'clock, till the gong called to breakfast, at eight o'clock. My days were spent, so far as I could get time, in searching the Scriptures. I read nothing else, all that winter, but my Bible; and a great deal of it seemed new to me. Again the Lord took me, as it were, from Genesis to Revelation. He led me to see the connection of things, the promises, the prophecies and their fulfillment; and indeed, the whole Scripture seemed to me all ablaze with light, and not only light, but it seemed as if God's word was instinct with the very life of God.

After praying in this way for weeks and months, one morning while I was engaged in prayer, the thought occurred to me, what if, after all this divine teaching, my will is not carried, and this teaching takes effect only in my sensibility? May it not be that my sen-sibility is affected, by these revelations from reading the Bible, and that my heart is not really subdued by them? At this point several passages of scripture occurred to me, much as this: "Line must be upon line, line upon line, precept upon precept, precept upon precept, here a little, and there a little, that they might go and fall backward, and be snared and taken." The thought that I might be deceiving myself, when it first occurred to me, it pierced me through like an arrow. It created a pang that I cannot describe. The passages of Scripture that occurred to me, in that direction, for a few moments greatly increased my distress. But directly I was enabled to fall back upon the perfect will of God. I said to the Lord, that if he saw it was wise and best, and that his honor demanded that I should be left to be deluded, and go down to hell, I accepted his will, and I said to him, "Do with me as seems good to you."

Just before this occurrence, I had a great struggle to consecrate myself to God, in a higher sense than I had ever before seen to be my duty, or conceived as possible. I had often before, laid my family all upon the altar of God, and left them to be disposed of at his discretion. But at this time that I now speak of, I had had a great struggle about giving up my wife to the will of God. She was in very feeble health, and it was very evident that she could not live long. I had never before seen so clearly, what was implied in laying her, and all that I possessed, upon the altar of God; and for hours I struggled upon my knees, to give her up unqualifiedly to the will of God. But I found myself unable to do it. I was so shocked and surprised at this, that I perspired profusely with agony. I struggled and prayed until I was exhausted, and found myself entirely unable to give her altogether up to God's will, in such a way as to make no objection to his disposing of her just as he pleased.

This troubled me much. I wrote to my wife, telling her what a struggle I had, and the concern that I had felt at not being willing to commit her, without reserve, to the perfect will of God. This was but a very short time before I had this temptation, as it now seems to me to have been, of which I have spoken, when those passages of Scripture came up distressingly to my mind, and when the bitterness, almost of death seemed, for a few moments, to possess me, at the thought that my religion might be of the sensibility only, and that God's teaching might have taken effect only in my feeling. But as I said, I was enabled, after struggling for a few moments with this discouragement and bitterness, which I have since attributed to a fiery dart of Satan, to fall back, in a deeper sense than I had ever done before upon the infinitely blessed and perfect will of God. I then told the Lord that I had such confidence in him, that I felt perfectly willing, to give myself, my wife and my family, all to be disposed of according to his own wisdom.

I then had a deeper view of what was implied in consecration to God, than ever before. I spent a long time upon my knees, in considering the matter all over, and giving up everything to the will of God; the interests of the church, the progress of religion, the conversion of the world, and the salvation or damnation of my own soul, as the will of God might decide. Indeed, I recollect, that I went so far as to say to the Lord, with all my heart, that he might do anything with me or mine, to which his blessed will could consent; that I had such perfect confidence in his goodness and love, as to believe that he could consent to do nothing, to which I could object. I felt a kind of holy boldness, in telling him to do with me just as seemed to him good; that he could not do anything that was not perfectly wise and good; and therefore, I had the best of grounds for accepting whatever he could counsel it to, in respect to me and mine. So deep and perfect a resting in the will of God, I had never before known.

What has appeared strange to me is this, that I could not get hold of my former hope; nor could I recollect, with any freshness, any of the former seasons of communion and divine assurance that I had experienced. I may say that I gave up my hope, and rested everything upon a new foundation. I mean, I gave up my hope from any past experience, and recollect telling the Lord, that I did not know whether he intended to save me or not. Nor did I feel con-cerned to know. I was willing to abide the event. I said that if I found that he kept me, and worked in me by his Spirit, and was preparing me for heaven, working holiness and eternal life in my soul, I should take it for granted that he intended to save me; that if, on the other hand, I found myself empty of divine strength and light and love, I should conclude that he saw it wise and expedient to send me to hell; and that in either event I would accept his will. My mind settled into a perfect stillness.

This was early in the morning; and through the whole of that day, I seemed to be in a state of perfect rest, body and soul. The question frequently arose in my mind, during the day, "Do you still adhere to your consecration, and abide in the will of God?" I said without hesitation, "Yes, I take nothing back. I have no reason for taking anything back; I went no farther in pledges and pro-fessions than was reasonable. I have no reason for taking anything back; I do not want to take anything back." The thought that I might be lost, did not distress me. Indeed, think as I might, during that whole day, I could not find in my mind the least fear, the least dis-turbing emotion. Nothing troubled me. I was neither elated nor de-pressed; I was neither, as I could see, joyful or sorrowful. My confi-dence in God was perfect, my acceptance of his will was perfect, and my mind was as calm as heaven.

Just at evening, the question arose in my mind, "What if God should send me to hell, what then?" "Why, I would not object to it." "But can he send a person to hell," was the next inquiry, "who accepts his will, in the sense in which you do?" This inquiry was no sooner raised in my mind than settled. I said, "No, it is impossible. *Hell could be no hell to me, if I accepted God's perfect will.*" This sprung a vein of joy in my mind, that kept developing more and more, for weeks and months, and indeed I may say, for years. For years my mind was too fall of joy to feel much exercised with anxiety on any subject. My prayer that had been so fervent, and protracted during so long a period, seemed all to run out into, "Thy will be done." It seemed as if my desires were all met. What I had been praying for, for myself, I had received in a way that I least expected. Holiness to the Lord seemed to be inscribed on all the exercises of my mind. I had such strong faith that God would accomplish all his perfect will, that I could not be careful about anything. The great anxieties about which my mind had been exer-cised, during my seasons of agonizing prayer, seemed to be set aside; so that for a long time, when I went to God, to commune with him — as I did very, very frequently — I would fall on my knees, and find it impossible to ask for anything, with any earnestness, except that his will might be done in earth as it is done in heaven. My prayers were swallowed up in that; and I often found myself smiling, as it were, in the face of God, and saying that I did not want anything. I was very sure that he would accomplish all his wise and good pleasure; and with that my soul was entirely satisfied.

Here I lost that great struggle in which I had been engaged, for so long a time, and began to preach to the congregation, in accordance with this my new and enlarged experience. There was a considerable number in the church, and that attended my preaching, who understood me; and they saw from my preaching what had been, and what was, passing in my mind. I presume the people were more sensible than I was myself, of the great change in my manner of preaching. Of course, my mind was too full of the subject to preach anything except a full and present salvation in the Lord Jesus Christ.

At this time, it seemed as if my soul was wedded to Christ, in a sense in which I had never had any thought or conception of before. The language of the Song of Solomon, was as natural to me as my breath. I thought I could understand well the state of mind he was in, when he wrote that song; and concluded then, as I have ever thought since, that song was unwritten by him, after he had been reclaimed from his great backsliding. I not only had all the freshness of my first love, but a vast accession to it. Indeed, the Lord lifted me so much above anything that I had experienced before, and taught me so much of the meaning of the Bible, of Christ's relations, and power, and willingness, that I often found myself saying to him, "I had not known or conceived that any such thing was true." I then realized what is meant by the saying, that he "is able to do exceeding abundantly above all that we ask or think." He did at that time teach me, indefinitely above all that I had ever asked or thought. I had no conception of the length and breadth, and height and depth, and efficiency of his grace.

It seemed then to me that that passage, "My grace is sufficient for you," meant so much, that it was wonderful I had never under-stood it before. I found myself exclaiming, "Wonderful! Wonderful! Wonderful!" as these revelations were made to me. I could un-derstand then what was meant by the prophet when he said, "His name shall be called Wonderful, Counselor, the mighty God, the everlasting Father, the Prince of peace." I spent nearly all the remaining part of the winter, till I was obliged to return home, in instructing the people in regard to the fullness there is in Christ. But I found that I preached over the heads of the majority of the people. They did not understand me. There was, indeed, a goodly number that did; and they were wonderfully blessed in their souls, and made more progress in the divine life, as I have reason to believe, than in all their lives before.

But the little church that was formed there was not composed of materials that could, to any considerable extent, work healthfully and efficiently together. The outside opposition to them was great. The mass even of professors of religion in the city, did not sympathize with them at all. The people of the churches generally were in no state to receive my views of sanctification; and although there were individuals in nearly all the churches, who were deeply interested and greatly blessed, yet as a general thing, the testimony that I bore was unintelligible to them.

Some of them could see where I was. One evening I recollect that Deacon P. and Deacon S., after hearing my preaching, and seeing the effect upon the congregation, came up to me, after I came out of the pulpit, and said, "Why, you are a great way ahead of us in this city, and a great way ahead of our ministers. How can we get our ministers to come and hear these truths?" I replied, "I do not know. But I wish they could see things as I do; for it does seem to me infinitely important that there should be a higher standard of holiness in Boston." They seemed exceedingly anxious to have those truths laid before the people in general. They were good men, as the Boston people well know; but what pains they really took, to get their ministers and people to attend, I cannot say.

I labored that winter mostly for a revival of religion among Christians. The Lord prepared me to do so, by the great work he wrought in my own soul. Although I had much of the divine life working within me; yet, as I said, so far did what I experienced that winter, exceed all that I had before experienced, that at times I could not realize that I had ever before been truly in communion with God. To be sure I had been, often and for a long time; and this I knew when I reflected upon it, and remembered through what I had so often passed. It appeared to me, that winter, that probably when we get to heaven, our views and joys, and holy exercises, will so far surpass anything that we have ever experienced in this life, that we shall be hardly able to recognize the fact that we had any religion, while in this world. I had in fact oftentimes experienced inexpressible joy, and very deep communion with God; but all this had fallen so into the shade, under my enlarged experience, that frequently I would tell the Lord that I had never before had any conception of the wonderful things revealed in his blessed Gospel, and the wonderful grace there is in Christ Jesus. This language, I knew when I reflected upon it, was comparative; but still all my former experiences, for the time, seemed to be sealed up, and almost lost sight of.

As the great excitement of that season subsided, and my mind became more calm, I saw more clearly the different steps of my Christian experience, and came to recognize the connection of things, as all wrought by God from beginning to end. But since then I have never had those great struggles, and long protracted seasons of agonizing prayer, that I had often experienced. It is quite another thing to prevail with God, in my own experience, from what it was before. I can come to God with more calmness, because with more perfect confidence. He enables me now to rest in him, and let everything sink into his perfect will, with much more readiness, than ever before the experience of that winter.

I have felt since then such a freedom, joy and delight in God, and in his word, a steadiness of faith, a Christian liberty and over-flowing love, this I had only experienced, I may say, occasionally before. I do not mean that such exercises had been rare to me before; for they had been frequent and often repeated, but never abiding as they have been since. My bondage seemed to be, at that time, entirely broken; and since then, I have had the freedom of a child with a loving parent. It seems to me that I can find God within me, in such a sense, that I can rest upon him and be quiet, lay my heart in his hand, and nestle down in his perfect will, and have no carefulness or anxiety. I speak of these exercises as habitual, since that period, but I cannot affirm that they have been altogether unbroken; for in 1860, during a period of sickness, I had a season of great depression, and wonderful humiliation. But the Lord brought me out of it, into an established peace and rest.

A few years after this season of refreshing, that beloved wife, of whom I have spoken, died. This was to me a great affliction. However, I did not feel any murmuring, or the least resistance to the will of God. I gave her up to God, without any resistance whatever, that I can recollect. But it was to me a great sorrow. The night after she died, I was lying in my room alone, and some Christian friends were sitting up in the parlor, and watching out the night. I had been asleep for a little while, and as I awoke, the thought of my bereavement flashed over my mind with such power! My wife was gone! I should never hear her speak again, nor see her face! Her children were motherless! What should I do? My brain seemed to reel, as if my mind would swing from its pivot. I rose instantly from my bed, exclaiming, "I shall be deranged if I cannot rest in God" The Lord soon calmed my mind, for that night; but still, at times, seasons of sorrow would come over me, that were almost overwhelming.

One day I was upon my knees, communing with God upon the subject, and all at once he seemed to say to me, "You loved your wife?"

"Yes," I said. "Well, did you love her for her own sake, or for your sake? Did you love her, or yourself? If you loved her for her own sake, why do you sorrow that she is with me? Should not her happiness with me, make you rejoice instead of mourn, if you loved her for her own sake?" "Did you love her," he seemed to say to me, "for my sake? If you loved her for my sake, surely you would not grieve that she is with me. Why do you think of your loss, and lay so much stress upon that, instead of thinking of her gain? Can you be sorrowful, when she is so joyful and happy? If you loved her for her own sake, would you not rejoice in her joy, and be happy in her happiness?"

I can never describe the feelings that came over me, when I seemed to be thus addressed. It produced an instantaneous change in the whole state of my mind. From that moment, sorrow, on account of my loss, was gone forever. I no longer thought of my wife as dead, but as alive, and in the midst of the glories of heaven. My faith was, at this time, so strong and my mind so enlightened, that it seemed as if I could enter into the very state of mind in which she was, in heaven; and if there is any such thing as communing with an absent spirit, or with one who is in heaven, I seemed to commune with her. Not that I ever supposed she was present in such a sense that I communed personally with her. But it seemed as if I knew what her state of mind was there, what profound, unbroken rest, in the perfect will of God. I could see that was heaven; and I experienced it in my own soul. I have never to this day, lost the blessing of these views. They frequently recur to me, as the very state of mind in which the inhabitants of heaven are, and I can see why they are in such a state of blessedness.

My wife had died in a heavenly frame of mind. Her rest in God was so perfect, that it seemed to me that, in leaving this world, she only entered into a fuller apprehension of the love and faithfulness of God, so as to confirm and perfect forever, her trust in God, and her union with his will. These are experiences in which I have lived, a great deal, since that time. But in preaching, I have found that nowhere can I preach those truths, on which my own soul delights to live, and be understood, except it be by a very small number. I have never found that more than a very few, even of my own people, appreciate and receive those views of God and Christ, and the fullness of his free salvation, upon which my own soul still delights to feed. Everywhere, I am obliged to come down to where the people are, in order to make them understand me; and in every place where I have preached, for many years, I have found the churches in so low a state, as to be utterly incapable of apprehending and appreciating, what I regard as the most precious truths of the whole Gospel.

When preaching to impenitent sinners, I am obliged, of course, to go back to first principles. In my own experience, I have so long passed these outposts and first principles, that I cannot live upon those truths. I, however, have to preach them to the unrepentant, to secure their conversion. When I preach the Gospel, I can preach the atonement, conversion, and many of the prominent views of the Gospel, that are appreciated and accepted, by those who are young in the religious life; and by those also, who have been long in the church of God, and have made very little advancement in the knowledge of Christ. But it is only now and then, that I find it really profitable to the people of God, to pour out to them the fullness that my own soul sees in Christ. In this place, there is a larger number of persons, by far, that understand me, and devour that class of truths, than I have found elsewhere; but even here, the majority of professors of religion, do not understandingly embrace those truths. They do not object, they do not oppose; and so far as they understand, they are convinced. But as a matter of experience, they are ignorant of the power of the highest and most precious truths of the Gospel of salvation, in Christ Jesus.

I said that this winter in Boston, was spent mostly in preaching to professed Christians, and that many of them were greatly blessed in their souls. I felt very confident that, unless the foundations could be relayed in some sense, and that unless the Christians in Boston took on a higher type of Christian living, they never could prevail against Unitarianism. I knew that the orthodox ministers had been preaching orthodoxy, as opposed to Unitarianism, for many years; and that all that could be accomplished by discussion, had been accomplished. But I felt that what Unitarians needed, was to see Christians live out the pure Gospel of Christ. They needed to hear them say, and prove what they said by their lives, that Jesus Christ was a divine Savior, and able to save them from all sin. Their professions of faith in Christ, did not accord with their experiences. They could not say that they found Christ in their experience, what they preached him to be. There is needed the testimony of God's living witnesses, the testimony of experience, to convince the Unitarians;

and mere reasonings and arguments, however conclusive, will never overcome their errors and their prejudices.

The orthodox churches there, are too formal; they are in bondage to certain ways; they are afraid of measures, afraid to launch forth in all freedom, in the use of means to save souls. They have always seemed to me, to be in bondage in their prayers, in so much that what I call the spirit of prayer, I have seldom witnessed in Boston. The ministers and deacons of the churches, though good men, are afraid of what the Unitarians will say, if, in their measures to promote religion, they launch out in such a way as to wake the people up. Everything must be done in a certain way. The Holy Spirit is grieved by their yielding to such a bondage.

I have labored in Boston in five powerful revivals of religion; and I must express it as my sincere conviction, that the greatest dif-ficulty in the way of overcoming Unitarianism, and all the forms of error there, is the timidity of Christians and churches. Knowing, as they do, that they are constantly exposed to the criticisms of the Unitarians, they have become overcautious. Their faith has been depressed. And I do fear that the prevalence of Unitarianism and Universalism there, has kept them back from preaching, and holding forth the danger of the impenitent, as president Edwards presented it. The doctrine of endless punishment, the necessity of entire sanctification, or the giving up of all sin, as a condition of salvation — indeed the doctrines that are calculated to arouse men, are not, I fear, held forth with that frequency and power, that are indispensable to the salvation of that city.

CHAPTER 28

FIRST VISIT TO ENGLAND

He exclaimed,
"There, that is worth coming
to England for!"

Having had repeated and urgent invitations to visit England, and labor for the promotion of revivals in that country, I embarked with my wife[1], in the autumn of 1849, and after a stormy passage, we arrived at Southampton, early in November. There we met the pastor of the church in Houghton, a village situated midway between the market towns of Huntington and Saint Ives. A Mr. Potto Brown, a very benevolent man, of whom I shall have occasion to speak frequently, had sent Mr. James Harcourt, his pastor, to meet us at Southhampton.

Mr. Potto Brown was, by parentage and education, a Quaker. He and a partner were engaged in the milling business, and belonged to a congregation of Independents, in Saint Ives. They became greatly affected in view of the state of things in their neighborhood. The Church, as it is called in England, seemed to them to be effecting very little for the salvation of souls. There were no schools, outside of the church schools, for the education of the poor; and the mass of the people were greatly neglected. After much prayer and consultation with each other, they agreed to adopt measures for the education of the children, in the village where they lived, and in the villages around them, and to extend this influence as far as they could. They also agreed

---

1 - *After death of his first wife, Mr. Finney had re-married. His second wife became Mrs. Elizabeth F. Atkinson, of Rochester.*

to apply their means, to the best advantage, in establishing worship, and in building up churches independent of the Establishment.

Not long after this enterprise was commenced, Mr. Brown's partner died. His wife, I believe, had died before him; and his partner committed his family, consisting of several sons and daughters, to the fraternal care of Mr. Brown, who committed them to the training of a judicious widow lady, in a neighboring village. Mr. Brown's partner, at his death, begged him not to neglect the work which they had projected; but to pursue it with vigor and singleness of eye. Mr. Brown's heart was in the work. His partner left a large property to his children. Mr. Brown himself had but two children, sons. He was a man of simple habits, and expended but little money upon himself, or his family. He employed a school teacher, in the village where he resided, and built a chapel there for public worship. They called a man to labor there as a minister, who held hyper-Calvinistic views; and consequently he labored year after year, with no results, such as met the expectations of Mr. Brown.

Mr. Brown had frequent conversations with his minister, about the want of good results. He was paying his salary, and laying out his money in various ways, to promote religion, by means of Sunday schools, and teachers, and laborers; but few or none were converted. He laid this matter before his minister so frequently, that he finally replied, "Mr. Brown, am I God, that I can convert souls? I preach to them the Gospel, and God does not convert them; am I to blame?" Mr. Brown replied, "Whether you are God or no God, we must have conversions. The people must be converted." So this minister was dismissed. Rev. James Harcourt was employed. Mr. Harcourt is an open-communion Baptist, a talented man, a rousing preacher, and an earnest laborer for souls. Under his preaching, conversions began to appear, and the world went on hopefully. Their little church increased in numbers and in faith; and the heaven was extending gradually, but perceptibly, on every side.

They soon extended their operations to neighboring villages, with good results. But still they did not know how to promote revivals of religion. The children of his partner, who had been left under his charge, had grown up to be young men and women, and were not converted. There were three daughters and three sons, a fine family, with abundance of property; but they were unconverted. Mr. Brown had a large number of very interesting and influential friends, in that country, for whose salvation he felt a very deep interest. He was also very anxious about the children of his deceased partner, that they might be converted. For the education of his sons he had employed a teacher in his family; and a considerable number of young men, of respectable families, from neighboring towns, had studied with his sons. This little family school, to which the young men who were sons of his friends, in various parts of the county, had been invited, had created a strong bond of interest between Mr. Brown and these families. Mr. Harcourt's labors, for some reason, did not reach these families. He was successful among the poorer and lower classes, was zealous and devoted, and preached the Gospel. As Mr. Brown said, "He was a powerful minister of Jesus Christ." But still he wanted experience, to reach the class of persons that Mr. Brown had more particularly on his own heart. These brethren frequently talked the matter over, and inquired how they could reach that class of persons, and draw them to Christ. Mr. Harcourt said that he had done all that he could, and that something else must be done, or he did not see this this class of persons would be reached at all.

He had read my revival lectures, and he asked me if I could not come and labor with them. This led to my receiving a very earnest request from Mr. Brown, to visit them. He conversed also with many other people, and with some ministers; which lead to my receiving numerous letters, of pressing invitations to visit England. At first, these letters made but little impression upon me, for I did not see how I could go to England. At length the way seemed to open for me to leave home, at least for a season; and as I have said, in the autumn of 1849, my wife and myself went to England. When we arrived there, and had rested a few days, I began my labors in the village chapel. I soon found that Mr. Brown was altogether a remarkable man. Although brought up a Quaker, he was entirely catholic in his views, and was laboring, in an independent way, directly for the salvation of the people around him. He had wealth, and his property was constantly and rapidly increasing. His history has reminded me many times of the proverb: "There is that scatters and yet increases; there is that withholds more than is meet, and it leads to poverty." For religious purposes, he would spend his money like a prince, and the more he spent, the more he had to spend.

While we were there, he threw his house open morning, noon, and evening, and invited his friends, far and near, to come and pay him a visit. They came in great numbers, so that his table was surrounded, at nearly every meal, with various persons who had been invited in, that I might have conversation with them, and that they might attend our meetings.

A revival immediately commenced, and spread among the people. The children of his partner were soon interested in religion, and converted to Christ. The work spread among those that came from the neighboring villages. They heard and gladly received the word. And so extensive and thorough was the work, among Mr. Brown's particular friends, whose conversion he had been longing and praying for, that before I left, he said that every one of them was converted, that the Lord had not left one of them out, for whom he had felt anxiety, and for whose conversion he had been praying.

The conversion of this large number of persons, scattered over the country, made a very favorable impression where they were known. The house of worship at Houghton was small, but it was packed at every meeting; and the devotedness and engagedness of Mr. Brown and his wife, were most interesting and affecting. There seemed to be no bounds to their hospitality. Their schoolmaster was a religious man, and would run in every day, and almost every meal, and sit down with us, to enjoy the conversation. Gentlemen would come in, from neighboring towns, from a distance of many miles, early enough to be there at breakfast. The young men who had been educated with his sons, were invited, and came; and I believe every one of them was converted. Thus his largest desires in regard to them, were fulfilled; and very much more among the masses was done, than he had expected. Mr. Harcourt, had at that time several preaching places, beside Houghton, in the neighboring villages. The savor of this work at Houghton, continued for years. Mr. Harcourt informed me, that he preached in a praying atmosphere, and with a meeting state of feeling around him, as long as he remained in Houghton.

I did not remain long in Houghton at this time; several weeks, however. Among the brethren who had written, urging me to come to England, was a Mr. Roe, a Baptist minister of Birmingham. As soon as he was informed that I was in England, he came to Houghton, and spent several days, attending the meetings and witnessing the results. About the middle of December, we left Houghton, and went to Birmingham, to labor in the congregation of Mr. Roe. Here, soon after our arrival, we were introduced to Rev. John Angell James, who was the principal dissenting[2] minister in Birmingham. He was a good, and a great man, and wielded a very extensive influence in that city, and indeed throughout England.

When my revival lectures were first published in England, Mr. James wrote an introduction to them, highly commending them. But when I arrived in Birmingham, I was informed that, after Mr. James had publicly recommended them, in meetings of ministers, and by his pen, he had been informed, by men belonging to certain circles on this side of the Atlantic, that those revivals that had occurred, under my ministry especially, had turned out very disastrously; and that to such an extent had these representations been made to him, that he had taken back what he had said publicly, in favor of those revival lectures.

However, when he saw me in Birmingham, he called the Independent ministers to a breakfast at his house, and requested me to attend. This is the common way of doing things in England. When we assembled at his house, after breakfast was concluded, he said to his ministerial brethren, that he had been impressed that they were falling greatly short of accomplishing the end of their ministry; that they were too well satisfied to have the people attend meeting, pay the minister's salary, keep up the Sunday school, and move on with an outward prosperity; while the conversions, in most of the churches, were very few, and after all, the people were going to destruction. I was told by Mr. Roe, with whom I was at that time commencing my labors, that there were, in Mr. James' own congregation, not less than fifteen hundred impenitent sinners. At the breakfast at Mr. James', he expressed himself very warmly, and said that something must be done.

Finally, the ministers agreed upon holding meetings, as soon as I could comply with their request, in the different Independent churches, in succession. But for some weeks, I confined my labors to Mr. Roe's congregation, and there was a powerful revival, such a movement as they had never seen. The revival swept through the congregation with great power, and a very large proportion of the impenitent were turned to Christ. Mr. Roe entered heart and soul into the work. I found him a good and true man. He was not at all sectarian, or prejudiced in his views; but he opened his heart to divine influence, and poured out

---

2 - *Dissenters – Christians who separated from the Church of England in 16th – 18th centuries.*

himself in labors for souls, like a man in earnest. Day after day he would sit in the vestry of his church, and converse with inquirers, as they came to visit him, and direct them to Christ. His time was almost entirely taken up with this work, for many days.

As I had to preach again in the evening, I was glad to have the rest. I soon accepted the invitations of the ministers, to labor in their several pulpits. The congregations were everywhere crowded; a great interest was excited; and the numbers that would gather into the vestries after preaching, under an invitation for inquirers, was large. Their largest vestries would be packed with inquirers, whenever a call was made to resort thither for instruction. As to mean, I used the same there that I had done in this country. Preaching, prayer, conversation, and meetings of inquiry, were the means used.

But I soon found that Mr. James was receiving letters from various quarters, warning him against the influence of my labors. He had acquaintances on this side of the Atlantic; and some of them, as I understood him, had written him letters, warning him against my influence. Besides, from various parts of his own county, the same pressure was made upon him. He was very frank with me, and told me how the matter stood; and I was as frank with him. I said to him, "Brother James, your responsibility is great. I am aware that your influence is great; and these letters show both your influence and your responsibility, in regard to these labors. You are led to think that I am heretical in my views. You hear my preaching, whenever I preach; and you know whether I preach the Gospel or not."

I had taken with me my two published volumes of Systematic Theology. I said to him, "Have you heard me preach anything that is not Gospel?" He said, "No, not anything at all." "Well," said I, "Now I have my Systematic Theology, which I teach to my classes at home, and which I everywhere preach; and I want you to read it." He was very earnest to do so. I soon saw that there was a very venerable looking gentleman with him, from evening to evening, at our meetings. They would attend meeting together; and when I called for inquirers, they would go in, and stand where they could get a place, and hear all that was said. Who this venerable gentleman was, I was not aware. For several nights in succession, they came in this way; but Mr. James did not introduce me to the person that was with him, nor come near, to speak with me, at those meetings.

After things had gone on in this way, for a week or two, Mr. James and his venerable friend called at our lodgings. He introduced me to Dr. Redford, informing me, at the same time, that he was one of their most prominent theologians; that he had more confidence in Dr. Redford's theological acumen, than he had in his own; and that he had requested him to visit Birmingham, attend the meetings, and especially to unite with him in reading my Theology. He said they had been reading it, from day to day; and Dr. Redford would like to have some conversation with me, on certain points of theology. We conversed very freely on all the questions to which Dr. Redford wished to call my attention; and Dr. Redford said, very frankly, "Brother James, I see no reason for regarding Mr. Finney, in any respect, as unsound. He has his own way of stating theological propositions; but I cannot see that he differs, on any essential point, from us."

Dr. Redford remained some time longer at Birmingham. He then went home, and, with my consent, took with him my Systematic Theology; and said he would read it carefully through, and then write to me his views respecting it. I observed that he was indeed at home in theology, was a scholar and a Christian, and a thoroughly educated theologian. I was, therefore, more than willing to have him criticize my theology, that if there was anything that needed to be retracted or amended, he might point it out. I requested him to do so, thoroughly and frankly. He took it home, gave himself up to a thorough examination of it, and read the volumes patiently and critically through. I then received a letter from him, expressing his strong approbation of my theological views, saying there were a few points upon which he would like to make some inquiries; and he wished me, as soon as I could get away from Birmingham, to come and preach for him. I continued in Birmingham, I think, about three months. There were a great many interesting conversions in that city; and yet the ministers were not then prepared to commit themselves heartily to the use of the necessary means, to spread the revival universally over the city.

There was one case of so interesting a character, that I will call attention to it. I suppose it is generally known in this country, that Unitarianism in England, was first developed and promulgated in Birmingham. That was the home of old Dr. Priestley, who was one of the principal, if not one of the first Unitarian ministers in England. His congregation I found still in existence, in Birmingham. One evening before I left Birmingham, I preached on this text: "You stiff-necked and uncircumcised in heart and ears, you do always resist the Holy Ghost." I dwelt first upon the divinity and personality of the Holy Ghost. I then endeavored to show in how many ways, and on how many points, men resist the divine teaching; that when convinced by the Holy Spirit, they still persist in taking their own course; and that in all such cases they are resisting the Holy Spirit. The Lord gave me liberty that night, to preach a very searching discourse. My object was to show, that while men are pleading their dependence on the Holy Spirit, they are constantly resisting him.

I found in Birmingham, as I did everywhere in England, that the greatest stress was laid upon the influence of the Holy Spirit. But I nowhere found any clear discrimination between a physical influence of the Spirit, exerted directly upon the soul itself, and that moral, persuasive influence, which he in fact exerts over the minds of men. Consequently, I found it frequently necessary, to call the attention of the people to the work in which the Holy Spirit is really engaged, to explain to them the express teachings of Christ upon this subject: and thus to lead them to see that they were not to wait for a physical influence, but to give themselves up to his persuasive influence, and obey his teachings. This was the object of my discourse that evening.

After I arrived at our quarters, a lady who was present at the meeting, and who came into the family where we were guests, remarked that she observed a Unitarian minister present in the congregation. I remarked that must have sounded strangely in the ears of a Unitarian. She replied, she hoped it would do him good. Not long after this, and when I was laboring in London, I received a letter from this minister, giving an account of the great change wrought in his religious experience, by means of that sermon. This letter I give, as follows:

August 16, 1850

REV. AND DEAR SIR: — Learning, from the Banner, that you are about to take your departure from England, I feel it would be somewhat ungrateful, if I allow you to go, without expressing the obligation I am conscious of being under to you, for the benefit I received from a sermon of yours, preached in Steelhouse Lane, Birmingham. I think it was the last sermon you preached, and was on resisting the Holy Spirit; but I have never been able to find the text. Indeed, in the interest of the points that most concerned me, I thought no more about the text, for two or three days after. In order that you may understand the benefit I received from the sermon, it is necessary that I should recount, briefly, my peculiar position at the time.

I was educated at one of our dissenting colleges, for the ministry among the Independents. I entered upon the ministry, and continued to exercise it about seven years. During that time, I gradually underwent a great change in my theological views. The change was produced, I think, partly by philosophical speculations, and partly in the deterioration that had taken place in my spiritual condition. I would say with deepest sorrow, my piety never recovered the tone it lost in my passage through college. I attribute all my sorrows principally to this. My speculations led me, without ever having read Dr. Williams' book on divine sovereignty and equity, to adopt fundamentally his views. The reading of his book, fully perfected my system. Sin is a defect, rising out of the necessary defectibility of a creature, when unsupplied with the grace of God. The fall of man, therefore, expresses nothing but the inevitable original imperfection of the human race. The great end of God's moral government, is to correct this imperfection by education, and revelation, and to ultimately perfect man's condition. I had already, and long previously, adopted Dr. Jenkyn's views of spiritual influence.

Under the guidance of such principles, you will understand, without my explaining how, sin became a mere misfortune, tempo-rarily permitted; or rather a necessary evil, to be remedied by infinite wisdom and goodness; how eternal punishment became a cruelty, not for one moment to be thought of, in the dispensation of a good being, and how the atonement became a perfect absurdity, founded upon unphilosophical views of sin. I became thoroughly Unitarian, and in the beginning of the year 1848, I professed my Unitarianism, and became minister of a church. The tendencies of my mind, however, were fortunately too logical, for me long to be able to rest in Unitarianism. I pushed my conclusions to simple deism, and then found they must go still farther. For this

I was not prepared. My whole soul started back in horror. I reviewed my principles. A revolution took place in my whole system of philosophy. The doctrine of responsibility was restored to me, in its strictest and literal sense, and with it a deep consciousness of sin. I need not enter into minute details, with reference to my struggles and mental sufferings.

About two weeks before I heard you, I saw clearly I must some day or the other, readopt the evangelical system. I never had doubted it was the system of the Bible. I became Unitarian, upon purely rationalistic grounds. But now I found I must accept the Bible, or perish in darkness. You may imagine the agonies of spirit I had to endure. On the one hand were convictions, becoming stronger every day, the sense of sin, and the need of Christ, obtaining a firmer hold over my heart, and the miserable condition of withholding the truth I knew, from the people looking up to me for instruction. On the other hand, if I professed myself, I instantly, in the sight of all parties, especially with that great majority having no sympathy with such struggles, ruined my character, by my apparent fickleness, and threw myself, my wife and children upon the world. I could not make up my mind to this alternative. I had resolved to wait, gradually to prepare the people's minds for the change, and by exercising a more rigid economy, for some months, to make provision for our temporal wants, during the period of transition. In this state of mind, I heard your sermon. You will recollect it, and easily comprehend the effect it produced. I felt the truth of your arguments. Your appeals came home irresistibly to my heart, and that night, on my way home, I vowed before God, come what would, I would at once consecrate myself afresh to that Savior, whose blood I had so recently learned to value, and whose value I had done so much to dishonor.

The peace of mind I now enjoy, does indeed surpass all understanding. I never before found such an absorbing pleasure, in the work of the ministry. I enter fully into the significance of what Paul says, "If any man be in Christ he is a new creature." I cannot tell you therefore, with how many feelings of gratitude, your name will be associated in my soul. I bless God for the kind providence that brought me to hear you. It seems to me now, more than probable, had I not heard you, my newly awakened religious life would soon have been destroyed, by continued resistance to my deep convictions. My conscience would again have become hardened, and I should have died in my sins. Through the grace of God, I shall trace up to you, any usefulness God may hereafter crown my labors with, and I feel it would be unjust to withhold from you, the knowledge of this fruit of your labors. May God, of his infinite mercy and grace, grant you a long life of even greater usefulness, than he has yet blessed you with.

Yours very truly,

When I received this letter, I was laboring with Rev. John Campbell in the old Tabernacle of Whitefield in London. I handed it to him to read. He read it over with manifestly deep emotion, and then exclaimed, "There, that is worth coming to England for!"

From Birmingham I went to Worcester, I think about the middle of March, to labor with Dr. Redford. I have said that he had read my Systematic Theology, and had written to me that he wished to have some conversation with me, on certain points. I had with me, my replies to the various criticisms which had been published, and these I handed to Dr. Redford. He read them through, and then called on me and said, "Those replies have cleared up all the questions on which I wished to converse; therefore, I am fully satisfied that you are right." After that, in no instance, that I recollect, did he make a criticism upon any part of my Theology. Those who have seen the English edition of that work, are aware that he wrote a preface to it, in which he commended it to the Christian public.

At the time I refer to, when he had read through my replies to those revenues, he expressed a strong desire that the work should be immediately published in England; and said that he thought the work was greatly needed there, and would do great good. His opinion had great weight in England, upon theological questions. Dr. Campbell, I remember, affirmed in his newspaper, that Dr. Redford was the greatest theologian in Europe. I remained in Worcester several weeks, and preached for Dr. Redford, and also for a Baptist congregation in that city. There were many very striking conversions; and the work was interesting indeed.

Some wealthy gentlemen in Worcester, laid before me a proposition to this effect. They proposed to erect a movable tabernacle, or house of worship; one that could be taken down and transported from place to place upon the railway, and, at slight expense, set up again, with all its seats, and all the furniture of a house of worship. They proposed to build it, one hundred and fifty feet square, with seats so constructed as to provide for five or six thousand people. They said if I would consent to use it, and preach in it from place to place, as circumstances might demand, for six months, they would be at the expense of building it. But on consulting the ministers at that place, they advised me not to do it. They thought it would be more useful for me to occupy the pulpits, in the already established congregations, in different parts of England, than to go through England preaching in an independent way, such as was proposed by those gentlemen.

As I had reason to believe the ministers generally would disapprove of a course then so novel, I declined to pledge myself to occupy it. I have since thought that I probably made a mistake; for when I came to be acquainted with the congregations, and places of public worship, of the Independent churches, I found them generally so small, so badly ventilated, so situated, so hedged in and circumscribed by the Church — I mean, of course, the Establishment — that it has since appeared to me doubtful whether I was right; as I have been of opinion that I could, upon the whole, have accomplished much greater good in England, by carrying as it were, my own place of worship with me, going where I pleased, and providing for the gathering of the masses, irrespective of denominations. If my strength were now as it was then, I should be strongly inclined to visit England again, and try an experiment of that kind. Dr. Redford was greatly affected by the work in Worcester; and at the May anniversaries in London, he addressed the Congregational union of England and Wales, and gave a very interesting account of this work. I attended those May meetings, being about to commence labor with Dr. John Campbell, in London.

Dr. Campbell was a successor of Whitefield, and was pastor of the church at the Tabernacle in Finsbury, London, and also of the Tottenham Court Road chapel. These chapels are both in London, and about three miles apart. They were built for Mr. Whitefield, and occupied by him for years. Dr. Campbell was also at that time editor of the British Banner, the Christian Witness, and of one or two other periodicals. His voice was such that he did not preach, but gave his time to the editing of those papers. He lived in the parsonage in which Whitefield resided, and used the same library, I believe, that Whitefield had used. Whitefield's portrait hung in his study in the Tabernacle. The savor of his name was still there; yet I must say that the spirit that had been upon him, was not very apparent in the church, at the time I went there. I said that Dr. Campbell did not preach. He still held the pastorate, resided in the parsonage, and drew the salary; but he supplied his pulpit by employing, for a few weeks at a time, the most popular ministers that could be employed, to preach to his people. I began my labors there early in May. Those who are acquainted with the workings of such a constant change in the ministry, as they had at the Tabernacle, would not expect religion in the church, to be in a flourishing condition.

Dr. Campbell's house of worship was large. It was compactly seated, and could accommodate full three thousand persons. A friend of mine took particular pains to ascertain which would hold the greatest number of people, the Tabernacle in Moorfields or Finsbury, or the great Dexter Hall, of which everybody has heard. It was ascertained that the Tabernacle would seat some hundreds more than Exeter Hall.

CHAPTER 29

LABORS IN THE TABERNACLE, MOORFIELDS, LONDON

I could not stop praying; the spirit of prayer
would almost draw me out of myself,
in pleadings for the people, and for the city at large.

I had accepted Dr. Campbell's cordial invitation to supply his pulpit for a time, and accordingly, after the May meetings I put in, in earnest, for a revival; though I said no such thing to Dr. Campbell, or anybody else, for some weeks. I preached a course of sermons designed to convict the people of sin, as deeply and as universally as possible. I saw from Sunday to Sunday, and from evening to evening, that the word was taking great effect. On Sunday day, I preached morning and evening; and I also preached on Tuesday, Wednesday, Thursday and Friday evenings. On Monday evening, we had a general prayer meeting in the Tabernacle. At each of those meetings I addressed the people on the subject of prayer. Our congregations were very large; and always on Sunday, and Sunday evenings, the house was crowded.

Religion had so declined throughout London, at that time, that very few weekly sermons were preached; and I recollect that Dr. Campbell said to me once, that he believed I preached to more people, during the week evenings, than all the rest of the ministers in London together. I have said that Dr. Campbell had the salary belonging to the pastor, in his congregation. But this salary, he did not use for himself, at least more than a part of it; because he supplied the pulpit at his own expense, while he performed such parochial duties, as it was possible for him to perform, under such a pressure of editorial labors. I found Dr. Campbell to be an earnest, but a very belligerent, man. He was always given to controversy. To use an American expression, he was given to "pitching into" everybody and everything that did not correspond with his views. In this way he did a great deal of good; and occasionally, I fear, some harm.

After preaching for several weeks, in the manner that I have described, I knew that it was time to call for inquirers. But Dr. Campbell, I perceived, had no such idea in his mind. The practice in that church, is to hold a communion service, every alternate Sunday evening. On these occasions they would have a short sermon, then dismiss the congregation; and all would retire, except those that had tickets for the communion service, who would remain while that ordinance was celebrated.

On the Sunday morning to which I have referred, I said to Dr. Campbell, "You have a communion service tonight, and I must have a meeting of inquiry at the same time. Have you any room, anywhere on the premises, to which I can invite inquirers after preaching?" He hesitated, and expressed doubts whether there were any that would attend such a meeting as that. However, as I pressed the matter upon him, he replied, "Yes, there is the infant school room, to which you might invite them." I inquired how many persons it could accommodate. He replied, "From twenty to thirty, or perhaps forty." "O," I said, "that is not half large enough. Have you not a larger room?" At this he expressed astonishment; and inquired if I thought that there was interest enough in the congregation, to warrant any such invitation as I had intended to give. I told him there were hundreds of inquirers in the congregation. But at this he laughed, and said it was impossible. I asked him if he had not a larger room. "Why yes," he said, "there is the British schoolroom. But that will hold fifteen or sixteen hundred; of course you don't want that." "Yes," said I, "that is the very room. Where is it?" "O," said he, "surely you will not venture to appoint a meeting there. Not half as many would attend, I presume, as could get into the infant schoolroom." Said he, "Mr. Finney, remember you are in England, and in London; and that you are not acquainted with our people. You might get people to attend such a meeting, under such a call as you propose to make, in America; but you will not get people to attend here. Remember that our evening service is out, before the sun is down, at this time of year. And do you suppose that in the midst of London, under an invitation to those that are seeking the salvation of their souls, and are anxious on that subject, that they will single themselves out, right in the daytime, and under such a call as that, publicly given, to attend such a meeting as that?" I replied to him, "Dr. Campbell, I know what the state of the people is, better than you do. The Gospel is as well adapted to the English people as to the American people; and I have no fears at all, that the pride of the people will prevent their responding to such a call, any more than it would the people in America."

I asked him to tell me where that room was; and so to specify it, that I could point it out to the people, and make the appeal that I intended to make. After a good deal of discussion, the doctor reluctantly consented; but told me expressly, that I must take the responsibility on myself, that he would not share it. I replied that I expected to take the responsibility, and was prepared to do so. He then gave me particular directions about the place, which was but a little distance from the Tabernacle. The people had to pass up Cowper street toward City road, a few rods, and turn through a narrow passage, to the British schoolroom building. We then went to meeting; and I preached in the morning, and again at evening; that is, at six o'clock, if I recollect the hour. I preached a short sermon, and then informed the people what I desired. I called upon all who were anxious for their souls, and who were then disposed, immediately, to make their peace with God, to attend a meeting for instruction, adapted to their state of mind. I was very particular, in regard to the class of persons invited. I said, "Professors of religion are not invited to attend this meeting. There is to be a communion service here; let them remain here. Careless sinners are not invited to this meeting. Those, and those only, are expected to attend, who are not Christians, but who are anxious for the salvation of their souls, and wish instruction given them directly, upon the question of their present duty to God." This I repeated, so as not to be misunderstood. Dr. Campbell listened with great attention; and I presume he expected, since I had restricted my appeal to such a class, that very few, if any, would attend. I was determined not to have the mass of the people go into that room; and furthermore, that those who did go, should go with the express understanding, that they were inquiring sinners. I was particular on this point; not only for the sake of the results of the meeting, but to convince Dr. Campbell that his view of the subject was a mistaken one. I felt entirely confident, that there was a great amount of conviction in the congregation, and that hundreds were prepared to respond to such a call, at once. I was perfectly confident that I was not premature, in making such a call. I therefore proceeded very particularly to point out the class of persons whom I wished to attend, and the manner in which they would find the place. I then dismissed the meeting, and the congregation retired.

Dr. Campbell nervously and anxiously looked out of the window, to see which way the congregation went; and to his great astonishment, Cowper street was perfectly crowded with people, pressing up to get into the British schoolroom. I passed out, and went up with the crowd and waited at the entrance, till the multitude went in. When I entered, I found the room packed. Dr. Campbell's impression was, that there were not less than fifteen or sixteen hundred present. It was a large room, seated with forms or benches, such as are often used in schoolrooms.

There was near the entrance a platform, on which the speakers stood, whenever they had public meetings, which was of frequent occurrence. I soon discovered that the congregation were pressed with conviction, in such a manner that great care needed to be taken, to prevent an explosion of irrepressible feeling. It was but a very short time before Dr. Campbell came in himself. Observing such a crowd gather, he was full of anxiety to be present; and consequently hastened through with his communion services, and came into the meeting of inquiry. He looked amazed at the crowd present, and especially at the amount of feeling manifested. I addressed them for a short time, on the question of immediate duty; and endeavored, as I always do, to make them understand that God required of them then to yield themselves entirely to his will, to ground their weapons of rebellion, make their submission to him as their rightful sovereign, and accept Jesus as their only Redeemer.

I had been in England long enough to feel the necessity of being very particular, in giving them such instructions as would do away their idea of waiting God's time. London is, and long has been, cursed with hyper-Calvinistic preaching. I therefore aimed my remarks at the subversion of those ideas, in which I supposed many of them had been educated; for but few persons present, I supposed, belonged properly to Dr. Campbell's congregation. Indeed, he had himself told me that the congregation which he saw from day to day, was new to him; that the masses who were thronging there were as much unknown to him as they were to me. I tried therefore in my instructions, to guard them on the one hand against hyper-Calvinism, and on the other against that low Arminianism in which I supposed many of them had been educated.

I then, after I had laid the gospel net thoroughly around them, prepared to draw it ashore. As I was about to ask them to kneel down, and commit themselves entirely and forever to Christ, a man cried out in the midst of the congregation, in the greatest distress of mind, that he had sinned away his day of grace. I saw that there was danger of an uproar, and I hushed it down as best I could, and called on the people to kneel down; but to keep so quiet, if possible, that they could hear every word of the prayer that I was about to offer. They did, by a manifest effort, keep so still as to hear what was said, although there was a great sobbing and weeping in every part of the house.

I then dismissed the meeting. After this I held similar meetings, with similar results, frequently on Sunday evening, while I remained with that congregation, which was in all nine months. The interest rose and extended so far, that the inquirers could not be ac-commodated in that large British schoolroom; and frequently when I saw that the impression on the congregation was very general and deep, after giving them suitable instructions, and bringing them face to face with the question of unqualified and present surrender of all to Christ, I would call on those that were prepared in mind to do this, to stand up in their places, while we offered them to God in prayer. The aisles in that house were so narrow and so packed, that it was impossible to use what is called the anxious seat, or for people to move about at all in the congregation.

Frequently when I made these calls, for people to arise and offer themselves while we offered them in prayer, many hundreds would arise; and on some occasions, if the house seated as many as was supposed, not less than two thousand people sometimes arose, when an appeal was made. Indeed, it would appear from the pulpit as if nearly the whole congregation arose. And yet I did not call upon church members, but simply upon inquirers to stand up and commit themselves to God.

In the midst of the work, a circumstance occurred which will il-lustrate the extent of the religious interest connected with that congregation at that time. The circumstance to which I allude was this: The dissenters in England had been for a good while endeavoring to persuade the government to have more respect in their action, than they were wont to do, to the dissenting interest in that country. But they had always been answered in a way that implied that the dissenting interest was small, as compared with that of the established church. So much had been said on this subject that the government determined to take measures to ascertain the relative strength of the two parties, that is, of the dissenters and the church of England. On a certain Saturday night, without any previous warning or notice whatever, that should lead the people anywhere to understand or even suspect the movement, a message was secretly sent to every place of worship in the kingdom, requesting that individuals should be selected to stand at the doors of all the churches, and chapels, and places of worship in the whole kingdom, on the next Sunday morning, to take the census of all that entered houses of worship of every denomination. Such a notice was sent to Dr. Campbell; but I did not know it till afterward. In obedience to directions, he placed men at every door of the Tabernacle, with instructions to count every person that went in, during the morning service. This was done, as I understood, throughout the whole of Great Britain. In this way they ascertained the relative strength of the two parties; in other words, which had the most worshippers on Sunday, the dissenters or the established church. I believe this census proved that the dissenters were in a majority. But however this may be, Dr. Campbell told me that the men stationed at the doors of the Tabernacle, reported several thousand more than could at any one time get into the house. This arose from the fact that multitudes entered the doors, and finding no place to sit or stand, would give place to others. The interest was so great, that a place of worship that would hold many thousands, would have been just as full as the Tabernacle.

Whence they all came, Dr. Campbell did not know, and no one could tell; but that hundreds and thousands of them were convert-ed, there is no reason to doubt. Indeed, I saw and conversed with vast numbers, and labored in this way to the full limit of my strength.

On Saturday evening, inquirers and converts would come to the study for conversation. Great numbers came every week, and conversions multiplied. People came, as I learned, from every part of the city. Many people walked several miles every Sunday to attend the meetings. Soon I began to be accosted in the streets, in different parts of the city, by people who knew me, and had been greatly blessed in attending our meetings. Indeed, the word of God was blessed, greatly blessed in London at that time.

One-day Dr. Campbell requested me to go in, and make a few remarks to the scholars in the British schoolroom. I did so, and began by asking them what they proposed to do with their education, and dwelt upon their responsibility in that respect. I tried to show them how much good they might do, and how great a blessing their education would be to them and to the world, if they used it aright, and what a great curse it would be to them and to the world, if they used it selfishly. The address was short; but that point was strongly urged upon them. Dr. Campbell afterward remarked to me, that a goodly number, I forget now how many, had been received to the church, who were at that time awakened, and led to seek the salvation of their souls. He mentioned it as a remarkable fact, because, he said, he had no expectation that such a result would follow.

The fact is, that the ministers in England, as well as in this country, had lost sight, in a great measure, of the necessity of pressing present obligations home upon the consciences of the people. "Why," said Dr. Campbell, when he told me of this, "I don't understand it. You did not say anything but what anybody else might have said just as well." "Yes," I replied, "they might have said it; but would they have said it? Would they have made as direct and pointed an appeal to the consciences of those young people, as I did?" This is the difficulty. Ministers talk about sinners; and do not make the impression that God commands them, now to repent; and thus they throw their ministry away.

Indeed, I seldom hear a sermon that seems to be constructed with the intention of bringing sinners at once, face to face with their present duty to God. You would scarcely get the idea from the sermons that are heard, either in this country or in England, that ministers expect or intend, to be instrumental in converting, at the time, anybody in the house.

A fact was related to me some time ago, that will illustrate what I have just said. Two young men who were acquaintances, but had very different views of preaching the Gospel, were settled over congregations, at no great distance from each other. One of them had a powerful revival in his congregation, and the other had none. One was having continual accessions to his church, and the other none. They met one day, and he who had no accession to his church, inquired of his brother the cause of the difference between them; and asked if he might take one of his sermons and preach it to his people, and see if it had any different effect from his own. The arrangement was made; and he preached the borrowed sermon to his people. It was a sermon, though written, yet constructed for the purpose of bringing sinners face to face with their duty to God. At the close of the service he saw that many were very much affected, and remained in their seats weeping. He therefore made a profound apology, saying he hoped he had not hurt their feelings, for he did not intend it.

My own mind was greatly exercised, in view of the moral desolation of that vast city of London. The places of worship in the city, as I learned, were sufficient to accommodate only a small part of the inhabitants. But I was greatly interested in a movement that sprang up among the Episcopalians. Numbers of their ministers came in, and attended our meetings. One of the rectors, a Mr. Allen, became very much engaged, and made up his mind that he would try to promote a revival in his own great parish. As he afterward informed me, he went around and established twenty prayer meetings in his parish, at different points. He went to preaching with all his might, directly to the people. The Lord greatly blessed his labors, and before I left, he informed me that not less than fifteen hundred persons had been hopefully converted in his parish. Several other Episcopal ministers were greatly stirred up, and quickened in their souls, and went to holding protracted or continuous services. When I left London, there were four or five different Episcopal churches that were holding daily meetings, and making efforts to promote a revival. In every instance, I believe, they were greatly blessed and refreshed. It was ten years before I visited London again to labor; and I was told that the work had never ceased; that it had been going on, and enlarging its borders, and spreading in different directions. I found many of the converts, the second time I visited there, laboring in different parts of London in various ways, and with great success.

I have said my mind was greatly exercised about the state of London. *I was scarcely ever more drawn out in prayer for any city or place than I was for London.* Sometimes, when I prayed, in public especially, it seemed, with the multitudes before me, as if I could not stop praying; and that the spirit of prayer would almost draw me out of myself, in pleadings for the people, and for the city at large. I had hardly more than arrived in England, before I began to receive multitudes of invitations to preach, for the purpose of taking up collections for different objects: to pay the pastor's salary, to help pay for a chapel, or to raise money for the Sunday school, or for some such object. And had I complied with their requests, I could have done nothing else. But I declined to go, in answer to any such call. I told them I had not come to England, to get money for myself or for them. My object was to win souls to Christ.

After I had preached for Dr. Campbell about four months and a half, I became very hoarse; and my wife's health also became much affected by the climate, and by our intense labors. And here I must commence more particularly, a recital of what God did by her.

Up to this time she had attended and taken part only in meet-ings for women; and those were so new a thing in England that she had done but little thus far in that way. But while we were at Dr. Campbell's, a request was made that she would attend a tea-meeting of poor women, without education and without religion. Tea-meetings, as they are called, are held in England, to bring together people for any special object. Such a meeting was called by some of the benevolent Christian gentlemen and ladies, and my wife was urgently requested to attend it. She consented, having no thought that gentlemen would remain in the meeting, while she made her address. However, when she got there, she found the place crowded; and, in addition to the women, a considerable number of gentlemen, who were greatly interested in the results of the meeting. She waited a little, expecting that they would retire. But as they remained, and expected her to take charge of the meeting, she arose, and, I believe, apologized for being called to speak in public, informing them that she had never been in the habit of doing so. She had then been my wife but a little more than a year, and had never been abroad with me to labor in revivals, until we went to England. She made an address at this meeting, as she informed me after she came to our lodgings, of about three quarters of an hour in length, and with very manifest good results. The poor women present seemed to be greatly moved and interested; and when she had done speaking, some of the gentlemen present arose, and expressed their great satisfaction at what they had heard. They said they had had prejudices against women speaking in public; but they could see no objection to it under such circumstances, and they saw that. it was manifestly calculated to do great good. They therefore requested her to attend other similar meetings, which she did. When she returned, she told me what she had done, and said that she did not know but it would excite the prejudices of the people of England, and perhaps do more harm than good. I feared this myself, and so expressed myself to her. Yet I believe I did not advise her to keep still, and not attend any more such meetings; but after more consideration I encouraged it. From that time, she became more and more accustomed, while we remained in England, to that kind of labor; and after we returned home, she continued to labor wherever we went. Upon this I shall have occasion to enlarge, when I speak of the revivals in which she bore a very prominent part.

There were a great number of most interesting cases of conversion in London at that time, from almost all classes of society. I preached a great deal on confession and restitution; the results of which were truly wonderful. Almost every form of crime was thus searched out and confessed. Hundreds, and I believe thousands of pounds sterling were paid over to make restitution.

Everyone acquainted with London is aware that from early in November till the next March, the city is very gloomy, and has a miserable atmosphere either to breathe or to speak in. We went there early in May. In September my friend Brown, of Houghton, called on us, and seeing the state of health that we were both in, he said, "This will never do. You must go to France, or somewhere on the continent where they cannot understand your language; for there is no rest for you in England as long as you are able to speak at all." After talking the matter over, we concluded to take his advice, and go for a little while to France. He handed me fifty pounds sterling, to meet our expenses. We went to Paris, and various other places in France. We sedulously avoided making any acquaintances, and kept ourselves as quiet as possible. The influence of the change of climate upon my wife's health, was very marked. She recovered her full tone of strength very rapidly. I gradually got over my hoarseness; and after an absence of about six weeks, we returned to our labors in the Tabernacle, where we continued to labor till early in the next April, when we left for home. I left England with great reluctance. But the prosperity of our college seemed to require that I should return. We had become greatly interested in the people of England, and desired very much to remain there, and protract our labors. We sailed in a large packet ship, the Southampton, from London. On the day that we sailed, a multitude of people who had been interested in our labors, gathered upon the wharf. A great majority of them were young converts. The ship had to wait for the tide, and for several hours there was a vast crowd of people in the open space around the ship, waiting to see us off. Tearing away from such a multitude of loving hearts, completely overcame the strength of my wife. As soon as the ship was clear of the dock, she retired to our stateroom. I remained upon the deck and watched the waving of handkerchiefs, until we were swept down the river, out of sight. Thus closed our labors in England, on our first visit there.

CHAPTER 30

LABORS IN HARTFORD AND IN SYRACUSE

*...soon the boy began to inquire what they
should have for breakfast.
She said, "I do not know, my son;
but the Lord will provide."*

We arrived at Oberlin in May, 1851, and after the usual la-bors of the summer, we left in the autumn for New York City, expecting to spend the winter, as I had been invited to do, in labor in Rev. Dr. Thompson's church, in the old Broadway Tabernacle. But after preaching there a short time, I found so many hindrances in the way of our work, especially the liability to the interruption of our evening services, by the practice of letting the Tabernacle for public lectures, that I despaired of success in the effort to promote a general revival. I therefore left, and accepted an invitation to go to Hartford, and hold a series of meetings. I was invited by Rev. William W. Patton, who was then pastor of one of the Congregational churches of that city.

Very soon after I began my labors there, a powerful revival in-fluence was manifested among the people. But there was at this time an unhappy state of disagreement existing between Dr. Hawes and Dr. Bushnell. The orthodoxy of Dr. Bushnell, as is well-known, had been called in question. Dr. Hawes was himself of the opinion that Dr.

Bushnell's views were highly objectionable. However, both Dr. Hawes and Dr. Bushnell attended our meetings, and manifested a great interest in the work, which they saw had fairly begun. They invited me to preach in their churches, which I did. Still the lay brethren through the city felt as if the disagreement among the ministers was a stumbling block in the way; and there was a considerable urgency expressed to have the ministers come more fraternally together, and take a united stand before the people, to promote the work. The people generally did not sympathize with Dr. Hawes' strong views, in regard to the orthodoxy of Dr. Bushnell. Being informed of this, I had a fraternal conversation with Dr. Hawes and told him that he was in a false position, and that the people felt tried with his laying so great stress upon what he called the errors of Dr. Bushnell, and that they very generally, I believed, did not justify him in the position that he occupied. Dr. Hawes was a good man, and manifestly felt his responsibility in this matter very deeply.

One evening I had been preaching, I think, for Brother Patton, and the three congregational ministers were present. After meeting they followed me to my lodgings, and Dr. Hawes said, "Brother Finney, we are satisfied that the Spirit of the Lord is poured out here; and now, what can we as ministers do to promote this work?" I told them freely what I thought; that a great responsibility rested upon them, and it seemed to me that it was for them to say, whether the work should become general throughout the city or not; that if they could reconcile their differences, and come out before the churches, and be united and take hold of the work, a great obstacle would be removed; and that I thought we might expect the work to spread rapidly on every hand. They saw their position; Dr. Hawes and Dr. Bushnell came to an understanding to lay aside their difficulties, and go on and promote the work. I should say here, that I believe Brother Patton had never sympathized with the strong views held by Dr. Hawes; and I should also say, that Dr. Bushnell himself did not seem to have any controversy with Dr. Hawes; and the obstacle to be removed from before the public seemed to be, mostly, in the unwillingness of Dr. Hawes, cordially to cooperate with the other ministers, in the work.

Dr. Hawes was too good a man to persist in anything that would prevent his doing whatever he could consistently do, to promote the work. Therefore, from that time we seemed to work together, with a good measure of cordiality. The work spread into all the congregations, and went on very hopefully, for a number of weeks. But there was one peculiarity about that work that I have never forgotten. I believe every Sunday that I was in that city, it stormed furiously. Such a succession of stormy Sundays I almost never witnessed. However, our meetings were fully attended; and for a place like Hartford the work became powerful and extensive.

Those who are acquainted with Hartford know how fastidious and precise the people are in regard to all they do. They were afraid of any measures other than prayer meetings, and preaching meetings, and meetings for inquiry. In other words, it was out of the question to call on sinners to come forward, and break away from the fear of man, and give themselves publicly to God. Dr. Hawes was especially very much afraid of any such measures. Consequently, I could do no such thing there. Indeed, Dr. Hawes was so much afraid of measures, that I recollect, one night, in attending a meeting of inquiry in his vestry, the number of inquirers present was large; and at the close I called on those that were willing to give themselves up to God, to kneel down. This startled Dr. Hawes; and he remarked before they knelt down that none were requested to do so unless they did it cheerfully, of their own accord. They did kneel down, and we prayed with them. Dr. Hawes remarked to me, as the inquirers rose and were dismissed: "I have always felt the necessity of some such measure, but have been afraid to use it. I have always seen," said he, "that something was needed to bring persons to a stand, and to induce them to act on their present convictions; but I have not had courage to propose anything of the kind." I said to him that I had found some such measure indispensable, to bring sinners to the point of submission.

In this revival there was a great deal of praying. The young converts especially, gave themselves to very much prayer. One evening, as I learned, one of the young converts after the evening services, invited another to go home with him, and they would hold a season of prayer together. The Lord was with them, and the next evening they invited others, and the next evening more still, until the meeting became so large that they were obliged to divide it. These meetings were held after the preaching service. The second meeting soon became too large for the room, and that again was divided. And I understood that these meetings multiplied, until the young converts were almost universally in the habit of holding meetings for prayer, in different places, after the preaching service. Finally, to these meetings they invited inquirers, and such as wished to be prayed for. This led to quite an organized effort, among the converts, for the salvation of souls.

A very interesting state of things sprung up at this time in the public schools. As I was informed, ministers had agreed that they would not visit the public schools, and make any religious efforts there, because it excited jealousy on the part of different denominations. One morning a large number of lads, as I was told, when they came together, were so affected that they could not study, and asked their teacher to pray for them. He was not a professor of religion, and sent for one of the pastors, informing him of the state of things, and requesting him to come and hold some religious service with them. But he declined, saying that there was an understanding among the pastors that they would not go to the public schools, to hold any religious services. He sent for another, and another, as I was informed; but they told him he must pray for the scholars himself. This brought a severe pressure upon him. But it resulted, I believe, in his giving his own heart to God, and in his taking measures for the conversion of the school. I understood there was a goodly number of the scholars, in the various common schools, that were converted at that time.

Everyone acquainted with the city of Hartford knows that its inhabitants are a very intelligent people, that all classes are educated, and that there is, perhaps, no city in the world where education of so high an order is so general as it is in Hartford. When the converts came to be received, some six hundred, I believe, united with their churches. Dr. Hawes said to me before I left, "What shall we do with these young converts? If we should form them into a church by themselves, they would make admirable workers for the salvation of souls. If, however, we receive them to our churches, where we have so many elderly men and women, who are always expected to take the lead in everything, their modesty will make them fall in behind these staid Christian men and women; and they will live as they have lived, and be inefficient as they have been." However, as I understood, the young converts, of both genders, formed themselves into a kind of city missionary society, and organized for the purpose of making direct efforts to convert souls throughout the city. Such efforts as this, for instance, were made by numbers of them. One of the principal young ladies, perhaps as well-known and as much respected as any lady in the city, undertook to reclaim, and if possible save, a class of young men who belonged to prominent and wealthy families, but had fallen into bad habits, and into moral delay, and had lost the respect of the people.

The position and character of this young lady rendered it possible and proper for her to make such an effort, without creating a suspicion of any impropriety on her part. She sought an opportunity to converse with this class of young men; and, as I understood, brought them together for religious conversation and prayer, and was very successful in reclaiming numbers of them. If I have been rightly informed, the converts of that revival were a great power in that city for good; and many of them remain there still, and are very active in promoting religion.

Mrs. Finney established prayer meetings for ladies, which were held in the vestry of the churches. These meetings were largely attended, and became very interesting. The ladies were entirely united, and very much in earnest, and became a principal power, under God, in promoting his work there.

We left there about the first of April, and went to the city of New York on our way home. There I preached a few times for Rev. Henry Ward Beecher, in Brooklyn; and there was a growing and deepening religious influence among the people, when I arrived, and when I left. But I preached but a few times, because my health gave way, and I was obliged to desist. We came home, and went on with our labors here as usual, with the almost uniform result of a great degree of religious influence among our students, and extending more or less generally to the inhabitants.

The next winter we left Oberlin at the usual season, and started East to occupy a field of labor to which we had been invited. While we were in Hartford, the previous winter, we had a very pressing invitation to go to the city of Syracuse to labor. The minister of the Congregational church came down to Hartford, to persuade me, if possible, to return with him. I could not see it my duty to go at that time, and thought no more about it. But on our way East at this time, we met this minister at Rochester. He was not then the pastor of the Congregational church in the city of Syracuse. But he felt so much interest for them, that he finally induced me to promise him that I would stop there, and spend at least one Sunday. We did so, and found the little church very much discouraged. Their number was small. The church was mostly composed of persons of very radical views, in regard to all the great questions of reform. The Presbyterian churches, and the other churches generally, did not sympathize at all with them, and it seemed as if the Congregational church must become extinct.

I preached one Sunday, and learned so much about the state of things as to be induced to remain another Sunday. Soon I began to perceive a movement among the dry bones. Some of the leading members of the Congregational church began to make confession to each other, and public confession of their wanderings from God, and of other things that had created prejudice against them in the city. This conciliated the people around them, and they began to come in, and soon their house of worship was too narrow to hold the people; and although I had not expected to stay more than one Sunday, I could not see my way clear to leave, and I kept on from Sunday to Sunday. The interest continued to increase and to spread. The Lord removed the obstacles, and brought Christian people nearer together.

The Presbyterian churches were thrown open to our meetings, and conversions were multiplied on every side. However, as in some other cases, I directed my preaching very much to the Christian people. There had been very little sympathy existing between them; and a great work was needed among professors of religion, before the way could be prepared outside of the churches. Thus I continued to labor in the different churches, until the Second Presbyterian church was left without a pastor; after which we concentrated our meetings there in a great measure, and held on throughout the winter.

Here again Mrs. Finney established her ladies' meetings with great success. She generally held them in the lecture room of the first Presbyterian church, I think, a commodious and convenient room for such meetings. A great many very interesting facts occurred in her meetings that winter. Christians of different denominations seemed to flow together, after a while, and all the difficulties that had existed among them seemed to be done away. The Presbyterian and the Congregational churches were all without pastors while I was there, and hence none of them opened their doors to receive the converts. I was very willing that this should be so, as I knew that there was great danger, if they began to receive the converts, that jealousies would spring up and mar the work.

As we were about to leave in the spring, I gave out notice from the pulpit, on my own responsibility, that on the next Sunday we should hold a communion service, to which all Christians, who truly loved the Lord Jesus Christ, and gave evidence of it in their lives, were invited. That was one of the most interesting communion seasons I ever witnessed. The church was filled with communicants. Two very aged ministers, Fathers Waldo and Brainard, attended and helped at the communion service. There was a great melting in the congregation; and a more loving and joyful communion of the people of God, I think I never saw anywhere.

After I left, the churches all secured pastors. I have been informed that that revival resulted in great and permanent good. The Congregational church built them a larger house of worship; and have been, I believe, ever since a healthy church and congregation. The Presbyterian churches, and I believe the Baptist churches, were much strengthened in faith and increased in numbers.

The work was very deep there among a great many professors of religion. One very striking fact occurred which I will mention. There was a lady by the name of C., the Christian wife of an unconverted husband. She was a lady of great refinement, and beauty of character and person. Her husband was a merchant, a man of good moral character. She attended our meetings, and became very much convicted for a deeper work of grace in her soul. She called on me one day, in a state of very anxious inquiry. I had a few moments of conversation with her, and directed her attention especially to the necessity of a thorough and universal consecration of herself and of her all to Christ. I told her that when she had done this, she must believe for the sealing of the Holy Spirit. She had heard the doctrine of sanctification preached, and it had greatly interested her; and her inquiry was how she should obtain it. I gave her the brief direction which I have mentioned, and she got up hastily and left me. Such a pressure was upon her mind, that she seemed in haste to lay hold of the fullness there was in Christ. I do not think she was in my room more than five or ten minutes, and she left me like a person who has some pressing business on hand. In the afternoon she returned as full of the Holy Spirit, to all human appearance, as she could be. She said she hurried home from my room in the morning, and went immediately to her chamber, and cast herself down before God, and made a thorough consecration of herself and of her all to him. She said she had clearer apprehensions by far of what was meant by that, than she had ever had before; and she made a full and complete resignation of herself and everything into the hands of Christ. Her mind became at once entirely calm, and she felt that she began to receive of the fullness of the Holy Spirit. In a very short time she seemed to be lifted up above herself, and her joy was so great that she could hardly refrain from shouting. I had some conversation with her, and saw that she was in danger of being over excited. I said as much as I dared to say, to put her on her guard against this, and she went home.

A few days afterwards her husband called on me one morning with his sleigh, and asked me to take a ride with him. I did so, and found that his object was to talk with me about his wife. He said that she was brought up among the Friends, and when he married her, he thought she was one of the most perfect women that he ever knew. But finally, he said, she became converted and then he observed a greater change in her than he thought was possible; for he thought her as perfectly moral in her outward life before as she could be. Nevertheless, the change in her spirit and bearing, at the time of her conversion, was so manifest, he said, that no one could doubt it. "Since then," he said, "I have thought her almost or quite perfect." "But," said he, "now she has manifestly passed through a greater change than ever. I see it in everything," said he. "There is such a spirit in her, such a change, such an energy in her religion, and such a fullness of joy and peace and love!" He inquired, "What shall I make of it? How am I to understand this? Do such changes really take place in Christian people?"

I explained it to him as best I could. I tried to make him understand what she was by her education as a Quaker, and what her conversion had done for her; and then told him that this was a fresh baptism of the Holy Spirit, that had so greatly changed her at that time. She has since passed away to heaven; but the savor of that anointing of the Holy Spirit remained with her, as I have been informed, to the day of her death.

There is one circumstance that I have often heard Mrs. Finney relate, that occurred in her meetings, that is worth notice here. Her ladies' meetings were composed of the more intelligent ladies in the different churches. Many of them were probably fastidious. But there was an elderly and uneducated old woman that attended their meetings, and that used to speak, sometimes, apparently to the annoyance of the ladies. Somehow she had the impression that it was her duty to speak at every meeting; and sometimes she would get up and complain of the Lord, that he laid it upon her to speak in meeting, while so many ladies of education were allowed to attend and take no part. She wondered why it was that God made it her duty to speak; while these fine ladies, who could speak so much to edification, were allowed to attend and "have no cross," as she expressed it, "to take up." She seemed always to speak in a whining and complaining manner. The part that she felt it her duty to take in every meeting, a good deal annoyed and discouraged my wife. She saw that it did not interest the ladies; and it seemed to her rather an element of disturbance.

But after things had gone on in this way for some time, one day this same old woman arose in meeting, and a new spirit was upon her. As soon as she opened her mouth it was apparent to everybody that a great change had come over her. She had come to the meeting full of the Holy Ghost, and she poured out her fresh experience, to the astonishment of all. The ladies were greatly interested in what the old woman said: and she went forward with an earnestness in relating what the Lord had done for her, that carried conviction to every mind. All turned and leaned toward her, to hear every word that she said, the tears began to flow, and a great movement of the Spirit seemed to be visible at once throughout the meeting. Such a remarkable change wrought immense good, and the old woman became a favorite. After that they expected to hear from her; and were greatly delighted from meeting to meeting to hear her tell what the Lord had done, and was doing for her soul.

I found in Syracuse a Christian woman whom they called "Mother Austin," a woman of most remarkable faith. She was poor, and entirely dependent upon the charity of the people for subsistence. She was an uneducated woman, and had been brought up manifestly in a family of very little cultivation. But she had such faith as to secure the confidence of all who knew her. The conviction seemed to be universal among both Christians and unbelievers, that mother Austin was a saint. I do not think I ever witnessed greater faith in its simplicity than was manifested by that woman. A great many facts were related to me respecting her, that showed her trust in God, and in what a remarkable manner God provided for her wants from day to day. She said to me on one occasion, "Brother Finney, it is impossible for me to suffer for any of the necessaries of life, because God has said to me, 'Trust in the Lord and do good: so shalt thou dwell in the land, and verily thou shalt be fed.'" She related to me many facts in her history, and many facts were related to me by others, illustrative of the power of her faith.

She said, one Saturday evening a friend of hers, but an impenitent man, called to see her; and after conversing awhile he offered her, as he went away, a five-dollar bill. She said that she felt an inward admonition not to take it. She felt that it would be an act of self-righteousness on the part of that man, and might do him more harm than it would do her good. She therefore declined to take it, and he went away. She said she had just wood and food enough in the house to last over the Sunday, and that was all; and she had no means whatever of obtaining any more. But still she was not at all afraid to trust God, in such circumstances, as she had done for so many years.

On the Sunday day there came a violent snowstorm. On Monday morning the snow was several feet deep, and the streets were blocked up so that there was no getting out without clearing the way. She had a young son that lived with her, the two composing the whole family. They arose in the morning and found themselves snowed in, on every side. They made out to muster fuel enough for a little fire, and soon the boy began to inquire what they should have for breakfast. She said, "I do not know, my son; but the Lord will provide." She looked out, and nobody could pass the streets. The lad began to weep bitterly, and concluded that they should freeze and starve to death. However, she said she went on and made such preparations as she could, to provide for breakfast, if any should come. I think she said she set her table, and made arrangements for her breakfast, believing that some would come in due season. Very soon she heard a loud talking in the streets, and went to the window to see what it was, and beheld a man in a single sleigh, and some men with him shoveling the snow so that the horse could get through. Up they came to her door, and behold! they had brought her a plenty of fuel and provision, everything to make her comfortable for several days. But time would fail me to tell the instances in which she was helped in a manner as striking as this. Indeed, it was notorious through the city, so far as I could learn, that Mother Austin's faith was like a bank; and that she never suffered for want of the necessaries of life, because she drew on God.

CHAPTER 31

LABORS IN WESTERN
AND IN ROME, 1854-1855

He affirmed, that
"neither Finney nor hell
could convert him."

The next winter, at Christmas time, we went again to Western, Oneida county, where as I have already related, I commenced my labors in the autumn of 1825. The people were at this time again without a minister; and we spent several weeks there in very interesting labor, and with very marked results.

Among the striking things that occurred in the revival this time, I will mention the case of one young man. He was the son of pious parents, and had long been made the subject of prayer. His parents were prominent members of the church. Indeed, his father was one of the elders of the church; and his mother was a godly, praying woman. When I commenced my labors there, to the great surprise and grief of his parents, and of the Christian people generally, he became exceedingly bitter against the preaching, and the meetings generally, and all that was done for the promotion of the revival. He committed himself with all the strength of his will against it; and affirmed, as I was told, that "neither Finney nor hell could convert him." He said many very hateful and profane things, until his parents were deeply grieved; but I am not aware that he had ever been suspected of any outward immorality.

But the word of God pressed him from day to day, till he could stand it no longer. He came one morning to my room. His appearance was truly startling. I cannot describe it. I seldom ever saw a person whose mind had made such an impression upon his countenance. He appeared to be almost insane; and he trembled in such a manner that when he was seated, the furniture of the room was sensibly jarred by his trembling. I observed, when I took his hand, that it was very cold. His lips were blue; and his whole appearance was quite alarming. The fact is, he had stood out against his convictions as long as he could endure it. When he sat down, I said to him, "My dear young man, what is the matter with you?" "O," said he, "I have committed the unpardonable sin." I replied, "What makes you say so?" "O," said he, "I know that I have; and I did it on purpose."

He then related this fact of himself. Said he, "Several years ago a book was put into my hands called, 'The pirate's own book.' I read it, and it produced a most extraordinary effect upon my mind. It inspired me with a kind of terrible and infernal ambition to be the greatest pirate that ever lived. I made up my mind to be at the head of all the highway robbers, and bandits, and pirates whose history was ever written." "But," said he, "my religious education was in my way. The teaching and prayers of my parents seemed to rise up before me, so that I could not go forward. But I had heard that it was possible to give the Spirit of God away, and to quench his influence so that one would feel it no more. I had read also that it was possible to sear my conscience, so that would not trouble me; and after my resolution was taken, my first business was to get rid of my religious convictions, so as to be able to go on and perpetrate all manner of robberies and murders, without any compunction of conscience. I therefore set myself deliberately to blaspheme the Holy Ghost." He then told me in what manner he did this, and what he said to the Holy Ghost; but it was too blasphemous to repeat.

He continued: "I then felt that it must be that the Spirit of God would leave me, and that my conscience would no more trouble me. After a little while I made up my mind that I would commit some crime, and see how it would affect me. There was a schoolhouse across the way from our house; and one evening I went and set it on fire. I then went to my room, and to bed. Soon, however, the fire was discovered. I arose, and mingled with the crowd that gathered to put it out; but all efforts were in vain, and it burnt to the ground." To burn a building in that way, was a state prison offense. He was aware of this. I asked him if he had gone farther in the commission of crime. He replied, "No." And I think he added, that he did not find his conscience at rest about it, as he had expected. I asked him if he had ever been suspected of having burnt it. He replied that he did not know that he had; but that other young men had been suspected, and talked about. I asked him what he proposed to do about it. He replied that he was going to the trustees to confess it; and he asked me if I would not accompany him.

I went with him to one of the trustees, who lived near; and the young man asked me if I would not tell him the facts. I did so. The trustee was a good man, and a great friend of the parents of this young man. The announcement affected him deeply. The young man stood speechless before him. After conversing with the trustee for a little while, I said, "We will go and see the other trustees." The gentleman replied, "No, you need not go; I will see them myself, and tell them the whole story." He assured the young man that he himself would freely forgive him; and he presumed that the other trustees, and the people in the town, would forgive him, and not subject him or his parents to any expense about it.

I then returned to my room, and the young man went home. Still he was not at rest. As I was going to meeting in the evening, ho met me at the door and said, "I must make a public confession. Several young men have been suspected of this thing; and I want the people to know that I did it, and that I had no accomplice, that nobody but God and myself knew it." And he added: "Mr. Finney, won't you tell the people? I will be present, and say anything that may be necessary to say, if anybody should ask any questions; but I do not feel as it I could open my mouth. You can tell them all about it."

When the people were assembled, I arose and related to them the facts. The family was so well known, and so much beloved in the community, that the statement made a great impression. The people sobbed and wept all over the congregation. After he had made this full confession he obtained peace. Of his religious history since I know not much. I have recently learned, however, that he retained his hold upon Christ, and did not seem to backslide. He went into the army during the rebellion, and was slain at the battle of Fort Fisher.

In giving my narrative of revivals thus far, I have passed over a great number of cases of crime, committed by persons who came to me for advice, and told me the facts. In many instances in these revivals, restitution, sometimes to the amount of many thousands of dollars, was made by those whose consciences troubled them, either because they had obtained the money directly by fraud, or by some selfish overreaching in their business relations.

The winter that I first spent in Boston, resulted in making a great many such revelations. I had preached there one Sunday in the morning upon this text: "Who covers his sins shall not prosper;" and in the afternoon on the remainder of the verse: "But who confesses and forsakes them, shall find mercy." I recollect that the results of those two sermons were most extraordinary. For weeks afterwards, persons of almost all ages, and of both sexes, came to me for spiritual advice, disclosing to me the fact that they had committed various frauds, and sins of almost every description. Some young men had defrauded their employers in business; and some women had stolen watches, and almost every article of female apparel. Indeed, it seemed as if the word of the Lord was sent home with such power at that time in that city, as to uncover a very den of wickedness. It would certainly take me hours to mention the crimes that came to my personal knowledge through the confessions of those that had perpetrated them. But in every instance the persons seemed to be thoroughly penitent, and were willing to make restitution to the utmost of their ability.

But to return from this digression, to Western. The revival was of a very interesting character; and there was a goodly number of souls born to God. The conversion of one young lady there I re-member with a good deal of interest. She was teaching the village school. Her father was, I believe, a skeptic; and as I understood, she was an only daughter, and a great favorite with her father. He was a man, if I was rightly informed, of considerable influence in the town, but did not at all attend our meetings. He lived on a farm away from the village. Indeed, the village is very small, and the inhabitants are scattered through the valley of the Mohawk, and over the hills on each side; so that the great mass of inhabitants have to come a considerable distance to meeting.

I had heard that this young woman did not attend our meetings much, and that she manifested considerable opposition to the work.

In passing the schoolhouse one day I stepped in to speak with her. At first she appeared surprised to see me come in. I had never been introduced to her, and should not have known her, if I had not found her in that place. She knew me, however, and at first appeared as if she recoiled from my presence. I took her very kindly by the hand, and told her that I had dropped in to speak with her about her soul. "My child," I said, "how is it with you? Have you given your heart to God?" This I said while I held her hand. Her head fell, and she made no effort to withdraw her hand. I saw in a moment that a subduing influence came over her, and so deep and remarkable an influence, that I felt almost assured that she would submit to God right on the spot.

The most that I expected when I went in, was to have a few words with her that I hoped might set her to thinking, and to appoint a time to converse with her more at large. But the impression was at once so manifest, and she seemed to break down in her heart so readily, that with a few sentences quietly and softly spoken to her, she seemed to give up her opposition, and to be in readiness to lay hold on the Lord Jesus Christ. I then asked her if I should say a few words to the students; and she said, yes, she wished I would. I did so, and then asked her if I should present herself and her students to God in prayer. She said she wished I would, and became very deeply affected in the presence of the school. We engaged in prayer, and it was a very solemn, melting time. The young lady from that time seemed to be subdued, and to have passed from death unto life. She did not live long before she passed, I trust, to heaven.

These two seasons of my being in Western were about thirty years apart. Another generation had come to live in that place from that which lived there in the first revival in which I labored there. I found, however, a few of the old members there. But the congregation was mostly new, and composed principally of younger people who had grown up after the first revival.

As in the case of the first revival, so in this, the people in Rome heard what was passing in Western, and came up in considerable numbers to attend our meetings. This led after a few weeks, to my going down and spending some time in Rome.

CHAPTER 32

REVIVAL IN ROCHESTER
IN 1855

A few souls had been
wrestling with God
until they felt that they were
on the eve of a great revival.

In the autumn of 1855, we were called again to the city of Rochester to labor for souls. At first I had no mind to go, but a messenger arrived with a pressing request, bearing the signatures of a large number of persons, both professors of religion and non-professors. After much deliberation and prayer, I consented. We commenced our labors there, and it was very soon apparent that the Spirit of God was working among the people. Some Christians in that place, and especially the brother who came after me, had been praying most earnestly all summer for the outpouring of the Spirit there. A few souls had been wrestling with God until they felt that they were on the eve of a great revival.

When I stated my objections to going to labor in Rochester again, the brother who came after me set that all aside by saying, "The Lord is going to send you to Rochester, and you will go to Rochester this winter, and we shall have a great revival." I made up my mind with much hesitancy after all. But when I arrived there, I was soon convinced that it was of God. I began preaching in the different churches. The first Presbyterian church in that city was Old School, and they did not open their doors to our meeting. But the Congregational church, and the two other Presbyterian churches with their pastors, took hold of the work and entered into it with spirit and success. The Baptist churches also entered into the work at this time; and the Methodist churches labored in their own way, to extend the work. We held daily noon prayer meetings, which were largely attended, and in which a most excellent spirit prevailed.

Soon after I commenced my labors there, a request was sent to me, signed by the members of the bar and several judges — two judges of the court of appeals, and I believe one or two judges of the supreme court who resided there — asking me to preach again a course of lectures to lawyers, on the moral government of God. I complied with their request. I began my course to lawyers this time by preaching first on the text: "Commending ourselves to every man's conscience in the sight of God." I began by remarking that the text assumed that every man has a conscience. I then gave a definition of conscience, and proceeded to show what every man's conscience does truly affirm; that every man knows himself to be a sinner against God; that therefore he knows that God must condemn him as a sinner; and that every man knows that his own conscience condemns him as a sinner. I was aware that among the lawyers were some skeptics. Indeed, one of them had a few months before declared that he would never again attend a Christian meeting, that he did not believe in the Christian religion, and he would not appear to do so; that it placed him in a false position, and his mind was made up to pay no more respect to the institutions of Christianity.

I shaped my lectures from evening to evening, with the design to convince the lawyers that, if the Bible was not true, there was no hope for them. I endeavored to show that they could not infer that God would forgive them because he was good, for his goodness might prevent his forgiving them. It might not on the whole be wise and good to pardon such a world of sinners as we know ourselves to be; that left without the Bible to throw light upon that question, it was impossible for human reason to come to the conclusion that sinners could be saved. Admitting that God was infinitely benevolent, we could not infer from that, that any sinner could be forgiven; but must infer from it, on the contrary, that impenitent sinners could not be forgiven. I endeavored to clear the way so as to shut them up to the Bible as revealing the only rational way in which they could expect salvation.

At the close of my first lecture, I heard that the lawyer to whom I have referred, who had said he would never attend another Christian meeting, remarked to a friend as he went home, that he had been mistaken, that he was satisfied there was more in Christianity than he had supposed, and he did not see any way to escape the argument to which he had listened; and furthermore that he should attend all those lectures, and make up his mind in view of the facts and arguments that should be presented.

I continued to press this point upon their attention, until I felt that they were effectually shut up to Christ, and the revelations made in the Gospel, as their only hope. But as yet, I had not presented Christ, but left them shut up under the law, condemned by their own consciences, and sentenced to eternal death. This, as I expected, effectually prepared the way for a cordial reception of the blessed Gospel. When I came to bring out the Gospel as revealing the only possible or conceivable way of salvation for sinners, they gave way, as they had done under a former course of lectures, in former years. They began to break down, and a large proportion of them were hopefully converted.

What was quite remarkable in the three revivals that I have witnessed in Rochester, they all commenced and made their first progress among the higher classes of society. This was very favorable to the general spread of the work, and to the overcoming of opposition.

There were many very striking cases of conversion in this revival, as in the revival that preceded it. The work spread and excited so much interest, that it became the general topic of conversation throughout the city and the surrounding region of country. Merchants arranged to have their clerks attend, a part of them one day, and a part the next day. The work became so general throughout the city that in all places of public resort, in stores and public houses, in banks, in the street and in public conveyances, and everywhere, the work of salvation that was going on was the absorbing topic. Men that had stood out in the former revivals, many of them bowed to Christ in this. Some men who had been open Sunday-breakers, others that had been openly profane, indeed, all classes of persons, from the highest to the lowest, from the richest to the poorest, were visited by the power of this revival and brought to Christ. I continued there throughout the winter, the revival increasing continually, to the last. Rev. Dr. Anderson, president of the University, engaged in the work with great cordiality, and, as I understood, a large number of the students in the University were converted at that time. The pastors of the two Baptist churches took hold of the effort, and I preached several times in their churches.

Mrs. Finney was well acquainted in Rochester, having lived there for many years, and having witnessed the two great revivals in which I had labored, that preceded this. She took an absorbing interest in this revival, and labored, as usual, with great zeal and success. As on former occasions, I found the people of Rochester, like the noble Bereans, ready to "hear the word with all readiness of mind, and to search the Scriptures daily, whether these things were so." Many of the ladies in Rochester exerted their utmost influence to bring all classes to meeting and to Christ. Some of them would visit the stores and places of business, and use all their influence to secure the attendance, at our meetings, of the persons engaged in these establishments. Many men connected with the operations of the railroad were converted, and finally, much of the Sunday business of the roads was suspended, because of the great religious movement in the city and among those employed upon the roads.

The blessed work of grace extended and increased until it seemed as if the whole city would be converted. As in the former revivals, the work spread from this center to the surrounding towns and villages. It has been quite remarkable that revivals in Rochester have had so great an influence upon other cities and villages far and near.

The means used to promote this revival were the same as had been used in each of the preceding great revivals. The same doctrines were preached. The same measures were used, with results in all respects similar to what had been realized in the former revivals. There was manifested, as there had previously been, an earnest and candid attention to the word preached; a most intelligent inquiry after the truth as it really is taught in the Bible. I never preached anywhere with more pleasure that in Rochester. They are a highly intelligent people, and have ever manifested a candor, an earnestness, and an appreciation of the truth excelling anything I have seen, on so large a scale, in any other place. I have labored in other cities where the people were even more highly educated than in Rochester. But in those cities the views and habits of the people were more stereotyped; the people were more fastidious, more afraid of measures than in Rochester. In New England I have found a high degree of general education, but a timidity, a stiffness, a formality, and a stereotyped way of doing things, that has rendered it impossible for the Holy Spirit to work with freedom and power.

When I was laboring in Hartford I was visited by a minister from central New York who had witnessed the glorious revivals in that region. He attended our meetings and observed the type and progress of the work there. I said nothing to him of the formality of our prayer meetings, or of the timidity of the people in the use of measures, but he remarked to me, "Why, Brother Finney, your hands are tied, you are hedged in by their fears and by the stereotyped way of doing everything. They have even put the Holy Ghost into a strait jacket." This was strong, and to some may appear irreverent and profane, but he intended no such thing. He was a godly, earnest, humble minister of Jesus Christ, and expressed just what he saw and felt, and just what I saw and felt, that the Holy Spirit was restrained greatly in his work by the fears and the self-wisdom of the people. Indeed, I must say, I do not think the people of New England can at all appreciate the restraints which they impose on the Holy Spirit, in working out the salvation of souls. Nor can they appreciate the power and purity of the revivals in those places where these fears, prejudices, restraints, and self-wisdom do not exist.

In an intelligent, educated community, great freedom may be given in the use of means, without danger of disorder. Indeed, wrong ideas of what constitutes disorder, are very prevalent. Most churches call anything disorder to which they have not been accustomed. Their stereotyped ways are God's order in their view, and whatever differs from these is disorder and shocks their ideas of propriety. But in fact nothing is disorder that simply meets the necessities of the people. In religion as in everything else, good sense and a sound discretion will, from time to time, judiciously adapt means to ends. The measures needed will be naturally suggested to those who witness the state of things, and if prayerfully and cautiously used, let great freedom be given to the influences of the Holy Spirit in all hearts.

CHAPTER 33

REVIVALS IN BOSTON
IN 1856-1958

"We have had enough instruction;
now, it is time for us to pray."

The next autumn we accepted an invitation to labor again in Boston. We began our labors at Park street, and the Spirit of God immediately manifested his willingness to save souls. The first sermon that I preached was directed to the searching of the church; for I always began by trying to stir up a thorough and pervading interest among professors of religion; to secure the reclaiming of those that were back-slidden, and search out those that were self-deceived, and if possible bring them to Christ.

After the congregation was dismissed, and the pastor was standing with me in the pulpit, he said to me, "Brother Finney, I wish to have you understand that I need to have this preaching as much as any member of this church. I have been very much dissat-isfied with my religious state for a long time; and have sent for you on my own account, and for the sake of my own soul, as well as for the sake of the souls of the people." We had at different times protracted and very interesting conversations. He seemed thoroughly to give his heart to God. And one evening at a prayer and conference meeting, as I understood, he related to the people his experience, and told them that he had been that day converted. This of course produced a very deep impression upon the church and congregation, and upon the city quite extensively. Some of the pastors thought that it was injudicious for him to make a thing of that kind so public. But I did not regard it in that light. It manifestly was the best means he could use for the salvation of his people, and highly calculated to produce among professors of religion generally a very great searching of heart.

The work was quite extensive that winter in Boston, and many very striking cases of conversion occurred. We labored there until spring, and then thought it necessary to return to our labors at home. But it was very manifest that the work in that city was by no means done; and we left with the promise that, the Lord willing, we would return and labor there the next winter. Accordingly, the next autumn we returned to Boston.

In the meantime, one of the pastors of the city, who had been in Europe the previous winter, had been writing some articles, which were published in the Congregationalist, opposing our return there. He regarded my theology, especially on the subject of sanctification, as unsound. This opposition produced an effect, and we felt at once that there was a jar among the Christian people. Some of the leading members of his church, who the winter before had entered heart and soul into the work, stood aloof and did not come near our meetings; and it was evident that his whole influence, which was considerable at that time in the city, was against the work. This made some of his good people very sad.

This winter of 1857-1958 will be remembered as the time when a great revival prevailed throughout all the Northern states. It swept over the land with such power, that for a time it was estimated that not less than fifty thousand conversions occurred in a single week. This revival had some very peculiarly interesting features. It was carried on to a large extent through lay influence, so much so as almost to throw the ministers into the shade. There had been a daily prayer meeting observed in Boston for several years; and in the autumn previous to the great outburst, the daily prayer meeting had been established in Fulton street, New York, which has been continued to this day. Indeed, daily prayer meetings were established throughout the length and breadth of the Northern states. I recollect in one of our prayer meetings in Boston that winter, a gentleman arose and said, "I am from Omaha, in Nebraska. On my journey east

I have found continuous prayer meetings all the way. *It's about two thousand miles from Omaha to Boston; and on our whole way, we saw people praying everywhere."*

In Boston we had to struggle, as I have intimated, against this divisive influence, which set the religious interest a good deal back from where we had left it the spring before. However, the work continued steadily to increase, in the midst of these unfavorable conditions. It was evident that the Lord intended to make a general sweep in Boston. Finally, it was suggested that a businessmen's prayer meeting should be established, at twelve o'clock, in the chapel of the Old South church, which was very central for business men. The Christian friend, whose guests we were, secured the use of the room, and advertised the meeting. But whether such a meeting would succeed in Boston at that time, was considered doubtful. However, this brother called the meeting; and to the surprise of almost everybody the place was not only crowded, but multitudes could not get in at all. This meeting was continued, day after day, with wonderful results. The place was, from the first, too strait for them, and other daily meetings were established in other parts of the city.

Mrs. Finney held ladies' meetings daily at the large vestry of Park street. These meetings became so crowded, that the ladies would fill the room, and then stand about the door on the outside, as far as they could hear on every side.

One of our daily prayer meetings was held at Park street church, which would be full whenever it was open for prayer; and this was the case with many other meetings in different parts of the city. The population, large as it was, seemed to be moved throughout. The revival became too general to keep any account at all of the number of conversions, or to allow of any estimate being made that would approximate the truth. All classes of people were inquiring everywhere. Many of the Unitarians became greatly interested, and attended our meetings in large numbers.

This revival is of so recent date that I need not enlarge upon it, because it became almost universal throughout the Northern states. A divine influence seemed to pervade the whole land. Slavery seemed to shut it out from the South. The people there were in such a state of irritation, of vexation, and of committal to their peculiar institution, which had come to be assailed on every side, that the Spirit of God seemed to be grieved away from them. There seemed to be no place found for him in the hearts of the Southern people at that time. It was estimated that during this revival not less than five hundred thousand souls were converted in this country.

As I have said, it was carried on very much through the instrumentality of prayer meetings, personal visitation and conversation, by the distribution of tracts, and by the energetic efforts of the laity, men and women. Ministers nowhere opposed it that I am aware of. I believe they universally sympathized with it. But there was such a general confidence in the prevalence of prayer, that the people very extensively seemed to prefer meetings for prayer to meetings for preaching. The general impression seemed to be, "We have had enough instruction; now, it is time for us to pray." The answers to prayer were constant, and so striking as to arrest the attention of the people generally throughout the land. It was evident that in answer to prayer the windows of heaven were opened and the Spirit of God poured out like a flood. The New York Tribune at that time published several extras, filled with accounts of the progress of the revival in different parts of the United States.

I have said there were some very striking instances of conversion in this revival in Boston. One day I received an anonymous letter, from a lady, asking my advice in regard to the state of her soul. Usually I took no notice whatever of anonymous letters. But the handwriting, the manifest talent displayed in the letter, together with the unmistakable earnestness of the writer, led me to give it unwonted attention. She concluded by requesting me to answer it, and direct it to Mrs. M., and leave it with the sexton of the church where I was to preach that night, and she should get it. I was at this time preaching around from evening to evening in different churches. I replied to this anonymous letter, that I could not give her the advice which she sought, because I was not well enough acquainted with her history, or with the real state of her mind. But I would venture to call her attention to one fact, which was very apparent, not only in her letter but also in the fact of her not putting her name to it, that she was a very proud woman; and that fact she needed thoroughly to consider.

I left my reply with the sexton, as she requested, and the next morning a lady called to see me. As soon as she came in, she informed me that she was the lady that wrote that anonymous letter;

and she had called to tell me that I was mistaken in thinking that she was proud. She said that she was far enough from that; but she was a member of the Episcopal church, and did not want to disgrace her church by revealing the fact that she was not converted. I replied, "It is church pride, then, that kept you from revealing your name." This touched her so deeply that she arose, and in a manifest excitement left the room. I expected to see her no more; but that evening I found her, after preaching, among the inquirers in the vestry. In passing around, I observed this lady. She was manifestly a woman of intelligence and education, and I could perceive that she belonged to cultivated society. But as yet I did not know her name; for our conversation that morning had not lasted more than a minute or two, before she left the room as I have related. As I observed her in passing around, I remarked to her quietly, "And you here?" "Yes," she replied, and dropped her head as if she felt deeply. I had a few words of kind conversation with her, and it passed for that evening.

In these inquiry meetings I always urged the necessity of immediate submission to Christ, and brought them face to face with that duty; and I then called on such as were prepared to commit themselves unalterably to Christ, to kneel down. I observed when I made this call, that she was among the first that made a movement to kneel. The next morning, she called on me again at an early hour. As soon as we were alone, she opened her mind to me and said, "I see, Mr. Finney, that I have been very proud. I have come to tell you who I am, and to give you such facts in regard to my history, that you may know what to say to me." She was, as I had supposed, a woman in high life, the wife of a wealthy gentleman, who was himself a skeptic. She has made a profession of religion, but was unconverted. She was very frank in this interview, and threw her mind open to instruction very cordially; and either at that time or immediately after, she expressed hope in Christ, and became a very earnest Christian. She is a remarkable writer, and could more nearly report my sermons, without shorthand, than any person I ever knew. She used to come and sit and write my sermons with a rapidity and an accuracy that were quite astonishing. She sent copies of her notes to a great many of her friends, and exerted herself to the utmost to secure the conversion of her friends in Boston and elsewhere. With this lady I have had much correspondence. She has always manifested that same earnestness in religion, that she did at that time. She has always some good work in hand; and is an earnest laborer for the poor, and for all classes that need her instruction, her sympathy, and her help. She has passed through many mental struggles, surrounded as she is by such temptations to worldliness. But I trust that she has been, and will be, an ornament to the church of Christ.

The revival extended from Boston to Charlestown and Chelsea. In short it spread on every side. I preached in East Boston and Charlestown; and for a considerable time in Chelsea, where the revival became very general and precious. We continued to labor in Boston that winter, until it was time for us to return to our labors at home in the spring. When we left, the work was in its full strength without any apparent abatement at all.

The church and ministry in this country had become so extensively engaged in promoting the revival, and such was the blessing of God attending the exertions of laymen as well as of ministers, that I made up my mind to return and spend another season in England, and see if the same influence would not pervade that country.

CHAPTER 34

SECOND VISIT
TO ENGLAND

---

*...people felt that if there were not more
or less conversions every week,
something was entirely wrong.*

We sailed for Liverpool in the steamer Persia, in December, 1858. Our friend Brown came to Liverpool to meet us, to induce us to labor in Houghton for a season, before we committed ourselves to any other field. Immediately on our arrival, I received a great number of letters from different parts of England, expressing great joy at our return and inviting us to come and labor in many different fields. However, I spent several weeks laboring in Houghton and Saint Ives, where we saw precious revivals. In Saint Ives they had never had a revival before. In Houghton we had labored during our first visit to England, and saw a very interesting work of grace.

At this time, we found at Saint Ives a very singular state of things. There was but one Independent church, the pastor of which had been there a good many years, but had not succeeded in doing much as a minister. He was a mysterious sort of man. He was very fond of wine and a great opposer of total abstinence. We held our meetings in a hall which would accommodate more people, by far, than the Congregational church. I sometimes preached, however, in the church; but it was a less desirable place to preach in than the hall, as it was a very small and incommodious house.

The revival took powerful effect there, notwithstanding the position of the minister. He stood firmly against it until the interest became so great that he left the town, and was absent, I know not where, for several weeks. Since that time the converts of the revival, together with my friend Brown, and some of the older members of the church, have put up a fine chapel, and the religious condition of the place has been exceedingly different from what it ever had been before.

Mr. Harcourt, the former pastor at Houghton, had proved him-self a very successful minister, and had been called to London, to Borough Road chapel. Here I found him on my second visit to England. He had been awaiting, with anxiety, our return to England; and as soon as he heard we were there, he used most strenuous efforts to secure our labors with him in London. The church over which he presided in London, had been torn to pieces by most ultra and fanatical views on the subject of temperance. They had a lovely pastor, whose heart had been almost broken by their feuds upon that subject, and he had finally left the church in utter discouragement. Their deacons had been compelled to resign, and the church was in a sad state of disorganization. Brother Harcourt informed me that unless the church could be converted, he was satisfied he never could succeed in doing much in that field.

As soon as we could leave Saint Ives we went to London, to see what could be done in his church and congregation. We found them, as he had represented, in so demoralized a state that it seemed questionable whether the church could ever be resuscitated and built up. However, we went to work, my wife among the ladies of the congregation, and I went to preaching, and searching them, to the utmost of my strength. It was very soon perceptible that the Spirit of God was poured out, and that the church was very generally in a state of great conviction. The work deepened and spread till it reached, I believe, every household belonging to that congregation. All the old members of the church were so searched that they made confession one to another, and settled their difficulties; and Mr. Harcourt told me, before I left, that his church was entirely a new church; that the blessing of God had been universal among them so that all their old animosities were healed; and that he had the greatest comfort in them.

Indeed, the work in that church was really most wonderful. I directed my labors, for several weeks, to the church itself. Mr. Harcourt had been praying for them, and laboring with them, till he was almost discouraged; but the blessing at last came, in such fullness, as to meet the longings of his heart. His people were reconverted and cemented together in love, and they learned to take hold of the work themselves.

Some years after my return to this country, Mr. Harcourt came over and made us a visit. This was a little while after the death of my dear wife. He then told me that the work had continued in his church up to that time, that his people felt that if there were not more or less conversions every week, something was entirely wrong. They were frightened if the work was not perceptibly and constantly going forward. He said they stood by him, and he felt every Sunday as if he was in the midst of a praying atmosphere. Indeed, his report of the results of that revival up to the time of his leaving, was deeply interesting. Considering what the church had been, and what it was after the revival, it is no wonder that Mr. Harcourt's heart was as full as it could hold, of thanksgiving to God, for such a blessing.

In this place, as had been the case before at Dr. Campbell's, there were great revelations made of iniquity that had been covered up for a long time, among professors of religion. These cases were frequently brought to my notice by persons coming to me to ask for advice. Not only did professors of religion come, but numbers that had never made a profession of religion, who became terribly convicted of sin.

Soon after I began my labors at this time in London, a Dr. Tregelles, a distinguished literary man and professed theologian, wrote to Dr. Campbell, calling his attention to what he regarded as a great error in my theology. In treating upon the conditions of salvation, I had said in my Systematic Theology, that the atonement of Christ was one of the conditions. I said that God's infinite love was the foundation or source from which the whole movement sprung, but that the conditions upon which we could be saved, were the atonement of Christ, faith, and repentance. To this statement Dr. Tregelles took great exceptions.

Strange to tell, instead of going to my theology, and seeing just what I did say, Dr. Campbell took it up in his paper and agreed with Dr. Tregelles, and wrote several articles in opposition to what he supposed to be my views. They, both of them, strangely misunderstood my position, and got up in England, at this time, a good deal of opposition to my labors. Dr. Campbell, it appeared, after all, had no doubt of my orthodoxy. Dr. Redford insisted that my statement of the matter was right, and that any other statement was far from being right. However, I paid no attention, publicly, to Dr. Campbell's strictures on the subject. He afterwards wrote me a letter, which I have now in my possession, subscribing fully to my orthodoxy and to my views; but saying that, unfortunately, I made discriminations in my theology that common people did not understand. The fact is, a great many people understood them better than the Doctor did himself.

He had been educated in Scotland, and was, after the straightest sect, a Scotch theologian; consequently my new school statements of doctrine puzzled him, and it took him some time to understand them. I found when I first arrived in England that their theology was to a very great extent dogmatic, in the sense that it rested on authority. They had their Thirty-nine Articles in the Established church, and their Westminster Confession of faith; and these they regarded as authority. They were not at all in the habit of trying to prove the positions taken in these "standards," as they were called; but dealt them out as dogmas. When I began to preach they were surprised that I reasoned with the people. Dr. Campbell did not approve it, and insisted that it would do no good. But the people felt otherwise; and it was not uncommon for me to receive such intelligence as this, that my reasonings had convinced them of what they had always doubted; and that my preaching was logical instead of dogmatic, and therefore met the wants of the people.

I had myself, before I was converted, felt greatly the want of instruction and logical preaching from the pulpit. This experience always had a great influence upon my own preaching. I knew how thinking men felt when a minister took for granted the very things that needed proof. I therefore used to take great pains to meet the wants of persons who were in this state of mind. I knew what my difficulties had been, and therefore I endeavored to meet the intellectual wants of my hearers. I told Dr. Campbell this; but at first he had no faith that the people would understand me and appreciate my reasonings. But when he came to receive the converts, and to converse personally with them, he confessed to me again and again his surprise that they had so well understood my reasonings. "Why," he would say, "they are theologians." He was very frank, and confessed to me how erroneous his views had been upon that subject.

After I had finished my labors at Borough Road chapel, we left London and rested a few weeks at Houghton. Such was the state of my health that I thought I must return home. But Dr. F., an excellent Christian man living in Huntington, urged us very much to go to his house and finish our rest, and let him do what he could for me as a physician. We accepted his invitation and went to his house. He had a family of eight children, all unconverted. The oldest son was also a physician. He was a young man of remarkable talents, but a thorough skeptic. He had embraced Comte's philosophy, and had settled down in extreme views of atheism, or I should say of nihilism. He seemed not to believe anything. He was a very affectionate son; but his skepticism had deeply wounded his father, and for his conversion he had come to feel an unutterable longing.

After remaining at the doctor's two or three weeks, without medicine, my health became such that I began to preach. There never had been a revival in Huntington, and they really had no conception of what a revival would be. I occupied what they called "Temperance Hall," the only large hall in the town. It was immediately filled, and the Spirit of the Lord was soon poured out upon the people. I soon found opportunity to converse with young Dr. F.. I drew him out into some long walks, and entered fully into an investigation of his views; and finally, under God, succeeded in bringing him to a perfect standstill. He saw that all his philosophy was vain. At this time, I preached one Sunday evening on the text: "The hail shall sweep away the refuges of lies, and the waters shall overflow the hiding places. Your covenant with death shall be disannulled, and your agreement with hell shall not stand." I spent my strength in searching out the refuges of lies, and exposing them; and concluded with a picture of the hailstorm, and the descending torrent of rain that swept away what the hail had not demolished. The impression on the congregation was at the time very deep. That night young Dr. F. could not sleep. His father went to his room, and found him in the greatest consternation and agony of mind. At length he became calm, and to all appearance passed from death unto life. The prayers of the father and the mother for their children were heard. The revival went through their family, and converted every one of them. It was a joyful house, and one of the loveliest families that I ever had the privilege of residing in. We remained at their house while we continued our labors in Huntington.

The revival took a very general hold of the church, and of professors of religion in that town, and spread extensively among the unconverted; and greatly changed the religious aspect of the town. There was then no Congregational church there. There were two or three churches of the Establishment, one Methodist, and one Baptist, at that time in Huntington. Since then the converts of that revival, together with Mr. Brown and his son, and those Christians that were blest in the revival, have united and built, as I understand, a commodious chapel at Huntington, as they did at St. Ives.

Mr. Brown had pushed his work of evangelization with such energy, that when I arrived in England the second time, I found that he had seven churches in as many different villages in his neighborhood, and was employing preachers, and teachers, and laborers, to the number of twenty. His means of doing good have fully kept pace with his princely outlays for souls. When I first arrived in England, he was running a hired flouring mill, with ten pairs of stones; the second time I was there, in addition to this, he was running a mill which he had built at Saint Ives, at an expense of twenty thousand pounds sterling, with sixteen pairs of stones. He afterward built, at Huntington, another mill of the same capacity. Thus God poured into his coffers as fast as he poured out into the treasury of the Lord.

On Christmas Eve, 1859, we arrived at Bolton, a city of about thirty thousand inhabitants, lying a few miles from Manchester. It is in the heart of the great manufacturing district of England. It lies within the circle of that immense population, that spreads itself out from Manchester, as a center, in every direction. It is estimated that at least three millions of people live within a compass of sixty miles around about Manchester.

In this place the work of the Lord commenced immediately. We were received as guests by Mr. J. B.. He belonged to the Methodist denomination; was a man of sterling piety, very uncertain in his views and feelings. The next evening after we arrived, he invited in a few friends for religious conversation and prayer; and among them a lady, who had been for some time in an inquiring state of mind. After we had had a little conversation we concluded to have a season of prayer. My wife knelt near this lady of whom I have spoken, and during prayer she observed that she was much asserted. As we rose from our knees, Mrs. Finney took her by the hand, and then beckoned to me across the room to come and speak with her. The lady had been brought up, as I afterwards learned, a Quakeress; but had married a man who was a Methodist. She had been for a long time uneasy about the state of her soul; but had never been brought face-to-face with the question of present, instantaneous submission.

I responded to the call of my wife, and went across the room and spoke with her. I saw in a moment that her distress of mind was profound. I therefore asked her if she would see me a little time, for personal conversation. She readily complied, and we crossed the hall into another room; and then I brought her face to face, at once, with the question of instant submission, and acceptance of Christ. I asked her if she would then and there renounce herself, and everything else, and give her heart to Christ. She replied, "I must do it sometime; and I may as well do it now." We knelt immediately down; and so far as human knowledge can go, she did truly submit to God. After she had submitted we returned to the parlor; and the scene between herself and her husband was very affecting. As soon as she came into the room he saw such a change manifested in her countenance, that they seemed spontaneously to clasp each other in their arms, and knelt down before the Lord.

We were scarcely seated before the son of Mr. B. came into the parlor, announcing that one of the servants was deeply moved. In a very short time, that one also gave evidence of submission to Christ. Then I learned that another was weeping in the kitchen, and went immediately to her; and after a little conversation and instruction, she too appeared to give her heart to God. Thus the work had begun. Mrs. B. herself had been in a doubting and discouraged state of mind for years; and she, too, appeared to melt down, and get into a different state of mind almost immediately. The report of what the Lord was doing, was soon spread abroad; and people came in daily, and almost hourly, for conversation. The first week of January had been appointed to be observed as a week of prayer, as it has been since from year to year; and the different denominations agreed to hold Union meetings during the week.

Our first meeting was in the chapel occupied by Mr. Davison, who had sent for me to come to Bolton. He was an Independent, what we in this country call a Congregationalist. His chapel was filled the first night. The meeting was opened by a Methodist minister, who prayed with great fervency, and with a liberty that plainly indicated to me that the Spirit of God was upon the congregation, and that we should have a powerful meeting. I was invited to follow him with some remarks. I did so, and occupied a little space in speaking upon the subject of prayer. I tried to impress upon them as a fact, that prayer would be immediately answered, if they took the stumbling blocks out of the way, and offered the prayer of faith. The word seemed to thrill through the hearts of Christians. Indeed, I have seldom addressed congregations upon any subject that seemed to produce a more powerful and salutary effect, than the subject of prayer. I find it so everywhere. Praying people are immediately stirred up by it, to lay hold of God for a blessing. They were in this place. That was a powerful meeting. Through the whole of that week the spirit of prayer seemed to be increasing, and our meetings had greater and greater power. About the third or fourth day of our meetings, I should think, it fell to the turn of a Mr. Best, also a Congregational minister at Bolton, to have the meeting in his chapel. There, for the first time, I called for inquirers. After addressing the congregation for some time, in a strain calculated to lead to that point, I called for inquirers, and his vestry was thronged with them. We had an impressive meeting with them; and many of them, I trust, submitted to God.

There was a temperance hall in the city, which would accommodate more people than any of the chapels. After this week of prayer, the brethren secured the hall for preaching; and I began to preach there twice on the Sunday, and four evenings in the week. Soon the interest became very general. The hall would be crowded every night, so that not another person could get so much as within the door. The Spirit of God was poured out copiously.

I then recommended to the brethren to canvass the whole city; to go two and two, and visit every house; and if permitted, to pray in every house in the city. They immediately and courageously rallied to perform this work. They got great numbers of bills, and tracts, and posters, and all sorts of invitations printed, and began the work of canvassing. The Congregationalists and Methodists took hold of the work with great earnestness.

The Methodists are very strong in Bolton, and always have been since the day of Wesley. It was one of Wesley's favorite fields of labor; and they have always had there an able ministry, and strong churches. Their influence was far in the ascendancy there, over all other religious denominations. I found among them both ministers and laymen, who were most excellent and earnest laborers for Christ. But the Congregationalists too entered into the work, with great spirit and energy; and, while I remained there, at least, all denominational disagreements seemed to be buried. They gave the town a thorough canvassing; and the canvassers met once or twice a week to make their reports, and to consider farther arrangements for pushing the work. It was very common to see a Methodist and a Congregationalist, hand in hand, and heart in heart, going from house to house, with tracts, and praying wherever they were permitted, in every house, and warning men to flee from the wrath to come, and urging them to come to Christ.

Of course in such a state of things as this, the work would spread rapidly among the unconverted. All classes of persons, high and low, rich and poor, male and female, became interested. I was in the habit, every evening I preached of calling upon inquirers to come forward and take seats in front of the stand. Great numbers would come forward, crowding as best they could through the dense masses that filled every nook and corner of the house. The hall was not only large on its ground floor, but had a gallery, which was always thronged. After the inquirers had come forward, we engaged in a prayer meeting, having several prayers in succession while the inquirers knelt before the Lord.

The Methodist brethren were very much engaged, and for some time were quite noisy and demonstrative in their prayers, when sinners came forward. For some time, I said nothing about this, lest I should throw them off and lead them to grieve the Spirit. I saw that their impression was, that the greater the excitement, the more rapidly would the work go forward. They therefore would pound the benches, pray exceedingly loud, and sometimes more than one at a time. I was aware that this distracted the inquirers, and prevented their becoming truly converted; and although the number of inquirers was great and constantly increasing, yet conversions did not multiply as fast as I had been in the habit of seeing them, even where the number of inquirers was much less.

After letting things pass on so for two or three weeks, until the Methodist brethren had become acquainted with me, and I with them, one evening upon calling the inquirers forward, I suggested that we should take a different course. I told them that I thought the inquirers needed more opportunity to think than they had when there was so much noise; that they needed instruction, and needed to be led by one voice in prayer, and that there should not be any confusion, or anything bordering on it, if we expected them to listen and become intelligently converted. I asked them if they would not try for a short time to follow my advice in that respect, and see what the result would be. They did so; and at first I could see that they were a little in bondage when they attempted to pray, and a little discouraged, because it so crossed their ideas of what constituted powerful meetings. However, they soon seemed to recover from this, because I think they were convinced that although there was less apparent excitement in our prayer meetings, yet there were many more converted from evening to evening.

The fame of this work spread abroad, and soon persons began to come in large members from Manchester to Bolton to attend our meetings; and this, as was always the case, created a considerable excitement in that city, and a desire to have me come thither as soon as I could. However, I remained in Bolton I think about three months, perhaps more. The work became so powerful that it broke in upon all classes, and every description of persons.

Brother B. had an extensive cotton mill in Bolton, and employed a great many hands, men and women. I went with him down to his mill once or twice, and held meetings with his operatives. The first time we went we had a powerful meeting. I remained with them till I was much fatigued, and then returned home, leaving Brother still to pray with, and instruct them. When he came home he reported that not less than sixty appeared clearly to be converted that evening, among his own hands. These meetings were continued till nearly all his hands expressed hope in Christ.

There were a great many very striking cases of conviction and conversion at the time. Although I kept cool myself, and endeavored to keep the people in an attitude in which they would listen to instruction, and would act understandingly in everything they did;

still in some instances, persons for a few days were too much excited for the healthy action of their minds, though I do not recollect any case of real insanity.

One night as I was standing on the platform and preaching, a man in the congregation rose up and crowded his way up to the platform, and said to the congregation, "I have committed a robbery." He began to make a confession, interrupting me as I was preaching. I saw that he was overexcited; and brother Davison who sat on the platform stepped up and whispered to him, and took him down into a side room and conversed with him. He found that he had committed a crime for which he was liable to be transported. He gave him advice, and I heard no more of it that evening. Afterwards the facts came more fully to my knowledge. But in a few days the man obtained a hope.

One evening I preached on confession and restitution, and it cre-ated a most tremendous movement among business men. One man told me the next day that he had been and made restitution, I think, of fifteen hundred pounds, in a case where he thought he had not acted upon the principle of loving his neighbor as himself. The consciences of men under such circumstances are exceedingly tender. The gentleman to whom I have just referred, told me that a dear friend of his had died and left him to settle his estate. He had done so, and simply received what the law gave him for his labor and expense. But he said that in hearing that sermon, it occurred to him that as a friend and a Christian brother, he could better afford to settle that estate without charging anything, than the family could afford to allow him the legal fees. The Spirit of God that was upon him led him to feel it so keenly, that he immediately went and refunded the money.

There was a case in Rochester, in New York, that I have forgotten to mention, but that may just as well be mentioned in this place, of the same kind. An extremely tender conscience led a man to see and feel keenly on the subject of acting on the principle of loving our neighbor as ourselves, and doing to others as we would that they should do to so. A man of considerable property was converted in one of the revivals in Rochester, in which I labored, who had been transacting some business for a widow lady in a village not far distant from Rochester. The business consisted in the transfer of some real estate, for which he had been paid for his services some fifteen or sixteen hundred dollars. As soon as he was converted he thought of this case; and upon reflection he thought he had not done by that widow lady and those fatherless children, as he would wish another to do by his widow and fatherless children, should he die. He therefore went over to see her, and stated to her his view of the subject as it lay before his mind. She replied that she did not see it in that light at all; that she had considered herself very much obliged to him indeed, that he had transacted her business in such a way as to make for her all she could ask or expect. She declined, therefore, to receive the money which he offered to refund.

After thinking of it a little he told her that he was dissatisfied, and wished that she would call in some of her most trustworthy neighbors, and they would state the question to them. She did so, called in some Christian friends, men of business; and they laid the whole matter before them. They said that the affair was a business transaction, and it was evident that he had transacted the business to the acceptance of the family and to their advantage; and they saw no reason why he should refund the money. He heard what they had to say; but before he left the town he called on the lady again and said, "My mind is not at ease. If I should die and leave my wife a widow and children fatherless, and a friend of mine should transact such a piece of business for them, I should feel as if he might do it gratuitously, inasmuch as it was for a widow and fatherless children." Said he, "I cannot take any other view of it than this." He laid the money upon her table, and left.

Another case occurs to me now, which illustrates the manner in which the Spirit of God will work in the minds of men, when their hearts are open to his influence. In preaching in one of the large cities on a certain occasion, I was dwelling upon the dishonesties of business, and the overreaching plans of men; and how they justify themselves in violations of the golden rule. Before I was through with my discourse, a gentleman arose in the middle of the house and asked me if he might propose a question. He then supposed a case; and after he had stated it, asked me if that case would come under the rule that I had propounded, I said, "Yes, I think that it clearly would." He sat down and said no more; but I afterwards learned that he went away and made restitution to the amount of thirty thousand dollars. I could relate great numbers of instances in which persons have been led to act in the same manner, under the powerfully searching influences of the Spirit of God.

But to return from this digression; the work went on and spread in Bolton until one of the ministers who had been engaged in directing the movement of canvassing the town, said publicly that they found that the revival had reached every family in the city; and that every family had been visited. If we had any place of worship large enough, we should probably have had ten thousand persons in the congregations from evening to evening. All we could do was to fill the hall as full as it could be crowded, and then use such other means as we could to reach the multitudes in other places of worship.

I recollect a striking case of conversion among the great mill owners there. I had been told of one of them that was a very miserly man. He had a great thirst for riches, and had been spoken of as being a very hopeless case. The revival had reached a large number of that class of men; but this man had seemed to stand out, and his worldly-mindedness and his miserly spirit had seemed to eat him up. But contrary to my expectations, and to the expectations of others, he in his turn called on me. I invited him to my room, and had a very serious conversation with him. He acknowledged to me that he had been a great miser; and that he had once said to God, that if he would give him another hundred thousand pounds, he would be willing to be eternally damned. I was very much shocked at this; but could see clearly that he was terribly convicted of the sinfulness of that state of mind.

I then repeated to him a part of the sixth chapter of Matthew, where Christ warns men against laying up treasure on earth, and recommends them to lay up treasure in heaven. I finally came to that verse: "But seek first the kingdom of God and his righteousness, and all these things shall be added unto you." He leaned toward me, and appeared to be as much interested as if it were all new to him. When I repeated to him this verse, he said to me, with the utmost earnestness, "Do you believe that?" I said, "Be sure I believe it. It is the word of God." "Well then," said he, "I'll go it;" and sprang upon his feet in the utmost excitement. "If that is true," said he, "I will give up all to Christ at once." We knelt immediately down, and I presented his case to God in prayer; and he seemed to break down like a child. From that time, he appeared to be a very different man. His miserly feelings all seemed to melt away. He took hold of that work like a man in earnest, and went and hired, at his own cost, a city missionary, and set him to work to win souls to Christ.

At this place, also, Mrs. Finney's meetings were very largely attended. She held them, as she always did, in the daytime; and sometimes I was informed that at her meeting of ladies, Temperance Hall would be nearly full. The Christian ladies of different denominations took hold with her and encouraged her; and great good, I trust, was done through the instrumentality of those ladies' meetings.

My wife and myself were both of us a good deal exhausted by these labors. But in April we went to Manchester. In Manchester the Congregational interest, as I was informed, rather predominates over that of other denominations. As is well-known, the manufacturing districts have a stronger democratic element than other parts of England. Congregationalism, therefore, is more prevalent in Manchester than in any other city that I visited. I had not been long there, however, before I saw that there was a great lack of mutual confidence among the brethren. I could see that there was a jar among the leaders; and frequently, to my grief, I heard expressions that indicated a want of real heart union in the work. This I was soon convinced was a great difficulty to be overcome; and that if it could not be overcome, the work could never be as general there as it had been in Bolton. There soon was manifest a dissatisfaction with some of the men who had been selected to engineer the work, and provide for carrying on the general movement.

This grieved the Spirit and crippled the work. And although from the very first the Spirit of God attended the word; yet the work never so thoroughly overcame the sectarian feeling and disagreements of the brethren generally, that it could spread over the city in the way it had done at Bolton. When I went to that city I expected that the Methodist and Congregational brethren would work harmoniously together, as they had at Bolton; but in this I found myself mistaken. Not only was there a want of cordiality and sympathy between the Methodists and Congregationalists; but also a great lack of confidence and sympathy among the Congregationalists themselves. However, our meetings were very interesting, and great numbers of inquirers were found on every side; and whenever a meeting was appointed for inquirers, large numbers would attend. Still what I longed to see was a general overflowing of the Spirit's influences in Manchester, as we had witnessed in Bolton. The difficulty was, there was not a good spirit manifested at that time, by the leading men in the movement.

I did not learn the cause — perhaps it was something in myself. But although I am sure that large numbers of persons were converted, for I saw and conversed with a great number myself that were powerfully convicted, and to all appearance converted; yet the barriers did not break down so as to give the word of the Lord, and the Spirit of the Lord, free course among the people.

When we came away, a meeting was called for those who had been particularly blessed during those meetings; and the number in attendance was, I believe, very much larger than was expected by the ministers themselves. I am confident that they were surprised at the numbers present, and at the spirit of the meeting. Indeed, I do not think that any of the ministers there were aware of the extent of the work, for they did not generally attend our meetings. They did not follow them from place to place, and were seldom seen in the meetings of inquiry. We continued in Manchester till about the first of August; and the revival continued to increase and spread up to that time.

But the strength of both myself and my wife had become exhausted, and some of the leading brethren proposed to us to suspend our labors, and go down into Wales and rest a few weeks, and then return to Manchester and resume our labors. What they proposed was, to secure a large hall, and thus to go on with our meetings in an independent way. They thought, and I thought myself, that we should secure a greater amount of good in that way than by laboring with any particular congregation. Denominational lines are much more strongly marked in that country than they are in this. It is very difficult to get people of the church of England to attend a dissenting place of worship. The Methodists will not generally and freely attend worship with other denominations. Indeed, the same is true of all denominations in England, and in Scotland. Sectarian lines are much more distinctly drawn, and the members of the different churches keep more closely within their lines, than in this country. I am persuaded that the true way to labor for a revival movement there, is to have no particular connection with any distinct denomination; but to preach the true gospel, and make a stand in halls, or even in streets when the weather is favorable, where no denominational feelings and peculiarities can straighten the influences of the Spirit of God.

On the second of August, 1860, we left Manchester and went down to Liverpool. A goodly number of our friends went down with us, and remained overnight. On the morning of the third, we left in the Persia for New York. We found that large numbers of our friends had assembled from different parts of England, to bid us goodbye. We took an affectionate and an affecting leave of them, and the glorious old steamer rushed out to sea, and we were on our way home.

CONCLUSION.

Those who have read the preceding pages, will naturally inquire in reference to the closing years of a life so full of labor and of usefulness.

After Mr. Finney returned from England, for the next ten years, he served as a pastor of the First church in Oberlin, and lecturer in the seminary. At the same time, as professor of Pastoral Theology, he gave a course of lectures each summer term, on the pastoral work, on Christian experience, or on revivals. He resigned the pastorate in 1872, but still retained his connection with the seminary, and completed his last course of lectures in July 1875, only a few days before his death. He preached, from time to time, as his strength permitted; and during the last month of his life, he preached one Sunday morning in the First church, and another in the Second.

Notwithstanding the abundant and exhausting labors of his long public life, the burden of years seemed to rest lightly upon him. He still stood erect, as a young man, retained his faculties to a remarkable degree, and exhibited to the end the quickness of thought, and feeling, and imagination, which always characterized him. His life and character perhaps never seemed richer in the traits and the beauty of goodness, than in these closing years and months. His public labors were of course very limited, but the quiet power of his life was felt as a benediction upon the community, which, during forty years, he had done so much to guide and mold and bless.

His last day on earth was a quiet Sunday, which he enjoyed in the midst of his family, walking out with his wife at sunset, to listen to the music, at the opening of the evening service in the church nearby.

Upon retiring he was seized with pains which seemed to indicate some affection of the heart; and after a few hours of suffering, as the morning dawned, he died, August 16th, 1875, lacking two weeks of having completed his eighty-third year.

The foregoing narrative is just a brief story of Mr. Finney's life. He was an evangelist, a preacher of righteousness, who served God with passion. To set forth the results of his life in details, would require another volume, which will probably never be written; but other generations will reap the benefits, without knowing the source whence they have sprung.